Notes From the Brink:
A Collection of Columns About Policy at Home and Abroad

Jeff Robbins

Creators Publishing
Hermosa Beach, CA

Notes From the Brink: A Collection of Columns About Policy at Home and Abroad
Copyright © 2024 CREATORS PUBLISHING
All rights reserved. No part of this book may be reproduced or transmitted in any form or by any means, electronic or mechanical, including photocopying, recording or by any information storage and retrieval system, without permission in writing from the author.

Cover design by Little Shiva

CREATORS PUBLISHING
737 3rd St
Hermosa Beach, CA 90254
310-337-7003

Although the author and publisher have made every effort to ensure that the information in this book was correct at press time, the author and publisher do not assume and hereby disclaim any liability to any party for any loss, damage or disruption caused by errors or omissions, whether such errors or omissions result from negligence, accident or any other cause.

ISBN (print): 978-1-962693-10-3
ISBN (ebook): 978-1-962693-11-0

First Edition
Printed in the United States of America
1 3 5 7 9 10 8 6 4 2

"Tough, honest and courageous are the words that best describe Jeff Robbins' columns reprinted in *Notes from the Brink*. Robbins, an outstanding lawyer and dedicated public servant, attacks each issue with passion, wisdom and a clear moral compass. He analyzes, explains and challenges the issues of the day, be they political, ideological or cultural. Read it; you will be a better, wiser citizen."
— **Abraham Foxman, former national director of the Anti-Defamation League**

"An essential voice in today's world. This collection of columns by Jeffrey Robbins, covering topics from the Middle East to the health of democracy, is a gift to us all and a must-read."
— **David Harris, former CEO of American Jewish Committee**

"Courageous voices give us more than cynicism and outrage. They give us insight. That's what Robbins consistently delivers in these columns. Read his courageous voice and see a bit more clearly through the haze."
— **Deval Patrick, former governor of Massachusetts**

"Jeff Robbins' *Notes from the Brink* is a moveable feast. Robbins is a Renaissance man, steeped in law and history, while thankfully also a master of satire:
When a certain political figure solemnly pronounces that 'character counts,' 'that takes not only the cake but the entire bakery.'
In groundless attacks on prominent women, 'the chutzpah paled before the misogyny.'

And a presidential condemnation of violence was 'a performance so patently insincere it made videotaped confessions by hostages held captive by Hezbollah seem voluntary by comparison.'

You hardly know whether to laugh or cry and will likely wind up doing both."
— **William Weld, former governor of Massachusetts**

TABLE OF CONTENTS

FOREWORD	1
INTRODUCTION	3

2019

Democrats Misfire When Taking Aim at Joe Biden Remarks	5
Pete Buttigieg Shapes up as Serious Democratic Contender	7
Details of Trump Ukraine Extortion Will Not Be Pretty	9
After Silence, Christian Magazine Calls Trump out for Moral Failure	11

2020

Fake Views: GOP Senators' Professed Anger Phony as Can Be	13
Celebrity Trumps: The Sad Implosion of Alan Dershowitz	15
Tale of 2 Heroes: Sen. Romney and Col. Vindman Remind America What It's About	17
Lemming Complex: The Bernie Bros Demand That the Democrats Jump off a Cliff	19
Art of the Self-Inflicted Wound: Pro-Palestinians Keep on Targeting Palestinians	21
Truth Decay: Con Job Central Confronts a Public Health Crisis	23
Dennis Ross Warns That What Happens in the Mideast Rarely Stays There	25
Overexposed: The Lying Game Catches up With Our President	27
Branch Covidian: The Virus Denier in Chief Tries a Rewrite	29
His Finest Hour: Andrew Cuomo Reminds Us How It's Done	31
Just Another Hoax: The President Who Doesn't Want Us to Know What Went Wrong	33

Jesus, Take the Wheel: The President Says, 'I'll Be the Oversight'	35
Mussolini in the Mirror: The President Declares He Has 'Total Authority'	37
Voodoomeister: Trump Takes a Spin as Medicine Man	39
Hate Wave: Strange Thanks for Communities of Color Carrying Us on Their Backs	41
Cowardly Lyin': Trump Minion Declares Mike Flynn Innocent of the Crime to Which He Already Pleaded Guilty	43
Leader Lost: Remembering Al Lowenstein	45
Mafia Don: The President Guards His Swamp	47
Bottomless: The President Reminds Us How Low He'll Go	49
Titanic: Ship of Fools Springs a Leak	51
In His Own Right: Amid a Pandemic, Joe Kennedy III Turns Heads	53
Exit Ramp: As Dumpster Fire Worsens, Voters Seem Ready to Give Trump the Boot	55
The Silencer: With the Stakes Getting High, the President Tightens the Muzzle	57
Good and Smart: Warren's Bill Boosting Low-Income Renter Households Makes Sense	59
Powerful Dissent: Conservative Patriots Take on a Dirty President	61
Weisswash: Out of Line, Out of Place, Out of Work at The New York Times	63
Scoundrel Time: As November Nears, Americans Contemplate Their Disaster in Chief	65
Perjury Troop: A Chuckling Attorney General Lies to Congress	67
Yo, Semites! No Doubt About It: Biden's the One	69
It's Bigot Time: Rattled by Kamala Harris, Trump and Friends Go Full White Power	71
Da, He Did: GOP-Led Senate Panel Confirms Trump Colluded With Russia for Election Interference	73
Unending Shootings of Blacks Show America Is Not What We Thought It Is	75
Nuts: The President Who Was Unfit for Service	77
Looking Under the Hood: Time for Congress to Investigate the Performance of Health Care Executives	79

Liar and Losers: The President Deceives, and Americans Take the Hit	81
When the Shoe Fits: Biden Invokes the F-Word for Trump, and He's Not Wrong	83
Trashed: On His Way out the Door, the President Leaves America a Mess	85
Mensch on the Bench: Remembering Massachusetts Chief Justice Ralph Gants	87
The Full Mussolini: The Proto-Fascist in Chief Goes for Broke	89
Agent Orange: Our Adversaries' Man in the White House	91
Stain Removal: Americans Get a Chance for a Deep Cleaning	93
Debased but Not Done: America Wrestles Its Strongman to the Ground	95
Banana Republicans: Trump and His Party Take America Hostage	97
Democracy Subversion to Dye for: Trump Shoots America to Kill	99
Fingers Crossed, Eyes Forward: Biden Team Vows to Show That America Is Back	101
Repairing the Arts: Yet Another Challenge for an Administration Tasked With Repairing the Country	103
Confederacy of Dunces: Trump World Takes Its Leave	105
The Splendid and the Vile: Enter Joe and Jill Biden, Spelling Relief	107
Jail Time for Bonzo: America Needs To Have Donald Trump Face the Music	109

2021

Whatever It Takes: Time for an All-Out National Assault on Hunger	111
Shame: Trump's Apologists Owe America an Apology	113
Teachable Moment: America Gets Its Own Chance to Say, 'Never Again'	115
Family Tradition: Jewish Agency's Bougie Herzog Takes On the Protection of World Jewry	117
Married to the Mob: The GOP Becomes the Party of the Kooks	119
Block the Vote: The GOP's Suppression Obsession	121
Dead Souls: Those Who Gave Us Donald Trump Would Do It Again	123
Lucky Once More: America Finds Itself a Leader	125

Rumpled Giant of the Senate: Carl Levin's Life and Times	127
Campus Bullies: The Extreme Right Aren't the Only Ones With an Anti-Semitism Problem	129
Taking On the Vile Factor: Biden Moves Against Anti-Asian American Hate	131
POTUS Pokes the Bear: No Longer Servile, the US Stirs to Challenge Putin	133
Time to Go: Protecting Voters' Rights Means Easing the Filibuster's Stranglehold	135
Rump Party: The Face of the GOP Is Not a Pretty One	137
Revenge of the Nerd: Across the Divide, Bernie Sanders Breaks Through	139
Looney Tunes: The Rot on the Right Isn't Going Away Anytime Soon	141
His Own Man: Angus King Refuses to Give Up on Bipartisanship	143
Pipe Dream: Biden's Call for Republican Bipartisanship Is Fervent, But Futile	145
Champion: As Long As Anti-Semitism Isn't Going Anywhere, Neither Is Abe Foxman	147
Complicit: The Left's Indulgence of Hamas Guarantees Palestinians and Israelis Will Continue to Suffer	149
The Keeper: In a GOP Dominated By Frauds and Cowards, Liz Cheney's a Profile in Courage	151
Renewal: With a Community Assist, Baseball Brings a Win to Worcester	153
Fresh Blood, Old Bias: New Israeli Leaders Confront the Stubborn Inanity of the Left	155
Believer: Prime Time Paul Zine No Longer Thinks COVID-19 Is Up for Debate	157
Hubris Factor: Progressive Elites Bet the Farm That America Believes What They Believe	159
Pride Time: Biden Puts a Bully Pulpit to Good Use	161
Tourist Visit: The GOP Keeps on Riding the Hogwash Express	163
Teacher's Story: At 88, Bob Gardiner Answers the Bell One More Time	165
Public Enemies: The 'COVID's a Hoax; Vaccinations Are a Plot' Crowd Is Enough To Make You Sick	167
Small-Town Hero: Remembering John Glenn's Right Stuff	169

Sweet and Spineless: Ben and Jerry's Caves to the Anti-Israel Mob	171
Pandemic Perpetuators: The Enablers of the Coronavirus's Spread Keep On Enabling	173
First Under Fire: Freedom of Speech Gets Squeezed From Both Sides	175
Snark Attack: The Afghanistan Blame Game Obscures an Urgent Need To Restore American Credibility	177
Duet: Boston's Catholic and Jewish Communities Reunite to Welcome Afghan Refugees	179
Backfire: Parole for Sirhan Would Be the Wrong Message at the Wrong Time	181
Foul Spirit: George W. Bush Mourns 9/11 and Warns of Our Jihadis Within	183
Reckless Disregard: Senate Hearings Showcase the FBI's Doltish Indifference to Predatory Molestation of Gymnasts	185
It's the Bullying, Stupid: The Anti-Israel Lobby Targets Jewish Kids on Campus	187
Circular Firing Squad: The Democrats' Internal Warfare Threatens To Send Them Back to the Wilderness	189
Soul Erosion: Americans Confront a Nation They Never Knew	191
Jail Bait: Steve Bannon Bets That His Middle Finger to Congress Won't Land Him in the Slammer	193
Burned at Both Ends: A Good President Finds Himself Torpedoed by the Right and Sniped at By the Left	195
Fresh Air: The New Boston Takes Charge	197
Sour Smell of Success: A President Under Attack for Doing What He Was Elected To Do	199
Just a Little Treason: Trump and Co. Play Hide-the-Putsch	201
Debasement (Continued): The GOP Descends To Lower and Lower Levels	203
Untruth And Consequences: The Hamas Caucus Gets It Wrong on Gaza	205
Beginnings and an Ending: For Better and Worse, New Winds Change Massachusetts' Landscape	207
Bright Spot: Adam Schiff Reminds Us There's Daylight After Midnight	209
Guilty Party: Big Don's Cosa Nostra Takes The Fifth	211

Merchant of Death: Public Health Be Damned, Fox News Goes for the Money — 213

2022

Unhappy Anniversary: Marking the Deplorables' Opening Act — 215

Shaken Faith: Failed by the System, Baby Rehma's Parents Try to Change It — 217

Birds of a Feather: For Both the Far Left and the Far Right, Antisemitism's the Thing — 219

Flimflam: Biden's Critics Take Chutzpah to New Levels — 221

Badge of Honor: Police Killings Remind Us What We Owe the Blue — 223

Sheep And Black Sheep: The GOP Goes Full Hezbollah — 225

Royal Flush: More Hidden Document Tricks from the Shredder-In-Chief — 227

Testing, Testing: Putin Bets the West Will Wobble — 229

Tools: Putin's Useful Idiots Find a New Way to Degrade Democracy — 231

Patriotic Interlude: In a Rare Moment of Consensus, the GOP Gathers 'Round the Flag — 233

Bad Bet: Putin Confronts an America That Has Edged Closer Together — 235

Ukrainian Takeaway: A Strong National Defense and American Leadership Are as Needed as Ever — 237

With Malice Toward Some: Violent, Frontal or Merely Sly, The Assaults on Jewry Keep Coming — 239

Heroes And Crooks: Ukraine Teaches Americans A Thing or Two and More — 241

High Achievers: America's Diplomats Do Us Proud on Ukraine — 243

On the Edge: Democracy in the Balance, Here and Elsewhere — 245

Two Steps Backward: Discrimination against Asian Americans Spikes, and Spikes Again — 247

Honoring Albright: Making Certain the Ukrainians Win — 249

White Knight: The Producer Who Brought 'The Music Man' to Life — 251

In the Belly of the Beast: An Israeli Hero Goes to Harvard — 253

Senator Scrappy: New Hampshire's Maggie Hassan Tells Mitch McConnell to Bring It On	255
Sorry State: Texas Massacre Highlights America's Gun Disease	257
Weak Knees and Atrocity Fatigue: Putin Pins His Hopes on a Wavering West	259
High Crime in Prime Time: The Jan. 6 Committee Lays a Corrupt President Bare	261
Prelude to a Perp Walk: 'Team Normal' Takes the Stand	263
Bum Rap: Slimed by the Right, Sniped at by the Left, Joe Biden Presses On	265
Courting Dissolution: An Unprincipled Gang of Justices Threatens to Take America Down	267
Political Asylum: The Jan. 6 Committee Spotlights America's Crazy Problem	269
Family Visits: Biden's Mideast Trip Starts Warm, Ends Chilly	271
Symptoms of a Different Kind: Biden's May Be Mild, but the Former Guy's Aren't	273
Damned Either Way: Merrick Garland Weighs the Mother of All Indictments	275
J Street Blues: The Group That Wants to Be AIPAC	277
Rap Sheet: If It's Friday, It Must Be the Espionage Act	279
Armed and Dangerous: Domestic Extremism Grows, and the GOP Goes Along for the Ride	281
I Spy: A Former Guy with The Look of a Crook	283
Fall Awakening: As Alarm About the GOP Rises, The Red Wave Recedes	285
Special Privileges: The Judge Granting Trump a Special Master Handed Him a Special Deal	287
Frozen Hearts Club: The DeSantis Human Trafficking Show Lays an Egg	289
Safe Space for Bigots: The University of Vermont Gets the Federal Investigation It Deserves	291
Loose Cannon: Trump's Mar-A-Lago Judge Says 'You've Got a Friend In Me'	293
Reckless Disinterest: Iranians Get Oppressed as Their Regime Gets Coddled	295

Letter From Sing Sing: Trump's Subpoena Response Sounds Like He's Already in Solitary	297
Land Of Oz: America Barrels Toward a Crossroads	299
Bloody Hands and Guilty Parties: Just Another Tourist Visit to The Pelosi Home	301
Officious Nonsense and Putin Apologists: Biden Bears a Cross on Ukraine	303
Bad Night for Crazy: Trumpism Stalls -- For Now	305
Schadenfreude Express: Democrats Should Beware Of Hubris	307
Murder, Then Sweets: The Palestinians Reelect Benjamin Netanyahu	309
Dog Days for Donald: Migraines Mount for the Former President	311
So Much For 'Dementia Joe': Biden Comes Out on Top, Again	313
Dishonorable Mention: Referred for Criminal Prosecution, Trump Enters the Realm of Humpty Dumpty	315
Champion for the Disabled: Jim Brett Keeps Fighting	317

2023

Art of the Con: On Trumpism's Wings, Mr. Santos Goes to Washington	319
Hunger Pain: Jim McGovern Prods America to Get Food on Everyone's Table	321
Send in the Clowns: Biden's Mistakes Invite the GOP Circus	323
White Wash: Ron DeSantis Will Decide What Your Children Learn About Black History	325
Demagogues' Devil: Targeted by MAGA World, Adam Schiff Resumes Punching	327
Grace And Disgrace: Black America Suffers Another Outrage	329
Bulwark: University of Haifa Helps Israel Hold the Line	331
Sly Fox: Libel Lawsuit Documents Network's Sad Embrace of Trash, For Cash	333
Hacks and Heroes: The Fight Against Putin Highlights The Good, The Great and The Ugly	335
Lucky Hank, Lucky Us: An American Hero Leaves Behind a Gift	337

Indecent Exposure: The Rot That Is the Republican Party Reclaims Center Stage	339
Arresting Developments: Donald Trump Prepares to Face the Music	341
At The Ramparts: Under Siege from Autocrats and Crooks, Fighters for Democracy Hang Tough	343
Multiple Bookings: Mr. 'Lock Her Up' Ponders A Lockup	345
Smell Test Alert: The Embarrassing Case of Clarence Thomas Gets More Embarrassing	347
Unjaded: Celebrating the Irish, Joe Biden Celebrates America	349
Unhidden Gem: Mouna Maroun Leads Israeli Arabs Down the Path She's Blazing	351
A Question of Rape: Donald Trump Goes on Trial	353
Tuesdays With Charlie: A Golden Retriever Goes to College	355
Discredited Suisse: Congress Spotlights a Bank's Attempt to Obscure Its Nazi Links	357
Sauce for the Goose: Democrats Scramble to Whitewash a Scandal of Their Own	359
Sociopath Versus Sycophants: The GOP's Field of Contenders Takes Shape	361
The Center Stirs: With A Crucial Debt Deal, Score One for The Adults	363
Toast: A Crooked President Betrays His Country	365
Fast Asleep: 'Cabaret' Sounds a Wake-up Call	367
Clown Show: House Republicans Censure Adam Schiff, and It's Perfect	369
In The Dock: A Discredited Court May Be a Harbinger of Worse to Come	371
Claptrap: Israel Has Some Nerve Challenging Murder, Incorporated in Jenin	373
The Brawler: Chris Christie's Not Mincing Words	375
National Zoo: Under MAGA's Gavel, There's Debasement in The House	377
Boss Man: America Has a Problem, and the Problem Is Us	379
Right To Lie: Trump Claims First Amendment Protection for A Coup D'etat	381
Blowin' Smoke: Hunter's Hubris Heightens GOP Hooey	383

Cruel Limbo: Frozen in Uncertainty, Loyal Afghan Allies Wait for the Safety They Deserve	385
Mugged: America Digests the Specter of Inmate No. PO1135809	387
'Ain't Rabbit No More': New Biography Highlights Dr. King's Enduring Legacy	389
Giving Irish: A Nation and a Vibrant Community Celebrate One Another	391
Pulp Fiction: Bowing to Trump, the GOP Launches a Phony Impeachment Inquiry	393
Difficult and Necessary: Arming Ukraine Is Costly and Also Our Only Option	395
Flop House: The GOP's 'Impeachment Inquiry' Lays an Egg	397
Slaughter Incorporated: Coddled by the Left and Armed by Iran, Hamas Stages a Massacre	399
Blast-Off: Israel's Critics Depart Planet Earth	401
Hail to a Chief: The President Overrides the Kindergarten	403
Tools' Paradise: Academia Says It's Down with Mass Slaughter	405
Bit of Blackmail: The Hamas Lobby Tells Biden to Bend, or Else	407
See No Evil: On American Campuses, It's Tiki Torch Time	409
No Surrender: Lacking Other Options, Israel Needs to Finish the Job	411
The Truman Show: Another Uncool President Makes His Mark	413
Masks Off: The Hamas Defense Forces Show the Unmistakable Bigotry on the Left	415
Ain't Budging: Attacked from The Left on Israel, Biden Stands His Ground	417
Immunity Disorder: The Man Who Would Be King Comes Out and Says So	419
Tunnel Vision: Congress Prepares to Investigate Taxpayer Subsidies of Hamas	421

2024

Genocide Jujitsu: The Hamas Lobby Flips the Facts	423
Dead Center: On America's Right and On Its Left, A Certain Madness	425

Tick Tock: As the Hostages' Lives Count Down, Hamas Has Reason To Smile	427
Married to the Mob: Democrats Can't Cater to the Fringe	429
Corrupt Enterprise: A Poisoned, Poisonous UN Agency in Gaza Faces the Music	431
Baked Squad: Hard-Left Democrats May Be in for a Thinning	433
The President's Tightrope: Biden Steers Between the Necessary and the Popular	435
Qatar Connection: American Universities Have Some Explaining To Do	437
Ostrich Days: Democracy on the Line, Americans Decide Whether to Fight or Fold	439
College Daze: On Campuses As In Newsrooms, Orthodoxy Rules	441
Hate Rape: The Kids Say It's OK	443
Blessed Mission: From Soul and Heart They Serve	445
The Bibi Bogeyman: Democrats' Feeble Wobble on Hamas Risks Sinking Biden	447
Mourning Joe: Losing Lieberman, We Lose a Principled Independent	449
Hot Air Buffoons: Talking Heads Hand Out Hogwash on Gaza	451
Mindless or Spineless: The Unbearable Lightness of Being Elizabeth Warren	453
Trouble in River City: Elitism and Arrogance Threaten a Backlash Against Democrats	455
ABOUT JEFF ROBBINS	457

FOREWORD
Written by Seth Klarman

  The musician Jelly Roll noted at last year's Country Music Association Awards that "your windshield is bigger than the rearview mirror for a reason. What's in front of you is so much more important that what's behind you." True, but if you want to understand what you're seeing in the windshield, knowing what came before is invaluable. How did we get here? Why are things the way they are? What lessons can we learn from the past to help us make better choices about the future?

  In the morning, the Boston Herald is the first newspaper I read for two reasons. One is the sports news, where the trials and tribulations of our local teams are carefully dissected. The other is Jeff Robbins' latest weekly column, which is invariably a stiff dose of impeccably reasoned analysis in a world that has increasingly drifted from its moorings. Jeff is one of my favorite editorialists for the same reason that he is one of my best friends: He's clear-headed, candid, incisive, entertaining, wise and deeply principled. His writing is always grounded and sensible, but also unpredictable. His arguments have prompted me to rethink issues and change my mind. And, on the rare occasion when I think he's gotten something wrong, he's open to hearing another perspective and doing his own rethinking.

  Jeff is consistent and resolute in his defense of American democracy and in his belief in American exceptionalism. He is proudly Jewish, a relentless fighter against antisemitism (and other hatreds) and a stalwart supporter of the right of Israel to exist while being unafraid to critique Israel when her policies veer off course.

  Jeff, with his lifelong interest in national affairs, background in human-rights advocacy and training as a lawyer, infuses his well-written editorials with the tenacity and logic of a legal brief, lining up fact after fact, one after the other, to make an irrefutable point. He pulls no punches and lets the editorial chips fall where they may.

  In times like these, when too often the world seems turned inside-out and upside-down, when, unfortunately, many Americans seem to want to burn the whole thing down, it is particularly important to maintain perspective. Ask yourself, and challenge others to consider: Is American democracy worth fighting for? Is Ukraine worth defending? Should America be a beacon for freedom and a bulwark against tyrants? Should we stand with Israel when she is under attack? Should we do the right thing even when it's hard and unpopular? Damn straight, Jeff Robbins says. And he says it every week, always in a fresh way, with passion and intelligence, nudging his readers to care about what he cares about and see things through his crystal-clear lens.

Society today faces myriad serious challenges, such as deep-rooted social divisions, climate change, and an unwillingness or inability to tackle long-term problems, just to name a few. Too often we suffer from unserious leaders who are more focused on popularity and theatrics than on getting things done. To our current morass, Jeff Robbins applies his keen mind and sharp pen, identifying issues, enlightening us and suggesting a path forward.

Whether you are a regular or occasional reader of Jeff's columns, or even if you are unfamiliar with his work, the volume in your hands is a great way to catch up on the past five years, jumpstart your understanding of today's most pressing issues and become a fan of Jeff Robbins.

Looking through the windshield almost halfway through 2024 is already daunting: There's a presidential matchup no one really seems to want, a worryingly divided electorate, a sweeping rollback of the right of women to control their own bodies, looming threats to LGBTQ rights, rising religious bigotry, an emboldening of authoritarians across the globe, and a radical rearrangement of political alliances and voting patterns. Trying to keep up with all of this can be like driving on a back road at night with your headlights off. But reading this compilation of columns is like having Jeff on the passenger side, helping you navigate difficult terrain and unprecedented road conditions—and with no rest stops in sight. With Jeff, you're more likely to arrive unscathed at the desired destination.

The past five years have gone by in a blink for many of us. Readers of the Boston Herald know they did not pass by unremarked, thanks to the incisive pen of Jeff Robbins, a consistent voice of reason in an often-unreasonable world.

INTRODUCTION

"It's always darkest...before it turns pitch-black," the late Sen. John McCain was fond of quipping. History, practically by definition, consists of difficult times that, one way or the other, have been overcome, or at least endured. Still, it does appear as though much that we cherish is on the brink.

At home, it seems no exaggeration to say that the future of democracy as we have known it, even in its far-from-perfect incarnation, lies in real and present danger, threatened by extremism in new and newly toxic forms and by direct challenges to the rule of law.

Abroad, democracy is also under assault, as Vladimir Putin's armies, two years into their punishing invasion of Ukraine, threaten to subjugate a fledgling democracy, in turn raising fears among the democracies of Western Europe that they may be next. Many Americans revert to the unwise, downright dangerous position that defending democracy is none of America's business, while millions actually seem perfectly content to let Putin overrun Ukraine and anything else he decides to overrun.

In the Middle East, savage forces whose very reason for being is to annihilate the Jewish state invaded Israeli villages on a peaceful Saturday morning, slaughtering some 1,200 Israelis as they danced at a holiday peace festival or slept in their beds, mutilating many more and kidnapping 250 others. Hamas and its backers worldwide have succeeded in portraying themselves as "freedom fighters" worthy of the support of "progressives," while those whom they have victimized are portrayed as being the perpetrators of a "genocide."

In the meantime, falsity is peddled as truth with an intensity and an abandon that we've never quite known before, with no particular reason to think that this state of affairs will self-correct.

Still, there are plenty of people out there fighting for good, and that is reason for hope.

These weekly columns span the period from 2019 through the spring of 2024, encompassing, among other things, COVID, a momentous presidential campaign, an attempted American coup, a historic surge in domestic extremism, the Russian invasion of Ukraine and Hamas' assault on Israel. I am grateful to the Boston Herald and to Creators for the opportunity to write them.

I am indebted to many, but to no one as much as my children, Alex and Tali, and to my magnificent wife, Joanne, whose gift at giving love exceeds even her gift at editing, which is saying something.

Democrats Misfire When Taking Aim at Joe Biden Remarks

June 25, 2019

    Those who count on Democrats' penchant for self-cannibalization to pave the way for President Donald Trump's second term were buoyed by the harsh criticism leveled at former Vice President Joe Biden over a handful of words uttered at a New York fundraiser last week. Reflecting on the dispiriting state of American political discourse, the presidential candidate gave an entirely appropriate illustration of how corrosive things have gotten — in the process leading the kamikaze wing of his party to prove his point.

    Biden, chosen by former President Barack Obama to serve as his vice president, endorsed by civil rights icon Rep. John Lewis and other black congressional leaders, and blowing his rivals for the Democratic presidential nomination away among black voters, spent last week defending himself against charges that he is somewhere between racially insensitive and an outright racist. The reason: At the fundraiser, Biden ruminated about having attempted early in his Senate career to find common ground even with segregationists whose politics he reviled, using as examples Southern Sens. James Eastland and Herman Talmadge — the latter whom Biden labeled "one of the meanest guys I ever knew." As for Eastland, whose opposition to civil rights Biden pointed out disgusted him, Biden said: "He never called me 'boy.' He always called me 'son.'" Nothing about Biden's observation suggested he was remembering Eastland's use of "boy" fondly, or that he was sentimental about the belittling language used by Southern whites for black males. The 10 words seized upon by Biden's rivals to paint him as a segregationist sympathizer were likelier to have been uttered sardonically and at Eastland's expense.

    Biden then finished his point, which was this: Though he abhorred what Eastland and Talmadge represented, he wanted to try to locate discrete areas on which they might work together. "At least there was some civility," said Biden, who is hardly off his rocker for being shaken by the ugliness that has engulfed not only Washington but the entire nation, of a sort to which he was then subjected. A frenzy of Biden bashing ensued, courtesy of those seemingly bent on demonstrating just how markedly intellectual dishonesty has supplanted levelheadedness. Sen. Cory Booker, polling at 2%, wasted no time trying to resuscitate a candidacy headed nowhere. He called Biden's remarks "insulting," accused him of "usage of words that harms folks" and called upon Biden to apologize. Biden, of course, had said nothing insulting or harmful to black Americans, as black Biden supporters like Lewis and South Carolina Rep. Jim Clyburn observed. And it required no well-honed sense of irony to note that Booker, no anti-Semite, was caught on video days later answering a question about whether he would be willing to meet with notorious anti-Semite Louis Farrakhan. "I'm not one of those people who says I wouldn't sit down with anybody to hear what they have to say," Booker replied.

Sen. Elizabeth Warren added some disingenuousness of her own to the mix. "I'm not here to criticize other Democrats," she told The Washington Post, "but it's never OK to celebrate segregationists. Never." Biden had not "celebrated" segregationists in any shape or form. Rep. Alexandria Ocasio-Cortez then accused Biden of "waxing nostalgic" about segregationists, an accusation not only false but also dishonest. Her charge of racial insensitivity was particularly rich given her invocation of the phrases "Never again!" and "concentration camps" to compare the inhumane detention centers maintained at our borders with the Nazi death camps where millions of Jews were herded into gas chambers and incinerated during the Holocaust.

Disingenuousness is not the best of all possible looks for Democrats headed into 2020. And hubris that it will be overlooked by the electorate is not the best of all possible strategies.

Pete Buttigieg Shapes Up as Serious Democratic Contender

November 1, 2019

The conventional wisdom about South Bend Mayor Pete Buttigieg's presidential candidacy has seemed incontestable: He may be smart, sensible and appealing, but he hasn't a prayer of winning the 2020 Democratic presidential nomination. With Buttigieg's surge in polls of potential Iowa caucusgoers, however, that bit of conventional wisdom, like other conventional wisdom that has imploded in recent presidential campaigns, may end up as stale as last month's bread. The hard fact is that Buttigieg could win the February Iowa caucuses. And if he does, his candidacy, fueled by momentum, a potentially endless flow of campaign contributions and the advantage of seeming the fresh face in an old and tired Democratic field, could reshape the Democratic nominating process overnight.

Friday's New York Times/Siena College poll found Buttigieg in a statistical tie for first place in Iowa, in a dead heat with Sen. Elizabeth Warren, Sen. Bernie Sanders and former Vice President Joe Biden. This was no outlier; an Iowa State University poll taken the previous week had him in a strong second place, with 20% of surveyed caucusgoers in his camp. That was on the heels of yet another poll showing him essentially tied for first place. Buttigieg's Iowa surge is real, and it has been boosted by the young mayor's intrinsic likability, his "barnstormers'" tours across the Hawkeye State and millions of dollars of cash on hand provided by a highly successful fundraising effort.

Nor did Buttigieg hurt himself with a fine performance at Iowa Democrats' Liberty & Justice Celebration in Des Moines on Friday night. Over 2,000 of his supporters showed up at the arena in which the gathering was held, and, not for the first time, their candidate delivered the cleanest, clearest rebuke to President Donald Trump. "(T)he purpose of the presidency," Buttigieg told the audience, "is not the glorification of the president but the unification of the American people." The clean-cut Afghanistan veteran, who has exuded Midwestern decency since launching his candidacy, presents to many Americans as the equivalent of a deep, cleansing bath after the slime shower inflicted on the nation over the past three years. "Pete comes across to people as absolutely authentic," said former

Democratic National Committee Chairman Steve Grossman, who has endorsed Buttigieg. "Likability trumps almost everything else in American politics. It is highly possible that Pete can do extraordinarily well in Iowa."

A Buttigieg victory in Iowa is a distinct possibility and one that would upend the political card table. Biden's still-strong national poll numbers notwithstanding, he is in trouble. His cash on hand to slug it out in the early-primary states and still prevail in the cross-country nomination battle to follow is very low, his fundraising hampered by dependence on maxed-out big donors. His candidacy is startlingly devoid of support from young or even middle-aged voters; the New York Times/Siena poll found that only 2% of Iowa Democrats under age 45 support the former vice president. He appears headed to a fade-out, and a likely fourth-place finish in Iowa will hasten his fade.

A Buttigieg win would deal a blow to Warren's basic strategy: to win Iowa, ride a momentum-driven rocket into New Hampshire, win there and roll over a flattened Biden to win the nomination. Instead, it would be Buttigieg who would be poised to win New Hampshire in a multicandidate field. Warren would have to duke it out with Buttigieg in primary states across the country that feature Democratic primary voters more hospitable to Buttigieg's more moderate views than those of Warren, whose hold on progressive Democrats will be challenged by Sanders right through the Democratic convention.

Expecting the unexpected has proven the safest course in recent presidential elections. Buttigieg's sudden emergence as a serious contender in Iowa is a reminder of how many surprises are out there waiting to surprise us.

Details of Trump Ukraine Extortion Will Not Be Pretty

November 11, 2019

By the time acting U.S. Ambassador to Ukraine Bill Taylor appears before the House Intelligence Committee tomorrow to publicly detail President Donald Trump's extortion of Ukraine for his own personal political gain, the president's team of malarkey artists will have taken their customary best shot at character assassination, spewing the kind of nonsense that most fourth graders instinctively know is beneath them. Trump will have an uphill battle discrediting Taylor's profoundly damaging testimony, but one can rest assured that the facts will not deter him.

Taylor has been the classic patriot, and his personal courage in serving and defending his country contrasts rather sharply with the Prince of Bone Spurs' occupation of the Oval Office. Taylor's career began at West Point, and he spent six years as an infantry officer including with the 101st Airborne Division in Vietnam before going on to serve Republican and Democratic presidents alike in high-level diplomatic assignments. Taylor is the quintessential straight arrow, quite a difference from the sleaze stew that is the Trump administration.

The relentless campaign by the president and his allies to bamboozle America down to its shoes regarding his flagrant extortion of Ukraine has been every bit as corrupt as the extortion itself. First they claimed, laughably, that the whistleblower account of the president's demand that Ukraine investigate Joe Biden's son, who was serving on the board of Ukrainian energy company Burisma, was hearsay. This was followed by the White House's own "rough transcript" of Trump's July 25 call to Ukrainian President Volodymyr Zelensky, which confirmed the whistleblower account, followed quickly by further confirmation in Trump's own admissions and those of his chief of staff.

Next, the president maintained, equally laughably, that his demand for Ukraine's "investigation" was not linked to the release of congressionally mandated aid for Ukraine. But the July 25 transcript ("I would like you to do us a favor though") did not lie, even if the president always does, and his chief of staff admitted that Trump's demand precisely constituted a quid pro quo. Then followed a procession of State Department officials who, rejecting

Trump's instructions that they keep their mouths shut about what they knew, confirmed in dispiriting detail that this was nothing more than a stickup, and one conceived, initiated and carried out by the president himself.

This week most Americans will get their first look at Bill Taylor's testimony about admissions by Trump's megadonor buddy and Ambassador to the European Union Gordon Sondland, personally dispatched by Trump to tell Ukraine how things were going to be: no investigation of Biden's son, no aid. Taylor will testify that Sondland told Ukraine's president's top aide "that the security assistance money would not come until President Zelensky committed to pursue the Burisma investigation." This, in turn, came straight from Trump himself. Taylor said: "Ambassador Sondland told me that President Trump had told him that he wants President Zelensky to state publicly that Ukraine will investigate Burisma and alleged Ukrainian interference in the 2016 U.S. election." There was no ambiguity, no difference of interpretation and nothing subtle about it. As Ambassador Taylor has already testified, "Sondland said everything was dependent on such an announcement. ... He said that President Trump wanted President Zelensky 'in a public box' by making such a public statement about ordering such investigations."

On the merits, this is a high crime and an abuse of office that cries out for Trump's impeachment and removal. He will never be removed, of course: The Republican Senate caucus, like its House counterpart, is chockablock with political eunuchs too petrified of Trump to act honestly on the evidence. But Trump, who decried the closed-door Intelligence Committee depositions as "secret," now denounces the decision to hold public hearings, where the evidence against him will be laid out for all to see. No wonder. The evidence against him is not going to be pretty.

After Silence, Christian Magazine Calls Trump out for Moral Failure

December 23, 2019

One of the numerous questions that will dog historians seeking explanations for this period in American history is why so many devout Christians, who work hard to incorporate Christ's teachings into their own lives and the life of their community, embrace President Donald Trump, a man whose life makes such a mockery of those teachings. Indeed, we have saddled ourselves with a president who seems the very personification of moral rot.

He has cheated small-business men, contractors and employees. He has defrauded students and conned charities. He has clearly committed sexual harassment and not only admitted it but bragged about it — on videotape. Hush money has been paid to women with whom he is alleged to have committed adultery in order to silence them including a porn star who says he cheated with her on his third wife shortly after she gave birth to their son.

There has been his taunting of women, of a reporter with disabilities, even of American patriot John McCain, whom Trump actually ridiculed for being captured while fighting for our country in Vietnam — a war that Trump evaded by using his family's wealth to cook up a clearly phony story about bone spurs. There have been the lies — not merely hundreds of them but thousands of them. Last week, the man actually mocked a dead World War II veteran, who served honorably in Congress for decades, by suggesting to supporters that he is in hell, ridiculing the man's grieving widow at Christmastime.

One shudders to think of the effect Donald Trump is having on America's children, and one wonders how those who profess to care about children have stayed so silent about him for so long. Last week, however, the silence was broken by Christianity Today, a prominent evangelical magazine founded by the Rev. Billy Graham, which called for Trump's removal from office on moral principle.

"That he should be removed," editorialized the magazine on Thursday, "is not a matter of partisan loyalties but loyalty to the Creator of the Ten Commandments." The editor of Christianity Today, Mark Galli, emphasized on Sunday that this was wholly a judgment on Trump's morality, and one reluctantly reached.

"I'm not really ... making a political judgment about him," said Galli, whose publication has a reported 4.3 million website visitors monthly as well as several hundred thousand print subscribers. "I am making a moral judgment that he's morally unfit, or even more precisely, it's his public morality that makes him unfit."

"We have reserved judgment on Mr. Trump for years now," the magazine wrote. "But the facts in this instance are unambiguous: The president of the United States attempted to use his political power to coerce a foreign leader to harass and discredit one of the president's political opponents. That is not only a violation of the Constitution; more importantly, it is profoundly immoral."

But more damningly still, the magazine laid out Trump's failure to meet acceptable moral standards in unsparing fashion. "The reason many are not shocked about this," it wrote, "is that this president has dumbed down the idea of morality in his administration. He has hired and fired a number of people who are now convicted criminals. He himself has admitted to immoral actions in business and his relationship with women, about which he remains proud. His Twitter feed alone — with its habitual string of mischaracterizations, lies, and slanders — is a near perfect example of a human being who is morally lost and confused."

"Morally lost and confused" is surely a gentle, and charitable, way of putting it. But it is nevertheless an important statement by a respected publication of faith that there are limits to the silence that has so sadly protected an immoral president. Christianity Today has done the nation its readers love and revere a very great service.

Fake Views: GOP Senators' Professed Anger Phony as Can Be

January 28, 2020

Rep. Adam Schiff, lead House manager of the impeachment case against President Donald Trump, delivered a tour de force last week, painfully, crushingly detailing the president's obvious guilt and decimating his defenses. It's fair to say, however, that this did not go over all that agreeably with Senate Republicans who, determined to sidestep the evidence of Trump's abuse of power and obstruction of Congress, opted for phony professions of outrage at being called to account.

Leading the charge was Sen. Susan Collins, whose depressing forfeiture of a once-meaningful reputation for independence has led former admirers to shake their heads at what fear of a Republican primary can do to a person's conscience. Collins claimed to be appalled at Congressman Jerry Nadler's use of the phrase "cover up" to describe conduct by Senate Republicans that can't easily be described otherwise. Trump's "defense" of the mountain of evidence against him is the patently false assertion that none of it is "first-hand." But Republicans have not merely looked the other way at Trump's blanket order that the documents reflecting his conduct be withheld and the aides to whom he gave orders be gagged; presented with a simple request that the documents be turned over and the aides be required to tell the truth, they made the request impossible. For his part, the president does not hide the fact that he is hiding the facts. "We're doing very well," Trump boasted about the impeachment proceedings last week. "(H)onestly, we have all the material. They don't have the material."

Collins is upset about the phrase "cover-up." Too bad. That is precisely what it is, and her objection to a phrase that fits the GOP's conduct like a glove makes her look ridiculous. Evidently, in the United States Senate, which Collins claims to revere, it is now permissible to block the truth and impermissible to speak it.

But it wasn't only the apt use of "cover-up" that Collins and colleagues find offensive. It was Schiff's reference to a CBS News report that said Republican senators had been warned, "Vote against the president and your head will be on a pike." "That's not true," shouted Collins, and Alaska Republican Sen. Lisa Murkowski complained, "That's where he lost me."

Whether the White House used the word "pike" or "spear," there is no doubt that the message has been delivered — forcefully and repeatedly: If Republicans stand up to Trump, they will sleep with the fishes, politically speaking. "I talk to Republicans all the time, quietly, individually," said Democratic Sen. Sherrod Brown on Friday. "(M)any of them tell me that Trump's a liar ... but they're all afraid of him." Republicans' professions of outrage at reports that they are afraid of Trump are, quite simply, as phony as a $3 bill.

Indeed, "phony" is the word that rushes to mind when listening to Trump's defenses, and one hardly knows which among them is the most laughable. One potential prize winner: Trump's contention that he had not demanded a quid pro quo from Ukraine. Knowing that he was guilty of the demand, he uttered the words "no quid pro quo" in a conversation in which he expressly confirmed that he was demanding a quid pro quo. This bit of idiocy would not survive scrutiny by fifth graders. "In other words," observes Brown University constitutional scholar Corey Brettschneider, "if the president is robbing a bank and says, 'I am not robbing a bank,' we should believe him."

Despite the hokum and the fraud served up by the White House's smoke-blowing machine, polls show that most Americans get what is going on here. Two surveys released before Schiff buried Trump found that 51% want Trump removed right now. Republican senators will no doubt succeed in preventing that. They are unlikely, however, to prevent a verdict from being rendered against them by history.

Celebrity Trumps: The Sad Implosion of Alan Dershowitz

February 4, 2020

The road leading to President Donald Trump's acquittal from charges of which he is plainly guilty is littered with a trail of public figures selling their souls and abandoning their consciences. Few have been more dispiriting, however, than retired law professor Alan Dershowitz, whose reputation imploded in national view during Trump's impeachment trial, all seemingly because of an unquenchable thirst for limelight. Dershowitz's embarrassing performance in the service of a corrupt president who positively basks in a totalitarian's view of his own power (speaking of the Constitution, he said, "I have an Article 2, where I have the right to do whatever I want as president") left Dershowitz looking like a sad and simple toady, so enthralled by media attention that he is willing to say anything for anyone in order to get it.

From its outset, the Trump presidency provided Dershowitz the welcome opportunity for attention, and he has taken advantage of it. He has been ubiquitous on cable television, sounding somewhere between silly and ridiculous on the president's behalf, arguing that the poor beleaguered Trump was being persecuted by those bent on trampling his civil liberties. As impeachment proceedings got underway, Dershowitz found himself in increasing demand and was tapped to be on Trump's defense team, an appointment he appeared to relish. His pitch: However accurately the articles of impeachment passed by the House summarize Trump's conduct, Trump cannot be impeached because he has not committed a statutory crime. Before you could say, "egg on his face," a clip surfaced of Dershowitz proclaiming the precise opposite with equal self-assurance in 1999. "It certainly doesn't have to be a crime," Dershowitz had said. "If you have somebody who completely corrupts the office of the president and who abuses trust and who poses great danger to our liberty, you don't need a technical crime."

Faced with this direct contradiction from his own lips, Dershowitz launched a series of cringeworthy "clarifications" that damaged his credibility further. "I wasn't wrong. I have a more sophisticated basis for my argument," he explained to one interviewer. "I didn't do research back then. I relied on what professors said," he told another. "I am much more correct right now," he insisted to a third, a line that may live on for its hubris and its inanity.

From there, Dershowitz proceeded to the well of the Senate to declare on behalf of President Trump that Trump could demand whatever he wanted of whomever he wanted as long as he believed it would get him reelected. "If a president does something which he believes will help him get elected in the public interest, that cannot be the kind of quid pro quo that results in impeachment," announced Dershowitz. This concept of American democracy evoked Mussolini more than Jefferson. Once again, Dershowitz tried to backtrack, falsely denying what he had said and then accusing those who had heard him of "distortion."

In his needy zeal for the spotlight, Dershowitz has self-eviscerated, eliminating his credibility on an issue that, one imagines, matters more to him than Trump does. For decades, Dershowitz has ably made the progressive case for Israel, challenging its critics on the left and arguing, frequently under fire, that those who genuinely care about democratic values should regard Israel, which has broadly preserved those values, with respect, rather than hatred. Dershowitz's unprincipled defense of the attempted dismantling of democracy by a president contemptuous of it has served to decommission him as an advocate for Israel; his association with Israel hurts Israel, rather than helps it, which is too bad for it and too bad for him.

In fairness, Donald Trump has had quite a team of enablers, and Dershowitz is far from the only one who has contributed to our crisis by letting his country down. He is a reminder of how much, and how quickly, work needs to be done to restore our nation to the one we once took for granted.

Tale of 2 Heroes: Sen. Romney and Col. Vindman Remind America What It's About

February 11, 2020

Last week provided more confirmation that America lies in intensive care, its recovery in doubt. It featured the defense lawyer for the president of the United States informing Americans that their president is free to threaten anyone he chooses with whatever consequences he wants in order to extract anything he wants in return, and is still immune from impeachment so long as he believes it will help him remain in office — an interpretation of American democracy at once novel and totalitarian. It included Republicans at the State of the Union acting like frat boys, chanting, "Four more years!" to convey their enthusiasm for a president who is not merely clinically megalomaniacal but also conclusively demonstrated to be epically corrupt.

Then there was the National Prayer Breakfast, at which our president expressly rejected the keynote speaker's gentle requests that he reflect on the teachings of Christ and try, maybe just a little bit, to incorporate them. And the oh-so-presidential "celebration" of his Senate acquittal on charges of abuse of power and obstruction of Congress, so conclusively documented that even some Republicans who were too intimidated by the president to vote to convict him openly admitted that the charges were true. Standing at a lectern embossed with the presidential seal, Donald Trump once again modeled pure dignity and grace for the American people, using obscenities and calling the FBI "scum." Trump also denounced those who had proven his guilt, calling them "the crookedest, most dishonest, dirtiest people I've ever seen." Those were remarkable words indeed given the numerous individuals he has seen at quite close range, including his former personal lawyer, his former campaign manager, his former national security adviser and his longtime political confidante, who have been convicted of felonies and are either headed to federal prison or already reside there.

It isn't merely Trump who reflects the advanced state of our national disease but his base, whose size and psyche have destroyed our heretofore self-congratulatory self-image. Trump World regards as really neat that which the decent among us instinctively know is indecent. Thus, for instance, the president and his enthusiasts feel it is clever to riff childishly on U.S. Rep. Adam Schiff's last name, with the moniker "Shifty Schiff" the least juvenile of the insults. When Schiff's fellow House manager Rep. Jerrold Nadler tweeted that he would miss some of the impeachment proceedings in order to help his wife cope with pancreatic cancer, some of his fellow countrymen replied that they looked forward to his return so he could be tried for treason. A spate of polls showed that 49% of Americans view Trump favorably. Former Massachusetts Gov. Deval Patrick, a candidate for his party's presidential nomination, has taken to saying, "This time, it's about the character of the country," and he is right.

But there was also good news, and there were people to be proud of. Sen. Mitt Romney, the sole Republican in Congress to be honest about Donald Trump, who reminded Americans what patriotism and political courage look like. Romney's vote to convict Trump has already generated the viciousness that is Trump World's calling card, but it has also earned him a degree of admiration reserved for few politicians, one that will endure in history. Ditto for Lt. Colonel Alexander Vindman, the son of a Ukrainian family who came to America fleeing totalitarianism because, in America, "right matters." Vindman fought for his nation, told the truth and was kneecapped by a president who dodged military service by having his wealthy family pay for a "bone spurs" diagnosis.

Mitt Romney and Alexander Vindman are saving graces, individuals we can point to when telling our children and grandchildren what America has been, what it has meant and why it deserves to be rescued. They are examples that provide some hope as we struggle to save a country that has long provided hope to so many.

Lemming Complex: The Bernie Bros Demand That the Democrats Jump off a Cliff

February 18, 2020

Bernie Sanders is as principled a major presidential candidate as we have seen. He has had the courage of his convictions for several decades, ceaselessly hammering away at issues of economic justice in ways that have opened millions of Americans' eyes to truths that have seemed too unpleasant to confront.

And if he becomes the Democratic presidential nominee, the likely consequence is four more years of President Donald Trump, the most dangerous, most damaging president we have ever had.

The hard fact is that in order to deny Trump a second term, whoever is the Democratic nominee must score the equivalent of a royal flush. She or he must hold every single state carried by Hillary Clinton in 2016, and flip Pennsylvania, Michigan and Wisconsin. Each of those three. Without losing a single state carried by Clinton in 2016. Not New Hampshire, where Trump lost by less than 3,000 votes. Not Nevada, which he lost by only 27,000 votes. Not Minnesota, which he lost by only 45,000 votes. Otherwise, we are looking at a second Trump inaugural.

Sanders argues that he, uniquely, is positioned to generate such broad enthusiasm among hitherto disenfranchised or disengaged voters that a tidal wave of support for the Democratic ticket will sweep Trump out to sea. "To win, we need energy, we need excitement, we need the largest voter turnout in American history," Sanders has said. "I think we are the campaign to do that."

Problem is, the data from Iowa and New Hampshire — a limited sampling, to be sure, but two states where Sanders spent massive amounts of time and resources in 2016, and still is in 2020 — throws some ice water on Sanders' argument. In 2008, 239,000 voters participated in the Iowa caucuses; this year, only 176,000 did, a drop-off of about 20% despite the disaster of the past three years. Sanders received just 26% of that sharply reduced turnout.

In New Hampshire, a state in which Sanders is virtually a third senator, he had a highly energized army of supporters and the benefit of a powerful political apparatus. Though the primary turnout increased from 250,000 in 2016 to 300,000 in 2020, the number of Democratic primary voters casting votes for Sanders dropped by 50%, from 153,000 in 2016 to only 76,000 this year. The Vermont senator eked out a win of fewer than 4,000 votes over Pete Buttigieg, the 37-year-old ex-mayor of a small Indiana city with no ties to New Hampshire and no natural base there. Compared with Sanders' 26% of the New Hampshire vote — which, at this rate, will earn him the moniker One Quarter Bernie — an aggregate 52% of the votes were cast for Buttigieg, Sen. Amy Klobuchar and former Vice President Joe Biden, all of whom in varying degrees pitched themselves as the "anti-Bernie" in the race. The apparent queasiness about Sanders among Democrats does not augur well for Sanders, especially if the theory that Sanders will generate a turnout blowout fizzles out.

Then there is the little matter of Sanders' self-identification as a socialist. The Sanders camp waves that aside, arguing that this will pose no impediment to his election. They are in a dreamland. Asked late last month about the cost to taxpayers of his proposal to make all health care and all college free, Sanders confessed to being clueless. "You don't know how much your plan costs?" journalist Norah O'Donnell asked Sanders. "You don't know," he replied. "Nobody knows. This is impossible to predict." This quote, and plenty more where that came from, is going to hurt Sanders badly, and there is no use pretending otherwise.

It may well be that this should not be the case. Perhaps in an America of the not-so-distant future, things will be otherwise. But we are not there. Where we are is in serious trouble, and Bernie Sanders as nominee is not going to get us out of it.

Art of the Self-Inflicted Wound: Pro-Palestinians Keep on Targeting Palestinians

February 25, 2020

With the same sad inevitability of death and taxes, a body that professes to care about the Palestinians but is mostly rabidly opposed to Israel took action this month that followed a familiar pattern: invoking the plight of Palestinians while doing them damage. For the umpteenth time, the source of the disconnect was the United Nations Human Rights Council, a bureaucracy long recognized by Democratic and Republican administrations alike as so debilitated by hypocrisy in general and anti-Israel bias in particular that it has precious credibility left. The action: The council published a blacklist of companies, including American ones, that in some fashion "do business" with Jews living in Israeli settlements. Everyone, including Palestinian negotiators, acknowledges that some of those settlements will formally become part of Israel in any eventual peace deal. The purpose: to support the anti-Israel boycott, divestment and sanctions movement, the vehicle of choice for those whose detestation of Israel outpaces their concern for the welfare of Palestinians.

For starters, the U.N.'s encouragement of the boycotting of businesses that engage with Israeli settlements on the West Bank largely hurts Palestinians. According to a report issued by the watchdog group Palestinian Media Watch based on interviews with Palestinian workers and lawyers, and the Palestinian Bureau of Statistics, Palestinians prefer working for Israeli companies on the West Bank to Palestinian ones. Israeli employers pay substantially higher wages and provide Palestinians with the same health care benefits, sick leave and vacation time as Israelis. The boycotts of these companies, therefore, disproportionately harm Palestinians. This did not stop the vapid endorsements of the council's move by Palestinian leaders, who compete with one another to find slogans that make the least sense. "A timely message for those who push us toward chaos and lawlessness," Husam Zomlot, the head of the Palestinian Mission to the United Kingdom tweeted about a boycott that may separate Palestinians who want to work from the jobs that permit them to do so. He was trumped by Palestinian Foreign Minister Riyad al-Malik, who labeled the U.N.'s call for a boycott "a victory for international law and diplomatic efforts," a head-scratcher if ever there was one.

The history of Palestinian self-harm is long, wearying and depressing. Had Palestinian leaders accepted the independent Palestinian state created for them by the U.N. in 1947, there would never have been any Israeli settlements on the West Bank. Had they chosen to create a Palestinian state when Israel had no presence on the West Bank, likewise no settlements. Had they accepted the Palestinian state on virtually all of the West Bank and all of Gaza with a capital in East Jerusalem offered by Israel in 2000, 2001 and again in 2009, ditto. The narrative insistently peddled by Israel's detractors that Jewish settlements are the source of the unending Palestinian-Israeli conflict isn't merely ahistoric. It's balderdash.

It reflects no love for the knot of right-wing religious zealots who have Israel's democracy in their grip to point that out. One may be repulsed by Israeli Prime Minister Benjamin Netanyahu's noxious authoritarianism, or by how the love fest between him and President Donald Trump is degrading American empathy for Israel, and still stipulate the obvious: Given that the Palestinians reject an independent Palestinian state over and over, offered to them by left-leaning Israeli leaders and centrist ones, it ain't Netanyahu or West Bank settlements that pose the real problem.

Whether it is boycotts bathed in the clever rhetoric of human rights but guaranteed to hurt Palestinians most of all, or the organized terrorizing of Jewish kids on college campuses aimed at browbeating them into abandoning their support for a Jewish national homeland, the BDS movement has made intimidation its trademark. As Arab and African states have drawn closer and closer to Israel, and patience in the Mideast for the Palestinian preference for victimhood over statehood has waned, BDS has grown ever angrier and ever less credible. This is too bad for Palestinians, and too bad for the prospects for peace.

Truth Decay: Con Job Central Confronts a Public Health Crisis

March 3, 2020

One thing you have to say about President Donald Trump: Three years into his presidency, people don't believe a word he says. Not his Cabinet. Not Kellyanne Conway. Not the bartender at Mar-a-Lago.

The president has never seemed bothered that everyone appears to know he lies constantly; after all, half of America finds his unrepentant dissembling somehow refreshing. But his dishonesty on every subject under the sun did not position him terribly well to reassure Americans or the stock market about the coronavirus when he finally felt obliged last week to say something about it. What limited credibility he retains seemed to evaporate by the minute during last Wednesday's press conference, at which his disinterest in facts and disregard for them were on display. Trump's assertion that the number of coronavirus cases in the United States was "going substantially down, not up," echoed by his economic advisor's boast that "We have contained this," was flatly contradicted by various top officials of the Centers for Disease Control and Prevention. Each stated that more cases are expected. "It's not so much a question of if this will happen anymore," said Nancy Messonnier, director of the National Center for Immunization and Respiratory Disorders, "but rather more a question when this will happen and how many people in this country will have severe illness."

But it continued. We are "rapidly developing a vaccine," Trump proclaimed. A top CDC official shut that down as well. No vaccine would be ready for "a year to a year and a half," he said. Then there was this Trump tweet during a week in which the market lost 10% of its value: "Stock market starting to look pretty good to me," eye-rolling malarkey.

By Friday, Trump sounded like a cross between Captain Queeg and Mr. Magoo, prattling incoherently on the White House lawn. "We're ordering a lot of supplies," he told reporters. "We're ordering a lot of, ah, elements that, frankly, we wouldn't be ordering unless it was something like this. But we're ordering a lot of different elements of medical. We are working on cures, and we're getting some very good results. As you know, they're working as rapidly as they can on a vaccine for the future. And with that I think I can head out."

By "head out" he meant fly to South Carolina, where he told a rally that all this talk about the coronavirus was actually a "hoax." His son and namesake were likewise on message, accusing Democrats of hoping that the virus would kill "millions of people so that they can end Donald Trump's streak of winning."

Within hours, the death of the first American from the virus necessitated the hastily organized press conference, slapped together so the president could appear presidential and hopefully divert attention from the fact that, yet again, his claim of "hoax" was the hoax. Duplicity watchers did not leave the press conference empty-handed: The president who, in order to gin up his base before the 2018 midterms, conjured up the story about a fictitious caravan of terrorist marauders advancing on our southern border actually berated Democrats and the media for inciting "panic."

If Team Trump believed naming Vice President Mike Pence to lead the national response to the virus would engender trust, it was hard to know who the team thought it was kidding. There are department store mannequins that appear better equipped to handle matters of magnitude than Pence, whose area of specialization seems to be standing uncomprehendingly at his boss's side at events and, when called upon to talk, mouthing meaningless bromides.

The lesson is that credibility in a president isn't just good form and morally preferable. It lies at the heart of good governance. That this president so plainly lacks it is another reason why, for the good of the country, he has got to go.

Dennis Ross Warns That What Happens in the Mideast Rarely Stays There

March 10, 2020

Dennis Ross is anything but partisan, and the veteran diplomat, appointed by both Republican and Democratic presidents to high-level foreign policy positions, is an unusual species. A deep knowledge of America's role in the Mideast accumulated over 30 years helping to oversee that role on behalf of former Presidents Ronald Reagan, George H. W. Bush, Bill Clinton and Barack Obama has made him the go-to expert for journalists and presidential candidates alike seeking guidance on the region's mind-numbing complexities.

Ross has watched with interest, and no small amount of concern, as candidates who otherwise have little in common use the same sort of hyped-up language to convey their determination to "extricate" the United States from the Mideast. President Donald Trump is wont to use the "This is none of our business" formulation. Sen. Bernie Sanders' pithy applause line is "No more wars!" Both are appealing to the strong sentiment, found in equal measure on the American right and left, that the United States needs to disengage from the Mideast as fast as possible. It is an impulse that is easy to understand; after all, a profound weariness exists across the political spectrum, born of the calamitous loss of life and treasure we have sustained over the past two decades in attempts to impose order on a region riven by medievalism, irrationality and blood thirst.

Ross gets this. In between stints helping to run American foreign policy in the Mideast for four presidents, he has authored a series of books on the area, most recently co-authoring, with David Makovsky, "Be Strong and of Good Courage," an account of critical decision-making by Israeli prime ministers. "There is a legitimate reason why (the desire to disengage from the Mideast) exists," Ross says. "We spent heavily, we lost heavily and things got worse. We've made terrible mistakes. But simply washing our hands (of the region) will be another terrible mistake."

Ross says: "(T)he worst pathologies in the world are in the Middle East. The problem is that in the Mideast the Las Vegas Rules don't apply. What happens in the Mideast doesn't stay in the Mideast." Ross believes that American abandonment of the region, while politically popular in many quarters, is a recipe for disaster. "When vacuums form in the Mideast," he says, "they are filled by the worst kind of forces." He points out that this is not speculation: Russia, Turkey and Iran are well underway filling those vacuums. It is "much better to prevent vacuums in the first place." And asserting that the region is "none of our business" is "unhelpful," he says, which is diplomatic-speak for hugely foolish. "It will become our business," says Ross, "and we will pay a higher price and our options will be sharply reduced" if we simply place our hands over our eyes.

Asked what the next president's priority should be in the Mideast, Ross doesn't hesitate. It is "adopting policies with those who have been our partners to improve their governance. Poor governance spawns rage and extremist ideologies." Countries where the risks of failing to improve governance converge with opportunities to do so are Egypt, Saudi Arabia, Jordan, Morocco, the Emirates and Bahrain. At the same time, Ross says, the United States is strategically obliged and well served to "contest those who use terror, intimidation and violence" in the region, singling out Iran. But he stresses that neither the delicate, painstaking work of improving governance nor that of confronting Iran's ever-growing threat can be achieved without partners. "The key for us," says Ross, "is to have partners, local partners, allies. If you withdraw, you'll have no allies, no partners."

Like most highly respected diplomats, Ross is a man of balance, and of nuance. We are not much into balance or nuance these days. But this does not stop the ever-optimistic Ross from making the case for them.

Overexposed: The Lying Game Catches up With Our President

March 17, 2020

Nothing screams "reassuring" during a growing pandemic quite as much as seeing one's president unable to read a short speech written in large letters in his native language after he spent weeks deriding mounting evidence of the pandemic as "fake news." That was America's experience last week as it watched President Donald Trump struggle to get through the blather-heavy remarks hastily cobbled together for him to deliver to an increasingly anxious nation. It was, tweeted MSNBC's Chris Hayes in real time, "like he's reading a foreign language phonetically."

Trump's stab at looking presidential was as devoid of credibility as any performance he has ever given, and that is saying something. No one watching it, save the most hopelessly gullible, could have believed the president had the vaguest idea what he was doing. It was enough to trigger the only wave of nostalgia for former President Herbert Hoover on record, and it was no wonder that within minutes, stock markets tanked and American civil society began announcing that it was shutting down.

It didn't take a Ph.D. in public relations to recognize that Trump's address was the Hindenburg disaster of spin control. His team quickly attempted a do-over, arranging a Rose Garden press conference for him. There the president was joined by a gaggle of CEOs, none of whom appeared to know what he was doing there, each of them tasked with affirming their general willingness to help their country with statements 30 seconds or less.

But it was not much of an improvement over the Oval Office address. For weeks Trump had been dismissing the very idea that the novel coronavirus is worth worrying about, let alone preparing for. "We have it totally under control," he told an interviewer on Jan. 22. "It's one person coming in from China. It's going to be just fine." On Feb. 2 he trotted out the same snake oil. "We pretty much shut it down coming in from China," the president said. During February and into March, he was accusing Democrats calling for action to combat the virus of promoting "fake news," once again accusing those who saw reality differently of promoting a "hoax."

Asked in the Rose Garden by PBS reporter Yamiche Alcindor about his 2018 dismantling of the White House unit tasked with addressing global health crises, and whether he was prepared to take any responsibility for his administration's failure to prepare for the pandemic, the president displayed that stand-up guy quality for which he is famous. "I think it's a nasty question," he snapped. "When you say me, I didn't do it. We have a group of people in this administration." Pressed by NBC's Kristen Welker whether he accepts any responsibility for our ill-preparedness, The Prince of Bone Spurs was true to character. "I don't take responsibility at all," he said, ever the role model. Then there was the White House's strange rollout of a poster board with a graphic touting a website that Americans could supposedly access for coronavirus testing, developed by Google and ready for use "very quickly." This was news to Google, which quickly corrected him. Turns out its subsidiary has merely agreed to try to develop a pilot website, which is not ready and won't be ready anytime soon.

It was Vice President Mike Pence, head of the president's coronavirus task force, who inadvertently captured the alternate universe in which Trump World resides. "This day should be an inspiration to every American," he proclaimed at the press conference with a perfectly straight face. It was a reminder that something was seriously unhealthy in America even before the coronavirus hit, and will remain amiss even after the virus is defeated.

Branch Covidian: The Virus Denier in Chief Tries a Rewrite

March 24, 2020

When it comes to pithy lines about dishonesty, writer Mary McCarthy's takedown of playwright Lillian Hellman remains a timeless classic. "Everything she writes is a lie," said McCarthy, "including 'and' and 'the.'" McCarthy died before Donald Trump became president, and wherever she is, she is undoubtedly glad she did. But any literary exaggeration by Hellman is mere chicken feed compared with the steady flow of falsehoods to which the nation is subjected daily by the president, who's responsible for bringing the word "pathological," previously used only by medical professionals, into common usage. As Trump likes to say: "No one could have imagined it. We've never seen anything like it." On the matter of presidential lying, at least, President Trump is spot on. Last week's front-runner for Exhibit A was Trump's claim that he recognized the coronavirus as a public health crisis way before others. "I felt it was a pandemic long before it was called a pandemic," he informed us. This, of course, was the usual hogwash from the perennial hogwash peddler.

Asked on Jan. 22, "Are you worried about a pandemic at this point?" the man who knew it was a pandemic before everyone else replied: "No, not at all. And we have it totally under control." Asked on Jan. 31 whether he was concerned about the coronavirus, Trump said, "Well, we've pretty much shut it down." On Feb. 10, he denied that there was anything to worry about. "A lot of people think it goes away in April," he said. On Feb. 26, the president told us that the virus was about to disappear. "Within a couple of days it's going to be down to close to zero," he said. On Feb. 28, he offered this inanity: "Almost everybody that we see is getting better, and it could be everybody." The next day, the president tried to sell America the epidemiological Brooklyn Bridge, stating that a coronavirus vaccine would be available "very quickly" and "very rapidly." On March 2, he doubled down with this lie: "They're going to have a vaccine relatively soon."

On March 6, he lied about the availability of coronavirus testing. "As of right now and yesterday," he said, "anybody who needs a test gets a test. They're there. They have the tests, and the tests are beautiful." The same day, asked by a reporter, "What do you say to Americans who are concerned you're not taking this seriously enough and that your statements don't match what your health experts are saying?" he snapped and replied, "That's CNN fake news." On March 15, when asked about the virus, the president lied: "It is something we have tremendous control over."

In government as in other sectors, denial and lying go hand in hand with incompetence, and the Trump administration's handling of the coronavirus is a historic example. Warned directly of the approaching pandemic in January, it did nothing to prepare the public or the health system to confront it. Asked on March 16, "On a scale of one to 10, how would you rate your response to this crisis?" Trump didn't hesitate to congratulate himself. "I'd rate it 10," he said. Shocker. In the meantime, he continued to refuse his authority to commandeer the production of desperately needed masks, protective equipment and ventilators, on which American lives depend. Instead, he told the nations' governors that they are on their own: "The federal government is not supposed to be out there buying vast amounts of items and then shipping. You know, we're not a shipping clerk."

Let's face it: The Trump presidency is in shambles. The ceaseless lying is a big reason why. The incompetence will not stop until the lying does, and it was obvious long ago that the lying will not stop until someone else occupies the Oval Office.

His Finest Hour: Andrew Cuomo Reminds Us How It's Done

March 31, 2020

In "The Splendid and the Vile," his new book about former Prime Minister Winston Churchill's stewardship of Britain through the desperate early months of World War II, Erik Larson details the seemingly hopeless circumstances confronting the country. Germany had overrun Europe and was poised to begin a bombing campaign aimed at obliterating British cities and, if that didn't force England's surrender, to invade England. By late 1941, 45,000 Britons had been killed and 52,000 injured. Three hundred thousand British soldiers were trapped at Dunkirk, certain to be captured or annihilated. German submarines were preventing supplies from reaching Britain, which was effectively on its own.

Churchill was defiant. "We shall not fail or falter," he proclaimed. "We shall not weaken or tire. Neither the sudden shock of battle nor the long-drawn trails of vigilance and exertion will wear us down." His people knew that he was as tireless as he was asking them to be. "Papa has served them with his heart (and) his mind," Churchill's daughter wrote in her diary, "and they have given him in his finest and darkest hour their love and confidence."

It is fair to say that Americans have not been similarly blessed during the current crisis. The Daily Dissemble, the White House "briefings" on the novel coronavirus, are substantially mixtures of misrepresentation and nonsense. The president has two signature specialties. One is making claims demonstrated within 24 hours to be misleading or simply false. The other is settling upon a truly meaningless banality ("It's very important that our economy be strong. A strong economy is very, very important. Really important.") and just repeating it endlessly, as though doing so makes it less meaningless. Both have been on full display during these briefings.

One bright spot has been New York Gov. Andrew Cuomo, who, like Churchill, has had to deliver continuously dreadful news while inspiring confidence. Americans confined to their homes have taken to tuning in to the governor's daily press conferences not only to hear about the state of things in New York but also to get reminded of what leadership looks like. It has been 90 years since Americans made it a regular point to listen to what a leader had to say. Our grandparents and great-grandparents gathered to listen to then-

President Franklin Roosevelt's fireside chats during the Great Depression because they felt they could trust him: to tell the truth, to know what he was doing, to have a plan of action, to empathize with them. Cuomo brings these qualities to his briefings, and Americans living nowhere near New York tune in because of it.

In truth, even a leader merely playing with the proverbial full deck of cards would be a sight for sore eyes for Americans, who have been deprived of this for three years. But Cuomo has been just what the doctor ordered. In contrast to the president's profound unreliability, Cuomo exudes command: Here is Plan A. Here is why it is urgent that Plan A work. Here are the problems that we face making Plan A work. Here is what we are doing to solve those problems. Here is Plan B.

Cuomo, a tough political gut fighter, has provided both humanity and inspiration while showcasing hands-on management. "This is going to be a long day, and it's going to be a hard day, and it's going to be an ugly day, and it's going to be a sad day," Cuomo told the National Guard before deploying it to assist reeling New Yorkers. He reaffirmed the words of his late father and predecessor, Gov. Mario Cuomo, on what a democratic government is supposed to mean. It is, he reiterated, "family, mutuality, the sharing of benefits and burdens for the good of all, feeling one another's pain, sharing one another's blessings — reasonably, honestly, fairly, without respect to race or sex or geography or political affiliation." Cuomo's management and words have reassured a deeply anxious nation, one that is grateful to him for his finest hour.

Just Another Hoax: The President Who Doesn't Want Us to Know What Went Wrong

April 7, 2020

In the Broadway classic "Guys and Dolls," a gangster named Big Julie From Chicago informs participants in a crap game that they will be using dice specially made for him — with "invisible" spots. "These dice ain't got no spots on them," protests Nathan Detroit, the game organizer. "They're blank." But Big Julie, a practiced cheater as well as a thug, is ready. "I had the spots removed for luck," he replies. "But I remember where the spots formerly were. Do you doubt my memory?" "Big Julie," says Nathan with resignation, "I have great trust in you."

President Donald Trump channeled Big Julie From Chicago during his White House spin classes over the last few weeks, insisting — not for the first time — that he hadn't said things the entire world heard him say and insulting reporters who had the nerve to quote him back to him. "Don't be a cutie pie," snarled the leader of the free world at one reporter who asked him about the thousands of Americans dying each week. But he was particularly incensed at proposals that the country actually try to learn what the federal government knew about the pandemic, when we knew it, what we did about it and what we are doing.

One proposal circulating in Congress would create a National Commission on the COVID-19 Pandemic, "not just to look back at prior practices and mistakes but to learn lessons as quickly as possible to better protect the United States going forward." The bipartisan body would consist of five Republicans and five Democrats. To ensure that it would not interfere with our response or become a tool in the presidential election, its members would not even be appointed until after the inauguration, and the new president would appoint its chair. Presumably, if Trump is reelected, that would be Jared Kushner.

The commission's purpose would be to get the facts, which was generally regarded as a good thing in times past. After the Japanese attacked Pearl Harbor, then-President Franklin Roosevelt appointed a commission to investigate why we were so unprepared for it. After the terrorist attacks of Sept. 11, 2001, then-President George W. Bush approved a commission to investigate. Both presidents, one a Democrat and one a Republican, knew that these inquiries might well embarrass them. But both possessed the character and the maturity to know that finding the truth was critical to the welfare of the country they were elected to serve.

This president, however, is in what may charitably be called a league of his own, and he blasted the suggestion that we learn the truth about what happened with COVID-19, deploying his customary rubbish. "It's witch hunt after witch hunt," sniped Trump. "Everyone knows it's ridiculous." If the president has been honest with the American public, an inquiry shouldn't concern him. "Actually, throughout my life, my two greatest assets have been mental stability and being, like, really smart," he tweeted in 2018. Let's call that debatable on both counts.

If the president has been honest, he should welcome the investigation. He and his fellow geniuses would be free to blame the disastrous federal response to warnings about the pandemic, and response to the pandemic itself, on anyone they want: on the states, for foolishly supposing that the United States government would confront a global health catastrophe; on the impeachment proceedings, which the president claims distracted him; on former President Barack Obama's administration, which hadn't been in office for almost three years when the pandemic struck and which warned Trump's team about this in early 2017; or on UFOs. The idea is to have adults separating facts from falsehoods with expertise, integrity and the good of the nation in mind.

The president is unenthusiastic, and one may reasonably infer why. But we are in extremely tough shape, and this is no time for crap games or hiding spots.

Jesus, Take the Wheel: The President Says, 'I'll Be the Oversight'

April 14, 2020

It's human nature to be drawn to a train wreck, and President Donald Trump's daily press appearances with his COVID-19 task force have been must-see TV for horror show aficionados. The president is pumped at "the ratings" from housebound Americans tuning in, but his appearances are a draw in the same way live footage of the sinking of the Lusitania would be a draw. His answers to reporters' questions have been increasingly alarming as his severe unfitness to lead — long painfully obvious — has become inescapably clear.

"Antibiotics used to solve every problem, and now one of the biggest problems this world has is the germ has gotten so brilliant that the antibiotics can't keep up with it," babbled the president about a virus, which, by definition, cannot be treated with antibiotics. He continued: "People go to a hospital, and they catch — they go for a heart operation. That's no problem. But they end up from — from problems. You know the problems I'm talking about." Asked about what the metrics are for easing public health restrictions currently in place, the president pointed to his head and said, "The metrics are right here." For tens of millions of Americans whose mouths are agape over the inanity of the self-styled genius at the nation's helm during this time of crisis, MSNBC host Joy Reid summed it up best. "Jesus take the wheel," she tweeted.

The president's announcement last week that he alone would decide how the $500 billion allocated by Congress to large corporations hit by the virus would be distributed has not increased the nation's comfort level. Asked who would oversee the half-trillion-dollar program, Trump had just the answer to calm an anxious citizenry's nerves. "I'll be the oversight," he proclaimed. For starters, his record for honest dealing is not exactly gold-plated. Two years ago he was required to pay $25 million to settle charges that he defrauded thousands of students through a profit-making vehicle he called Trump University. Just four months ago, a New York court forced him to shut down his personal foundation and pay $2 million to eight charities for having illegally misused charitable funds for political purposes. The payoffs to porn stars, the hidden tax returns and the waterfall of false statements on every topic under the sun have all made one less than Pollyannaish about the specter of this president having unfettered discretion to hand out $500 billion.

Because the impact of COVID-19 on America's economy has been so devastating and the need for wise deployment of federal aid to remedy the devastation is so desperate, Congress established mechanisms to ensure that the distribution and administration of the funds be responsibly overseen. These included a special inspector general obliged to report his findings to Congress, a panel of inspectors general from multiple federal agencies and a congressional oversight committee. For reasons that require no detective to discern, Donald Trump does not favor oversight, and he wasted little time seeing to it that, for all intents and purposes, there wouldn't be any. He appointed one of his lawyers to be the special inspector general and announced that there would be no reports to Congress. He removed the inspector general who would have chaired the oversight panel. And since he has repeatedly ordered his administration to give the middle finger to congressional committees forced to subpoena information from federal agencies, he has made it plain that as long as he is president, congressional oversight will remain a virtual nullity.

Even middle schoolers know that accountability is the key to a properly functioning democracy, and that leaders who arrogate the right to operate in secret subvert it. The president's proclaiming, "I'll be the oversight," is yet another reason for Americans to worry at a time when they hardly need another one.

Mussolini in the Mirror: The President Declares He Has 'Total Authority'

April 21, 2020

"Democracy is beautiful in theory," wrote Italian dictator Benito Mussolini. "In practice it is a fallacy. You in America will see that one day." The fiery fascist did not have a perfect score in the prognostication department. For example, his decision to ally with Adolf Hitler worked out poorly for him, and he ended up summarily executed by a countryman and hung upside down in a town square.

Still, on whether Americans' commitment to preserving our democratic character would last forever, Mussolini appears to have a point, and President Donald Trump punctuated it again last week. Since it has always been Trump's position that he is free to do as he pleases without consequence, his claim that he has the power to do whatever he wants as president was unsurprising. "When someone is the president of the United States," he proclaimed, asserting that he could "open" or "close" states as he wishes, "the authority is total. And that's the way it's got to be. It's total. It's total."

As usual, the president was just making stuff up. "What provision in the Constitution gives the president the power to open or close states?" wondered one curious reporter. "Numerous provisions," jabbered Trump, who, like everyone else watching, knew that he had no idea what he was talking about. "We'll give you a legal brief if you want," he added. It's been a week, and we are still waiting for that legal brief. Don't hold your breath: The Constitution was actually written to guard against dictator wannabes deciding they are king. The 10th Amendment to the Constitution expressly contradicts Trump's claim to absolute authority, stating, "The powers not delegated to the United States by the Constitution nor prohibited by it to the States are reserved to the States respectively, or to the people."

Prevailed upon by aides to lighten up on an unfortunate totalitarian look, the president backpedaled the next day, allowing that the states actually get to decide what is necessary to keep their citizens from dying. But he was soon back at it, threatening "close-downs" of states that acted more vigorously to protect their people than he thought necessary. Asked what in the world he meant by a "close-down," the president once again made it up, sounding one part autocrat, one part buffoon. "We have the right to do whatever we want," babbled Trump, "but we wouldn't do that, but no, we would have the right to close down what they're doing if we want to do that, but we don't want to do that, and I don't think there'll be any reason to do that. But we have the right to do that."

The president has made a near fetish out of self-regard and seems determined to demonstrate it. He arranged to have his name appear on the "memo" line of emergency checks mailed to American families suffering from the economic meltdown, angling to take personal credit for funds appropriated by Congress. In the category of "Why should this day be different from any other?" he then lied about it. "Mr. President, why did you add your name to the coronavirus relief checks?" asked a reporter last week. "I don't know too much about that," replied Trump. "I don't understand how my signature got on the relief checks." But he offered that Americans would be relieved to see "Donald Trump" on the check. "I'm sure people are very happy to get a big, fat, beautiful check with my name on it," said our president, layering eye-popping personality disorder upon simple mendacity.

American democracy has endured quite a stress test these past three years. November's election will test just how much we have absorbed from civics lessons and 4th of July speeches. And it will determine, perhaps conclusively, what Americans see when we look in the mirror.

Voodoomeister: Trump Takes a Spin as Medicine Man

April 28, 2020

President Donald Trump's daily appearances at White House COVID-19 briefings have resolved a friendly dispute playing out at dinner tables across America: Is our president more aptly described as a danger or a dolt? There is no longer a need to quibble over this, and here's why: There's no incorrect answer.

The president's suggestion that we consider bombarding ourselves with ultraviolet light and injecting disinfectant to cure the coronavirus seems to have turned the light switch on for some Americans who had been laboring under the perfectly understandable presumption that he was compos mentis. On Thursday, Trump decided to reassure a deeply anxious country reeling under both pandemic and national economic collapse by sharing his thoughts about a potential solution. "Suppose we hit the body with a tremendous — whether it's ultraviolet or just very powerful light," said the leader of the free world, turning to two of his top medical advisors, whose blood appeared to drain from their faces on national television. "Supposing you brought the light inside the body, which you can do either through the skin or in some other way. I think you said you're going to test that, too. It sounds interesting." He continued: "Then I see the disinfectant, where it knocks it out in a minute. One minute. And is there a way we can do something like that, by injection inside or almost a cleaning? So it would be interesting to check that."

Quicker than you could say "25th Amendment," everyone in the world whose name is not Rush Limbaugh warned that the president's invitation to self-administer disinfectant was not merely stupid but dangerous. The American Cleaning Institute, fearing that this bit of presidential idiocy would cause yet more deaths on top of what we are experiencing, issued this statement: "Disinfectants are meant to kill germs or viruses on hard surfaces. Under no circumstances should they ever be used on one's skin, ingested or injected internally." Facing widespread mockery, the president chose the path most familiar to him. "I was asking a sarcastic and a very sarcastic question to the reporters in the room," he lied baldly the next day, despite video that made it obvious this was hogwash. The president's new press secretary, evidently determined to become a laughing stock even more rapidly than her numberless predecessors, offered this whopper in his defense: "The president gives specific facts."

This was hardly the president's first disastrous foray into dispensing medical opinions. For weeks he has endorsed the anti-malaria drug hydroxychloroquine as just the treatment for serious coronavirus cases. "(I)f somebody is in trouble you take it, I think," he said, tweeting that it had "a real chance to be one of the biggest game-changers in the history of medicine." Last week a nationwide study of the drug's use in veterans hospitals showed a greater rate of death of those who took it than those treated under standard protocols. And the Food and Drug Administration warned that it had dangerous side effects.

The president was likewise dead wrong in predicting that the virus would disappear with warmer weather. "Looks like by April, you know in theory when it gets a little warmer, it miraculously goes away," he opined. When Dr. Anthony Fauci, the nation's leading infectious disease expert, confirmed that it would return with a vengeance this fall, Trump asserted without explanation that Fauci was wrong.

The more interesting clinical question is why anyone would believe a word this president says. His former secretary of state pronounced him a "moron." His former chief of staff called him an "idiot," and his former secretary of defense said he has the understanding of a "fifth or sixth grader." Let's face it: This is not an especially good time to have a flashing "vacancy" sign in the Oval Office. And the evidence is that what we have is even worse.

Hate Wave: Strange Thanks for Communities of Color Carrying Us on Their Backs

May 5, 2020

COVID-19 has ripped off any cover that still obscures the deep inequalities burdening communities of color in America — inequalities that have, in a few months' time, become too obvious and too ugly for the rest of us to ignore. They are driven home by what we watch hour after hour on the news to which we are glued, and by what we can see around us. Americans at large are now clearly dependent for their sustenance, if not their survival, on their countrymen of color, on recent immigrants and on those with different-sounding names: medical personnel, food industry workers, public transit workers, nursing home workers and many others.

The communities carrying the nation on their backs happen to be the same ones suffering from the coronavirus in disproportionate numbers. In metropolitan areas across the country, black and Hispanic Americans account for wildly out-of-whack percentages of those stricken, a function of inferior access to health care, frequently inadequate housing and high-risk jobs. "People of color are being infected and dying from coronavirus at astounding rates," said Sen. Kamala Harris, D-Calif., who recently introduced the COVID-19 Racial and Ethnic Disparities Task Force Act to focus on assessing that impact and remedying it. "The very communities of color bearing the burden of this pandemic have been bearing the brunt of systematic inequities since long before COVID-19," says Boston City Councilor Michelle Wu. "Residents of color are over-represented in the case counts and also make up more of our frontline workers risking their health to keep everyone safe and sound." Those communities will also bear the brunt of the job losses soaring daily and the suffering associated with them.

But that isn't a heavy enough cross to bear, evidently. The Anti-Defamation League, long the gold standard of anti-bias organizations, warns that the upsurge in American hate dating to 2016 has spiked further since the virus' outbreak. "The blame game has already started," wrote ADL CEO Jonathan Greenblatt in a USA Today piece he co-authored with former presidential candidate Andrew Yang in March. "(T)here's now a serious risk that this kind of hateful rhetoric and outright scapegoating of minorities will take on a life of its own."

Two weeks ago, the ADL released a list of examples of the harassment and threats to which Asian Americans were subjected in the first half of April alone. These included racial slurs, physical assaults, threats of violence, racist graffiti and Facebook vitriol. Last week, the ADL reported on anti-Muslim bigotry in a time of pandemic, exposing "American anti-Muslim ideologues propagating a range of conspiracy theories aimed at stoking fear, claiming Muslims are defying social distancing rules and actively trying to spread the virus." The ADL has been front and center in pressuring social media platforms to clamp down on the white supremacy that continues to metastasize on the internet; Greenblatt has not hesitated to personally confront social media executives over their companies' role in enabling the dissemination of hate.

Greenblatt is peripatetic by nature and of necessity even during "normal" times. These days, he seems to be everywhere — here, focusing journalists on the venom being spewed, and there, partnering with other civil rights groups to push government and the private sector to do more. "Throughout history," he observed last week, "hateful actors attempt to seize the narrative around global health pandemics by placing blame on minority communities. The same is true with COVID-19."

The last few years have made it clear that we are not the America we had hoped we were, and the current crisis has opened our eyes to just how much has to be fixed. It isn't "only" a pandemic and economic convulsion. The coronavirus has spawned its own virus, a grotesque hatred directed at those to whom we owe so much, yet another challenge for a country badly in need of course correction.

Cowardly Lyin': Trump Minion Declares Mike Flynn Innocent of the Crime to Which He Already Pleaded Guilty

May 12, 2020

For some leaders, personal responsibility in disregarding warnings of an impending pandemic that has now killed 80,000 Americans and cratered the economy might stimulate reflection about the national good. Not so for Donald Trump, whose disastrous presidency continues to capsize the democratic institutions on which we have prided ourselves.

One of those is the U.S. Department of Justice, which has now officially joined other institutions whose reputations have been destroyed by President Titanic, abetted by the sad willingness of a sorry few to carry out kamikaze runs on their own legacies in order to curry favor with The Boss. Last week's announcement by Attorney General William Barr that — lo and behold! — there wasn't a basis to convict former national security advisor Michael Flynn of the crime to which he had twice pleaded guilty didn't just take the cake. It took most of what remains of the Justice Department's credibility since the president appointed Barr to protect him from impeachment and criminal investigations.

Barr has proved to be nothing if not dutiful. Within hours of receiving but not reading a 440-page report by special counsel Robert Mueller detailing voluminous evidence of 10 separate acts of obstruction of justice by the president, Barr proclaimed that Trump had done nothing wrong. This was unsurprising, since Barr had made the same proclamation before being appointed, which was what led to his appointment in the first place.

Barr's pronouncement so distorted the facts that the famously restrained Mueller wrote to him privately to complain about it. A federal judge appointed by a Republican castigated Barr for dishonesty in terms that would have made most attorneys check their law licenses. He concluded that Barr had "made a calculated attempt to influence public discourse about the Mueller report in favor of President Trump despite certain findings in the Mueller report to the contrary." But it got worse. "These circumstances generally and Attorney General's lack of candor specifically," ruled the judge, "call into question Attorney General Barr's credibility." Barr's self-abasement repeated after the White House whistleblower, corroborated by a parade of Trump administration officials, reported that the president attempted to extort the Ukrainian government by asking it to fabricate dirt on Joe Biden through a phony "investigation" so it would receive the American aid it needed to defend itself against Russia. Nothing here, announced Barr barely minutes after hearing about the matter.

So it was hardly a shocker that even after Flynn twice admitted under oath that he had committed the federal crime of lying to the FBI, the president's loyal appointee declared that Flynn was actually innocent of the crime. Flynn, who lied to the FBI while actually sitting in the White House, did not lie to the FBI about just anything. He lied about secret discussions he had with the Russian ambassador just after the 2016 election about foreign policy "arrangements." These were discussions that on their face violated one federal law while Flynn was violating another. "A very serious crime," said the federal judge before whom Flynn pleaded guilty. "Arguably, you sold your country out. I'm not hiding my disgust or my disdain."

But last week, Barr declared that, now that he thought about it, Flynn's lies were not "material" ones. Sure they weren't: Here was Trump's top foreign policy advisor lying about his illegal contacts with the Russian government at a time when the FBI was investigating whether Trump's team had improperly coordinated with the Russians. What could possibly have been "material" about that? Barr, as deep in the tank as one can be, was ready with a line that out-Aliced Alice in Wonderland. "I wanted to make sure that we restore confidence in the system," he said.

The upshot? Flynn, who led Trump supporters in the "Lock her up!" chant about Hillary Clinton, actually committed a crime. He will now skate, courtesy of a president for whom there is probable cause that he committed a series of crimes. There's a confidence booster for you.

Leader Lost: Remembering Al Lowenstein

May 19, 2020

In 1967, an unknown 38-year-old civil rights activist from New York took it upon himself to change the world, and then he did. Allard Lowenstein, a Yale-educated lawyer who had steadfastly avoided practicing law and was proud of having done so, was already a master of the quixotic. He had smuggled searing evidence about apartheid out of South Africa, managing to present it at the United Nations and forcing the United States to distance itself from its South African ally. Calling upon his credibility on campuses across America, he had spearheaded Freedom Summer, which drew hundreds of volunteers to Mississippi to register black voters in 1964.

Lowenstein was convinced that the Vietnam War was immoral and self-destructive, and that President Lyndon Johnson could be defeated for the 1968 Democratic presidential nomination by an anti-war candidate. There were at least some people who agreed with Lowenstein on the first point. Nobody agreed with him on the second. But Lowenstein, who combined a remarkable ability to bring crowds to their feet with shrewd, street-smart political skill, believed that he could supply the movement if a candidate could be found. "I try to make people realize how powerful their political strength is whenever they get discouraged," Lowenstein later reflected, vastly understating what he could do that others couldn't.

The rest, as they say, is history. Lowenstein first tried to persuade Robert Kennedy to challenge Johnson. When Kennedy declined, he pursued others. Finally, in late November 1967, Minnesota Sen. Eugene McCarthy succumbed to Lowenstein's arguments and announced his candidacy. Three months later, Johnson was toast, and on March 31, 1968, he withdrew from the race. American politics had been upended, and Lowenstein hadn't merely predicted it; he had made it happen. "For Al," Kennedy wrote in a note to Lowenstein soon after Johnson withdrew, "who knew the lesson of Emerson and taught it to the rest of us: that if a man plants himself on his convictions and there abides, the huge world will come 'round to him."

Lowenstein went on to win election to Congress before New York's Republican-controlled state legislature gerrymandered his congressional district in order to prevent his reelection. It suited his sense of humor that after losing, he was introduced at a prominent British university as "that famous American congressman whose seat has been redistributed." He led a national effort to register young people who had just won the right to vote, earning a coveted spot as No. 7 ("007" was how Lowenstein proudly described it) on then-President Richard Nixon's so-called enemies list (in which he was called a "Guiding force behind the 18-year-old 'Dump Nixon' vote drive"). He was later appointed U.S. ambassador to the United Nations Commission on Human Rights by President Jimmy Carter.

In 1980, a deranged former student shot and killed Lowenstein. Thousands whom he had inspired and changed forever spilled out of New York City's largest synagogue onto Manhattan's streets to mourn his loss and celebrate his life. Many who knew him, or heard him, think about him still.

Lowenstein was blessed with gifts that hardly anyone had, and with one that no one did: the ability to persuade those implacably opposed to his position to change their minds. This he did by overwhelming force of logic married to respect. But it also didn't hurt that he could make people laugh as hard as they had ever laughed — whether large audiences or individual college students conscripted to drive him to the next event. "His enormous warmth and humor made him appreciate others more than anyone I have ever known," said his wife, Jenny Littlefield.

Lowenstein, whose connection to students was deep, would have found it unimaginable that any young person could fail to appreciate the imperative of removing President Donald Trump from office as America's last clear chance at redeeming the country we love. Forty springs after his death, with so much riding on those who care about our future understanding their own strength, one misses Al Lowenstein more than ever.

Mafia Don: The President Guards His Swamp
May 26, 2020

Notorious mobster Albert Anastasia, proud founder of the modern American Mafia, is best remembered for two things. One is being shot to death while sitting in a Manhattan barber's chair during what proved to be a really bad shave. The second is his distinctive ill humor concerning those who informed law enforcement about his illegal activities. Hearing that an associate had provided information about a hit job Anastasia had ordered, Anastasia ordered another one. "I can't stand squealers," he said. "Hit that guy."

The Trump White House fairly trumpets the fact that The Anastasia Principle is its guiding one, enforced on direct orders from The Boss, President Donald Trump. It is straight out of the Gambino family playbook: he who is in a position to disclose the truth about the Trump administration and seems inclined to do so gets whacked.

The latest Trump administration official to sleep with the fishes for having done his job conscientiously is State Department inspector general Steve Linick, who got caught doing what the law requires inspectors general do: investigating waste, fraud, mismanagement and misconduct within the executive agencies. Linick, a highly regarded former assistant U.S. attorney in administrations of both parties, had the effrontery to perform his duties with integrity, a definite no-no in Trump World. He had investigated evidence that Mike Pompeo's State Department had illegally circumvented a congressional freeze on arms sales to Saudi Arabia. He had also inquired about Pompeo's use of State Department resources to walk his dog, Sherman, get his laundry done — and take taxpayer-funded trips back to his home state of Kansas, not generally regarded as a diplomatic hot spot requiring State Department travel. Trump fired Linick because Pompeo, under investigation by Linick, asked him to.

Pompeo at first kept mum about whether he had asked Trump to fire Linick. This became rather more difficult when Trump admitted that Pompeo had asked him to get rid of the troublesome inspector. Pompeo, not exactly the epitome of honesty, then attempted the line that he didn't even know Linick was investigating him. That laugher survived about 15 minutes, until the evidence emerged that he certainly did. Just another day in the lives of the folks who in 2016 peddled the hokum that they were all about draining the swamp.

Linick joins a series of inspectors general canned by Trump in recent weeks. All were sent packing because they were exercising the independence that Congress mandated they exercise so Americans' tax dollars could be respected, the law followed and the integrity of government preserved. This made them a threat to this president, who regards watchdogs holding his administration accountable with both loathing and fear.

The president's whack jobs are not administered only to inspectors general. Dr. Rick Bright, the high-ranking government scientist who had warned administration officials on Jan. 23 that the burgeoning pandemic had to be urgently addressed rather than waved aside, is another recent victim. "We're going to need vaccines and diagnostics and drugs," he told the Trump administration. "It's going to take a while and we need to get started." Here was what Donald Trump was telling America on Jan. 30: "We think we have (the coronavirus) very well under control. We have very little problem in this country." Bright continued to refuse to kowtow to an inane party line, bucking a White House demand that the demonstrably useless and potentially dangerous drug hydroxychloroquine be made "widely available" for COVID-19 patients. He was fired, patently in retaliation for his temerity in standing up for public health. The same fate has befallen others who tried to protect Americans from a pandemic, the response to which the Trump White House has so egregiously bungled.

More than a swamp, the Trump presidency has been a cesspool, one that the president has done everything in his power to protect. It will take an epic reclamation effort to clean it up.

Bottomless: The President Reminds Us How Low He'll Go

June 2, 2020

Until recently, it had been Sen. Joseph McCarthy who was the poster child for the thuggish impulse that occasionally rears its head in America — ebbing here, flowing there, but always present. If he has accomplished nothing else, President Donald Trump has supplanted McCarthy as the embodiment of the American thug, rising and reigning with the help of those who either thrill to his bullying or lack the courage to challenge it.

McCarthy's principal tools were dishonesty and viciousness, and he wielded them freely for over three years before Americans finally decided they had had enough. The turning point was unexpected. During Senate hearings in 1954, Boston attorney Joseph Welch responded to McCarthy's savaging of a young lawyer who had once joined a legal services organization that defended alleged Communists by posing to McCarthy this simple, almost naive question: "Have you no sense of decency, sir, at long last?" McCarthy had been bullying innocent people for years, so it is unclear why Welch's gentle appeal to "decency" triggered a sudden shift in public opinion against him.

Trump may have self-administered a takedown with his untethered, false insinuation that former Republican Rep. Joe Scarborough murdered a former staffer in 2001. This, of course, is pure junk, Trump's specialty. The autopsy conducted on the staffer, a young woman who was happily married to a man who still misses her dearly today, confirmed that she died when a heart condition caused her to fall and hit her head. Scarborough was 800 miles away. His only "crime" is criticizing Trump, including by pointing out — go figure — that he has little regard for the truth.

Illustrating the point, Trump has tweeted repeatedly that the "case" should be "re-opened," making McCarthy look scrupulous by comparison. It is bad enough that Trump has defamed Scarborough; he has also inflicted deep pain on the woman's family, who has been begging him to stop trashing her — to no avail.

Republican Sen. Mitt Romney called Trump's accusation "vile" and "baseless". "Enough already," Romney tweeted, speaking for every decent American. The conservative Wall Street Journal called Trump's accusation "ugly even for him." The president, it editorialized, "is debasing his office, and he's hurting the country in doing so." Republican Rep. Adam Kinzinger stated the all too obvious, tweeting, "Completely unfounded conspiracy. Just stop."

Trump could care less. He knows that most of his base finds his pathology electrifying rather than loathsome. But pathology is what drives this presidency. For instance, Trump has settled on "Sleepy Joe" as a derisive moniker for former Vice President Joe Biden. It is both a witless insult and a curious one from a president who sits by himself in his residence until it is nearly time for lunch, flipping cable television channels and machine-gunning tweets that read as though they were composed by a third grader. His insult is the more ironic where Trump not only lacks the energy to read intelligence briefs but also, by all accounts, possesses neither the capacity nor the inclination to read anything at all. Indeed, if watching him struggle while attempting to read the cards placed for him on the presidential podium is any indication, our president's very ability to read is open to earnest debate.

To say that Joe Biden easily surpasses Trump in the mental acuity department is to damn Biden with faint praise, but the same is also obviously true on the physical side of the ledger. This is what makes Trump's insults so peculiar. Biden is physically fit, while Trump — how shall we put this — is not. It does not look as though Donald Trump has done a situp since the second Eisenhower administration, but that has not stopped him from continually deriding others' physical appearance.

Last week, Rush Limbaugh summed up what Donald Trump is about, and he meant it as a compliment. "Trump is just throwing gasoline on a fire, and he's loving watching the flames," said Limbaugh admiringly.

Just what you want in a president of the United States.

Titanic: Ship of Fools Springs a Leak

June 9, 2020

It wasn't the best of weeks for President Donald Trump. On Friday, he proclaimed it a "great day" for George Floyd, who had been murdered by Minneapolis police the week before. "Hopefully George is looking down right now and saying 'This is a great thing that's happening to our country,'" said Trump as Americans took to the streets in all 50 states to protest the persistence and scope of American racism, and as tens of millions remained jobless.

The president, who dodged the military draft, claiming that bone spurs unfortunately required him to pass on serving his country in Vietnam, devotes considerable energy to projecting a tough-guy persona. That persona took something of a hit when demonstrations outside the White House grew large and loud and it emerged that Our Strong Man was rushed to an underground bunker. This wasn't a great look for someone wanting to avoid the appearance of Saddam Hussein in his final days, and the derision was swift.

As usual, Trump decided to lie about it, calling his emergency retreat more like an "inspection" than anything else. This triggered yet more mockery, with skeptics questioning the president's sudden interest in ensuring that the cots in his bunker had hospital corners and the table tops had been appropriately polished with lemon Pledge.

Things went directly from bad to worse, morphing into a political consultant's version of a Hitchcock movie. Desperate to appear very tough very quickly, Team Trump had troops use horses and tear gas to rout peaceful protesters from the park facing the White House so the president could stride manfully to St. John's Episcopal Church and pose in front of it holding a Bible upside down. It was the Daily Double of grotesquerie: deploying American military might to assault Americans doing nothing more than exercising their First Amendment rights to protest in order that Trump could use a church and a Bible as political props. Any disagreement about whether he looked more like a tin-pot totalitarian or a dolt was quickly put to rest: He looked like both. Perhaps most damaging was that, by brandishing a Bible, in which he is wholly disinterested and whose contents he is wholly unfamiliar with, he looked like a simple phony.

Trump spokesmen took spins at spinning, but only the unwaveringly gullible were buying it, and there seemed fewer of those than usual. Press secretary Kayleigh McEnany broke new ground in the jaw-dropping-comparisons department, likening Trump's use of troops against American protesters to stage a photo opportunity to Winston Churchill's walking among Londoners to observe the rubble left by Nazi bombers. This proved too much for scores of retired American military officials, who stepped forward to denounce Trump. Most prominent of these was retired four-star Marine Gen. James Mattis, Trump's own former secretary of defense, who said he was "angry and appalled" at Trump's conduct. Referring to Trump, Mattis urged Americans to hold accountable "those in office who would make a mockery of our Constitution" and said, "We are witnessing the consequences of three years without mature leadership."

Trump wasn't the only one caught in the headlights. Secretary of Defense Mark Esper, in charge of the troops who had attacked their fellow Americans, dutifully accompanied Trump to St. John's and stood beside him. Later realizing that he hadn't merely entered eunuch territory but had fully occupied it, Esper announced that he had been confused at the time, and that the president hadn't told him what they were doing. "I didn't know where I was going," said our secretary of defense. This was at least a step up from the original disclaimer apparently settled on by Esper after conferring with his aides: that he thought the president was taking him to Chuck E. Cheese.

Abraham Lincoln had his team of rivals. Donald Trump has his sycophants who are too intimidated to say what they know and what Americans increasingly sense: He is off his rocker, and we are paying for it.

In His Own Right: Amid a Pandemic, Joe Kennedy III Turns Heads

June 16, 2020

The inhabitants of Chelsea, Massachusetts, have known tough times for a long time, long before the COVID-19 pandemic hit them hard. Almost half of Chelsea's population consists of recent immigrants, largely from Latin America, and almost 1 in 5 lived below the poverty line even before the virus struck and wiped out the economy. Massachusetts has suffered badly from the coronavirus, and the Chelsea community has suffered worst of all, its densely packed residents infected at the highest rate in the state. "I have been dropping off food boxes for people at their homes during the pandemic and I have seen up to twelve people living in a two bedroom apartment," says Gladys Vega, executive director of the Chelsea Collaborative. "That's our reality."

Chelsea is not in United States Rep. Joseph P. Kennedy III's district. And though Kennedy is running for a Democratic seat in the United States Senate, Chelsea, with its massive immigrant population, has few voters to offer someone in the middle of a Democratic primary battle. But that has not stopped Kennedy, who spent two years as a Peace Corps volunteer in the Dominican Republic and speaks Spanish fluently, from focusing on Chelsea's plight with an intensity unsurprising to many who have watched Kennedy since his election to Congress in 2012. "When the epidemic hit Chelsea," says Roy Avellaneda, president of the Chelsea City Council, "Joe was right there. He called me up and said 'Hey, I know you're in a tough spot.' He just came in with his team, funneling money to relief organizations, volunteering, preparing food, handing it out."

Kennedy raised $30,000 for food and housing relief for Chelsea, part of more than $100,000 he has raised for pandemic relief throughout Massachusetts since April. But even more importantly, he did what he has come to be known for doing: He showed up whether or not there were any votes in it for him. On Mother's Day, he joined Chelsea City Councilor Judith Garcia in delivering hot meals and gifts to 20 Chelsea mothers who had contracted COVID-19 and were quarantined apart from their families. "It was a small way to let them know our community is with them and praying for their speedy recovery," said Kennedy, who had the satisfaction of seeing the women smile from the windows in their converted motel rooms.

Since his election to Congress, Kennedy has turned heads and made admirers out of cynics, in part because he so consistently shows up where politicians do not ordinarily go. Drawn to the hurting and the marginalized, he is wont to spend time at shelters, food banks, group homes and drug rehabilitation centers — everywhere, it seems, where likely voters aren't. Early on in his relationship with Kennedy, Avellaneda concluded that the young man identified viscerally with those shunted aside. "When I talked to him," Avellaneda recalls, "I could see all the adrenaline that he wants to fight with is there." There is adrenaline, but there is also anger. "Our system can't continue to tell people 'Hey, just try a little harder or just wait a little longer'," says Kennedy, his voice steely, "or, 'Eventually we're going to get to you.'"

Ten weeks before the Massachusetts primary pitting the young congressman against incumbent Sen. Edward Markey, Kennedy leads in the polls. This is less a knock on Markey than a reflection of the work Kennedy has done. Markey's supporters have tried to turn Kennedy's famous last name against him, accusing him of being "a progressive in name only" and "entitled." The first charge is ridiculous and the second unjust. Serious and thoughtful, Kennedy has conducted himself in a way that seems anything but entitled. There is no doubt that his last name helped launch his political career. But there is also no doubt that he is where he is because of what he is.

Exit Ramp: As Dumpster Fire Worsens, Voters Seem Ready to Give Trump the Boot

June 23, 2020

It's been another bad stretch for Donald Trump. The president's terrible, horrible, no-good, very bad week began with his labored shuffle down a short, modestly inclined ramp after giving an even more labored speech at West Point, one eliciting an audience response somewhere between tepid and silent. It was an event commandeered by Trump himself. He was trying to appear a wee bit presidential after having been hustled to his emergency bunker when peaceful protests across the street grew loud and his manly stride to a church to hold a bible as though it were kryptonite boomeranged.

Problem was, it looked an awful lot like a ramp too far; there are track meets that could have been held in the amount of time it seemed to take the president to get down that ramp. Coupled with his inability minutes earlier to raise a glass of water with one hand, this led to a fresh wave of doubt about his capacity, doubt which, to be fair, he has generated virtually nonstop since taking office. Characteristically, he made matters worse. "The ramp that I descended after my West Point commencement speech was very long & steep," he tweeted, "and most importantly was very slippery." The thing is, lying just isn't as easy as it used to be, what with the advent of videotape. Everyone could see that the ramp was actually very short, not remotely steep and, unless it had been inexplicably slicked with Vasoline for the occasion, not at all slippery. Not since Jimmy Carter claimed to have used a canoe paddle to battle an amphibious attack rabbit to a draw had a presidential attempt at bravado seemed so pathetic.

Before you could say, "How did this guy get elected?" an ad was out that brutally contrasted a barely ambulatory Trump with footage of an athletic Joe Biden running through the White House with former President Barack Obama, finishing up by clinking glasses of ice water. The tag line: "Biden. He can run and drink water."

Rampgate wasn't even the week's low point for Trump. Former national security adviser John Bolton's account of his time observing the president hit bookstores, and his portrait of president-as-narcissistic-ignoramus was ugly though hardly groundbreaking. "I don't think he's fit for office," Bolton told ABC. "I don't think he has the competence to carry out the job." Bolton joined a list of Trump appointees who eventually abandoned ship after reaching the same conclusion about Trump. They include Trump's former secretary of state (Trump is "a moron"), chief of staff ("an idiot") and secretary of defense (Trump has "the understanding of a fifth or sixth grader"). Keen observers may be able to make out the barest outline of a pattern here.

Three years of corruption and chaos seem to have registered on American voters, who appear ready to ring the gong on The Trump Show and begin cleaning up. A Fox News poll last week showed Biden leading Trump by 12 points, in line with other polls. Other polls showed Trump's favorability ratings in the 30s. Barely a third of Americans believe what Trump says, and what those individuals are thinking is anybody's guess. Biden has begun to pull away from Trump in battleground states and establish solid leads in states he does not even need to win. States that should be layups for the president have turned into toss-ups, with polling there showing him and Biden essentially tied.

In the meantime, Biden raised more money in May than Trump, a surprising and telling development. And after Trump officials proclaimed that a million Americans had signed up for tickets to attend his kickoff rally in deep-red Oklahoma on Saturday night, only 6,200 showed up. There is an eternity to go before the election. But at this rate, the jig may be up for Donald Trump, and it is looking as though he knows it.

The Silencer: With the Stakes Getting High, the President Tightens the Muzzle

June 30, 2020

It isn't easy being Donald Trump these days: so many people to silence and so little time. Muzzling those who have damaging evidence on you can be exhausting in the best of circumstances, and keeping a lid on so much incriminating information springing from so many different sources would make anyone cranky. The president has had to block the disclosure of his tax returns, stonewall congressional subpoenas, fire a slew of inspectors general investigating corruption in his administration and launder $130,000 in hush money to buy the silence of a porn star with whom he was having an "alleged" affair four months after his third wife gave birth to their son. And that's just for starters. It is never a good sign when the United States Marine Band has to be pointedly reminded not to play "Hail to the One-Man Racketeering Enterprise" when the president appears.

Last week, a New York state judge rejected an effort, clearly orchestrated by Trump, to block his niece Mary Trump from publishing her forthcoming book about how he conducts himself. "Too Much and Never Enough: How My Family Created the World's Most Dangerous Man" — out on July 28, available wherever books are sold — is causing concern in Trump World, and understandably so. After all, who among us has not forced family members to sign nondisclosure agreements preventing them from telling the truth about us and then filed a lawsuit to keep them quiet? The legal battle over whether Mary Trump gets to speak or get gagged is not yet over. The president hopes to fare better suppressing his niece's book then he did suppressing that of his former national security adviser John Bolton, in which Bolton depicts a president historically unfit to protect Americans from hostile nations and seemingly disinterested in doing so. Trump, Bolton flatly told CNN's Jake Tapper, is "dangerous enough that he shouldn't get a second term."

Nothing invigorates Trump's machinations to hide evidence quite like his concern that the evidence may place him in criminal jeopardy, a concern that is far from fanciful. Cheating family members is one thing. Felony charges are another, and it is likely not lost on Trump that, with his poll numbers looking grim, he may not be president on Jan. 21, 2021. If he isn't, it is not only Air Force One that he will be losing but also the protection of the Justice Department's legal opinion that sitting presidents cannot be indicted.

This did not augur well for one Geoffrey Berman, the highly respected — and Republican — United States attorney for the Southern District of New York, who was informed one recent Friday night that, unbeknownst to him, he had "stepped down." Berman issued a statement saying that he had done no such thing, whereupon Trump dispensed with the pretense and fired him. It did not require Sherlock Holmes to decipher the reason: Berman and his office have never gotten the proverbial memo that their job was to protect Trump. It was Berman whose prosecutors convicted former Trump lawyer-fixer Michael Cohen, unceremoniously identifying Trump in the indictment as the "Individual 1" who had directed Cohen to commit felonious acts. It is Berman whose prosecutors have already charged Rudy Giuliani's Merry Men, Lev Parnas and Igor Fruman, and who are reportedly investigating Giuliani himself. This is not an episode of "Flip The Felon" that Donald Trump can be especially eager to see play out. In short: Bye-bye, Berman.

Recent polls indicate that there is only so much obstruction of justice most Americans can stomach. Last week's New York Times poll reflected that only 36% of voters are prepared to reelect Trump. That's just a few points above the percentage of Americans convinced that, pandemic or no pandemic, wearing a mask is the equivalent of donning Satan's Loincloth. The president's gag show has always been designed to bury evidence of his wrongdoing. But there is growing evidence that it is repelling his countrymen.

Good and Smart: Warren's Bill Boosting Low-Income Renter Households Makes Sense

July 7, 2020

While comfortable Americans are passing the pandemic studying their favorite restaurants' takeout schedules and strategizing Zoom techniques, tens of millions of our countrymen dramatically less fortunate are desperately trying to keep their families from being tossed into the street.

Jaimy Gonzalez of Chelsea, Massachusetts, is one of them. The El Salvadoran native immigrated to the United States 18 years ago. Since the pandemic struck, she has been unable to find work as a babysitter. She shares her apartment with three other adults and three children; the other adults are also out of work. Like millions of other households, Gonzalez's has been devastated by the pandemic, and like millions of other renters, she and her housemates, unable to pay the rent because of the economic collapse of the past four months, are on the brink of homelessness. Gonzalez recently told a New York Times reporter, "I was crying morning, afternoon and night thinking about how we were going to pay the rent, what we were going to do?"

For Gonzalez and so many others living in the most prosperous country on the planet, there is not yet an answer. The huge stimulus package passed by Congress in March provided a 120-day moratorium on evictions for tenants living in federally subsidized housing. That moratorium covered only about one-quarter of America's 44 million renter households, and its protections are set to expire later this month. The other three-quarters of renters have been dependent on a patchwork of state-enacted moratoriums, unemployment insurance and one-time government checks to stave off eviction. A study by analytics firm Amherst estimates that with the federal moratorium about to lapse; 20 state moratoriums having already expired and another 9 slated to follow shortly; and the official unemployment rate at 11% — not counting the severely underemployed — some 28 million renter families are close to having no place to live.

That is the reason for legislation recently introduced by Sen. Elizabeth Warren, joined by several of her Democratic colleagues in the Senate and the House of Representatives. The Protecting Renters From Eviction and Fees Act would shield renter households from eviction for nonpayment of rent until March 2021 — a year after the virus' onset. It would thus provide an additional eight months for those hit hardest by the global health crisis against which there is no defense, and those least able to sustain that hit and get on their feet. "Renters who have lost their jobs or had their income reduced shouldn't have to fear losing their homes in the middle of a pandemic," says Warren. "Housing is an absolute necessity to keep families safe during this crisis."

If there is a case against legislation that would protect tenants from eviction while fairly addressing the rights of landlords, it is difficult to apprehend. It is both unconscionable and self-destructive for the United States to abandon millions of its people to a fate consisting of not only homelessness but also hopelessness and hunger. Warren and her colleagues are dead right to confront the plight of low-income renter families who have been battered by the coronavirus pandemic, and to do so urgently.

"Every once in a while America reinvents herself," former Massachusetts Gov. Deval Patrick said in a July 4th statement. "How marvelous to think that (that reinvention) could be led by the outcasts and the despised and their sons and daughters." Cleaning up the national wreckage left by four years of President Donald Trump and restoring America to a path worthy of its forebears won't be easy. It will require the energy, and the civic and economic participation, of all Americans including those who have been left behind and are in danger of being jettisoned altogether. Protecting and boosting those families during a time of excruciating pain and profound need isn't merely the right thing to do. It is the smart thing.

Powerful Dissent: Conservative Patriots Take on a Dirty President

July 14, 2020

When the late film producer Julia Phillips published her 1991 expose of Hollywood's depravity in the 1970s and 1980s, she chose a title that correctly forecasted the movie establishment's retributive response. "You'll Never Eat Lunch in This Town Again" was summed up by one Hollywood power broker as "the longest suicide note in history."

The cadre of accomplished Republican political strategists who founded the Lincoln Project last December to organize against a historically crooked president from their own party knew they would be vilified, and they were right. Veterans of the presidential campaigns of George H.W. Bush, George W. Bush and John McCain, they penned a mission statement that befit their reputations for no-nonsense, no-punch-pulled messaging. "President Donald Trump and those who sign onto Trumpism," they wrote, "are a clear and present danger to the Constitution and our Republic." In the last eight months, the group's withering television and internet ads have shredded the president mercilessly, if appropriately, and they are helping to shape America's conversation about what it means to have a thoroughly corrupt president. In June alone, their ads attracted 108 million internet views, fueling the growth of a grassroots movement that has hundreds of thousands of followers. After one ad, titled "Mourning in America," spotlighted his epically awful handling of the pandemic, the president unleashed a tweet storm attacking the Lincoln Project as "LOSERS," thereby advertising how worried he is that they are anything but.

The Project's ads, like those of aligned groups like Republicans for the Rule of Law and Republican Voters Against Trump, are gems. Day after day, new ones eviscerate the president in a way that traditional political campaign ads cannot. "The productivity of the group has just been astonishing," journalist John Heilemann recently told an audience during The New England Council's "Politics & Eggs" series. "They have been relentlessly all over the President in every news cycle." Their focus has been on Trump's trashing of the values that resonate most with Republicans and Republican-leaning independents: patriotism, family and honesty. Naturally enough, Trump, a draft-dodging, thrice-married launderer of hush money paid to a porn star with whom he was allegedly having an affair, whose obstruction of justice approaches in volume that of sand on the proverbial seashore, provides the group with a robust inventory of material. It is diligently working its way through that material with something that is not quite rage and not quite delight but certainly resembles relish.

Each passing week replenishes the supply of reasons that principled conservatives have to want Donald Trump expunged from our national memory. Last week was no exception. On Friday, Trump commuted the prison sentence of Roger Stone, who, quite apart from his special status as the only man on Earth whose absence of a moral compass is so complete as to make Trump look like a Jesuit by comparison, was a key link between the Russian government and Trump's 2016 presidential campaign. Trump spoke with Stone repeatedly about the latter's efforts on his behalf. Questioned by congressional committees about his communications with Russian government intermediaries and with Trump, Stone lied so baldly that he was convicted on seven felony counts by a federal jury. He vowed to stay silent until his dying day about what he did and at whose direction, for which the grateful Trump not only praised him but also handed him a stay-out-of-jail card. It was, Republican Sen. Mitt Romney said, "unprecedented, historic corruption: an American president commutes the sentence of a person convicted by a jury of lying to shield that very president."

The president who conned voters with the line that he would "drain the swamp" has in fact created his very own sewage pond. "There's a freedom that comes with being loose of the bonds of partisanship," says Lincoln Project co-founder Reed Galen. He and his colleagues are modeling patriotism at a time when Americans, in a crisis and at a crossroads, are badly in need of it.

Weisswash: Out of Line, Out of Place, Out of Work at The New York Times

July 21, 2020

Not long ago, the student newspaper at an elite Northeast college reported that 93% of all outside speakers were from "the Left" and only 7% from "the Right." Asked whether this seemed consistent with their professed belief that academia should provide pluralistic venues for open marketplaces of ideas, the majority of students in one class were emphatic that the breakdown seemed about right to them and, if anything, unduly generous. One argued that students were within their right to establish a "code of acceptable opinion," and that such a code was crucial to ensure a "safe space" on campus.

Among the speakers who eluded the students' safety net were conservative journalist William Kristol, former Florida Gov. Jen Bush and former New York City Police Commissioner Raymond Kelly. None seemed likely by their appearances at the college to trigger search-and-destroy missions by marauding conservatives targeting campus progressives. When asked whether the desire of their fellow students to listen to speakers with differing views merited consideration, one person responded that no one was trying to prevent the speakers' views from being heard. After all, she said, anyone wanting to hear those speakers could always find some prior speech that they had given on YouTube.

There are toxins aplenty circulating in President Donald Trump's America, but he and his enablers are not responsible for all of them. This was illustrated last week by the resignation of New York Times columnist Bari Weiss, a gifted opinion writer who happens to hold opinions that are regarded as unacceptable by many of her fellow Times employees and as downright Neanderthal by some of the unhinged set in the Twittersphere. Weiss, a left-leaning centrist, was recruited away from the Wall Street Journal in 2017, ostensibly to provide some relief from the lockstep proclivities of The Times, which promotes viewpoints ranging all the way from very progressive to progressive. She had two strikes against her from the start. She is an unapologetic Zionist, which means she supports the right of Jews to self-determination in a national homeland after centuries of brutal persecution.

She is also attentive to metastasizing anti-Semitism, including on the far left. And she has had the guts to write about both.

This was distinctly unendearing to her Times colleagues, who regard Israel as the mother of all bogeymen and the subject of anti-Semitism as something between tiresome and annoying. "My own forays into WrongThink," Weiss wrote in her resignation letter, "have made me the subject of constant bullying by colleagues who disagree with my views. They have called me a Nazi and a racist; I have learned to brush off comments about how I'm 'writing about the Jews again.'" She reported that her friends at the paper were attacked by co-workers. "My work and my character," she wrote, "are openly demeaned on company-wide Slack channels where masthead editors regularly weigh in." The paper's management looked the other way at her mistreatment, thereby encouraging it. It is not the first time that Weiss has publicly denounced the insistence on "an orthodoxy already known to an enlightened few whose job is to inform everyone else." She has repeatedly been right and courageous in doing so. "Showing up for work as a centrist at an American newspaper should not require bravery," she wrote.

What was once merely the creeping tendency on the part of America's left to demand slavish obeisance to what Weiss calls a "predetermined narrative" regardless of the facts has turned into a kind of soft fascism in the Trump Era, in part in reaction to it. The blackballing and the bullying of those whose perspective is different is a sickness of its own. Putting America's pieces back together, let alone transforming America, when the Time of Trump comes mercifully to an end will be difficult enough. The kinds of assaults that were levied on Bari Weiss by those holding themselves out as progressives will make it very much harder.

Scoundrel Time: As November Nears, Americans Contemplate Their Disaster in Chief

July 28, 2020

Historians may mark the moment that best captured the America that now dangles from a cliff as the day when the president of the United States bragged that he had "aced" a dementia screening exam requiring him to name the current month and identify an elephant — and then refused to disclose the test results. If nothing else, President Donald Trump's unreassuring defense of his cognitive skills spawned the marketing of an impressive array of "Person. Woman. Man. Camera. TV." merchandise.

But there are so many moments to choose from that are fully capable of giving that one a run for its money. Each week provides Trump's countrymen a fresh supply of reasons to be frightened, repulsed or both by a leader not merely flagrantly corrupt but dangerous. Last week was another one.

With his popularity tanking, a debacle of a campaign rally in Tulsa and one in New Hampshire called on account of disinterest, Trump re-upped his threat to reject the results of any election in which he is defeated. "When somebody's the president of the United States," he informed us recently, "the authority is total, and that's the way it's got to be." This full-throated embrace of totalitarianism caused no stir among Trump's defenders, who increasingly resemble the wait staff in a Berchtesgaden bunker. Trump has openly proclaimed that there are no limits to what he believes he can do if he wants to do it. Fox's Chris Wallace asked him whether he would adhere to the most basic precept of democratic government: that leaders who lose elections voluntarily and peacefully turn power over to the winner. "I have to see," replied Trump. "No, I'm not going to say yes. I'm not going to say no."

The president doubled down on his utterly bogus claim that the upcoming election will be "rigged," the sort of proto-fascist rubbish that could plunge the nation into our worst internal crisis since the Civil War. Credit Donald Trump: He knows that a sizable chunk of America won't be the slightest bit disturbed by the jettisoning of hitherto fundamental American norms.

With the election approaching, Team Trump resurrected the so-called "coronavirus briefings," which, in actuality, are riff sessions at which the president uses the White House backdrop to air grievances and make stuff up. After months deriding the pandemic as a "hoax" that was nothing to worry about, and after it had infected 4 million Americans and taken 145,000 American lives, Trump announced that he was "in the process of developing a strategy" to address it.

Equally jarring was the president's friendly shoutout to Ghislaine Maxwell, charged with running a child sex-trafficking operation for Trump playmate Jeffrey Epstein. "I just wish her well, frankly," said our president to Maxwell, accused of transporting minors across state lines for sex with Epstein and his buddies. "I've met her numerous times over the years. But I wish her well." It required neither imagination nor cynicism to infer that Trump knows that Maxwell knows what he does not want others to know, and that Trump was making the same "keep quiet" reach-out he has made to convicted felons and Trump confidantes Michael Flynn, Paul Manafort and Roger Stone.

Trump has boasted of a lifetime committing sexual assault with impunity, and there is a video of Epstein and him leering at women at Epstein's Florida mansion, as well as numerous photos of them together. It is true there's no direct evidence that Trump availed himself of more than Epstein's friendship. But it is likewise true that when a waterfowl waddles like a duck and quacks like one, what we probably have is a duck. Trump's warm wishes to the keeper of Jeffrey Epstein's secrets brings more than the faint outline of a duck into relief, as well as the discernible sound of something quacking.

There is no gainsaying that what with pandemic, recession and a disaster in chief, Americans find themselves in a deep hole. The good news is that we soon have a chance to climb back out of it.

Perjury Troop: A Chuckling Attorney General Lies to Congress

August 4, 2020

Steven Calabresi is not what you'd call a "leftist." The co-founder of conservative legal group the Federalist Society worked for former Presidents Ronald Reagan and George H.W. Bush and has only voted for Republican presidential candidates, including Donald Trump. Now a law professor, Calabresi adamantly opposed last year's impeachment of President Trump on constitutional grounds.

But with the president's call to delay the election, premised on the phony claim that it will be "fraudulent," because he expects to lose it, Calabresi has had enough. "I am frankly appalled by the president's recent tweet seeking to postpone the November election," Calabresi wrote in an op-ed last week. "Until recently I had taken as political hyperbole the Democrats' assertion that President Trump is a fascist. But this latest tweet is fascistic and is itself grounds for the president's immediate impeachment again by the House of Representatives and his removal from office by the Senate."

Calabresi's break with America's totalitarian wannabe has doubtless earned him a slew of hate mail. The more Trump channels the brownshirts of 1930s Germany, the more zealously his defenders circle the wagons, resembling nothing so much as a sort of Kool-Aid Brigade, drinking whatever anti-democracy poison he urges them to drink.

But it is a testament to Kool-Aid's appeal that the Brigade remains robust. Its size and volume encourage Trump loyalists like Attorney General William Barr to lie — under oath, not under oath; in formal settings and casually — because they have concluded they can do so without consequence. Last week's venue was the House Judiciary Committee, where Barr was sworn to tell the truth, a chore he regarded more as annoyance than obligation. By now Barr has destroyed any reputation he ever had for relative probity. In March, a federal judge found that he had demonstrated a "lack of candor" in his public representations about the content of special counsel Robert Mueller's report, which was provided to him before the public could read it for itself. Barr, the judge ruled, had "distorted the findings" in a "calculated attempt to influence public discourse" by conning the public into thinking the report had "exonerated" Trump when it actually published voluminous evidence of 10 separate acts of obstruction of justice by Trump.

So it was unsurprising that Barr seemed comfortable, even jaunty, lying to Congress. When Barr was asked about his firing of Geoffrey Berman, the Manhattan federal prosecutor who has the evidence about Trump supplied by former Trump fixer Michael Cohen and whose office is investigating current Trump fixer Rudolph Giuliani, Barr insisted his risible letter announcing Berman was "stepping down" was accurate. "He may not have been aware of it, but he was stepping down," parried Barr with a self-satisfied grin. He later allowed that Berman, the respected Republican prosecutor who could not be trusted to protect the president, was "removed." Berman had "stepped down" the way Soviet dissidents under Josef Stalin "stepped down" from 14-story windows while being interrogated.

Having once admitted that it "would be a crime" for a president to reward someone who withheld evidence against him with a pardon, Barr denied that Trump's commutation of Roger Stone's prison sentence was even problematic. Stone was found guilty of lying to Congress when he falsely denied communicating with Trump's team about the emails hacked by Russia. But there was evidence that Stone spoke directly with Trump, among others, about them. Barr's own Justice Department asserted that Stone had lied to protect Trump — who had himself lied to Mueller about the conversations.

To recap: Stone lies to Congress to protect Trump, who had lied to Mueller. Stone brags that he has protected Trump, who praises him for it and then commutes his sentence. Barr lies to Congress that this is not evidence of a crime, when he has already admitted that it is.

An honorable, inspiring bunch, the Trump White House. Good for Steven Calabresi for reminding us what telling the truth looks like. It's occasionally hard to remember.

Yo, Semites! No Doubt About It: Biden's the One

August 11, 2020

No one has ever accused Abe Foxman of being derelict in defending Israel or soft when it comes to protecting the Jewish people. A Holocaust survivor who only narrowly escaped the fate suffered by 6 million Jews, Foxman served the Anti-Defamation League for a half-century, including 28 years as its national director. A force of nature, he became the face of the endless battle against anti-Semitism, melding bluntness and fearlessness with legendary tirelessness.

Whether he likes it or not, Foxman still finds himself to be someone to whom American Jews turn to ask the age-old Jewish question: Who and what is "good for the Jews"? Presidential elections inevitably spawn this question, and this election is no exception. Asked whether it is President Donald Trump or former Vice President Joe Biden whom American Jews should support, Foxman missed even fewer beats than usual. "I have always been asked before every election: who is better for Israel and the Jews?" Foxman says. "And my answer is always the same: Israel and the Jews need a strong, stable, credible and caring America. So vote for the candidate that will secure such an America." No longer encumbered by the need for discretion that comes with running a major nonprofit, Foxman says aloud what other Jewish leaders cannot. "There is no question in my mind," he continues, "that the answer this time to all those concerns is Joe Biden."

Polls consistently show that the overwhelming majority of American Jews agree with Foxman. One survey commissioned by the nonpartisan Jewish Electorate Institute earlier this year found that 68% of Jewish likely voters disapprove of Trump, and over 90% of those say they "strongly disapprove" of him. Seventy-one percent of American Jews disapprove of his "performance" addressing anti-Semitism and white nationalism.

As well they should. The president has zealously promoted a thug culture, one that threatens Jews as well as Black, Latino and Muslim Americans. This is a period of national shame, one that we will look back at with disgust. And that should surprise no one. When David Duke, the white supremacist leader and spokesman for Holocaust denial, declared in 2016 that whites would be committing treason if they did not vote for Trump, the object of Duke's desire was asked whether he would denounce white supremacy. Trump replied: "Well, just so you understand, I don't know anything about David Duke. OK? I don't know anything about what you're even talking about with white supremacy or white supremacists. So, I don't know."

Those with Israel's future in mind have watched Trump's embrace of her operate as a poison kiss, driving significant American constituencies away from the Jewish state in droves. Here's the problem: Narcissistic proto-fascists tend to be unappealing to those who happen to not be narcissists or proto-fascists. The damage Trump has done to Israel's standing in America, where support for Israel matters to Israel most, may be irreparable. Simply put, Israel deserves better friends than Donald Trump. It needs an American president with stature and credibility at its back. Trump isn't one. Biden is.

Foxman rightly observes that Jewish communities around the world are served well by an America that is democratic, respected and even feared, and served ill by an America that has lost its way and looks weak. Trump, himself a weakling, has turned America into a weakling as well, the object of international derision. Beholden to Russian President Vladimir Putin and afraid to confront him, even when it comes to the subversion of American elections, Trump has made America not great but pitiable. Instead of pressing China when COVID-19 emerged, he gushed about it. His ring kissing of North Korean dictator Kim Jong Un hasn't been merely embarrassing. It has been pathetic.

The speed at which America has plunged to laughingstock levels has been dizzying. Whether it will be able to reclaim its proper place as the world's preeminent democracy hinges on November's election, and American Jews are decidedly among those who know it.

It's Bigot Time: Rattled by Kamala Harris, Trump and Friends Go Full White Power

August 18, 2020

Joe Biden's selection of Sen. Kamala Harris as his running mate last week placed two facts on graphic display. The first is that President Donald Trump, who is rattled by accomplished women generally, is deeply rattled by Harris, a former prosecutor who, as a member of the Senate Judiciary Committee, drilled holes in experienced dissemblers like Attorney General William Barr and Supreme Court nominee Brett Kavanaugh. The second is that Trump's reelection chances hinge on two tactics: discouraging citizens of color from voting in November or preventing them from doing so altogether, and ginning up the largest possible turnout of white voters disposed to think that nonwhites threaten their way of life, if not their existence.

A recent Pew Research Center survey told us what we need to know about Trump's path to retaining power. It found that Biden leads Trump among Blacks 89% to 8%, among Hispanics 63% to 35% and among Asian Americans 67% to 31%. Among white men with college degrees, Biden is ahead 58% to 41%; among white women with college degrees, he leads 63% to 35%.

That leaves exactly one demographic that favors Trump: white Americans without college degrees, and he leads among them by nearly 2 to 1. Therein lies the simplicity of Trump's battle plan: suppressing the vote in communities of color, frightening the devil out of non-college-educated whites and pushing the view that he is the Preserver of White Power incarnate.

It worked for Trump in 2016, and he hopes it will work again in 2020. In the lead-up to Biden's widely expected choice of Harris, whose mother was born in India and father was born in Jamaica, Trump called the movement to affirm that Black lives matter "a symbol of hate," stoking certain whites' fear of Blacks with characteristic elegance. Touting his rollback of an Obama administration rule simply requiring local communities receiving federal funding to study racial discrimination and set goals for reducing segregation, Trump declared himself the savior of lily-white America. "I am happy to inform all of the people living their Suburban Lifestyle Dream," he tweeted, "that you will no longer be bothered or financially hurt by having low income housing built in your neighborhood." Suburbanites, he continued, "are thrilled that I ended the long running program where low income housing would invade their neighborhood." In order to make sure that no whites missed the message, he told reporters on July 31: "You build low-income housing, and you build other forms of housing — also having to do with zoning — and destroy people that have lived in communities in suburbia. For years, they've lived there, and they want to destroy their lives and destroy what they have."

If Trump has a distinctive hallmark, it is his lack of class, and he reminded us of it when the selection of Harris was announced. Born and raised in California, Harris is indisputably an American citizen. This did not stop Trump from pointedly encouraging the crackpot hogwash that Harris' citizenship is an "open question." "If she's got a problem, you would have thought that she would have been vetted by sleepy Joe," sneered Trump, thereby encouraging Americans to ingest the snake oil that Harris had "a problem" when she has none. It was the very same racist claptrap that Trump had promoted about Barack Obama. Harris and Obama are both Black, you see, which Trump hopes will suggest that their citizenship is dubious. Trump's Kool-Aid chorus picked up the refrain, with wingman Tucker Carlson acting like a juvenile delinquent by intentionally mispronouncing Harris' first name.

It's Bigot Time in America, and our president sees each news cycle as a new opportunity to hit a new low. "We are in a battle for the soul of the nation," says Joe Biden, and is he ever right.

Da, He Did: GOP-Led Senate Panel Confirms Trump Colluded With Russia for Election Interference

August 25, 2020

"Dear President Putin," wrote Donald Trump to Russian President Vladimir Putin on Dec. 19, 2007, to congratulate the former KGB officer on being named Time magazine's man of the year. "You definitely deserve it. As you probably have heard, I am a big fan of yours." And as the Republican-led United States Senate Select Committee on Intelligence confirmed last week after a bipartisan investigation, the feeling is assuredly mutual. Putin wanted Trump elected president, not Hillary Clinton, because Putin believed Trump would serve his interests and Clinton wouldn't. Putin, therefore, interfered with America's election to help Trump win and ensure Clinton did not. Not only did Trump welcome that help but he solicited it, and he and his closest aides actively colluded with the Russians and their intermediaries to secure it and capitalize on it. And then, as the Senate committee found, Trump made false statements under oath about that collusion to special counsel Robert Mueller in order to hide it.

Other than that, the Senate committee, chaired first by Republican Sen. Richard Burr and currently chaired by Republican Sen. Marco Rubio, "exonerated" the president of collusion. Generally, once you hear this president deny that X is true, you can rest easy knowing that X is absolutely true. The Senate report demonstrates that all the while Trump proclaimed "no collusion," the truth was "yes, collusion."

For starters, the committee established that the notorious June 2016 meeting hosted at Trump Tower by Trump's campaign manager, Paul Manafort, Trump son-in-law Jared Kushner and Donald Trump Jr. for the purpose of receiving Russian dirt on Clinton wasn't just with any old Russians. It included Russians who had "significant connections to the Russian government, including the Russian intelligence services." The links between one of them and the Kremlin were, the committee stated, "far more extensive and concerning than what had been publicly known." This, of course, was the meeting set up by Trump Jr., who responded to a Russian intermediary's promise to yield information damaging to Clinton with this inspirational, high-minded message: "If it's what you say it is, I love it."

Then there are the detailed findings about the close, longtime relationship between Manafort and Russian intelligence officer Konstantin Kilimnik; and between Manafort and Russian oligarch Oleg Deripaska, a Putin intimate who, according to the Senate, has acted as "a proxy for the Russian state and intelligence services" dating back to 2004, when Manafort met him. Manafort, convicted by a federal jury of tax and bank fraud, shared confidential Trump campaign information, including polling data and campaign strategies, with Kilimnik. Perhaps Kilimnik simply has a fascination with American political campaigns and put this information on his nightstand next to Theodore White's classic "The Making of the President 1960," but one may be forgiven for inferring that there are alternative explanations. The committee found evidence that Kilimnik was personally tied to Russia's operation carried out by Russian intelligence to interfere in our presidential election. And it concluded that Manafort's relationship with Kilimnik "represented a grave counterintelligence threat" to the United States.

Trump told the special counsel he did not recall anyone from the Trump campaign having had contact with his adviser Roger Stone, who liaised with Russian intelligence operatives about the Democratic emails the Russians had hacked and released through Wikileaks. The committee established that — surprise! — the denial was false. "(T)he Committee assesses that Trump did, in fact, speak with Stone about Wikileaks and with members of his Campaign about Stone's access to Wikileaks on multiple occasions," the committee found.

But Trump is ever ready with a most persuasive response, certain to keep his loyalists loyal for its sheer gravitas. Like everything else — the Mueller report, Trump's attempt to extort the Ukrainian president to obtain fabricated dirt on Joe Biden, the COVID-19 pandemic and much, much more — the Senate committee findings were — you guessed it! - "a hoax." Hooked on the Kool-Aid, incapable of seeing what is in front of their noses, the president's adherents continue to believe him.

Unending Shootings of Blacks Show America Is Not What We Thought It Is

September 1, 2020

Sixty-five years ago on Aug. 28, 14-year-old Emmett Till, while visiting his Mississippi relatives, was kidnapped, tortured, mutilated, murdered and dumped into the Tallahatchie River by white men after a complaint that the Black youngster had whistled in the proximity of a white woman. Till, who stuttered, had been taught by his mother to whistle softly before pronouncing certain problematic words, as a technique to alleviate his stutter. A witness to his murder heard the boy cry, "Mama, Lord, have mercy! Lord, have mercy!"

Till's body was dredged from the river, bloated and disfigured. His mother insisted he be placed in an open casket so everyone could see what had been done to him. Tried before an all-white, all-male jury, the defendants were acquitted after their lawyers told the jury that their "forefathers would turn over in their graves" if they were to convict. The jury took all of 67 minutes to acquit. One member said afterward, "We wouldn't have taken so long if we hadn't stopped to drink pop." Less than a year after the acquittal, the defendants told Look magazine that, of course, they had killed Till. "Well, what else could we do?" one of them said. "I just decided it was time a few people got put on notice. As long as I live and can do anything about it, (N-word) are gonna stay in their place. (N-word) ain't gonna vote where I live. If they did, they'd control the government."

The same week that Americans marked the grim anniversary of Emmett Till's murder, that segment of America that has not lost its sense of decency shuddered at the news that yet another Black countryman was brutalized by a white American — a law enforcement officer, no less — without apparent regard for human life. Millions have seen the video of a Kenosha, Wisconsin, police officer shooting 29-year-old Jacob Blake, an unarmed Black man walking away from the police, not once, not twice but seven times in the back, pulverizing his internal organs and leaving him paralyzed. "Daddy, why'd they shoot me so many times?" Blake asked his father from his hospital bed. "I don't want to be a burden on anybody," he told his mother. Like "I can't breathe," the words uttered by George Floyd 20 times as he begged for his life while police officers suffocated him on a

Minneapolis street in May, Blake's words all but make audible those of Emmett Till three generations ago: "Lord, have mercy."

For those of us who are white, the idea that America is suffused with racism has long been difficult to swallow. It is not the way we see ourselves, not the way we wish to see ourselves or the country we love. The charge that our cherished nation is afflicted with a national illness puts us in a defensive crouch.

But the unending litany of unjustified, unjustifiable violence by white police officers against Blacks has backed us into a corner, and it is time to admit it: We are not dealing with racist "incidents," or even lots of incidents, but rather a condition. And we cannot pretend that the recurring footage we see on national television is anything but the tip of the iceberg. It simply is not believable that what happened to Blake, Floyd and the dreadful list of notable others whose victimization has received national attention is not happening in cities and towns all across America, where videographers are absent and there is no media to draw attention.

The viciousness and the hatred that have, since 2016, grown too obvious to ignore predate Donald Trump's election. But a president with an atom-sized particle of either wisdom or love of country would search for ways of remedying our national disease rather than spreading it. This president has neither. So it will just have to be up to us to figure out how to do the job, and to start doing it as quickly as possible.

Nuts: The President Who Was Unfit for Service
September 8, 2020

On the morning of Dec. 22, 1944, German soldiers waving white flags approached American troops defending the Belgian city of Bastogne against the Nazi counterattack known as the Battle of the Bulge. The German army had the American defenders completely surrounded and outnumbered, and the Americans were rapidly running out of supplies by five to one.

The Germans had a message from their general to the American commander, Brig. Gen. Anthony McAuliffe: Surrender immediately or face "total annihilation." Their note was explicit. "In order to think it over," it stated, "a term of two hours will be granted beginning with the presentation of this note. If this proposal should be rejected one German Artillery Corps and six heavy battalions are ready to annihilate the U.S.A. troops in and near Bastogne."

McAuliffe was awakened with this news and initially misunderstood it. "They want to surrender?" he asked his operations officer. "No, sir," the officer replied, "they want us to surrender." Informed that the Germans demanded a written response, McAuliffe instructed that the following reply be delivered: "To the German commander: NUTS! The American commander."

McAuliffe and his troops were far from "losers" or "suckers," the terms reportedly used for our military men and women by a president who dodged the draft by making a phony claim that he had bone spurs to avoid serving his country. The Atlantic has detailed President Donald Trump's derision of those who served instead of ducking service, and the story, consistent with so many accounts by those who have observed Trump firsthand and through recordings of his public statements, is based on multiple sources. It has been backed by Fox News itself, not exactly central command of The Deep State Conspiracy. Americans have sacrificed their own lives to protect the rest of us since the nation's founding. Those who serve are not losers, and they are not suckers. They are our heroes.

One such individual was Capt. Eugene Rabinowitz of Brooklyn, New York, who was flying bombing missions over Germany at the same time McAuliffe was telling his German counterpart to stick it. The son of two Russian Jews who had come to America in the early 1900s to escape czarist pogroms, Rabinowitz went to work at an aircraft parts factory after graduating high school in 1942. Because the job was considered essential to the war effort, Rabinowitz could have used it to avoid putting his life on the line. He did not do so. He also did not claim to have bone spurs. He enlisted in the Army Air Corps and soon was given the command of a squadron of B-17s based in southeast England, charged with taking it to the Nazis.

Rabinowitz became close friends with a young man named Joe Scarpullo, the son of Italian immigrants, and Scarpullo became his wingman, flying a plane next to him in their bombing formation. After unloading their bombs on German targets during an early 1945 mission, Rabinowitz's plane was hit by German anti-aircraft fire, and his B-17, an easy target in the best of circumstances, could not keep up with the rest of the squadron. He radioed Scarpullo to leave him behind and head back across the English Channel to their base. "I've been hit," he told Scarpullo. "Don't wait for me!" Scarpullo radioed back, "I can't hear you." Rabinowitz repeated himself, only louder. "I can't hear you," said Scarpullo again. This went on until Rabinowitz realized that Scarpullo could hear him loud and clear but was not going to leave him behind. Scarpullo's plane accompanied Rabinowitz's all the way home.

The president has denied mocking the armed forces and our veterans, but you'd have to be quite a consumer of snake oil to believe him about that or anything else. If ever a more demonstrable liar has walked our Earth, it would be surprising. If these last four years have shown anything, it is that Donald Trump is profoundly unfit for service, and the reasons have nothing to do with bone spurs.

Looking Under the Hood: Time for Congress to Investigate the Performance of Health Care Executives

September 15, 2020

After the 2008 economic collapse, the U.S. Senate Permanent Subcommittee on Investigations launched a series of inquiries aimed at exposing the rot underlying the financial services industry. During one memorable hearing, then-Sen. Carl Levin grilled Goldman Sachs executives on their sale of investment products they knew to be dubious in order to increase their already eye-popping compensation. An exchange in which Levin used internal emails to show how Goldman Sachs officials sold products they knew to be "s——-ty deals" went viral.

Congress has a long history of conducting investigations to shed light on sharp or shoddy practices and the handsome compensation packages granted to the executives responsible for them. In 1933, a Senate committee investigating the roots of the Great Depression called banker J.P. Morgan to testify about his own salary and the dishonest practices that made that salary possible, generating public support for remedial legislation enacted during the New Deal.

The pandemic has exposed with new clarity the comparable rot that underlies the American health care system. Americans pay an estimated $4 trillion annually for health care, and the pandemic has unmasked a system that proved ill-equipped to cope with a major public health crisis while other countries could and did. The mind-boggling monies pouring into health care providers' coffers somehow leaves tens of millions of Americans unable to afford the health care they need and one serious illness away from ruin.

Meantime, one lucky group of individuals are health care CEOs, whose compensation packages often bear little relationship to the delivery of affordable health care and frequently are the product of incentives to overcharge and under-treat. For example, Boston is a mecca for not only health care but also executives' compensation arrangements, even as health care costs explode. A recent survey of nonprofit hospitals showed that as of 2018, the last year when their IRS filings are available, the CEOs of the city's 10 largest health care companies were paid salaries ranging from $1.7 million to $4.7 million. Dozens of other health care executives in Boston were paid similar amounts.

This does not include the appointments to health care company boards these CEOs are able to leverage for themselves by dint of their positions. These appointments pay handsomely, with stock grants and annual board fees over and above their compensation. They are hardly charitable in nature: The companies handing out the board seats seek hospital business, and they get it, in the form of participation in programs paid for by patients; research and clinical arrangements; and other lucrative benefits. On their face, these relationships are either blatant conflicts of interest or provide the compelling appearance of them. "It smells," Alan Sager, professor at Boston University's School of Public Health, says of this mutual back-scratching. "We don't know whether it is a mild stench or a revolting stench. The potential for conflicts of interest is there. It should be prohibited."

But the conflicts of interest are not even the only problem. "High health care CEO salaries," Sager says, "are like the froth on a toxic waste dump. It is visible on the surface, but it obscures what is even worse underneath." Hospital executives are often given free rein to run enterprises whose mandate is to increase the bottom line. "They are going to do things that are profitable," he says, and that tends to encourage procedures, billing and other conduct whose target is that bottom line. "What they frequently do," says Sager, "is put their financial self-interest first."

Whether it is examining potential conflicts of interest by health care executives, or strengthening whistleblower protections for health care personnel who report practices that are dishonest or jeopardize patient safety, Congress has a crucial role to play, and it is crucial that it play it. The new Congress that takes office in January should use its investigative powers to shine a much-needed spotlight on America's health care corporations, and on how they can better serve the patients who pay their executives' remarkable salaries.

Liar and Losers: The President Deceives, and Americans Take the Hit

September 22, 2020

"Once a country is habituated to liars," Gore Vidal once observed, "it takes generations to bring back the truth." Many of us don't have generations left. After four years during which President Donald Trump has waged thermonuclear war on the truth, we face the depressing reality of living out our days in a country in which, thanks to Trump and the cultlike embrace of him by far too many of our countrymen, corruption has not been merely normalized but legitimized. It is hard to imagine that the Good Lord ever created a less honest human being than The Donald, and even harder to imagine that anyone not seriously on the sauce believes a word he utters. But even 20,000 or so documented falsehoods into the Trump administration later, millions of Americans still do, which makes the grim reality of the America of 2020 that much grimmer.

The release of Bob Woodward's taped interviews with the president illustrates that the lying has left not only a heretofore-accepted American value system shattered but also tens of thousands of Americans needlessly dead. To no one's surprise, the tapes disclose a president who was quite deliberately lying to the American people over and over about the deadly virus he was trying to gull us into believing was a hoax. In refusing to take the steps to procure ventilators desperately needed to save lives and equipment badly needed to protect health care workers and others, and in staging rallies that eased his ego while endangering the lives of all those present and undermining health officials' frantic efforts to promote life-saving social distancing and mask wearing, the president mocked the very idea that any public health issue even existed. The virus was, he said, ever the used-car salesman, "going to disappear." It was "low-risk." It was "very much under control." He had "pretty much shut it down." It was no more than 15 cases, and "within a couple of days is going to be down to close to zero."

The virtuoso con artist was conning America, as all but the stoutly fact-resistant now know. Excerpts of Trump's taped admissions that his public pronouncements were hogwash, and that he knew it, were released, while more than 6.7 million Americans have been infected with the coronavirus; the number of new cases has increased by 10% in the last week in 31 states; and 200,000 Americans have been killed by the disease. As Trump was belittling the notion that the disease was even worth mentioning, he was confiding in Woodward, saying: "It's a horrible thing. It's unbelievable," and "It's so easily transmissible you wouldn't even believe it," and "This is deadly stuff." While demanding that states open schools and universities, and claiming that young people were "almost immune" to the virus, here was what our president was telling Woodward about those contracting COVID-19: "Now it's turning out that it's not just old people. Young people, too. Plenty of young people."

We have become so sufficiently used to having a pathological liar as president that neither the lying nor the lying about the lying much registers any longer. Despite a recording of Trump telling Woodward that he had downplayed the virus to the American people, White House press secretary Kayleigh McEnany, valedictorian at the Joseph Goebbels Institute of Public Relations, simply denied that he had said it. "To be honest with you, I wanted to always play it down," Trump told Woodward on March 19. "I still like playing it down." Princess Pinocchio, however, could not have cared less that the entire world heard him say it on tape. "The president never downplayed the virus," she told the White House press corps with a straight face on Sept. 9.

Donald Trump's legacy will be his unprecedented mendacity and the dissolution of faith that our leaders will feel a baseline obligation to speak truthfully. But it will also be the loss that has upended millions of American families, loss that would have been avoided had we only had a president with a modicum of moral character.

When the Shoe Fits: Biden Invokes the F-Word for Trump, and He's Not Wrong

September 29, 2020

In her 2018 book, "Fascism: A Warning," former Secretary of State Madeleine Albright, herself a refugee from totalitarians, cautioned that it is hubris at best and delusion at worst to imagine that fascism of the sort that ascended to power in 1930s Europe couldn't do the same here. The book was released two years into Donald Trump's presidency, and the ugly outlines of fascism were already discernible in Trump's conduct. Hitler, Albright wrote, "lied incessantly about himself and about his enemies." He duped millions of Germans into thinking that he "cared for them deeply when, in fact, he would have sacrificed them all." He strove to nullify limits on his power. He exhorted his supporters to harm his political opponents and delighted in the suffering of his victims.

There is a strong resistance to comparing anyone, no matter how vile, with fascist leaders, and with good reason. Four years of the Time of Trump, however, has made honoring this taboo more and more of a strain.

The famously cautious Joe Biden entered new territory on Saturday, saying aloud what most of the world has already concluded: America has a president who acts a very great deal like Nazi propaganda minister Joseph Goebbels. "He's sort of like Goebbels," Biden said of Trump. "You say the lie long enough — keep repeating it, repeating it, repeating it — it becomes common knowledge." That, of course, is precisely what Trump does. He has been doing it his entire life. He did it throughout the 2016 campaign. And he has done it day in and day out during his presidency. With the polls showing him trailing Biden badly and the election only weeks away, more lying is what America will get. It is the only trick this one-trick pony knows.

To be precise, however, Goebbels isn't the only fascist Trump resembles, and lying isn't the only trait he has in common with fascists. Another is his refusal to agree to honor an election in which American voters express their will that he leave office. Asked last week whether he would abide by the most basic of democratic norms — the peaceful transfer of power from incumbent to challenger — Trump replied, "We're going to have to see what happens." He added: "Get rid of the ballots and we'll have a very peaceful — there won't be a transfer, frankly. There'll be a continuation."

On Friday, Trump celebrated the painful injury suffered by MSNBC journalist Ali Velshi, who crumpled to the ground after being hit by a rubber bullet while reporting on protests in Minneapolis this spring. "It was the most beautiful thing," Trump told his cheering crowd. "It's called law and order."

During demonstrations in Kenosha, Wisconsin, following the police shooting of an unarmed Black man seven times in the back, a teenager allegedly shot to death two protesters with an assault rifle. Trump fabricated the usual hogwash. The teenager, Trump lied, was simply "trying to get away from them, I guess, it looks like."

Speaking in Minnesota last week, Trump channeled the "master race" rhetoric of German fascists of 80 years ago. "You have good genes. You know that, right?" he said, stroking his virtually all-white crowd. "A lot of it is about the genes, isn't it? Don't you believe? The racehorse theory." Seeking to whip up the nativist hatred of a Pittsburgh crowd, he targeted Ilhan Omar, a Somali refugee who is not only an American citizen but also a member of Congress. "How about Omar of Minnesota?" he asked mockingly. "She's telling us how to run our country. How's your country doing?"

When the similarities are so obvious, it is no longer the making of comparisons between Donald Trump and European fascists that seems inappropriate but refraining from making them. America has flirted with fascists and fascism before. It happened here in the run-up to World War II. It happened during the era of Joe McCarthy. But it's never been as bad as this.

Trashed: On His Way out the Door, the President Leaves America a Mess

October 6, 2020

In the classic movie "Annie Hall," the narrator tells the timeless joke of the two friends at a Catskills resort bemoaning the poor quality of the restaurant. "The food at this place is really terrible," one observes. "I know," replies her friend, "and such small portions." Americans living through the dumpster fire that is Donald Trump's presidency are rightly worried about whether our country will ever truly recover from it, and they confront a similar conundrum: Is it more precise to characterize this administration as loathsome or a disgrace?

Last week did not make the choice any easier. It featured a president whose signature character traits were on vivid display: The lying, the infantile personal attacks and the bullying interruptions triggered a national gag reflex, exactly what Americans want to experience watching their leader.

But that was only part of it.

Trump boasts about being a brilliant businessman and professes concern for working Americans. However, not so much, as all but the most ardent of Kool-Aid drinkers could have predicted. During his debate with Democratic nominee Joe Biden, he babbled nonsense in response to questions about The New York Times' reporting on his tax returns — the returns he has fought to keep hidden while assuring the uber-gullible that he intends to release them during this lifetime. Those returns confirm that Trump has been an astonishing business failure; owes unidentified creditors over $400 million; and has stiffed the Treasury by paying no federal income taxes for 10 of the last 15 years and only $750 each in two other years. Why anyone would imagine that someone who has so consistently stiffed students, contractors and employees wouldn't stiff Uncle Sam in spectacular fashion remains unclear.

But perhaps nothing stimulated collective waves of nausea more than the president's warnings that he was urging his supporters to storm polling places to "watch" for "election fraud." For starters, there is no election fraud and no reason to believe there will be any, as the president's own FBI director has himself reaffirmed. That fact matters not at all to a president whose assertions of fraud are themselves fraudulent. Moreover, the conduct he is urging his supporters to engage in is egregiously illegal. We also saw a president who yet again refused to condemn white supremacists, comprising his most rabid base of support. Challenged to implore one group of supporters, the neo-fascist Proud Boys, to renounce their violence on American streets, Trump instead instructed them to "stand by." He took pains to underscore his threat. "This is not going to end well," Trump warned twice. "This is not going to end well."

Meanwhile, the president who refuses to agree to honor the results of an election that he loses is reinforced by allies determined to discourage or outright prevent Americans from voting, knowing that keeping citizens from expressing their will is Trump's best shot at retaining the presidency. In Texas last Thursday, Republican Gov. Greg Abbott directed counties to permit only one drop-off box for absentee ballots. This means that in large counties, including the state's most populous one, voters may have to drive dozens of miles to hand-deliver those ballots. On the same day, two right-wing operatives were charged by the Michigan attorney general with a fraudulent robocall scheme by which 85,000 Black voters in Detroit were warned that voting by mail could subject them to arrest, debt collection and forced vaccination.

By the weekend, the president, who had torpedoed efforts to protect Americans from COVID-19, was hospitalized with it. Two hundred and ten thousand Americans have been killed by the pandemic he decided it was in his interest to ignore. "He did not just downplay the virus," noted historian Douglas Brinkley, "he paraded around like a peacock, making fun of those who took it seriously." The presidency that the country appears poised to flush away has left the America we thought we were in pieces. Putting it back together will be a tall order.

Mensch on the Bench: Remembering Massachusetts Chief Justice Ralph Gants

October 13, 2020

Lawyers are not generally known for their humility, and anyone who has spent much time in courts knows that lawyers fortunate enough to become judges can develop a certain, shall we say, arrogance. Some years ago, one Massachusetts trial judge announced to her courtroom, "I'm very smart. I really am," a memorable expression of self-admiration that remained distinctive until Donald Trump made proclamations like that commonplace.

But then there are those whose humility is an inspiration. Four days before the passing of United States Supreme Court Justice Ruth Bader Ginsberg shook the nation, Massachusetts experienced its own blow to the civic solar plexus with the death of Ralph Gants, the chief justice of its Supreme Judicial Court. Lawyers and litigants, community leaders and ordinary citizens mourned Gants' death in a reaction unusually intense and widespread for the passing of a judge. Flags across the Commonwealth were lowered as commenters on the websites of both right- and left-wing media outlets took a short break from one-upping one another with snark in order to praise Gants. Courts, law schools and lawyers' groups have already begun a series of events honoring Gants' memory, unlike any outpouring of appreciation Massachusetts has ever seen for a judge.

This would have surprised Gants, a wry, self-effacing man whose death at age 65 cut short a life spent trying to help others on a human level and enhance fairness on a judicial one. A graduate of Harvard College and Harvard Law School and a successful federal prosecutor, Gants would have had plenty of reason to regard himself as special, as he was appointed to be a trial judge at age 42. Tapped by Gov. Deval Patrick to be chief justice of the state's highest court, he built upon the reputation he already had by not only being a thoughtful jurist but also being kind to those who appeared before him. Invoking the Yiddish word for a person of honor and integrity, one cantankerous political figure whose conservative politics contrasted with Gants' liberalism greeted his appointment with grudging approval. "Ralph Gants is a mensch," she said, "and the bench needs a mensch."

It got a mensch in Gants, who hurled himself into launching programs aimed at dramatically improving access to the courts, crisscrossing

Massachusetts to prod lawyers to represent the powerless and court systems to better protect the disenfranchised. Weeks after the 2016 presidential election, Gants made a point of traveling to Boston's largest mosque to convey a message of support for 800 Muslim worshippers. "You do not stand alone," Gants told them. "You have a Constitution and laws to protect your right to practice your religion, to protect you from discrimination and the denial of your equal rights, and to protect you from acts of violence that might be committed because of your religion or your nation of origin."

Gants' identification with the underdog was visceral and deep. "He didn't care about credit," his family said in a statement. "He didn't care about self-promotion. He cared about the vulnerable. He cared about fairness."

Gants had a heart attack 10 days before his fatal one, and he was under doctors' orders to rest. It was consistent with his stubborn work ethic that the morning he died, he was on the phone with Boston attorney Susan Finegan, with whom he had collaborated closely on justice-related issues for a decade. "He called me to discuss his deep concern about the looming eviction crisis," Finegan says, "which he had called 'the greatest access to justice challenge of our lifetime.'"

Yale Law School professor Harold Koh, one of Gants' oldest friends, remembers Gants repeating the words of the federal judge for whom Gants had clerked 40 years earlier. "We can't make the whole world fair," the judge told Gants, "but we can make one small piece of the world a place where fairness, justice and civility rule." Gants told Koh long ago that he intended to live his life according to that precept, and he kept his word.

The Full Mussolini: The Proto-Fascist in Chief Goes for Broke

October 20, 2020

With two weeks to go until we choose our next president and polls continually indicating that Americans are suffering acid reflux at the thought of four more years of Donald Trump, the president has gone full Mussolini: He has threatened that "things will not go well" if Joe Biden defeats him and that he won't agree to peacefully leave office if that occurs. He tweeted unhinged conspiratorial hogwash that former President Barack Obama had Navy Seals killed in order to "cover up" the "fact" that Osama bin Laden is alive. And he has otherwise conducted himself like a power-obsessed lunatic. Late last week, Trump accused the Bidens of being part of an "organized crime family," a maniacal refrain dutifully repeated by his most untethered supporters, and called Sen. Kamala Harris, Biden's running mate, a "monster" and a "communist."

The thrice-married serial adulterer, who was heard on tape bragging about being able to sexually assault women without any consequences, and who has defrauded students, charities, employees and contractors, proclaimed this week National Character Counts Week. Coming from him, that takes not only the cake but the entire bakery. "We must resolve to build lives grounded in moral clarity," intoned Individual 1 (Trump) in the federal indictment issued by Trump's own Justice Department, which alleges that he directed his longtime fixer to pay $130,000 in hush money to a porn star with whom he allegedly had an affair just after his third wife gave birth to their son.

You cannot, as the expression goes, make this stuff up.

Trump's acolytes have left nothing in the locker room when it comes to rushing to debase themselves in the service of a bona fide proto-fascist. After Michigan Gov. Gretchen Whitmer acted decisively to stop the deadly spread of the coronavirus, which Trump had denied and disregarded, he urged his supporters to "liberate Michigan." Egged on by their man and resembling fascist Stormtroopers in 1930s Germany, hundreds of protesters, including armed militia men, stormed the Michigan State Capitol. Trump has loudly and repeatedly supported these "protests." After the FBI uncovered a plot by dangerous right-wing nut jobs to kidnap Whitmer, Trump refused to express sympathy for Whitmer or her family. In Michigan on Saturday, he gleefully mocked her. "They said she was threatened," Trump sneered. "Hopefully, you'll be sending her packing pretty soon." "Lock her up!" chanted Trump's Nuremberg-like crowd about the leader who sought to protect them from a deadly virus. "Lock 'em all up," replied Trump approvingly. Trump adviser and daughter-in-law Lara Trump unsurprisingly thought this was excellent. "He was having fun at a Trump rally," she told CNN.

The president has taken to threatening that if he loses the election, he will leave the United States. This seems like a good idea for the rest of us, as long as he chooses a country with which we have an extradition treaty. Not since Saddam Hussein fled Baghdad has there been so much evidence incriminating a deposed leader. Trump and his sons, American versions of Qusay and Uday Hussein, will leave behind evidence sufficient to keep federal and New York prosecutors busy for quite some time: tax fraud, bank fraud, mail fraud and fraud-fraud. And that's just for starters. If ground is ever broken on an Obstruction of Justice Hall of Fame, Trump will almost certainly be its first inductee. For this reason, a scenario in which the president purports to pardon himself before leaving office and a yearslong litigation about the validity of a self-pardon ensues is plausible.

Donald Trump does not have to work at channeling Mussolini. It comes naturally to him. But his is not the America that those who came before us could have imagined. It is indeed an America our forebears fought and died to guard against. Now Americans have two weeks to decide whether they will reclaim their country from what has been a national disgrace or lose it, likely for good.

Agent Orange: Our Adversaries' Man in the White House

October 27, 2020

When the Donald Trump era comes mercifully to a close, and after the national chore of fumigating the White House is well underway, Americans will need to address this question: Just how many foreign governments had our president in their pocket, and how did he land there?

First up will, of course, be Russia, which appears to have owned The Donald since before the 2016 election. It is established that President Vladimir Putin's government directed the hacking of Democratic Party computers and orchestrated the release of stolen emails to elect Trump. It is equally clear that Trump and his closest aides actively sought Russian help. Trump has refused to criticize Russia's assault on our country, just as he has refused to criticize Russia for its offers to pay for the murder of American troops.

Unless it is just a fondness for borscht, the most compelling explanation for Trump's servility is that Russia has something on him. It may simply be that Trump knows that Putin knows that Trump owes his election to Putin.

But with Trump $421 million in hock to unidentified creditors in unidentified countries, the answer may lie in his financial entanglements with Russia and his hope for future ones. At a 2008 conference, Donald Trump Jr. gave a shoutout to his family's financial relationship with Russia. "Russians make up a pretty disproportionate cross-section of a lot of our assets," Junior told attendees. A 2018 investigation by Reuters found that individuals with Russian passports or addresses owned almost $100 million worth of units in seven Trump properties alone. After Trump earned several million dollars from the 2013 Miss Universe pageant in Moscow, he proclaimed, "I have plans for the establishment of business in Russia."

Last week's disclosure that Trump has a secret bank account in China should by rights convince all but those ready to buy swamp land that the reason Trump has refused to show us his tax returns is not because of any "audit." The disclosure did not exactly allay concerns that Trump is subject to foreign influence, and his characteristically flagrant dishonesty about the account raises those concerns to DEFCON 1 levels. "The bank account you're referring to," he stammered when asked about it at last week's debate, "everybody knows about it; it's listed. It was open, and it was closed in 2015, I believe."

Ordinarily, the president is a one-falsehood-per-sentence-fragment kind of a guy, but on this occasion, he doubled his quotient. Contrary to Trump's claim, nobody knew about his Chinese bank account because he kept it secret; his financial disclosure forms do not identify it. And the account was not closed in 2015, or ever: a lawyer for his company confirms that it remains open to this day. As for what the monies that run through that Chinese account have paid for, Trump isn't saying.

A hidden financial relationship with China is not a good look for Trump, who licked China's boots over and over earlier this year when he waved aside the deadly virus originating in China and covered up by the Chinese government, causing horrific consequences for the American people. "China has been working very hard to contain the Coronavirus," Trump asserted on Jan. 24. "The United States greatly appreciates their efforts and transparency. It will all work out well. In particular, on behalf of the American people, I want to thank President Xi." Trump continued to heap praise on the Chinese government on Feb. 7, Feb. 10 and Feb. 13, and did so for weeks as the pandemic that that government had kept hidden took root here.

So much that has been unthinkable has come to pass in the time of Trump that it is sometimes difficult to keep it all straight. The indications that our commander in chief has been beholden to foreign interests is far too real to ignore. It will have to be part of our national self-reckoning if the upcoming election gives Americans a chance at a fresh start.

Stain Removal: Americans Get a Chance for a Deep Cleaning

November 3, 2020

Everything that anyone with a head or a heart needed to know about Donald Trump was obvious on the night of Nov. 25, 2015, when he mocked the severe physical disability of a journalist in front of a hooting, jeering South Carolina crowd. Trump had been caught making the false claim that "thousands and thousands" of Muslims in Jersey City, New Jersey, cheered the World Trade Center's collapse on Sept. 11, 2001. Scrambling to defend this lie, Trump cited a 2001 article written by reporter Serge Kovaleski. But Kovaleski had written no such thing and publicly stated as much.

So, Trump did what Trump does. Kovaleski has arthrogryposis, an incurable congenital disease that distorts the movement of his hands and arms. Like the cruelest of schoolyard bullies, Trump crudely imitated Kovaleski with a sneer on his face, reveling in the derisive, approving laughter he had elicited from his audience.

Trump's deeply rooted indecency was on vivid display, but so, too, was the indecency of the crowd that loved it, and of those who watched it from afar and decided they were perfectly OK with it. Nothing we have seen from Donald Trump since — the jaw-dropping dishonesty, the historic corruption, the obstruction of justice and the unadulterated narcissism — is revelatory. All of it is merely confirmatory.

The scene evoked others throughout history that depict ugly depravity. One remembers the sickening photographs of Nazis in 1930s Germany forcing frail elderly Jews to kneel and clean the streets, while their neighbors pointed and laughed. Over and over, we have asked: How could this have happened? How did Germans endorse the cruelty, embrace it, defend it and join in it?

In the 1985 movie classic "Witness," Philadelphia detective John Book, played by Harrison Ford, discovers that his longtime police chief has become just the kind of corrupt cop that the chief had long railed against. "Isn't that what you used to say about dirty cops?" Ford asks him. "Somewhere along the line, they lost the meaning?"

Over half of Americans tell pollsters that religion is very important to them, and most of the other half would nevertheless agree that faith-based values like honesty, fairness, charity, and kindness to strangers and the vulnerable matter to them — and are values they want to matter to their children. But tens of millions of our fellow countrymen have nonetheless defended and helped enable a president who has extended his middle finger to those values with a sneer. He has laughed at the rule of law and whipped up hatred against Americans of color and immigrants, dispensing xenophobic rhetoric with machine gun-like rapidity, stroking white supremacists and stoking white supremacism. The president whom these Americans adore has never read the Bible and could care less about it. He has taken a blow torch to values that form the cornerstone of all religious faiths. And yet, these Americans have not only looked the other way at his conduct; they have often rejoiced in it. In so doing, they have shown that somewhere along the line, they, too, have lost the meaning.

When dozens of his supporters tried to run a Biden-Harris campaign bus off the road in Texas this weekend, a little maneuver that could have killed people, Donald Trump gleefully praised them as "patriots." Trump has pointedly refused to agree to relinquish power peacefully if he loses the election; he gave notice that he would declare victory on election night regardless of whether the uncounted ballots would establish that he lost. His campaign filed suit to invalidate 125,000 votes duly cast pursuant to Texas law because he is afraid he will lose Texas if they are counted. His loyal defenders — in Congress, in the conservative media — profess their devotion to democracy. Their silence proves that is phony.

There is a stain on America. Donald Trump has put it there, but Americans have allowed him to do it. The good news is that we have the chance to remove it, and to start afresh.

Debased but Not Done: America Wrestles Its Strongman to the Ground

November 10, 2020

For those who have not yet perceived the flashing red lights and screaming emergency sirens in Donald Trump's America, the president's jolting meltdown at the White House lectern last Thursday should have triggered a revelation. "I'd like to provide the American people with an update on our efforts to protect the integrity of our very important 2020 election," began the president who has done everything he could conjure up to obliterate "the integrity of our very important 2020 election." Though he was obviously losing the election by Thursday, according to the entirely legal votes of a record-breaking number of Americans, he proclaimed, "If you count the legal votes, I easily win." Those able to summon the intestinal fortitude to watch this display saw the familiar cross between Charlie Chaplin and Benito Mussolini, but this time, he crossed that fine line separating swaggering demagogue from swaggering whack job.

In Lexington, Massachusetts, the next day, angry Trump supporters faced off against jubilant Joe Biden backers steps away from where the American Revolution got underway. The former waved American flags and chanted, "USA! USA!" But you had to wonder what concept of USA squares with declaring votes illegal because they happen to have been cast for one's opponent. The Biden supporters, comprised of people in their teens and 20s, countered with "This is what democracy looks like!" And it is a testament to their families and their teachers that, despite the daily debasement of democracy that we have been subjected to over the past four years, they have not forgotten what democracy is at least supposed to look like.

Indeed, young Americans provided a powerful boost to the broad coalition of citizens who made Joe Biden president-elect, voting in numbers that contradicted conventional wisdom. Credit as well Biden's former rivals for the Democratic nomination for swallowing their disappointment, parking their own ambitions and rallying behind the Biden-Harris ticket, focused like lasers on the existential threat that Trump has posed to the country. On the left, progressives such as Rep. Alexandria Ocasio-Cortez and others worked overtime to elect Biden first so they could advocate for policy enhancements later, while principled conservatives organized by The Lincoln Project, Bill

Kristol and others relentlessly made the case that traditional American values and support for Donald Trump do not mix. In Georgia, Stacey Abrams spearheaded a multiyear voter-registration effort that carried Biden to victory there.

Then there are Black Americans, whose rescue of this country is all the more moving given how badly and how long they have been mistreated by it. They have been ravaged by this pandemic both epidemiologically and economically, and they have experienced a season of police violence so outrageous as to shake the nation. This has included the suffocation of George Floyd and the shooting of Jacob Blake, wanton acts of violence by professed officers of the law. In the Year of our Lord 2020, a sneering president and his allies have not only openly denigrated the proposition that Black lives matter but also attacked as terrorists those who insist they matter.

Hemmed in by restrictions aimed at suppressing their votes, Blacks might have waved off this election with a steely "Well, now you know how we feel. If you want America saved from Donald Trump, do it yourselves."

But they didn't. By the millions, Black Americans waited in lines for hours to vote — in the heat; in the rain; in the cold; in Atlanta, Philadelphia, Detroit and Milwaukee. Unbowed by the pandemic, undeterred by injustice, they carried Joe Biden to the White House on their backs and are responsible for escorting Donald Trump out.

Our country has been degraded by the past four years; there is no question about it. But a majority of Americans determined that enough was enough. Thanks to that determination, the America that we love has been given a new lease on life.

Banana Republicans: Trump and His Party Take America Hostage

November 17, 2020

The news that President Donald Trump has not attended a White House Coronavirus Task Force meeting in five months recalled satirist Dorothy Parker's reaction upon hearing that Calvin Coolidge had died. "How could they tell?" she asked. It is not quite accurate to say that the president has checked out when it comes to the deadly surge of coronavirus cases consuming America, because he never checked in. Even Trump's admission that he had downplayed the virus because he did not want America to panic was dishonest; he had not "downplayed" the virus so much as he had deliberately lied about it. And he did so not because he was afraid Americans would panic but because he was afraid they would hold him accountable. After all, avoiding accountability has been Trump's life mission.

Until American voters rejected him on Nov. 3, Trump was able to declare mission accomplished. Once stripped of presidential immunity and the services of an attorney general functioning as a one-man, two-legged protection racket, ex-President Trump may find himself subject to accountability on steroids: foreclosure proceedings, IRS penalties, lawsuits arising from alleged sexual assaults and criminal investigations based on the compendium of obstruction of justice evidence assembled by Bob Mueller and the fraud buffet currently being examined by New York prosecutors.

Trump presently occupies himself by tweeting untethered drivel about how the election he resoundingly lost was "rigged" and "fraudulent," how he won it and all the other deceitful gibberish for which history will remember him. None of this is true, and Trump's fellow Republicans know it. That, however, doesn't translate into the minimal courage necessary to state publicly that Trump lost and Joe Biden won.

Judge after judge, disinclined to permit smoke to be blown up their robes, has thrown out the empty post-election lawsuits filed by Trump. As for Trump's sci-fi contrivance that there has been some sort of chicanery in the vote tabulation, that was promptly debunked by his own Department of Homeland Security. "There is no evidence that any voting system deleted or lost votes, changed votes or was in any way compromised," it stated.

Naturally, the facts have had little impact on those who comprise the Republican Party and are too terrified by Trump to place country over party. They are repeating the blather that he won the election and remaining silent about his refusal to cooperate in the presidential transition. "President Trump won this election, so everyone who's listening, do not be quiet," proclaimed House Minority Leader Kevin McCarthy, despite the obvious reality that Trump had lost. Secretary of State Mike Pompeo, tasked with promoting the rule of law abroad, refused to do so at home. When asked whether the refusal to cooperate in the transition could harm America, he said, "There will be a smooth transition to a second Trump administration."

The respectful acceptance of the peoples' will and full cooperation with an incoming administration is, of course, a democratic tradition that helps us heal wounds and binds us to one another as a single nation.

But it is more. Even in ordinary times, it is also crucial to discouraging hostile foreign powers and actors from exploiting confusion or gaps in our defenses. But when a riven nation is ravaged by an out-of-control pandemic, the national security imperative of a peaceful transition is greater still. Any president who gave a fig about his country would appreciate this.

"I did not believe how easily the Republican establishment, people who had been in Washington for a long time and had professed a belief in certain constitutional values and norms, would just cave," observed former President Barack Obama. Donald Trump and his party do not appear to care that we have taken on not just the appearance of a banana republic but some of its attributes. They have made a sad period in America's history even sadder.

Democracy Subversion to Dye for: Trump Shoots America to Kill

November 24, 2020

When Donald Trump's liar-for-hire Rudy Giuliani proclaimed last week that his master's election rejection was due to "a massive fraud," it wasn't only black liquid hair dye that leaked out. It was Giuliani's last remaining droplets of credibility, assuming any still remained after several years of crooked buffoonery in service of a crooked president. President Donald Trump, in insisting that he won an election he overwhelmingly lost, has abandoned any last pretense of caring about the country he leads. And Giuliani, flailing wildly in a fashion that called delirium to mind, matched The Boss grotesquerie for grotesquerie. "I know crimes. I can smell 'em," puffed the reported subject of an FBI investigation. Yet his client's conduct has provided criminal investigators with one amazing smorgasbord of incriminating evidence to pick over.

Trump is repeating over and over that the election was "stolen" by a combination of sorcerers, goblins and the Charles Manson family. In doing so, he hasn't merely enshrined himself as the most morally bankrupt public official in American history; he has made Joe McCarthy look like an Episcopal priest. By refusing to honor the most fundamental feature of democracy — the cooperative transfer of power by an incumbent to his elected successor — Trump has done more damage to American democracy than Russian President Vladimir Putin ever could, other than by military attack. He has invited hostile forces, jubilant at the harm he has inflicted on America's institutions, to take advantage of us, jeopardizing our national security.

By blocking the incoming Joe Biden team from organizing to immediately address a pandemic that now nearly strikes 200,000 Americans each day, Trump is consigning innumerable Americans to unnecessary sickness and, inevitably, death. History will record that the 45th president did not merely ignore COVID-19; stupidly dismiss it; refuse to mobilize to protect his countrymen from it; and lie to them about it. It will record that Trump has actually prevented his elected successor from promptly acting to safeguard the American people from the raging disease.

Donald Trump will not enter our pantheon of shame by himself. He has been coddled and enabled by Republican politicians more disposed to cower and grovel than honor the basic civics lessons we were all taught in elementary school.

There have been rare exceptions, and they have been notable. "Having failed to make even a plausible case of widespread fraud or conspiracy before any court of law," said Sen. Mitt Romney last week, "the president has now resorted to overt pressure on state and local officials to subvert the will of the people and overturn the election. It is difficult to imagine a worse, more undemocratic action by a sitting American president."

In Pennsylvania, federal judge Mathew Brann, a conservative Republican, did not permit personal politics to affect judicial review of Trump's attempt to overthrow that state's election by invalidating millions of properly cast ballots. Likening the president's "strained" legal attempt to undo a fair election to "Frankenstein's Monster," Judge Brann was blunt. Trump, he held, asks the court "to violate the rights of over 6.8 million Americans. It is not in the power of this Court to violate the Constitution."

But the grim truth is that the fault lies with us. By embracing a president who has subverted fundamental democratic norms, we have proven ourselves unworthy of the self-admiration with which we indulge ourselves. Our appreciation of what a democracy means, let alone our commitment to it, is in grave doubt.

Farah Pandith, the State Department's former special representative to Muslim communities, has called for a national initiative to promote democracy at home that rivals our much-ballyhooed initiatives abroad. We must, Pandith writes, "reintroduce ourselves" to democratic values.

She's right. It is hubris to suppose that what we have will long endure if we cavalierly permit the sort of travesty we have experienced over the past four years to recur. Nearly half of American voters have evinced a willingness to do just that. Plainly, America is in a hole it needs to dig itself out of.

Fingers Crossed, Eyes Forward: Biden Team Vows to Show That America Is Back

December 1, 2020

In March 1999, hundreds of human rights activists from around the world gathered in a hall in Geneva, Switzerland, to meet America's three principal representatives to the United Nations Human Rights Commission at its annual session to spotlight human rights violations. They were in Geneva to prod governments to replace rhetoric with responsibility, and years of knocking their heads against walls had left them hardened but still hopeful. They crowded into the hall to take the measure of the United States, which has long convinced itself of its own relative rectitude, feeling entitled to lecture other governments on how to conduct themselves. And they harbored the same complicated mixture of admiration and resentment that the name "America" has triggered across the globe since the end of World War II, with the ratio of one to the other prone to fluctuation based on current events and the nature of national U.S. leadership at that given moment.

The three representatives reflected America's diversity and its vast potential for doing good. Harold Hongju Koh, the son of Korean immigrants, was our assistant secretary of state for the Bureau of Democracy, Human Rights and Labor and was a prominent human rights advocate before assuming that post. Indeed, before joining the United States government, Koh had litigated against it, fighting on behalf of Haitian refugees interned at Guantanamo. George Moose, our ambassador to the United Nations organizations in Geneva, was an Africa expert who had served in significant diplomatic positions in Republican and Democratic administrations alike. Nancy Rubin, our ambassador to the commission, had spent decades advocating for women's rights.

The three weren't merely America's face but, from the perspective of those convinced that America can promote decency abroad, its soul. The excited buzz when the event ended left the United States delegation to the commission emotional — and proud.

Those present that day saw an America that people everywhere yearn to see: a country that means what it says about democracy and the rule of law; that conducts itself accordingly; that models compassion; and that strives, however imperfectly, to do the right thing.

That is not what anyone has seen in President Donald Trump's America, and President-elect Joe Biden and the foreign policy team he introduced last week know it. It is why Biden purposefully selected "America is back" as the organizing message for last week's roll-out. The world wants to know whether the desecration of American values that the Trump presidency wrought was a temporary spasm in the country's history or a way station on a permanent downward spiral.

Biden's secretary of state nominee, Antony Blinken, captured our complex challenge abroad perfectly, emphasizing that we need to find a way to simultaneously display "humility and confidence" in reengineering our relationships with the rest of the world. The personal story Blinken chose to illustrate what the United States is capable of meaning was likewise perfect. As a small boy, Blinken's stepfather escaped from a Nazi death march in the Holocaust's last days and hid in the Bavarian woods. He saw a tank with American markings on it. "He ran to the tank," Blinken recounted in accepting the nomination as our chief diplomat last week. "The hatch opened. An African American G.I. looked down at him. He fell to his knees and said the only three words he knew in English that his mother had taught him: 'God Bless America.' The G.I. lifted him into the tank, into America, into freedom."

"American democracy," historian Michael Beschloss remarked last week, "just went through a near-death experience." Our new president will face challenges as grave as those faced by former President Abraham Lincoln in 1861 and former President Franklin Roosevelt in 1933. But he has already set about confronting them with discipline and good judgment, constructing an administration with individuals who keenly appreciate what America aspires to be and who seem determined to help the country claw its way back.

Repairing the Arts: Yet Another Challenge for an Administration Tasked With Repairing the Country

December 8, 2020

When Alexander Kutik and his wife, Alla Zernitskaya, fled the Soviet Union in 1990, the two Belarussian musicians took with them two young sons, two suitcases and a shared faith in the power of music. Alexander was a trumpeter; Alla taught violin to children. The anti-Semitism that has forever been a poisonous fixture in Russia had given them no realistic alternative to leaving. They settled in western Massachusetts, refugees from a place that was dead in spirit and short on hope, eager to start fresh in a country that offered both.

Their younger son, Yevgeny, submitted to his mother's violin lessons in a big way. By age 18, Yevgeny Kutik was a nationally recognized concert violinist. Now 35, he is asked to perform all over the world. His breakthrough album, "Music from the Suitcase," was based on sheet music passed down in his family, which his mother stuffed into those two suitcases when they departed the imploding Soviet Union with less than $500 to their name.

Like that of hundreds of thousands of artists of every variety, Kutik's life changed abruptly with the pandemic's arrival earlier this year. "By late February," Kutik recalls, "the next concert suddenly canceled. Then the next concert canceled. By that point, the whole thing fell apart. All of a sudden, this work which you've spent your life developing evaporated overnight."

Kutik is quick to point out that he is one of the luckiest of the innumerable people in America's arts world whose lives have been upended and whose futures are in doubt. The pandemic has shut down venues all over America and, indeed, all over the world. Performers, writers, technicians, ticket takers, custodians and virtually everyone associated with the arts has seen their prospects placed under a cloud, their income slashed or eliminated. Food, rent, health care and retirement are now question marks for many. "I have colleagues who are truly suffering," says Kutik, and the suffering has infiltrated every nook and cranny in American arts and culture. "It's been 'You're on your own now. Good luck.'"

The pandemic's direct economic hit on the American arts extends to other linked industries, such as restaurants, lodging and travel. But the damage inflicted is not merely economic. America in December 2020 is experiencing many of the same troubles that beset it during the Great Depression: shaken confidence that we genuinely embrace the values we say we do; fissures and fractures along racial, demographic and political lines that make us all wonder about our national future; and the death around us both measured in lost lives and evident in depleted spirit. "It seems like our 'empathy muscle' is deteriorating," Kutik says. "What are the arts? The arts are actually the No. 1 pathway toward building empathy. If you cut arts during normal times, what do you do now? The more you cut, the less empathy, and then there's a downward spiral."

President-elect Joe Biden has been bequeathed quite a nightmare, with no shortage of dire needs to meet. The suffering in America's arts community is one of them. There is precedent for a national effort to rescue that community in calamitous times: The New Deal's Federal Project Number One sought to bolster the country's music, theater and fine arts sectors, to provide not only income but also the stimulation and magic so important to lifting the nation's wobbly psyche. Franklin Roosevelt's administration understood just how vital those sectors are to keeping a frayed nation united.

Yevgeny Kutik is hopeful. "People do love music," he says. "They do love art. After this collective hibernation, I really think there will be a rush, a Renaissance. But getting to that point will require a collective, all-hands-on-deck effort."

The Biden administration will have headaches aplenty, thanks to the disastrous presidency that precedes it. The new president has to figure out a way to repair the damaged arts industry, for all of our sakes.

Confederacy of Dunces: Trump World Takes Its Leave

December 15, 2020

It's been disclosed that the White House will be fumigated before Joe Biden moves in, and one hopes that the chemical agent will be extra-strength. It's unclear whether mere fumigation will be enough to remove the disease that Donald Trump has spawned in the American people's house. Even if one round suffices to rid the White House of COVID-19, it may take additional rounds to eliminate the other toxins that four years of epic corruption have produced in our body politic.

By God's grace, a vaccine will protect us from the coronavirus. But there is no vaccine for the disease of ugly anti-Americanism that has infected large swaths of America, promoted and spread by a president who cares not one whit about the country he purports to lead. The extent of the damage Trump has wrought was illustrated in yet one more new way last week, when the majority of Republicans in the House of Representatives and 18 Republican state attorneys general demanded that the Supreme Court, dominated by Republican appointees, declare the winner of the presidential election — Biden — the loser and declare the loser — Trump — the winner. Put another way, despite the fact that the voters, the states and the courts have all determined that Biden won the election fair and square and there is zero evidence to the contrary, these Republicans demanded that the election results be disregarded and Trump be installed for a second term.

The sad truth about these officials and the millions of Americans who support them is this: They either do not know what democracy is or do not approve of it; they either do not know what America is or reject it.

Indeed, some of them have begun to wonder whether, if America really insists on distinguishing between fact and fiction and insists on honoring elections, they belong elsewhere. Conservative commentator Candace Owens ruminated that if the election results aren't overturned, Trump supporters should simply take a page from the seven pro-slavery states that withdrew from the United States in 1861 and formally pull out of the country. "You actually don't need a bloody war to secede — just an agreement," she noted. Talk-radio host Rush Limbaugh, Trump ally extraordinaire, said: "I actually think that we're trending toward secession. ...

There cannot be a peaceful coexistence of two completely different theories of life, theories of government, theories of how we manage our affairs."

After the Supreme Court, including three justices appointed by Trump himself, quickly concluded that his bid to overthrow the election was too meritless to even consider, the head of Texas' Republican Party denounced the court, saying that it was time for the states whose attorneys general filed the frivolous lawsuit to form their own country. "Perhaps law-abiding states should bond together and form a union of states that will abide by the Constitution," he said, true to Trump World's near fetish for rubbish.

Say this for the Kool-Aid-drinking cultists at Jonestown: They may have drunk the poison, but they didn't try to destroy a country. Even lemmings have the common decency to jump off cliffs alone, without dragging others with them. The same cannot be said of those in MAGA Land, who seem to have seceded from America in spirit, if not formally.

"Before entering upon so grave a matter as the destruction of our national fabric, with all its benefits, its memories, and its hopes," implored Abraham Lincoln shortly after the secession that triggered the Civil War, "would it not be wise to ascertain precisely why we do it?" Those patriots and adults left in the Republican Party would do well to insist to their brethren that this question be asked — and asked again. The future of America may depend on it.

The Splendid and the Vile: Enter Joe and Jill Biden, Spelling Relief

December 22, 2020

In the reunion classic "The Big Chill," a criminal defense lawyer played by Mary Kay Place tries to find the words to convey to her old college friends just how awful her clients are and settles on the phrase "extreme repulsivos." Asked who she imagined she would be representing, Place replies, "I just didn't think they would be this guilty."

The outgoing Trump presidency has produced quite a rogue's gallery, none more disgraceful than the outgoing president himself. We are reminded of this on a daily basis. Last Friday, President Donald Trump held a White House meeting with convicted felon and all-around expert on who should be locked up Michael Flynn to discuss declaring martial law and ordering America's military to force new elections in the swing states won by President-elect Joe Biden. On the same day, news emerged that the president wanted to appoint as special counsel Nutcase-With-a-Law-License Sidney Powell, who has traversed the country making the fraudulent claim that the presidential election Trump lost was "rigged." The president wants to authorize Powell, whose right to continue to practice law is open to question, to use governmental power to pursue his untethered claim, which has been rejected as bogus by every court that has considered it.

Amidst the craziness, it is easy to overlook the promising news on the horizon. Biden and his wife, Dr. Jill Biden, the polar opposites of Donald Trump in every way, will soon occupy the White House, and not a moment too soon. They bring with them refreshingly old-fashioned American values that have seemed to be on newly vivid display since Nov. 3: an appreciation for patriotism the way we learned about it in civics class, small-towners' respect for others and devotion to family. The faith that has sustained them is welcome balm for a nation reeling under round after round of reasons to lose faith. It is perfectly in keeping with the unembarrassed mendacity President Trump has displayed in repeatedly accusing Joe Biden of threatening religion. Biden, a devout Catholic, attends Mass regularly, while Trump could not tell a Bible from a bacon cheeseburger. The footage of Biden attending church these days feels like a shot in the arm, a reminder to Americans of Biden's frequent exhortation to "keep the faith." And Dr. Jill Biden exudes warmth and humor at a time when the country badly needs both.

Foretelling what we have in store, MAGA World contrived a chance to demean the incoming first lady for having the temerity to use the standard title "Dr.," traditionally used to signify the achievement of earning a doctorate. It is obvious to all but the willfully blind that Dr. Biden is not only accomplished but also a mensch who has led her family through excruciating loss and trauma. Why, then, shouldn't she be targeted for mean-spirited belittling by the whackadoodles who have cheered on Team Trump?

Leading the charge was Fox News' most-watched flim-flam man, Tucker Carlson, who pronounced Biden "illiterate" and guilty of using "fake credentials" to "justify their power over you." Carlson is, of course, well-positioned to patronize Biden for her three graduate degrees inasmuch as he has none. But the chutzpah paled before the misogyny, an absolute must-have for anyone aspiring to hero status in Trump Land.

One of the curiosities of American history is that, at crisis points, we have lucked into electing badly underestimated presidents who proved to be just what the nation needed. Abraham Lincoln, who took the oath of office just weeks after the country had split apart, was one. Franklin Roosevelt, sworn in amidst economic calamity that was two and a half years underway and had no end in sight, was another. In the last six weeks, we've watched a president-elect about to lead a country ravaged by a pandemic, and a citizenry whose future is more uncertain than at any time in a century, project calm and discipline, humanity and decency.

There's been plenty of bad news. The good news for the country is that our new president looks like what the doctor ordered.

Jail Time for Bonzo: America Needs to Have Donald Trump Face the Music

December 29, 2020

President Donald Trump's presidential pardons last week went to a predictable assortment of loathsome characters: those who had lied about contacts with Russian intermediaries, corrupt Republican former Congressmen and war criminals. Another fortunate felon was Charles Kushner, Ivanka Trump's father-in-law, convicted of tax evasion and of hiring a prostitute to seduce his sister's husband to blackmail him out of testifying against Kushner.

Certain pardons passed from the realm of the stomach-turning into the realm of the quite-possibly-criminal. Former Trump campaign chairman Paul Manafort, convicted of a series of financial crimes, refused to speak about his contacts with Russian intelligence during the 2016 campaign. Trump confidante Roger Stone, an intermediary with those who released the Clinton campaign emails hacked by the Russians, was convicted for lying about his contacts with Trump campaign officials about the matter. Trump's signals to Manafort and Stone that their silence would be rewarded were reinforced by evidence that, after speaking to Trump's criminal defense lawyer, Manafort heard the message that if they kept their mouths shut, "we'll be taken care of." They did, and as Trump's pardons last week indicated, they were. At his confirmation hearing, Trump's attorney general nominee, William Barr, was asked whether "a president could lawfully issue a pardon in exchange for the recipient's promise not to incriminate him."

"No," answered Barr. "That would be a crime."

On top of the voluminous evidence amassed in Robert Mueller's report that Trump committed as many as 10 separate acts of obstruction of justice, the fact that Trump not only dangled pardons in front of Manafort and Stone in exchange for silence but also delivered them has revived a question likely to consume public debate in the coming months: Quite apart from New York prosecutors' independent investigation of Trump for violations of New York laws, should the incoming Justice Department investigate whether Trump violated federal ones?

It should.

To be sure, there is an argument that the Justice Department should "move on," stay as far away as possible from any investigation of Trump and let New York prosecutors make whatever prosecutorial judgments they choose to make. The country is fractured, the anger deep and the wounds open, badly in need of healing. A federal investigation into Trump will trigger accusations of retaliation, or worse.

But respect for democratic values has been ravaged over the past four years. Our commitment to those values and our ability to preserve them is in real doubt. If a former American president is to be given a pass from even a review of evidence of his criminality, it is unclear how America will be able to look at itself in the mirror, let alone look the world in the eye.

Other democracies have found preserving the rule of law more important than avoiding controversy, and on that basis have prosecuted former leaders. Israel, whose citizenry is even more polarized than ours and which faces internal challenges and external threats more grave, has repeatedly done so, concluding that the doctrine that no man is above the law demanded it. Former Prime Minister Ehud Olmert and former President Moshe Katsav were tried, convicted and imprisoned for obstruction of justice. The country's current prime minister, Benjamin Netanyahu, is presently under indictment for corruption.

France has likewise recognized that prosecuting former leaders when the evidence warrants it is fundamental to protecting its democratic character. Former French President Nicolas Sarkozy is on trial for offering a job to a judge in exchange for information about an investigation involving him. In 2011, former French President Jacques Chirac was convicted of using public funds to benefit his political party.

Scrupulous, professional and independent scrutiny of the evidence of obstruction of justice, campaign finance violations and fraud that is a matter of record may lead prosecutors to conclude that no prosecution of Trump is warranted. But it will be a test of our resolve to repair our battered democracy whether we discharge that painful responsibility or shirk it.

Whatever It Takes: Time for an All-Out National Assault on Hunger

January 5, 2021

The video gone viral of New Year's Eve at Mar-A-Lago with Donald Trump, Donald Trump Jr., Eric Trump and assorted Trumpettes dancing while a lounge lizard sang "Play That Funky Music (White Boy)" seemed certain to take first prize as the perfect coda of the Trump years. It was merely cringeworthy, however, and was quickly overtaken by a felonious phone call Donald Trump reportedly made to Georgia's secretary of state to demand that he "find" the votes necessary to enable Trump to claim he won an election he certifiably lost. Trump's call was just the latest sampling of the cornucopia of criminality that has characterized his presidency from start to finish.

But in the stiff competition for the most emblematic illustration of our current national embarrassment, honorable mention must surely go to U.S. Sen. John Cornyn, R-Texas, who, in the middle of a pandemic in which millions of Americans lack sufficient food to eat, tweeted out a picture of a "great tenderloin dinner" from a fancy steakhouse. "Highly recommend," Cornyn tweeted in a triumph of empathy for the more than 5 million of his fellow Texans who are without access to basic sustenance. Cornyn's homage to fancy steak meals came the same day that Senate Majority Leader Mitch McConnell blocked the Senate from voting to provide $2,000 in stopgap checks for Americans, over 50 million of whom have gone hungry this year. Seventeen million of those hungry Americans are children. The funds aimed at helping 1 in 6 Americans eat are, according to McConnell, simply "socialism for rich people."

President-elect Joe Biden has the unenviable task of clearing out one truly filthy Augean stable, a disastrous state of affairs brought to us largely by a calamity of a president. Biden cannot be expected to clean every corner of a stable most foul immediately, or simultaneously.

But the time is past ripe for an all-out national assault on hunger in America, a point driven home recently by U.S. Rep. Jim McGovern, D-Mass., who urged the president-elect to appoint a national hunger czar to lead a coordinated effort to eradicate hunger in America. "Appointing a high-level official in your Administration to oversee and coordinate a national anti-hunger strategy," wrote McGovern, co-chair of the House Hunger Caucus, "would be a turning point in the fight against hunger and signal your administration's firm commitment to an issue that millions of American families deal with every single day."

McGovern exhorted the incoming administration to take a number of specific steps to rescind measures taken by Team Trump to curtail eligibility for food assistance, including the Supplemental Nutrition Assistance Program, or SNAP. "With an unprecedented fifteen percent of Americans ... struggling with food insecurity," said McGovern, "there has never been a more pressing time to strengthen the country's social safety nets."

One hopeful aspect of the four-year debacle of a presidency we have endured is that it has forced many of us to focus on the need to reset, to quit relying on time-honored but fanciful self-flattery. Whether regarding the depth of racial injustice in the United States, the calcified, unequal economic opportunity or the rotted fidelity to democratic norms among our countrymen, it has been made crystal clear, if painfully, that we are not the country we professed to be or thought we were. The good news: We have a historic chance to take bold steps to better synchronize America's self-image with reality.

This is true with the not-so-secret secret that the world's richest nation is home to tens of millions of hungry people. "It is really a scandal," McGovern says. "These are our fellow citizens who don't even know where their next meal is going to come from. It's unbelievable."

It doesn't get any more basic than ensuring that our fellow Americans have enough to eat — this week, next week and always. McGovern and those who advocate for seizing the opportunity to eliminate hunger are right to believe that this is a whatever-it-takes moment.

Shame: Trump's Apologists Owe America an Apology

January 12, 2021

    The neo-fascist mob that bashed in Capitol Police officer Brian Sicknick's skull with a fire extinguisher, wielded lead pipes, ransacked Congress and terrorized members of Congress have a plausible claim that they were only following orders — those of the president of the United States. Donald Trump had told them it was their duty to come to Washington, D.C., on the day Congress would count the electoral votes that would make Joe Biden the next president, promising them a "wild" time if they did.

    He personally addressed them, exhorting them to go to the Capitol and express their hatred with all their might. "We are going to have to fight much harder," he told them. "You will never take back the country with weakness."

    Namesake and certified nitwit Donald Trump Jr. urged the crowd to make it painfully clear to legislators that they had better swallow the fraudulent fiction that his father had won the election. Or else, "We are coming for you," he said. Donald Trump lawyer and frantic pardon-seeker Rudy Giuliani was blunter yet, telling the thousands of storm trooper-wannabes that they should engage in "trial by combat."

    The mob did as it was told, savaging the Capitol and inflicting on the country one of the gravest acts of domestic terrorism in our history. But it was backed by innumerable enablers and fawners and acolytes, politicians and right-wing commentators and ordinary Americans alike, who have gushed and giggled as Trump has trashed decency and democratic values — not merely since Nov. 3 but daily over the last four years. These individuals bear a share of responsibility for our national shame.

    Some of them who have coddled Trump and defended him day after day for years now pronounce themselves shocked — shocked! — at last week's attack on America.

    It's a nice try. But they own it. And they owe their country an apology.

    The president assured the insurrectionists he assembled that he would accompany them to the Capitol, which doubtless reinforced their confidence that they were doing their Fuhrer's will. Evidently, however, he was stricken with a bout of Sudden Onset Bone Spurs (SOBS) and instead slipped back to the White House to watch on television while his people (to whom he said: "We love you. You're very special.") laid siege to the Capitol on his behalf. After 24 hours of unflattering media coverage of the attempted putsch, Trump was persuaded to tape a statement that he condemned violence, a performance so patently insincere that it made videotaped confessions by hostages held captive by Hezbollah seem voluntary by comparison.

To his credit, Sen. Pat Toomey, R-Pa., called out his fellow Republicans, who had hyped Trump's garbage claim that he won the election, stoking unhinged conspiracy theories that helped trigger Wednesday's assault and that leave our government vulnerable to further domestic extremism. These Republicans are, Toomey noted, "complicit in the big lie." But the Trump presidency has been rife with lies since its inception. The talk-show jocks, the Fox News celebrities, the Republican loyalists and the small-time right-wing commentators who thrilled to Trump's diseased machismo have done America incalculable damage.

The risible, Goebbels-like lying about a "rigged" election (it wasn't) that Trump won (he didn't) did not suffice to stir these individuals' somnolent sense of decency. But this was unsurprising. They supported Trump when he attacked Dr. Anthony Fauci, House Speaker Nancy Pelosi and Michigan Gov. Gretchen Whitmer, even when those attacks placed them in physical danger. They supported him when he called for retaliation against journalists and political opponents, when he mocked a reporter with a physical disability, when he derided war hero John McCain because McCain was captured while serving his country. They supported him when he tried to extort a foreign leader into fabricating an "investigation" intended to defame the likely Democratic presidential nominee, and when he fired devoted public servants for telling the truth.

Donald Trump's defenders do not merely share the blame for last week's events. They have let America down. And whether America will ever fully recover is an open question.

Teachable Moment: America Gets Its Own Chance to Say, 'Never Again'

January 19, 2021

Donald Trump's presidency involved no Holocaust, no concentration camps, no gas chambers. There was no genocide and no threat of one.

But what it did feature was bad enough — more than bad enough for America to stop, search its soul and commit itself to declaring, "Never again."

It featured a narcissistic sociopath of a president, a totalitarian wannabe who believed that his power was absolute, or should be. It featured an epic liar who employed The Big Lie with particularly destructive effect after he was voted out of office in order to defraud Americans into believing he had won — and who tried to coerce officials into conspiring with him to concoct a crooked election result. It featured a snarling, cruel and deeply dishonest man who obstructed justice with abandon, and who not only embraced toxic white supremacy but also stoked it, giving America its first real taste of fascism.

And it featured the spurning of the peaceful transfer of power that is the essence of any democracy by a president who summoned an extremist mob to Washington, D.C., on the day President-elect Joe Biden's election was to be acknowledged in accordance with our Constitution. Promising them a "wild" time and endorsing his lawyer's exhortation that they initiate "combat," the president personally directed the mob to proceed to the Capitol and use "strength" to "take your country back." The mob did as directed, smashing up the Capitol, assaulting dozens of police officers and murdering one, reportedly threatening to kidnap the speaker of the House and chanting to hang the vice president. But for pure, blessed serendipity and the heroism of a few individuals, we might have seen the kidnapping and assassination of top national officials, all incited by the leader of our own country.

And but for roughly 22,000 voters spread among Georgia, Wisconsin and Arizona who decided to vote for Joe Biden rather than Donald Trump, America would have four more years of such a person, whose contempt for democracy, arrogation of limitless power to himself and penchant for spreading poison might well have finished off the American experiment.

In taking up the second impeachment of Trump, the United States Senate has not merely the opportunity to say "never again" but the urgent obligation to do so. It's unlikely that 17 Republican senators will muster the courage to convict Trump of the incitement to violence and insurrection they know he committed. But a trial that lays out Trump's criminal conduct and what it wrought serves a crucial purpose. Trump's White House has been a house of un-American activities, and the country — and those who come after us — need to see the betrayal of America by Trump and his defenders for what it was.

Moreover, America needs to turn a spotlight on the witch's brew of white nationalism and neo-fascist extremism that make up Trump's hardcore base. There is a painful truth: Our country has an enemy within. Other countries that abandoned their traditions and disgraced themselves had to do the same in order to survive as democracies. Post-war Germany has spent decades facing up to its embrace of Nazism. Italy had to confront its romance with fascism. America must likewise face up to its dance with Trumpism — and, much more importantly, rid itself of it.

The impeachment trial, legislation to ban the naming of federal buildings after Trump and the elimination of federal subsidies for Trump's post-presidential activities: These are all part of what is needed to send a national message that Trumpism is a stain on our nation. Full, fair investigations into evidence that Trump committed federal or state crimes are important to show that we are truly a nation that respects law.

But it won't be enough. Extremism expert Farah Pandith has written that "(whether) we are trying to stop radicalization into Nazi groups or ISIS, the winning strategy (against extremism) is a combined effort of government, business, philanthropy and regular citizens." America's battle against Trumpism will be a long and difficult one. But it is one that simply must be won.

Family Tradition: Jewish Agency's Bougie Herzog Takes on the Protection of World Jewry

January 26, 2021

Israelis do not "do" royalty, to put it mildly. They are famously irreverent, deeply skeptical and distinctively if not scathingly critical of their leaders.

But if Israel recognized royal families, surely Isaac Herzog, known to Israelis as "Bougie," would qualify as a prince. His Irish-born father, Chaim Herzog, fought with the British Army during World War II before helping to found the Jewish state, ultimately serving for 10 years as its president. Bougie's grandfather, Ireland's chief rabbi, later became Israel's Ashkenazi chief rabbi. And his uncle, Abba Eban, was Israel's most famous diplomat and one of the best-respected international diplomats of the last century. "We carry a big lineage of serving the Jewish people," said Herzog recently, with some understatement. "We are a serving family."

Bougie Herzog has himself served in distinguished fashion. After several positions in Israel's government, he was elected to its Parliament in 2003. He rose to lead Israel's Labor Party and lost a close election to Israeli Prime Minister Benjamin Netanyahu in 2015.

In 2018, Herzog was named chairman of The Jewish Agency for Israel, known simply as The Jewish Agency, the world's largest Jewish nonprofit and the most important Jewish organization many American Jews have never heard of. Established in 1929, 19 years before Israel was born, its mission is to "ensure that every Jewish person feels an unbreakable bond to one another and to Israel no matter where they live in the world, so that they can continue to play their critical role in our ongoing Jewish story." One measure of the Agency's historic significance is the role it played in bringing Holocaust survivors and Jews expelled from Arab lands to the safety of a Jewish homeland after World War II. It has continued to spearhead the rescue of Jews persecuted and pursued in their native lands — from Europe to the Soviet Union to Ethiopia — ever since.

Another measure may be found in the names of those asked to lead it. David Ben-Gurion, Israel's first prime minister, headed the Agency from 1935 until the Jewish state was established in 1948. Herzog himself succeeded the great Natan Sharansky, the Soviet dissident and human rights leader who spent nine years in Soviet prisons before he was freed and emigrated to Israel.

Herzog says that the Agency is focused on three major challenges. The first is what he describes as "the famous rift": the disconnect between Israel and North American Jewry, a disconnect marked by dramatically different life experiences. American Jews are generally comfortable. Israelis' lives, by contrast, are in certain fundamental respects uncomfortable, as a function of the threats posed by the neighborhood in which the Jewish state resides. Although Israel's vaccination program has in recent weeks become the envy of the world, COVID-19 has hit Israel particularly hard. "Tourism has been devastated," Herzog says, and the pandemic has shrunk Israel's 2020 gross national product by an estimated 6.5%.

The second challenge is a tsunami of anti-Semitism worldwide, including, quite clearly, in the United States. Herzog points to the poisonous spread of white supremacism here, well illustrated by the Charlottesville, Virginia, riot; the shooting sprees at synagogues in Pittsburgh and California; and the recent mob attack on the United States Capitol.

The third is the need to cope with millions of people around the globe who, claiming that they have Jewish heritage, assert that they are therefore entitled to Israeli citizenship. Meanwhile, the pandemic has inflicted real suffering on Jewish communities within Israel and elsewhere. In response, the Agency has created the COVID-19 Loan Fund for Communities in Crisis, set up to help at-risk communities bridge the financial gaps that would otherwise threaten their ability to meet important needs.

"There is a new energy to help others," says Herzog. It is an energy that, by dint not merely of lineage but also of passion and savvy, he is well positioned to inspire.

Married to the Mob: The GOP Becomes the Party of the Kooks

February 2, 2021

The cliche of the moment is that the Republican Party is not only "divided" but "fractured," that an internecine war has split the party in two.

If only.

The truth is that the Republican Party is now officially the party of choice for political nut cases, including some genuinely dangerous ones. The overwhelming majority of Republicans continue to chug former President Donald Trump's Kool-Aid by the gallon, indulging if not parroting the fraud and poison spewed by Trump and his cult members, who repeat everything the disgraced demagogue says. The truth is that the GOP, once the party of Lincoln, is now the party of Jonestown.

It is mainly true of the Republican rank and file. And it is generally true of party leadership who, out of fear of Trump, continue to debase themselves by embracing him.

In the weeks between President Joe Biden's election and his inauguration, The Big Lie that Trump had won was effectively or expressly spread by the vast majority of Republicans, who dutifully promoted the party line. They knew it was false, and they knew that every time they repeated it, the delicate fabric of American democracy was torn in a new place. This, however, didn't stop many Republican officials from climbing aboard Trump's Garbage Express. Even after Trump supporters summoned to Washington to pressure Congress into rejecting the election results ransacked Congress and assaulted Capitol Police, more than three-fifths of the Republicans in the House of Representatives and eight in the Senate did the mob's bidding, refusing to certify Biden's election.

Trump's role in inciting that mob to stage a violent insurrection against our government is indisputable, so much so that congressional Republicans have been unable to dispute it. One might presume that the very fact that they cannot dispute it would lead them to hold him accountable for it. But that would presume a degree of honor that is not really a Republican thing these days. Of the 211 Republicans in the House, only 10, less than 5% of the Republican caucus, voted to impeach Trump on the charge of incitement of insurrection. While commentators remarked sunnily that this was historic, let's face it: 95% of Republicans lacked the guts and the patriotism to state that such conduct is incompatible with the American presidency.

Forty-five out of 50 Republican senators endorsed sweeping Trump's putsch attempt under the rug, voting to block an impeachment trial that would place before the nation just what he and his mob had done. It was hardly cause for celebration that five Republican senators dissented. Rather, that 90% of them had voted to give a would-be totalitarian a pass for unleashing hordes of felonious crackpots on our Capitol was yet more reason to conclude that the GOP is a dead letter.

Trump has no more ardent supporter than protege Marjorie Taylor Greene, the anti-Semitic, white supremacist and QAnon conspiracy theory-toting psycho who is the Third Reich's representative in Congress. In no particular order, Greene has promoted the hanging of former President Barack Obama and the assassination of House Speaker Nancy Pelosi, blamed California wildfires on lasers wielded from outer space by Jewish bankers, stalked a young survivor of the Parkland school shooting and informed us that what seemed like compelling evidence that a plane was flown into the Pentagon on 9/11 was actually a hoax. She alleges that either Bill or Hillary Clinton — it is not clear which — was responsible for the 1999 plane crash that killed John F. Kennedy Jr.

So it is perhaps small wonder that several months ago Trump pronounced Greene a "future Republican star" who is "strong on everything." It is a love fest: Over the weekend, Greene tweeted, "I had a GREAT call with my all time favorite POTUS, President Trump!" For his part, House Minority Leader Kevin McCarthy just appointed Greene to the House Education Committee, taken by the salutary effects someone with Greene's credentials could have on America's schoolchildren.

It is some grand old party. It is also, evidently, a morally dead one.

Block the Vote: The GOP's Suppression Obsession

February 9, 2021

Black History Month 2021 arrived just in time to cap a year in which white Americans' eyes have been opened in a new way to the burdens endured by communities of color. In the year since the pandemic broke into the open, a particularly harsh spotlight has shone on race in America, shattering the false confidence that allegations of systemic racism were overly aggressive or just plain overblown.

We have watched Black and brown Americans steer America through that pandemic — the health care, food and postal workers and many others on whom we have depended — even as those same Americans were infected and died at rates dramatically higher than their white counterparts. We saw, finally and inexplicably for the first time, the vulnerability to police violence that has long been a simple fact of life for nonwhite people, driven home at last for the rest of us in graphic, irrefutable fashion by the murder of George Floyd. In November and then again in January, we saw voters of color ignore or face down onerous obstacles to voting that, in many instances, existed precisely to exclude them. Some of those obstacles were pandemic-related, but others were placed there purposefully by politicians who were not only not interested in having Black and brown Americans vote but who, to the contrary, were affirmatively interested in having them not vote.

For those who tended to think that the term "voter suppression" was too extreme or too obscure, the 2020 election wasn't a wake-up call as much as it was a wake-up siren. We can mince words if we like, but Democrats want Black and brown Americans to vote; Republicans, not so much.

Republican enthusiasm for high voter turnout among communities of color, always dim, got considerably dimmer last Nov. 3, when those communities braved rain and snow to vote in Atlanta, Philadelphia, Detroit and Milwaukee, lifting Joe Biden to a narrow victory over Donald Trump.

So it is no wonder that those who ardently wish to prevent a recurrence are hard at work. According to the Brennan Center for Justice, since the beginning of this year 106 bills aimed at preventing Americans from voting have been introduced in 28 state legislatures across the country. These include measures to limit or terminate mail-in voting, shorten or eliminate early voting periods and impede voter registration. Others stiffen photo ID requirements, including actually requiring American citizens to present two forms of government-issued ID as a condition of choosing their leaders. An estimated 25 million eligible American voters lack one such ID, let alone two. They have no passports and, because they have no cars, are too old to drive or are disabled, do not have driver's licenses.

Voting rights advocates are not exactly ceding ground. The Brennan Center calculates that thus far in 2021, some 406 bills have been filed in 35 states seeking to expand mail-in voting, preserve or extend early voting and institute automatic voter registration for eligible citizens signing up with social service agencies or motor vehicle bureaus. A broad fight is underway in Congress, where Democratic control of the Senate may make it possible to break the chokehold on ballot access once and for all. The For the People Act, passed by the House last year but suffocated in the Senate, was reintroduced in early January. It would federalize virtually all of the provisions in the voting rights legislation pending in state legislatures. The John Lewis Voting Rights Advancement Act would revitalize key provisions of the Voting Rights Act of 1965 gutted by the Supreme Court's conservative majority during the Obama administration.

It is hard to imagine a more fitting or more overdue response to the suppression of votes in communities of color than a determined, comprehensive codification of voting rights measures both in the states and in Congress. Those bent on keeping those communities from fully participating in American elections will not go quietly. The rest of us shouldn't either.

Dead Souls: Those Who Gave Us Donald Trump Would Do It Again

February 16, 2021

No American with an ounce of patriotism could have watched the video of the animals who overtook the nation's Capitol without being revolted by what former President Donald Trump has done to the country we love. But plenty of Americans who profess to be patriots have watched this Trump impeachment trial not merely stone cold to the evidence, but actually falling over one another to proclaim their contempt for it.

After seeing the House impeachment managers meticulously document one of the worst days in American history — on which a violent mob summoned and directed by the president of the United States stormed our seat of government, assaulted police officers and threatened to execute the vice president and the speaker of the House — Republican Sen. Rick Scott proclaimed the presentation "a complete waste of time." Fellow Republican Sen. Marco Rubio said, "I think the trial is stupid." The evidence was "offensive and absurd," claimed the reliably spineless Republican Sen. Lindsey Graham. "They're peddling #fakenews during the impeachment trial," tweeted Republican Rep. Jim Jordan.

Trump loyalist and indefatigable attention-seeker Alan Dershowitz spied yet another opportunity for air time and seized it. "President Trump didn't incite people to come to the Capitol, he invited the people," Dershowitz told Fox News. As if to make certain that viewers appreciated his rhyme, he repeated it, determined to pound every available nail into the lid of the coffin in which his credibility officially resides. "Not incite, invite," he emphasized. Missouri Republican Sen. Josh Hawley, who famously flashed a fraternal power salute to the mob outside the Capitol on Jan. 6, ostentatiously signaled his disregard for the impeachment trial during the first day of the presentation of evidence. Leaving the Senate floor to sit above in the spectators' gallery, Hawley put his feet up on the chair in front of him, flipping through folders while his fellow senators sat in their seats on the Senate floor below, listening to the proceedings as the Senate rules required them to do.

Congressional Republicans too frightened of retaliation by Trump supporters if they held accountable a crooked sociopath may be cowards, but they're not fools. A poll taken in late January, over two weeks after the Trump mob overran the Capitol, showed that 81% of Republicans had a favorable opinion of the former president. Insurrection or no insurrection, 50% believed that Trump should play a "major role" in the Republican Party. A vote to impeach or convict Trump would surely subject the offending Republican legislator to a successful primary challenge. Political careers would come to screeching ends, and any hope of parlaying those careers into lucrative lobbying jobs would end, as well.

Besides, the truth is that Republicans still love Trump. The fraud, the cruelty, the infantile insults, the lying, the extortion, the contempt for America's civic institutions, the embrace of white supremacy — these don't bother most Republicans. Indeed, many Republicans find all of it enthralling, and that is the most dispiriting manifestation of the disease that grips America. Pro-Trump commentators have gushed and giggled as Trump subjected us to a national nightmare, and they would feel perfectly happy — even delighted — to have a reprise.

The conclusion seems inescapable: The Republican Party is profoundly sick, and likely incurable. For many who cherish the old ideal of two patriotic political parties, each with the good of America legitimately at heart, this is sad. But the current spectacle of a Republican Party so morally corrupt is sadder still. Earlier this month, dozens of former Republican officials held a Zoom call to discuss mounting a challenge to either take back the party or break from it. These included former officials from the administrations of former Presidents Ronald Reagan, George H. W. Bush, George W. Bush and Trump himself. One of them was Evan McMullin, former chief policy director for the House Republican Conference. "Large portions of the Republican Party are radicalizing and threatening democracy," McMullin told Reuters.

He is right, of course. And for the moment, those large portions of the Republican Party and their cheerleaders pose a clear and present danger to the country. The battle is over whether they win or the country does.

Lucky Once More: America Finds Itself a Leader

February 23, 2021

At moments of historic national crisis, America has had a knack for getting lucky. The first month of Joe Biden's presidency suggests that, thank goodness, we have gotten lucky once again.

When the nation split in two in 1860, there was no reason to expect that Abraham Lincoln was suited to the herculean task of restoring the Union. "There is no describing his lengthy awkwardness, nor the uncouthness of his movement," wrote Nathaniel Hawthorne after meeting President Lincoln in 1862. He was "the most shut-mouthed man who ever lived," wrote Lincoln's longtime law partner, William Herndon.

Lincoln was hardly the only badly underestimated American president to take office with the country in profound trouble. Franklin Roosevelt took the presidential oath in March 1933 with America in free fall, three years into economic collapse. He had been derided by those in the know as a privileged lightweight. Roosevelt, sniffed Supreme Court Justice Oliver Wendell Holmes, had a "second-class intellect," even if he had a first-rate temperament.

When Roosevelt died in April 1945, the new president inherited an ongoing world war and a European continent in rubble, and he faced a Soviet Union bent on occupying or dominating wide swaths of the globe. A failed haberdasher once dismissed by The New York Times as a "rube," Harry Truman was mocked for what was his supposed lack of worldliness. "To err is Truman," was just one phrase deployed by his political opponents to ridicule the president whose resolve and good judgment helped salvage Europe and safeguard America's security in the 75 years since.

As familiar a figure as Biden has been for the past half-century, it has been easy to sell him short, to somehow overlook the qualities that equip him so well to steer the country through an existential crisis that is medical, economic and civic all at the same time. We knew Biden, or thought we did, as the senator-since-forever who reliably went on at too-great length on C-SPAN. He was the well-credentialed candidate for the Democratic presidential nomination who could not get out of the starting gate in 1988 or in 2008. As Barack Obama's vice president, he was the sturdy if garrulous understudy to a president with historic magnetism. During most of the 2020 primary campaign, he drew small, tepid audiences that could only generously be termed "crowds." On the debate stage with his primary rivals, he seemed awkward and out of place, vying for attention with candidates with more pizazz, who took turns as the media darling of the month while poor old Joe stumbled and teetered, seemingly on the brink of one more flameout as a presidential contender. Then, after returning from the dead to secure the Democratic presidential nomination, "the former guy," as Biden calls Donald Trump, peddled the line that Biden had lost mental acuity, a bogus claim that was the product of crude mendacity and wishful thinking.

Many Americans bought it. Most didn't.

The blizzard of emergency bills and executive orders aimed at wrestling the pandemic to the ground, rescuing the American economy and shepherding Americans through their suffering is only one reason to be grateful for the Biden presidency one month into it. Those who watched last week's CNN town hall saw just what the proverbial doctor ordered: a humane, empathetic and deeply decent man who was immersed in policy and in command of the levers of power. Reassuring mothers, consoling a child, respecting the legitimacy of skeptics' concerns and kibbitzing with a professor who offered to teach him Yiddish (Biden evidently already has a head start), the president dispensed balm to a nation sorely in need of it. His visit on Saturday to former Republican presidential nominee Robert Dole, 97 years old and battling stage 4 lung cancer, was just exactly the kind of menschlichkeit — Yiddish for "humanity" — that America needs to see modeled.

The country has an immense amount of work ahead of it. But on the quality of its new leader, at least, we can at long last take a breather.

Rumpled Giant of the Senate: Carl Levin's Life and Times

March 2, 2021

Whether or not you enjoyed watching Carl Levin question witnesses during U.S. Senate hearings depended entirely on where you were sitting while he was doing it. If you were a Senate committee staffer sitting behind the senator from Michigan while he eviscerated arrogant or dissembling corporate executives whose weeks of preparation with high-powered lawyers failed to prevent the evisceration, it was something to behold. It wasn't only that no one else in Congress was better at questioning witnesses than Levin. No one even came close.

If, on the other hand, you were the witness being grilled by the rumpled former trial lawyer with the wry sense of humor and the glasses perched on the tip of his nose, it was an experience to be avoided, if possible. The trouble was, if Levin and the crack team of aides he assembled wanted you to testify, so that tax evasion schemes or disdain for investors could be exposed, chances were that you would be testifying. And that spelled bad news, because while other members of Congress were out at fundraisers, Levin would be up in his office late at night, sleeves literally rolled up, wading through documents too daunting for most investigators, let alone senators. One five-minute clip of Levin examining a visibly miserable Goldman Sachs executive about the investment bank's dubious sales techniques has been viewed millions of times on YouTube, likely including many viewers who watched it over and over.

The six-term senator, who melded Midwestern decency with razor-sharp intellect and a love of country passed down by immigrant forebears, published his memoir this week. "Getting to the Heart of the Matter: My 36 Years in the Senate" is an account of a splendid Senate career by one of its greats. But it is also a well-timed reminder of what the Senate is supposed to be: a place where the national good is earnestly considered, not a viper's nest for conspiracy theories and vitriol. Levin, a Democratic stalwart if ever there was one, was never a shrinking violet when it came to issues he cared about, and there were plenty of those. But his old-fashioned sense of fair play helped him forge productive relationships with Republicans and craft bipartisan legislation in the days before that phrase became an oxymoron.

These Republicans included Sen. Susan Collins and the late Sen. Arlen Specter, who found Levin an ally when it came to good government and national defense. "We developed a very strong bond of personal trust," recalls former Sen. John Warner. "Our word was our bond and the security of our nation was always foremost." Levin, once said the late John McCain, is "the model of serious purpose, principle and personal decency, whose example ought to inspire the service of new and returning senators."

Levin did not just rest on the respect he had earned across the aisle. He used it to craft consequential legislation, including on federal procurement reform, ethics in government and cracking down on tax cheats. A senior member of the Armed Services and Intelligence Committees, he was frequently and notably prescient. Asked in a Boston conference room in July 2001 what kept him up at night, he replied that it was the threat of an unconventional attack on America by foreign terrorists unlike anything we had ever experienced. In December 2002, he warned in a speech broadcast on C-SPAN that invading Iraq might make America feel better but would boomerang badly.

But it is likely as the master of the modern congressional investigation that Carl Levin will be best remembered. As chairman of the Senate's powerful Permanent Subcommittee on Investigations, he personified congressional oversight at its best: fair, rigorous, decent — and relentless. His memoir may be modest and unvarnished, like its author. But it recounts a career of public service that was as good as it has ever gotten.

Campus Bullies: The Extreme Right Aren't the Only Ones With an Anti-Semitism Problem

March 9, 2021

When Max Price was elected to Tufts University's student judicial body, he likely didn't expect to have to fight off a move to impeach him and remove him from office for being Jewish. And yet Price's recent experience simply replicates the kind of crude anti-Semitic intimidation now so commonplace on college campuses that it qualifies for "dog-bites-man" status, too routine to merit much attention.

Price's ordeal wasn't exactly ho-hum as far as he was concerned. A member of Tufts' Community Union Judiciary, Price was among those tasked with monitoring student-initiated referenda for misrepresentations of fact. When the Tufts chapter of Students for Justice in Palestine introduced a referendum demanding that Tufts "apologize" because a former university police chief traveled to Israel with the Anti-Defamation League for a seminar that included Israeli and Palestinian police officers, Price identified significant inaccuracies in the text.

This did not go over well with the SJP, which first demanded that Price be barred from consideration of the matter, and then that he be disciplined, impeached and removed from his position altogether. "I was ... called a racist, a fascist, a Nazi, an enemy of progress, slandered in the student newspaper," said Price. Over the course of two days, Price found himself interrogated at length about his Jewish identity and the beliefs that flowed from that identity. It was the kind of treatment that plainly never would have been tolerated had Price been Black or Latino, grilled on whether he was fit to pass on student governance issues on the basis that he had personal feelings about racial discrimination.

It was only when the Louis D. Brandeis Center shined a spotlight on the disgrace at Tufts that the SJP withdrew its bid to remove Price from office. "It was an attempt to place Jewish identity on trial," says Ken Marcus, chairman of the Center, a civil rights organization established to combat anti-Semitism. "Max Price refused to be silent." Marcus notes that college students are highly vulnerable to social harassment, and the intensification of anti-Semitism makes Jewish students particularly vulnerable. "Most undergraduates placed under the pressure Max felt would have given up," says Marcus. "And that's the whole point."

Jewish students all over America are regularly targeted by campus campaigns to stigmatize them and drive them underground for believing in a Jewish homeland and the right to Jewish self-determination. Last year, University of Southern California senior Rose Ritch resigned as vice president of the school's student government, "harassed for months by fellow students because they didn't like one of my identities." Hounded as a "Pro-Israel White Supremacist" and victimized by a social media drive to "impeach her Zionist a**," Ritch recounted her decision to resign last summer. "Because I openly identify as a Jew who supports Israel's right to exist as a Jewish state — i.e., a Zionist," she wrote, "I was accused by a group of students of being unsuitable as a student government leader." Resignation, she concluded, "was the only sustainable choice I could make to protect both my physical safety and my mental health."

This was no surprise for Rachel Beyda, the UCLA sophomore whose confirmation as a member of the student's council's judicial board was blocked after she was grilled on her "conflict of interest" as a Jew reviewing governance issues. "Given that you are a Jewish student and very active in the Jewish community," one student demanded to know, "how do you see yourself being able to maintain an unbiased view?" The council's rejection of Beyda was rescinded only when a faculty adviser pointed out that being Jewish was not a "conflict of interest."

What Price, Ritch and Beyda have endured is, unfortunately, the new normal. Recent years have exposed a whole lot of ugly, and the metastasis of anti-Semitism posing as progressivism on American campuses is very ugly indeed. If there is any chance of shrinking this cancer, it will come from those on campus with the sense of justice to resolve to call it what it is.

Taking On the Vile Factor: Biden Moves Against Anti-Asian American Hate
March 16, 2021

Shortly after the 2016 election, Mai, a Vietnamese American college student, was on a train in Miami when a large white man wearing a Make America Great Again cap approached her. "He just looked at me and spat at me," Mai says. "I just moved to a different car because I didn't want to cause any trouble." This sort of thing wasn't new. She has been taunted with slurs like "Chin Chong" and called a "Chink B———."

Since COVID-19 began, says Mai, now a Ph.D. student at a prestigious New England university, what has long been bad has gotten worse. Sitting in the front of a bus last year, she says, a passenger boarded, looked at her, muttered "Oh, heck, no" and got back off. Last week, two men followed her at a train station, loudly coughing at her. She has been told "Go back to your country," even though her country is America. "You just have to hope they don't hurt you," says Mai. "I try to stay silent or run away. I just pray every day that from the time I leave home to when I come home at night nothing scary will happen to me."

The sharp rise in physical assaults and verbal harassment directed at Asian Americans has once again garnered attention, and it is clear that this isn't "merely" vile people doing vile things, but a national disgrace. A recent report by the Center for the Study of Hate & Extremism at California State University, San Bernardino, found that anti-Asian hate crimes in 16 of America's largest cities rose by 149% last year. This was especially notable since hate crimes overall declined slightly, attributable to reduced public interaction during the pandemic. Harassment of Asian Americans is almost certainly underreported given the language limitations and the culture of silence and fear often extant in their communities.

In recent weeks, a fresh spate of anti-Asian American violence has intensified anxiety. Noel Quintana, a Filipino American, was slashed in the face with a box cutter on a New York City train, requiring about 100 stitches. "Nobody came, nobody helped, nobody made a video," he said afterward. In San Francisco, an 84-year-old Thai American, Vicha Ratanapakdee, was assaulted while on his morning walk and later died of his injuries. Iona Chong, a Chinese American epidemiologist, was called "Coronavirus" while jogging in

Oakland last year, and then, last December, shoved to the ground after delivering a Christmas gift.

"Everybody I know who is Asian is going through something similar to me," says Mai. Boston City Councilor Michelle Wu, the daughter of Taiwanese immigrants, is pointed about the ugliness. "Even before COVID-19 had reached the United States," says Wu, a candidate for mayor of Boston, "Chinatowns and Asian American and Pacific Islander communities across the country were hit by the virus of racism and xenophobia, crushing local businesses and fueling hate crimes."

Part of the horror of the pandemic has been seeing Asian Americans, an estimated 2 million of whom have been in the vanguard of our nation's response as frontline workers, subjected to schoolyard taunting by their president. Former President Donald Trump missed few opportunities to use phrases such as "China virus" and "Kung Flu" to describe the disease, relishing the glee that this pointless cruelty animated among his most ardent supporters.

President Joe Biden has wasted little time trying to make the virus-within-a-virus a top priority. Six days after taking office, he issued an executive order directing federal agencies to combat anti-Asian discrimination. On March 5, his Justice Department announced a battery of initiatives to focus investigative and prosecutorial resources against it. During his first national prime-time address, on March 11, Biden denounced "vicious hate crimes against Asian Americans who have been attacked, harassed, blamed and scapegoated. ... It's wrong," Biden emphasized. "It's un-American."

Biden's administration has a lot to tackle, to be sure. Part of its daunting task is confronting a decay of American decency. Its emphasis on shaming those guilty of targeting Asian Americans, and on prosecuting them, is an excellent start.

POTUS Pokes the Bear: No Longer Servile, the US Stirs to Challenge Putin

March 23, 2021

It is hard to imagine that, faced with aggressive, relentless assaults on American elections by the Kremlin, evidence of Russian bounties placed on the heads of American soldiers in the Mideast and bare-knuckled moves to re-gobble Ukraine, Ronald Reagan would have kissed Vladimir Putin's posterior. There was a time — lasting decades, in fact — when an American president lavishing praise on a former KGB agent running a Russian police state would have been denounced by Republicans as either a dolt or a dupe. Conservatives would have called him a weakling, a sell-out and a threat to our national security. And they would have been right.

Times have changed, however, and dramatically so. During the four years of former President Donald Trump's most curious romance with Putin, siding with the Russian president in his conflict with America in ways by turns cringeworthy and stomach-turning, the Grand Old Party sided with Trump in siding with Putin against the USA, lending new meaning to the expression "Politics makes strange bedfellows."

The last administration and its supporters left American credibility on the ropes and reaching for smelling salts. Credibility shredded over four years cannot simply be stitched back together overnight. The new administration understands that restoring America's influence abroad requires an end to the coddling of Russia, and that end has begun. In his first trip to the State Department, President Joe Biden provided a read-out of his telephone call with Putin and delivered a pointed message. "I made it clear to President Putin, in a manner very different from my predecessor," said Biden in his speech at Foggy Bottom, "that the days of the United States rolling over in the face of Russia's aggressive actions — interfering with our elections, cyberattacks, poisoning its citizens — are over. We will not hesitate to raise the cost on Russia."

Those were mere words, but they were words Putin hasn't heard for quite some time. When the American intelligence community unanimously confirmed that Russia had interfered in the 2016 election in order to elect Trump and defeat Hillary Clinton, Trump's announcement that he chose to believe Putin over his own government left one with two choices, each dispiriting: concluding that Trump was a nitwit or concluding that he was in the tank.

When Putin's government poisoned Russian opposition leader Alexei Navalny, Trump's silence and solicitude encouraged the Russians to believe after Navalny recovered and returned to Moscow that they could imprison him without consequences — and imprison him is just what they did. Biden has called Russia's oppression of Navalny what it is: an egregious human rights violation, the targeting of a political dissident for spotlighting Russian corruption. Biden called for Navalny's immediate, unconditional release. Seeking to galvanize a multilateral response to Russia, Biden urged the Munich Security Conference in February to confront "Russian recklessness," an effort he called "critical to protect our collective security." Within days, the European Union announced its imposition of sanctions on Russia in response to Navalny's jailing. Days later, the Biden administration announced its own set of sanctions against Russian companies and individuals, as well as other punitive measures. There is more to do, including using the presidential bully pulpit to shame Putin on the international stage, and the potential sanctioning of Putin cronies. The administration says that expanding its first round of sanctions is under review.

Biden's directness about Putin has been refreshing, though likely not to Putin. Asked by ABC's George Stephanopoulos last week whether he believed Putin was a killer, Biden replied, "I do," and said that Putin would "pay the price" for meddling in the 2020 election, which the intelligence community concluded earlier this month he had also clearly done. In retaliation, Putin recalled Russian Ambassador to the United States Anatoly Antonov back home to Moscow in diplomatic protest.

Ambassador Antonov should treat himself to a nice, long vacation with his family in Moscow and enjoy the home cooking. In the meantime, it is good to see that America is back.

Time to Go: Protecting Voters' Rights Means Easing the Filibuster's Stranglehold

March 30, 2021

Folk singer Phil Ochs was biting about one state's especially noxious mistreatment of Black Americans. "Here's to the land you've torn out the heart of," goes the refrain in "Here's to the State of Mississippi," Ochs' 1965 protest song. "Mississippi, find yourself another country to be part of."

Georgia has now taken center stage as our country's poster child for voter suppression. Last week, Republican Gov. Brian Kemp signed into law a bill that had rocketed through Georgia's Republican-controlled legislature. Its aim was to discourage voters of color from exercising their right to vote. This was accompanied by the usual straight-faced claptrap that the legislation was really intended to enhance "election integrity." Few over the age of 6 could have believed this: One of the bill's signature provisions was making it a crime to offer food or water to voters who might be waiting in line for hours in the hot Georgia sun to cast their ballot. Trying to help one's fellow Americans avoid heatstroke while waiting to vote does not exactly constitute election subversion.

Another "election integrity" provision authorizes the shutting down of voting in some cases as early as 5 p.m., exactly when working people get off work and are actually in a position to go vote. Another requires photo IDs to vote absentee, which will clearly disadvantage low-income voters who do not have driver's licenses because they do not have cars, either because they cannot afford them or because they live in inner cities.

As of mid-February, Republican legislators in 43 states had introduced over 250 bills that restrict access to the ballot. These would restrict mail-in and early voting and authorize the near-elimination of ballot drop-off boxes. Republicans insist that reducing voter turnout in communities of color is the furthest thing from their minds. Of course they do. As George Orwell wrote, a pickpocket does not go to the races with a sign that says "thief" on his lapel.

Enter the For the People Act, a bill passed by the U.S. House of Representatives to enact a series of federal safeguards against the kind of election manipulation that Republicans around the country are raising to an art form. According to one poll last month, 68% of Americans support the bill, including 57% of Republicans. Yet in a nation that has celebrated itself for having a representative government, the bill is presently slated to die in the Senate, strangled by the Senate procedural rule commonly referred to as the "filibuster." The term is something of a misnomer; the rule that guarantees gridlock actually simply provides that no bill can be voted upon unless 60 senators agree that it can. Put another way, Democrats need to find 10 Republican Senators to agree to a law that would safeguard communities of color against attempts to suppress their votes. Pigs will not only fly but circumnavigate the globe before that occurs. The only solution is to eliminate or modify the filibuster.

The filibuster rule is often defended as encouraging bipartisanship and good faith in Congress. But this is more of a hoot than a hope. Over 145 Republican members of Congress voted to block an election that they knew Joe Biden had won. Senate Republicans have made clear that, just as their single most important goal when Barack Obama was elected was to make him a one-term president, so too are they committed to stonewalling Biden's legislative agenda. One has to consume a fair amount of fairy dust to believe that bipartisanship and good faith are on congressional Republicans' minds these days.

The right to vote is the mother of our democracy, and it is in danger. Reforming the filibuster to permit the majority of both houses of Congress to protect communities of color against attempts to suppress their votes isn't procedural reform. It is the key to preserving the America that most of us cherish.

Rump Party: The Face of the GOP Is Not a Pretty One

April 6, 2021

Former House Speaker John Boehner's new book landed just in time to underscore the point that Republican Rep. Matt Gaetz has been making in spades: The Republican Party is a hot mess. In "On The House: A Washington Memoir," the Ohio Republican bluntly assesses the paltry intelligence and dubious character of many of the leading figures in the Republican caucus. "You could be a total moron and get elected just by having an R next to your name," wrote Boehner about the crop of House Republicans elected in the 2010 midterms. Boehner calls the Republican caucus "Crazytown," describing Texas Sen. Ted Cruz as "the new head lunatic leading the way."

With last week's reports that he is under investigation for sex trafficking, the spotlight is on Gaetz, who had become the darling of MAGA world for his role as Donald Trump's mini-me. No one on Earth, let alone in Congress, has backed Trump more vocally than Gaetz, who called him "the greatest president in my lifetime — one of the greatest presidents our country has ever had, maybe the greatest president our country has ever had."

The Florida congressman has denied any wrongdoing in a series of public statements by turns ill-advised and bizarre. "My family and I have been victims of an organized criminal extortion involving a former DOJ official seeking $25 million while threatening to smear my name," he tweeted. One intuitively senses that this is not an accurate or complete summary of Gaetz's legal situation.

Schadenfreude, defined as satisfaction at someone else's bad news, is generally to be resisted, but Gaetz has not made that easy. Before news of the federal investigation surfaced, he had amassed quite a record of foul behavior.

In 2018, he invited a Holocaust denier to be his guest at the State of the Union. In February 2019, the night before Trump fixer Michael Cohen was to testify to Congress, Gaetz tweeted at Cohen: "Do your wife & father-in-law know about your girlfriends? Maybe tonight would be a good time for that chat. I wonder if she'll remain faithful when you're in prison. She's about to learn a lot." This bit of "message-sending" earned him a rebuke from the House Ethics Committee. Later that year, he led 30 of his Republican colleagues in storming a closed, secure deposition of a Pentagon official testifying about Trump's withholding of military aid as a lever to extract Ukraine's announcement of an "investigation" into the Biden family.

In March 2020, he mocked concerns about COVID-19 by wearing a gas mask during a House debate over combating the pandemic. And hours after the Jan. 6 ransacking of the Capitol by a pro-Trump mob, he dutifully parroted the claptrap that the marauders were "masquerading as Trump supporters and were, in fact, members of the violent terrorist group antifa."

But Gaetz, a charlatan if ever there were one, has plenty of kindred spirits in the Republican congressional caucus, two-thirds of whom voted to overturn the presidential election because Trump had lost it. There's Rep. Marjorie Taylor Greene, who supported executing Barack Obama and Nancy Pelosi, and claimed that Hillary Clinton murdered a child in a satanic ritual. There's Rep. Lauren Boebert, who, asked about her endorsement of the nutcase conspiratorial movement QAnon, gushed that it is "motivating and encouraging and bringing people together stronger" and "it could be really great for our country." There's Rep. Mo Brooks, who exhorted the crowd of Trump supporters on Jan. 6 before they smashed up the Capitol: "Today is the day American patriots start taking down names and kicking ass. ... Are you willing to do what it takes to fight for America?" There's Rep. Paul Gosar, who promoted fraudulent "Stop the Steal" rallies and repeatedly called President Joe Biden "an illegitimate usurper."

The sad fact is that Gaetz and Gang are not outliers. They represent the core of the Republican Party, and not merely its hard core. As long as that remains true, America will have Crazytown to contend with.

Revenge of the Nerd: Across the Divide, Bernie Sanders Breaks Through

April 13, 2021

Bernie Sanders was never the most all-American of presidential candidates. The Brooklyn-born socialist senator from Vermont has a New York accent less thick than overpowering. Lecturing America relentlessly on its serious ills, he presented as a cross between Scrooge and the Grim Reaper, seemingly as likely to appeal to American voters as Leon Trotsky, with whom he appeared to share a hair stylist. He did not slap backs, could not tell jokes and spouted policy prescriptions that sounded right out of "Das Kapital."

First in 2016 and then again in 2020, he was underestimated, and even dismissed. New York Times reporter Amy Chozick recounts missing the meaning of Sanders' message in 2016, nearly blowing off the opportunity to interview him early in that campaign in favor of a physical fitness class. "I initially brushed Bernie off with such casual nonchalance, such ill-informed elite media snobbery," she has written, "that I almost canceled our first one-on-one coffee because I didn't want to miss abs-and-back day at boot camp."

Today it's clear that on issue after issue, Sanders' thunder on the left has carried the day among a majority of Americans, including substantial numbers of Republicans. Conservative attacks on Sanders-style proposals for universal health care, raising taxes on the wealthy, raising the federal minimum wage and other programs as "European socialism," once tried and true, are increasingly falling flat. The nation's near-death experience coping with an anti-democratic president, an upsurge in right-wing extremism and a devastating pandemic seems to have left many Americans convinced that more dramatic change than they had once been willing to contemplate is necessary to hold a weakened country together.

So say the polls, in any event.

In announcing his candidacy for the Democratic presidential nomination in 2019, for example, Sanders proclaimed "We say to the American people that we will rebuild our crumbling infrastructure: our roads, our bridges, our rail systems and subways ... and our airports," vowing to create millions of jobs in the process. And he promised to tax the rich to pay for it. "The wealthy and multinational corporations in this country," Sanders said, "will start paying their fair share of taxes."

Americans are with him. Asked last month whether they would support President Joe Biden's massive public infrastructure plan even after passage of a $1.9 trillion COVID-19 relief act, 73% of voters overall, including 57% of Independents and 61% of Republicans, told Data for Progress pollsters that they would. A Morning Consult poll two weeks ago found that 54% of Americans supported funding those improvements by raising taxes on those earning over $400,000 a year and raising the corporate tax rate. Unsurprisingly, this included 73% of Democrats. More notably, it included 52% of Independents and 32% of Republicans. Fifty-seven percent of voters told the pollsters that they would be more likely to support Biden's infrastructure plan if it included raising taxes on high earners; only 17% said it would make them less likely to do so. Forty-seven percent said they would be more likely to support the bill if it was paid for by raising corporate taxes, while only 21% said it would make them less likely to support it.

Raising taxes to invest in public infrastructure is not the only issue on which America's political sands are shifting. A poll taken last fall by the Kaiser Family Foundation concluded that 53% of Americans supported a national health plan which would insure everyone. This included 58% of Independents and 21% of Republicans. A contemporaneous Pew Research Center poll found that 63% of American adults believe that government bears responsibility for providing health care coverage for all, up from 2019. This included 34% of Republicans. And a recent Morning Consult poll found that a majority of Republicans support raising the federal minimum wage.

It has been a very long time since Bernie Sanders could be ignored. If once it could be said that he was ahead of his time, it must now be said that Americans are catching up to him.

Looney Tunes: The Rot on the Right Isn't Going Away Anytime Soon

April 20, 2021

Hot tempers at last week's House hearing on the battle against COVID-19 highlighted again the hatred that America's hard right continues to harbor for Dr. Anthony Fauci, director of the National Institute of Allergy and Infectious Diseases. It's both ironic and fitting that America's preeminent warrior against infectious diseases is despised by those infected by America's second-most dangerous disease: the anti-fact, anti-science, pro-conspiracy extremism that grips a slice of this country.

Testifying before a House committee last year, Fauci had the temerity to reiterate a warning with which every public health expert in the country agrees: We should "avoid crowds of any type no matter where you are because that leads to the acquisition and transmission. ... When you're in a crowd, particularly if you're not wearing a mask, that induces the spread. ... You should stay away from crowds, no matter where the crowds are."

You might suppose that with almost 32 million Americans infected and nearly 570,000 dead, even Trump loyalists who embraced the old con man's assurance that COVID-19 was a media "hoax" would make it a point to sound sober. And you might suppose that would apply to Rep. Jim Jordan, R-Ohio, who, as one of the Master of Mar-a-Lago's most stalwart acolytes, was reliably wrong about COVID-19 right from the start. At a March 2020 hearing of the House oversight committee, after Fauci warned bluntly that COVID-19 was going to get worse, Jordan insisted that "the risk to Americans remain low."

Jordan proved to be a chump, and Fauci proved to be prescient. But Washington is a town short on memory and even shorter on sheepishness; and Jordan, always sneering and rarely correct, could not contain his fury at Fauci, whose sin, in the eyes of the looneys who loathe him, was that he was right about the disease when they were wrong. In July, a snarling Jordan demanded to know whether Fauci believed two individuals in some New Jersey town should have been arrested for opening up their gym in violation of state law. "You think that's okay?" Jordan yelled, rambling about how neither church-goers nor hairstylists were attacking police or committing arson.

"Where does it get to?" Jordan thundered at Fauci last week. "When it comes down, what number do we get our liberties back? Tell me the number!" After his time for questioning witnesses had expired and the committee chair had recognized another member, Jordan kept going. "The American people want Dr. Fauci to answer the question!" he snapped. This prompted Rep. Maxine Waters to exclaim what many watching were silently thinking. "You need to respect the Chair and shut your mouth!" she told Jordan.

Jordan was not well-briefed on Americans' view of Fauci. A Morning Consult/Politico poll in February found that 60% of voters rate Fauci's handling of COVID-19 as "excellent" or "good," and only 17% said it was "poor."

But what a 17%!

The nutcases in our midst maintain that Fauci was behind the COVID-19 outbreak, likely in order to profit from vaccine sales. Fox personality Tucker Carlson saw fit last week to suggest that, like the virus itself, the vaccine is a hoax. "So maybe it doesn't work," Carlson told his audience, "and they're simply not telling you that." After Fauci cautioned that children should continue to wear masks when playing with children from multiple households, one Boston-area columnist who had supported Donald Trump's fraudulent pronouncements one after the other made it clear that no public health expert was going to tell him anything about public health. "Go away, you nuisance," he tweeted.

The virus-deniers and the anti-vaccination crowd have made the national effort to stop the suffering and rebuild the country more difficult than it already is. The Fauci-hatred that is the staple of domestic extremism is not merely irrational. It is yet another cross that America can ill afford to bear.

His Own Man: Angus King Refuses to Give Up on Bipartisanship

April 27, 2021

Angus King doesn't only have an independent streak. The United States senator from Maine has been an Independent for three decades. "The Democratic Party as an institution has become too much the party that is looking for something from government," King said in launching his successful bid for governor of the Pine Tree State in 1993. He spent much of his career in the private sector. He voted against Bernie Sanders' amendment to add a $15 hourly minimum wage provision into the American Rescue Plan and has endorsed his share of Republicans. King has a fondness for taking RV trips through rural America, which likely sets him apart from most members of the Senate's Democratic caucus.

This isn't to say that where King is likely to stand on any given issue is a jump ball. He aligns with his Democratic colleagues, with whom he typically votes. After King lambasted Donald Trump's handling of COVID-19 as the blend of stubborn obtuseness and bumbling ineptitude that it was, Trump lambasted him right back, calling King "worse than any Democrat," surely an honor on a par with making it onto Richard Nixon's enemies list.

Still, King's independent, cerebral approach lends him outsized credibility in the Senate, and he rejects the conventional wisdom that bipartisanship in the world's supposedly most deliberative body is dead. "A lot of things do get done on a bipartisan basis but they don't get covered," says King. He points to last year's budget deal and the Great American Outdoors Act, the land conservation legislation praised as "a conservationist's dream" by the National Parks Conservation Association.

But he is not naive about the partisan pingpong that chokes progress in Washington. "What happens is that the primary in so many states becomes the election," he explains. "In many states if you win the nomination you are going to be the Senator. If the primary is the election, who votes in the primary? The activists. And those people are at the edges of their party. One of the commonalities of activists on the right and the left is a distaste for compromise. You can lose your seat because you are someone who is willing to listen to the other side. That's an extremely dangerous place for the country to be."

King recalls a dinner he had with a conservative Republican incumbent who told him that he would probably face a primary challenge. "What are they going to charge you with?" King asked. "They are going to charge me with being reasonable," replied the Republican. "It makes it hard to solve problems," King laments, "not because of the substance of the matter, but because consorting with the enemy is considered an executable offense."

King was one of a handful of senators invited to the Oval Office last week to discuss President Joe Biden's infrastructure bill. Biden knew what he was doing. Not only is King effective at building bridges, but he has been beating the drum for providing broadband to areas shut off from digital access for a generation. "Rural America has taken a beating over the past 25 years," King says. "The pandemic exposed this. Broadband is the first thing that provides the promise of giving rural areas a future." As governor, in 2002, King launched the Maine Learning Technology Initiative, a groundbreaking program to provide laptops to all middle school students in the state. "I see broadband as important in the short term for telehealth and education and in the long term as a lifeline economically," says King, who is playing point in the negotiation of Biden's infrastructure package.

"I have found," says King, "if you have a difficult problem and you can gather people around a table and establish a common understanding of the facts, you can come up with a policy." Skeptical of the skeptics, King forges ahead, confident he can help prove them wrong.

Pipe Dream: Biden's Call For Republican Bipartisanship Is Fervent, but Futile

May 4, 2021

President Joe Biden's address to Congress last week wasn't merely a sobering recitation of the nation's most profound wounds and weaknesses, and it wasn't only a summary of the specific proposals he has made in his first 100 days to confront them. It was an old-fashioned call for bipartisanship by one who came of age in a different, better time. It was grounded in the premise that in the past, at least, national crises have moved enough partisans to suspend their partisanship that crisis didn't have to turn into catastrophe. And it came naturally to a president whose long life has positioned him to take the long view, who has experienced far more than a fair share of personal pain, and whose innate disposition is to find common ground.

Biden bent over backwards to thank congressional Republicans and extend an olive branch to them, even though there was little factual basis for doing so. He applauded Republican senators who had at least put forward an infrastructure package, saying, "I'd like to meet with those who have ideas that are different — they think are better. I welcome those ideas." On police reform, so necessary to address the no-longer-ignorable racism marbled throughout our criminal justice system, he said, "I know Republicans have their own ideas and are engaged in the very productive discussions with Democrats in the Senate."

But perhaps the most obvious example of giving credit where none was due came when the president praised both parties for providing the desperately needed COVID-19 relief afforded by the American Rescue Plan, which every single Republican in Congress opposed. Lockstep Republican opposition to the plan, of course, has not stopped Republicans from telling their constituents that they are responsible for its benefits. So it goes in "Crazytown," former House Speaker John Boehner's memorable term for the Republican caucus.

The fact that congressional Republicans uniformly opposed the relief America needed so badly in order to recover from the pandemic says everything one needs to know about the chances that Biden will receive cooperation from the GOP, a party that is one part hapless, three parts hallucinogenic. Last week, yet another poll found that 70% of Republicans believe that Donald Trump, not Biden, won the election. This is a reflection of the grip held on the GOP by Fox News, aptly described by CNN's Jim Acosta as a "B.S. factory," though he did not confine himself to the initials. Last Monday, Fox News was forced to admit that it had erred in claiming that Biden is trying to restrict Americans' red meat consumption. On Tuesday, the New York Post, Fox's Manure Inc. affiliate, had to revise an article that falsely claimed Vice President Kamala Harris' book was being distributed to migrant children. The reporter who wrote it resigned, apologizing that it was "an incorrect story I was ordered to write and which I failed to push back hard enough against."

Sen. Mitt Romney, a rock-ribbed Republican with the integrity to vote twice to impeach Trump, narrowly avoided a censure by Utah's state Republican convention, whose delegates peppered him with cries of "traitor" and "communist." After she walked a few steps to simply greet the president of the United States as he made his way down the aisle toward the House rostrum to deliver his address, Rep. Liz Cheney, the third-ranking House Republican, was targeted with a fresh round of vitriol from her colleagues, many of whom have vowed to boot her from Republican leadership.

Buoyed by the empirical likelihood that it will pick up seats in the 2022 midterms and knowing that it will not take much of a pickup to reclaim control of Congress, the GOP is committed to opposing Joe Biden, not helping him. If that means that Americans are the losers, so be it. The president will get no bipartisanship from Republicans, which is a sad thing for a nation that deserves better.

Champion: As Long as Anti-Semitism Isn't Going Anywhere, Neither Is Abe Foxman

May 11, 2021

For anyone who follows sports, the name "Tiger" means golf legend Tiger Woods. Music lovers know that "Yo Yo" means cellist Yo Yo Ma. For Jewish communities around the world, and for those with a stake in the never-ending battle to roll back anti-Semitism, "Abe" means Abraham Foxman, whose name has for decades been synonymous with the struggle against the planet's oldest prejudice.

Foxman, who just turned 81, is being honored in Washington, D.C., this month as part of American Jewish History Month, established by Congress and a presidential proclamation in 2006. A Holocaust survivor, saved as a child by his Polish Catholic nanny, Foxman immigrated to America at 10. After obtaining his law degree, he joined the Anti-Defamation League, founded in 1913 to combat discrimination against Jews and all others. He would go on to spend 50 years at the ADL, including 28 as its national director, helping to turn an already important civil rights organization into a household name. Since Foxman retired in 2015, the bully pulpit constructed by him has been ably wielded by Foxman's successor, Jonathan Greenblatt, who, in a time of Trumpism, has had no more chance to rest than Foxman ever did.

One of the qualities that enabled Abe Foxman to excel at what he did was his sheer energy. ADL delegations traveling abroad with him would wake to find that he had suddenly flown off somewhere, Air Foxman, to meet with the leader of a country not on the itinerary in order to work some 8-ball-in-the-side-pocket bit of international diplomacy, likely coordinated with whatever American administration was in power. Another was his capacity to strategize on multiple planes simultaneously, to look at the chessboard and say: If we do this, X will occur. That will trigger Y, which will in turn create the following options, from which we will choose Z.

Abe is by turns a sweet-talker and blunt as a hammer, often in the same sentence, sometimes within the same introductory clause. He is used to meeting with corporate heads and heads of nations alike, and one has the distinct impression that he never spoke differently to them than he did to anyone else.

Through famous for his high-profile battles against discrimination against Jews, Foxman used his platform more broadly, pouring resources into ADL's effort to expose white supremacy, placing the organization early and squarely on the side of LGBT rights and advocating for immigrants. Foxman, like Greenblatt, associates himself firmly with Rabbi Hillel's exhortation, "If I am only for myself, what am I?" which has earned each of them slings, arrows and angry donors.

But it is on the subject of the relentless cancer of anti-Semitism, metastasizing on the right and left and advancing on Jewry like a pincer, that Foxman's counsel is most frequently sought, for he has lived it, watched it and fought it for a lifetime. "There is no vaccine for anti-Semitism, no antidote for it," says Foxman, "and if we didn't develop one after we saw Auschwitz (we never will). We will have to continuously find ways to contain it by building a firewall, a consensus that it is immoral, un-Christian, un-Muslim and un-American."

Both the extreme left and the extreme right and their sympathizers bear the blame, Foxman emphasizes. "Both right and left have been responsible for horrific anti-Semitism," says Foxman. "Fascism and Communism have both hurt the Jewish people. There is no percentage in comparing them; they both have been deadly for the Jews. The anti-Semitism on the right and the left need to be challenged vigorously."

Foxman is no more worried about people not liking his straight talk than he ever was. The tributes that have rolled in from members of Congress are themselves a tribute to his authenticity. But they also reflect an appreciation that his life has been that of an authentic American hero.

Complicit: The Left's Indulgence of Hamas Guarantees Palestinians and Israelis Will Continue to Suffer

May 18, 2021

In a statement last week, a Hamas spokesman expressed the mentality behind the suffering in Gaza in a nutshell. "The decision to bomb Tel Aviv, Dimona and Jerusalem," he boasted about the 3,000 rockets Hamas has fired at Israeli communities in recent days alone, "is easier for us than drinking water."

You bet it is. As in the past, the calculation by Hamas, deemed a terrorist enterprise by the European Union, the United States and others, to use Palestinian civilians as human shields from which to attempt the murder of Israeli civilians, isn't just easy. It is a no-brainer.

Here is what Hamas knows: It will fire missiles at innocent Israelis, using innocent Palestinians in homes, hospitals and schools as collateral damage-in-waiting. No Israeli government can permit its civilians to be used as lambs to be slaughtered. The only way for it to stop the rockets is to stop those who fire them. Israel will try to minimize the harm to Gazans, even those whom Hamas is happy to sacrifice. Innocent Palestinians, whom Hamas has effectively designated for death, will die.

And that isn't all Hamas knows. It knows that the cycle of inanity on the left will be replayed again, with so-called progressives blaming not Hamas for firing the rockets but Israel for trying to protect itself from them.

Hamas' expectations were rewarded last week by Representatives Ayanna Pressley, D-Mass., and Alexandria Ocasio-Cortez, D-N.Y., who recited the customary blather. Disregarding the rocketing of Israeli civilians that was intended to elicit Israeli self-defense and which required it, Pressley chose to condemn Israeli "state violence" and called for an end to American aid to Israel. Ocasio-Cortez denounced President Biden for noting that Israel had no choice but to protect its civilians, demanding that the president "stand up" to Israel.

One supposes that neither Pressley nor Ocasio-Cortez has had their families forced into underground shelters while missiles aimed at annihilating them landed all around. The painful appearance is that neither congresswoman "sees" Israelis. Both seem to regard Israelis as somehow not quite human, perhaps three-fifths of a human being in the way that America's white Founding Fathers regarded Black people as three-fifths of a white person. Israeli life evidently holds little value or interest for Pressley, Ocasio-Cortez and some of their colleagues, whose silence about the large-scale attacks on Israeli civilians veers dangerously close to the implicit but pernicious racism to which they are sensitive — in contexts other than those involving the Jewish state.

"We cannot stand idly and complicitly by and allow the occupation and oppression of the Palestinian people to continue," said Pressley, opting for a platitude both sophomoric and inapposite. The idea that Hamas, which has consigned Palestinians to needless suffering since it seized control of the Gaza Strip in a 2007 coup, acts out of concern for Palestinians' welfare is risible. No one need take Israel's word for it; ask Palestinian President Mahmoud Abbas, Hamas' sworn enemy. Thumbing its nose at the opportunity to help construct a Palestinian state, Hamas has effectively enslaved Gazans in service of its own fanaticism. It is an organization that progressives should not indulge, let alone embrace.

Just as the congresswomen have no particular interest in standing in Israelis' shoes, so, too, are they disinterested in material facts. Were it otherwise, they would know that over the past two decades Israel has repeatedly agreed to an independent Palestinian state encompassing the West Bank and Gaza, in return for peace. Each time the offer was made, Palestinian leadership rejected it. Whether Pressley has the vaguest idea of this when she whitewashes the targeting of Israeli civilians by invoking "the occupation and oppression of the Palestinian people," one can only guess.

Israel has plenty of flaws, like everyone else. But the left's devil-may-care attitude toward the use of innocent Palestinians as human shields isn't merely foolish. It badly hurts those on both sides of the conflict.

The Keeper: In a GOP Dominated by Frauds and Cowards, Liz Cheney's a Profile in Courage

May 25, 2021

Addressing Suffolk University graduates on Saturday, retired Washington Post editor Martin Baron summarized the sociopolitical virus afflicting the nation in three sentences. "We learned in recent years that our institutions were more vulnerable to pressure and intimidation than we ever imagined," said Baron. "Many turned submissive when a powerful leader demanded it. Others went quiet for fear of reprisal."

Though Baron refrained from mentioning you-know-who or the not-so-Grand Old Party that continues to ask, "How high?" when Donald Trump tells it to jump, everyone knew what he was talking about. For, over four years, even Republican politicians who knew how sociopathic and anti-democratic their president was shilled for him or simply stayed silent, fearful of being primaried. When he demanded that state election officials declare him the winner of elections he had lost, they remained silent. When The Master of Mar-a-Lago declared that he had won the presidential election and that it had been "stolen" from him, assertions that were fraudulent, they nodded.

Trump then summoned a mob to Washington on Jan. 6, the day Congress was to certify the election results, promising them a good time and exhorted them to go down to the Capitol and show that "they're not going to take it any longer," that "we will stop the steal," and that they were ready to "fight like hell." He could not have been that much more explicit about what he wanted them to do for him. "So we're going to walk down Pennsylvania Avenue," he shouted. "And we're going to the Capitol... So let's walk down Pennsylvania Avenue."

The ensuing ransacking of the Capitol by Trump supporters was a dark day for America. It occurred as 147 Republican members of Congress did some ransacking of their own, voting to reject the election of Joe Biden, an election that the compos mentis among them knew Biden had won.

Among the phonies, frauds and cowards who dominate the Republican Party, one Republican stood out for her courage. That was

Wyoming Congresswoman Liz Cheney, who minced few words about what was transpiring. "We Republicans need to stand up for genuinely conservative principles," she declared, "and steer away from the dangerous and anti-democratic Trump cult of personality. History is watching. Our children are watching."

Guzzling Kool-Aid is a prerequisite for Republicans these days, and Cheney understood that by taking on the crazies who control her party she was assuring that she would be booted out of Republican leadership. "If you want leaders who will enable and spread (Trump's) destructive lies, I'm not your person," she told the Republican caucus. In a move that suited them perfectly, House Republicans decided to oust Cheney by voice vote, rather than have their individual votes recorded, a maneuver designed to permit them to appease The Donald on one hand while hiding from history on the other. For her part, Cheney has nothing to fear from history, which will treat her as the profile in courage that she is. "I will do everything I can to ensure that the former president never again gets anywhere near the Oval Office," she said defiantly after she was ousted.

The Republicans' sharp preference for fiction over truth continued on display this past week, with 175 out of 210 Republican members of Congress voting against having a bipartisan commission investigate "the facts and causes relating to" the Jan. 6 attack on the Capitol. One would not want to know the facts and causes relating to the unprecedented violent takeover of the Capitol by weapon-toting domestic extremists, after all.

But there is good news. Thirty-five Republicans — fully 1 out of 6 Republicans in the House — bucked their leadership's fierce opposition to finding out the truth, concluding that finding out the truth might actually be in the national interest. That's 35 out of 210 votes for the truth on the Republican side of the aisle in our House of Representatives. This counts as a good day.

Things are looking up.

Renewal: With a Community Assist, Baseball Brings a Win to Worcester

June 1, 2021

Even in ordinary times, the inside of a professional baseball stadium is a sight for sore eyes. These are extraordinary times, and not in a good way. So taking in a baseball game on a spring night in the spanking new stadium built by the Boston Red Sox' Triple A affiliate in Worcester, Massachusetts, provided a lift to the fans who streamed into Polar Park to participate in the premiere season of the recently arrived Worcester Red Sox. But the team's relocation should also provide a lift to those simply interested in how private-public partnerships executed with grit and vision can make a difference to communities that can use a boost, especially after 15 months of a pandemic.

The Worcester Red Sox, or WooSox, as they are known, are the new incarnation of the Pawtucket Red Sox, which had long played in a stadium in Pawtucket, Rhode Island, increasingly feeling the effects of Father Time. In 2018, team management, led by former Red Sox CEO Larry Lucchino, announced that it would relocate to a new stadium in Worcester.

There was one catch: There was no new stadium. What there was, says WooSox General Manager Dan Rea, was a determination on the part of team owners, Worcester city officials, Worcester civic leaders and the governor of Massachusetts to make the new team in a new park a win for Worcester — New England's second-largest city. "From the start," says Rea, "there was a willingness to work together."

That willingness to work together has come in mighty handy, because the logistical obstacles to opening Polar Park at all, let alone in time for the opening of the 2021 Triple A season, were of D-Day dimensions. The cost of turning a parking lot into a sparkling stadium was over $150 million. Over half was provided by the city of Worcester, with the city and the commonwealth pitching in to address a limitless list of other needs. Rea and a well-tuned team of young professionals drank daily and copiously from a fire hose of challenges, ranging from design to permitting to licensing to construction. Then there was the little matter of COVID-19, which greatly complicated the 15 months leading up to opening day and which shut down work for seven precious weeks. Team President Charles Steinberg, whose appreciation for baseball's impact on kids and families runs deep, conducted a series of "fan forums" designed to learn what the community wanted to see in their team and their stadium. "We realize that a baseball team has a social mission in the community," Rea says. "Worcester is a very diverse community in very different ways. We want our team to contribute to that diversity and reflect it."

The team is expected to bring 750,000 visitors to Worcester annually, with an infusion of revenue for existing and new retail establishments and plans underway for two new hotels and hundreds of new housing units, as well as a burst of jobs. Still, team owners know that benefits only for the usual suspects won't cut it. "If this ballpark benefits just a small subset of the population, we're not living up to our obligations," says Rea. This is welcome news for the Rev. Dr. Debora Jackson, dean of Worcester Polytechnic Institute's Business School, who praises the team for what she terms its "significant economic impact" but who will be watching to make sure the team follows through on its laudable intentions. "I want to make sure that the benefits are spread equitably to people who are often left out," says Jackson, hoping that the team will "ensure that women and minority-owned businesses get a part" of the opportunities generated by the new team in town.

Rea and company seem energized by the chance to do good, rather than exhausted by what has had to get done to get them here. For the moment, the WooSox and their partners have furnished some good news in a time sorely in need of it.

Fresh Blood, Old Bias: New Israeli Leaders Confront the Stubborn Inanity of the Left

June 8, 2021

Last week's formation of a new Israeli government, comprised of Parliament members from across the country's wide political spectrum, was good news for Israel, which needs to move on from long-time Prime Minister Benjamin Netanyahu. Reinforcing that good news was the election of Isaac Herzog, the widely respected former Labor Party leader, as Israel's new president.

Israeli leaders preside over a nation both hugely successful and hugely challenged. Among their challenges is an American left that increasingly embraces the narrative that the massive rocketing of Israeli civilians by Hamas is more or less fine and that Israeli attempts to stop it constitute war crimes. This inanity captivates American progressives, who have swallowed it whole.

New York Times columnist Nicholas Kristof illustrates the point. Each time Hamas has used Gazans as human shields to fire thousands of rockets at Israeli communities — in 2009, 2012, 2014 and just recently — Kristof's chose to bitterly criticize Israel because — shocker! — when Israel tried to stop the rocketing and reduced Hamas' ability to conduct it, Gazans, whom Hamas was happy to sacrifice for public relations gains, were killed. It requires no genius to grasp that Hamas wants to terrorize and kill Israelis and wants Gazans to die to dupe the left into blaming Israel. But Kristof and others, including some really smart people, seem not to get it.

Appearing on "Real Time with Bill Maher" last month, Kristof was left stammering when Maher asked him what he, Kristof, suggested Israel should do to defend itself from Hamas rockets. Seeking to self-resuscitate a few days later, Kristof wrote a column offering up the meaningless pablum that Israel should act "with more restraint and wisdom," a banality at once precious and witless. Would it constitute "wisdom" for Israel to simply permit Hamas to carpet Israeli civilians with thousands of rockets every time it saw fit, without trying to protect its civilians? As for "restraint," Kristof has not the foggiest idea of the extent to which Israel goes to avoid hurting civilians. Any serious person who gives it a minute's thought realizes that there is no way for Israel to stop Hamas from waging war against it without Gazans being hurt, particularly since Hamas intends for Gazans to be hurt.

Those who have somewhat more knowledge of what is entailed in trying to stop thousands of rockets than columnists and editorial writers praise Israel as the gold standard of military morality. General Martin Dempsey, President Obama's chairman of the Joint Chiefs of Staff, was among those with actual expertise who have hailed the "extraordinary lengths" to which the Israel Defense Forces go to minimize the harm to Gazans while trying to protect Israelis. "They did some extraordinary things to try to limit civilian casualties," said Dempsey in 2014, the last time Hamas fired thousands of rockets at Israelis only to have the left attack Israel. "The IDF is not interested in creating civilian casualties. They're interested in stopping the shooting of rockets and missiles out of the Gaza Strip and into Israel."

So true, so obvious, and just as true and obvious this last time as before. And still irrelevant as far as the left is concerned. Thankfully, not everyone on the Democratic left has lost their minds — or their spines. United States Representative Ritchie Torres, a Black, openly gay congressman representing the South Bronx, is not buying the hogwash being peddled by congressional colleagues like Ayanna Pressley, Alexandria Ocasio-Cortez and others, who hold themselves out as progressives while apologizing for Hamas' crimes against both Gazans and Israelis. "The hysterical demonization of Israel has set off a global wave of anti-Semitic violence and vitriol," said Torres days ago.

He is right. And a troubling number of Democrats share in the responsibility for it.

Believer: Prime Time Paul Zine No Longer Thinks COVID-19 Is up for Debate

June 15, 2021

At age 68, former wrestler Paul Zine still looks as though he could personally deconstruct a skyscraper with his bare hands. A personal trainer for the last 20 years, Zine went by the professional name "Prime Time Paul Zine" on the wrestling circuit. In his prime, he once bench pressed 512 pounds. Now, decades later and after too many shoulder surgeries to count stemming from his years in the ring, it looks like he can no longer lift more than 508.

Zine is real people through and through. He grew up in a Boston neighborhood that was seized by eminent domain in order to expand the Massachusetts Turnpike. His father worked for a half-century as a photo engraver for the old Record American, later the Boston Herald. After high school, Zine himself worked at the newspaper, then tried flight school, canine training and helping out in the family restaurant before launching a wrestling career at 32.

Zine makes no bones about his politics. "I'm an absolute conservative and an absolute Trump supporter," he says. "Hate me if you will." When the COVID-19 pandemic took over the news two winters ago, Zine was a full-fledged cynic, sharply inclined to view the warnings about shutdowns and social distancing as classic media hype, exaggerations hatched and promoted by a news business that wanted to take then-President Donald Trump down. Like many, he was offended by the idea of government telling everyone what to do and what not to do. "People don't like to feel forced to do things that they don't want to do, me included," he says. "People were told which way to walk in a grocery store. People don't like that. It's just human nature, especially in this country."

His own views about the coronavirus changed in a hurry this past March, when he contracted it. It began with a cough. "At first I didn't pay much attention to it ... And then the cough got a little worse. And it got worse every day. And then I was lightheaded and dizzy, and I became very, very weak." Before long, Zine was unable to stand, let alone walk.

He landed in the hospital twice. "As sick as I was, there was a time that I really didn't know that I was going to survive it," Zine continues. "I wouldn't wish that on anyone. It's just too dangerous."

His politics haven't changed. What has changed is his belief that COVID-19 is a media invention. "For those who think that," Zine adds, "I say, believe that at your own risk." The virus left him out of commission for seven weeks. Asked if his views have evolved, Zine is unhesitating. "Oh, yeah," he says. "You can't pooh-pooh it once you've had it. You take it very seriously. You may not have believed it before, but if you get it, you believe. Trust me. It's not politics. It's for real. It's not an issue that's up for debate anymore."

For all of the tangible signs that the worst is over, approximately 50% of Americans 12 and older are still not fully vaccinated and 39% have not even received a single shot. We will likely fall short of President Joe Biden's goal of administering at least one shot to 70% of all Americans by July 4, and American public health experts and the World Health Organization alike warn that a new strain of the virus, known as the Delta variant, is emerging as a potent threat. The good news is that the vaccines currently being administered are highly effective against it. The bad news is that tens of millions of Americans insist on just saying no to vaccination.

This is incomprehensible to Prime Time Paul Zine. "I understand that people don't want to have things injected in them," says Zine. However, "I don't think people have the right to endanger other people. You need to get vaccinated. I'm a Trump supporter, sure. But there are precautions you've got to take."

Hubris Factor: Progressive Elites Bet the Farm That America Believes What They Believe

June 22, 2021

Earlier this month, comedian Bill Maher delivered a biting commentary on self-styled progressives, mocking "the recurrent theme on the far left that things have never been worse." On privileged university campuses, Maher noted, progressive students "can't see that your dorm in 2021 is better than the South before the Civil War." Among progressive elites, woe unto the brave soul who points out that there are progressive talking points that simply do not withstand serious scrutiny. In such quarters, Maher says, "what you say doesn't have to make sense, or jibe with the facts or ever be challenged."

Maher's point was illustrated by the most recent deluge of thousands of Hamas rockets fired from Gaza at Israeli civilian centers. As always, Hamas attacks on Israel produce the confident, if bizarre, progressive orthodoxy that rocket attacks blanketing Israeli communities are somewhere between no big deal and perfectly fine, whereas Israel's efforts to protect its civilians by stopping them constitute war crimes.

With the 2022 midterm elections already in view, some Democrats willing to risk eternal damnation as Not Sufficiently Progressive worry that slavishly following the party's left may result in losing control of Congress in 2022 and the White House in 2024. It isn't hard to see why. Republicans have the wind at their backs, with historical precedent strongly suggesting that they will pick up seats in both houses of Congress. They need only a small handful of pickups in the House of Representatives to seize control there and a net gain of only a single seat to regain control of the Senate. As for 2024, the bravado about President Joe Biden's 7.1 million popular vote margin obscures this reality: Had only 6,000 Biden voters in Arizona, 6,000 in Georgia and 11,000 in Wisconsin voted instead for former President Donald Trump, the large con man would be five months into his second term.

A recent analysis of the 2020 election by three Democratic groups contained some serious warnings for Democrats. One was that although the Republican line that Democrats were "socialists" and favored eliminating law enforcement may drive Rachel Maddow-watchers berserk, it resonated, including among core Democratic constituencies. "Republican attempts to brand Democrats as 'radicals' worked," the authors concluded. The data firm Catalist calculated that Biden's percentage share of Latino voters decreased by 8% relative to Hillary Clinton's 2016 share, his share of Black voters fell 3% and his share of Asian American and Pacific Islander voters slipped 1%. In many key Congressional districts, Democratic candidates trailed Biden. "Some districts where 'law and order' or 'socialism' was a drumbeat also a saw a higher share of Latino/AAPI/Black voters who supported the GOP," the Democratic groups' report found.

These warnings may be dismissed by some Democrats who delude themselves that Cambridge, Massachusetts, is representative of the country and that the nation is just waiting to embrace the Democratic Socialists of America.

To be sure, the Republican Party is a hot mess, dominated by insurrectionists, charlatans and phonies. The Grand Old Party more closely resembles the Party of Putin than the Party of Lincoln. A new Economist/YouGov poll published on the very day Biden was meeting with Russia's poisoner-in-chief reported that the Russian president, Vladimir Putin, is more popular among Trump voters than the American president. Thirty percent of Republicans believe that it is "likely" that Trump will be reinstated as president within six months, and 70% of them believe the whacked-out hogwash that Trump won the 2020 election. Simply put, the GOP is barking mad, and the left believes that that ought to be enough to keep control of Congress and the presidency.

It should be. It won't be. The traditional reduced voter turnouts in midterm elections and Republican-orchestrated curtailments of voting across the country will complicate Democrats' efforts to hold onto Congress. Over-the-top rhetoric and the disconnected, even haughty assumptions by progressive Democrats that Americans believe what they believe run the risk of leaving them, and Democrats generally, sorely disappointed two Novembers from now.

Pride Time: Biden Puts a Bully Pulpit to Good Use

June 29, 2021

The expression commonly used to capture the unique power of a president to elevate America's character was coined by Theodore Roosevelt, according to historians. Reading aloud a message he had drafted for the American people, he mused to those present, "I suppose my critics will call that preaching, but I have got such a bully pulpit." In TR-speak, the word "bully" was early 20th-century white Anglo-Saxon Protestant for "superb."

In his first five months in office, President Joe Biden has employed his superb pulpit superbly, reminding us of who we are or, at least, who we could be.

Last week, our commander in chief hosted a commemoration of LGBTQ Pride Month at the White House, acknowledging a uniformed transgender lieutenant colonel and telling her in front of the entire country, "Thank you for your service to the nation." He wished a happy birthday to the husband of his Transportation Secretary Pete Buttigieg, the first openly gay Cabinet secretary to win Senate confirmation. Buttigieg put the occasion in crisp perspective. "Not that long ago," he observed, "well within the lifetimes of many people in this room, being 'outed' could be disqualifying from public service — any public service, not just being a Cabinet officer. Yet today here I am. Here you are. Here we are — standing in the East Room in the company of the president of the United States and the first lady, wishing each other happy Pride."

Binding together a country that has come apart and lost its moorings under the stress of four years of mean-spirited juvenile delinquency at the top is a daunting challenge, but one that clearly has the new president's focused attention. A week before the Pride Month event, Biden convened members of the Congressional Black Caucus and 94-year-old Opal Lee, a longtime advocate for a federal holiday recognizing the end of slavery in the United States, for a signing ceremony establishing June 19, or Juneteenth, as both a holiday and a day of national reflection. "Juneteenth marks both the long, hard night of slavery and subjugation and the promise of a greater morning to come," said Biden, who pronounced the holiday one "in which we remember the moral stain, the terrible toll that slavery took on America and continues to take." With that, he made official a day in which America would take note of what Black Americans have been forced to overcome. "I wish all Americans a happy Juneteenth," Biden said, choosing to close his remarks on an uplifting note.

In late May, with the increase in violence against Asian Americans during the pandemic too demonstrable to disregard, Biden took advantage of the presidential platform to spotlight anti-Asian hate crimes, confronting a sick phenomenon that has been stoked by the malign taunting of his predecessor. Once again, he deployed the White House stage, signing the COVID-19 Hate Crimes Act into law. "My message to all of those who are hurting is: We see you, and the Congress has said, we see you. And we are committed to stop the hatred and the bias," he said.

The same week, with a poisonous resurgence of antisemitism on both the right and the left emanating from white supremacists and certain self-professed progressives alike, Biden once again used the bully pulpit to stand up for those being bullied. "I will not allow our fellow Americans to be intimidated or attacked because of who they are or the faith they practice," said the president about the venom being unleashed at American Jews. "We cannot allow the toxic combination of hatred, dangerous lies and conspiracy theories to put our fellow Americans at risk."

"Pride is back at the White House," proclaimed Biden at last week's LGBTQ event. It's true. We once again have a president with values we can respect. It is a fragile pride, an endangered pride and by no means a fully secure one. But after a long drought of optimism, it is something to feel optimistic about.

Tourist Visit: The GOP Keeps on Riding the Hogwash Express

July 6, 2021

The poor soul responsible for selecting the most laughable falsehood to have emanated from Trump World is going to have his work cut out for him. The sheer volume of hooey to the effect that former President Donald Trump won the election that he lost, that the election he lost was stolen from him and that he and his troops were not responsible for the January 6 insurrection at the Capitol makes it difficult to pick a winner in the No-Lie-Is-Too-Brazen Competition.

Surely, however, Rep. Andrew Clyde, R-Ga., is in the running. "Watching the TV footage of those who entered the Capitol and walked through Statuary Hall," Rep. Clyde offered recently, "showed people in an orderly fashion staying between the stanchions and ropes taking videos. If you didn't know that TV footage was a video from January the 6th, you would actually think it was a normal tourist visit."

Congress is no place for idiots, but you wouldn't know it watching most Republicans dodge, duck and dissemble about not only one of the blackest but most humiliating days in American history. The footage that Americans have watched for six months ought to have made clear to all but the mendacious and the witless that, far from resembling a "tourist visit," Jan. 6 resembled a neo-fascist riot aimed at stopping the certification of the presidential election — the election, that is, that occurred on Planet Earth.

Last week's release of a report on the Jan. 6 attack compiled by a New York Times video team makes the stomach turn anew. Based largely on footage from the rioters themselves and supplemented by body camera video from police officers, the report illustrates how horrifying the attack was, and how fragile the democracy we have just spent the weekend celebrating really is.

It begins with a busload of Trump troops traveling to Washington reciting the Pledge of Allegiance, though one wonders to what. "It's so much more than rallying for President Trump," says one. "It's really rallying for our way of life." They were urged to come to Washington on the day mandated by the Constitution for counting presidential electors in order to stop the count from taking place, with the promise of a "wild" time by their leader. "This election was a fraud," lied Trump, who exhorted them to march on the Capitol. Trump consigliere Steve Bannon, saved from a fraud conviction by a presidential pardon, had told them what was expected of them. "All hell is going to break loose tomorrow," he boasted. "Everyone is going to remember who actually stands in the breach and fights tomorrow and who goes running off like a chicken," crowed Trump advisor Jason Miller.

"As soon as Trump is done (speaking), we're storming the Capitol," announced one of the mob leaders on the 6th. "Pass it on." And pass it on they did. The Times video records cries of "Take the Capitol!" and "We will take the building!" as the rioters overwhelmed the Capitol Police and breached Congress in eight separate locations. "You gonna stop us?"

Over several hours, the mob that Trump built Tased, gassed, beat, trampled, dragged and crushed the police that they profess to care about, injuring some 150 officers. The Justice Department has charged 500 of them with crimes, including 100 with assaulting law enforcement officers. FBI Director Christopher Wray estimates that "hundreds" more criminal investigations are underway.

Against this backdrop, the party of patriotism and law enforcement once again opposed letting Americans know what happened on January 6 and why. After blocking a bipartisan commission to investigate the riot, congressional Republicans almost unanimously opposed an investigation by a congressional committee — wait for it — because it would be "partisan."

And there you have the GOP's position. No bipartisan investigation. No congressional investigation. No investigation. Jan. 6 was just a normal tourist visit to the Capitol. That's their story, and they're sticking to it.

Teacher's Story: At 88, Bob Gardiner Answers the Bell One More Time

July 13, 2021

Bob Gardiner hoped for a career in aeronautics until advanced mathematics at Colgate University interfered. "My dreams of being an aeronautical engineer were destroyed by calculus," says the 88-year-old resident of Lenox, Massachusetts, one of the jewel communities in the western part of the state. As a lark he took an English literature class, and the teacher changed his life. "It came to me suddenly that I wanted to do what he was doing," remembers Gardiner.

For almost a half-century Gardiner taught English to high school students at Cheshire Academy, an independent school in Connecticut; teaching and his wife Ruth were his life's pillars. "I came alive as a teacher," Gardiner says. "The only other place I came alive was in my marriage with Ruth."

Gardiner attended a grade school with a total of 25 students in it, housed in a one-room schoolhouse. Eight decades later he remembers the influence of one of his boyhood teachers, Emma Heath. "There was one kid who remained in the second grade for three years," he says, recalling the respect accorded to the boy by Mrs. Heath. Her lesson, one that Gardiner tried to impart to the 3,000 high schoolers he would teach, was: "You are important to yourself. You are important to me. You matter."

After Colgate came the Army ("I was supposed to go to Korea, but I ended up in Puerto Rico") and a master's degree. He was given the choice between teaching and a job that offered him three times a teacher's salary. His father advised him that he should explore teaching. "I bless him for that," says Gardiner.

Teaching high school students for almost 50 years was a labor of love for Gardiner. "It meant paying attention to them," he says of his students. "What were they like? What were they thinking? What were they capable of achieving?"

Gardiner delayed retirement until he was 71. He and Ruth moved full time to the Berkshires, drawn there by the music. "My wife," he says proudly, "was made of music." A trained pianist, "she didn't have the psyche for performing publicly." After school, Gardiner would slip into their house and, without her knowing he was there, listen to her play the piano and sing.

The love between Bob and Ruth was a lifetime love. They met when he was 14 and she was 21. ("If we go there," Gardiner warns, noticing his interviewer's arched eyebrows, "you're going to need a lot more paper."). In 2005, a year after Bob retired, Ruth was diagnosed with dementia, and Bob became her caregiver until she died in 2011. After they received the brutal diagnosis in a Boston hospital, they sat in their car before starting their long ride home. "You can get good care in a nursing home," he told Ruth. "But the only place you can get love is at home. So you're going to stay home."

This past May, ten years after Ruth's death, a member of Bob's church sidled up to him. He was working on the production of a film called "Skelly," with a cast of kids aged 12 to 17. The Screen Actors Guild required that a teacher supervise their studies while they were not filming. Was he interested? "I didn't ask any questions, I just said 'yes'," Gardiner says.

For three weeks this spring Gardiner was in a kind of heaven, even though heaven meant spending up to 10 hours a day overseeing high schoolers' studies. "These were teenagers," says Gardiner, relishing the memory even while nursing himself back from exhaustion. "They were full of energy."

When he arrived for his last day of "classes," the students and their parents gave Gardiner a standing ovation. "My gratitude is unbounded," he told them.

He will remember that ovation forever. "It was an acknowledgement of the importance of 'relationship'," he says. "And that's at the heart of a good relationship. It's also at the heart of a good life."

Public Enemies: The 'COVID's a Hoax; Vaccinations Are a Plot' Crowd Is Enough to Make You Sick

July 20, 2021

As the coronavirus that has thus far killed over 608,000 Americans spread across the country in March 2020, the president of the United States felt quite comfortable lying to his countrymen about it. "We're prepared, and we're doing a great job with it," he told reporters on March 10, 2020, "and it will go away." COVID-19, he informed us, was a nothingburger.

As is his predilection, former President Donald Trump's straight-faced pronouncement was part flimflam, part drivel. His loyalists worshipped the flimflam and savored the drivel. Thirty-four million Americans have since been infected with the virus, and the nation struggles to recover from a devastating recession, nationwide business shutdowns and unemployment that neared Great Depression levels, all caused by the disease.

Though Trump is no longer positioned to administer a wrecking ball to this fragile country, legions of his followers continue to wage guerrilla warfare against it. They do so by denigrating vaccination, spreading falsehoods about the vaccine and blocking the circulation of information that conclusively demonstrates that vaccination is the way to protect their families, their friends, their country — and themselves — from illness.

And they are succeeding. Despite the vaccine's widespread availability and the clear proof that it virtually eliminates the risk of becoming seriously ill with COVID-19, 50% of eligible Americans are still not fully vaccinated. These include millions of Americans who are brainwashed by internet garbage peddled by the far right. A new survey conducted for The Economist found that 1 of 5 Americans believes that COVID-19 vaccines are being used by the government to "microchip the population." That translates to over 40 million Americans. Publications with titles like "COVID-19 vaccines are weapons of mass destruction" flood the right-wing zones, and Fox personalities like Laura Ingraham pass up few opportunities to mock this COVID-19 thing as just one big left-wing contrivance, not to be taken seriously. "They just can't let the pandemic go," smirked Ingraham about coverage of the recent surge in cases. "At some point, they're going to have to break the addiction."

At a recent Conservative Political Action Committee conference in Dallas, the crowd cheered when a speaker celebrated the fact that the Biden administration had not met its goal of getting 70% of American adults at least one shot by July 4. In Florida, which now accounts for 20% of the nation's new COVID-19 cases, Republican governor and presidential candidate-in-waiting Ron DeSantis hopes to capitalize on the unhinged vitriol that prevails among Republicans about Dr. Anthony Fauci, the director of the National Institute of Allergies and Infectious Diseases, who for months urged Americans to wear masks and socially distance. These were measures that every reputable public health expert believed then and now were critical to saving lives. Not DeSantis, whose state has seen over 2.3 million people infected with the disease. His political action committee is selling T-shirts and beer koozies reading "Don't Fauci my Florida."

In Tennessee, one of 35 states that just saw the rate of new cases increase 50% over previous weeks, the state's top immunization official was fired for distributing a memorandum accurately pointing out that under Tennessee law, minors deemed "mature" by health care providers could be eligible for the vaccine without parental consent. Republican officials announced that they were halting the distribution of information about the vaccine to teenagers. This despite the warnings of public health experts of the kind that the right has ridiculed for the last 18 months. "We're losing time here," said Dr. Francis Collins, director of the National Institutes of Health. "The delta variant is spreading; people are dying; we can't actually just wait for things to get more rational."

You don't have to be Madame Curie to discern that getting vaccinated means avoiding serious illness. Over 99% of those now hospitalized with COVID-19 are unvaccinated. "This is not just a matter of people expressing opinions that might be wrong," says Collins. "This is life or death." Put another way, unlike some people, the data does not lie.

Small-Town Hero: Remembering John Glenn's Right Stuff

July 27, 2021

On July 4, 1997, Sen. John Glenn hosted a lunch for his staff in his hideaway office underneath the Capitol dome. Born in New Concord, Ohio, population 1,800, the plumber's son turned war hero turned astronaut Glenn felt America's birthday in his bones, and he was in good spirits.

At the time, Glenn was the ranking Democrat on a Republican-controlled Senate committee investigating former President Bill Clinton's administration for alleged fundraising improprieties during Clinton's 1996 reelection campaign. The Democrats had engaged in the same routine, legal but sometimes malodorous practices in which both parties have historically engaged, dangling access to top officials in order to stroke large donors. The Republicans, barely recovered from the shock of seeing Clinton defeat former President George H.W. Bush in 1992, fairly levitated with rage at Clinton's easy defeat of Bob Dole the previous November. They professed to be shocked — shocked! — that the Democrats had solicited campaign contributions in the exact same way Republicans had. And they saw an opportunity to blacken former Vice President Al Gore and undermine his prospects for succeeding Clinton in 2000. The political charges and countercharges were not only predictable but old as the hills.

It was, in short, nothing more than politics, and Glenn, though given a central role in the investigation as the senior Democrat on the committee, was barely able to mask his disinterest. Almost 76, the first American to orbit the earth was far more interested in lobbying NASA to permit him to return to space, arguing that this would enable scientists to better study the effects of aging. Glenn had to pass a rigorous, highly invasive series of physical examinations, ones which, to put it delicately, involved no shortage of tubes and other unpleasant objects being run through parts of the body that God did not create in order to have tubes and other unpleasant objects run through them.

"How long will you be up there if NASA lets you do it?" one of Glenn's committee lawyers asked him.

"Seven to 10 days," Glenn replied.

"So, you have to spend weeks having tubes run through you in order to win the right to have tubes run through you for seven to 10 days in space?" asked the uncomprehending lawyer, suddenly without any appetite.

"Pretty much," said Glenn.

"Haven't you heard of Club Med?" his lawyer asked.

"For me," Glenn replied, "this would be Club Med."

Glenn was made of different stuff. He quit college to enlist after the United States entered World War II, flew 149 combat missions for his country in that conflict and then in Korea, winning a crateful of military honors. After the Soviet Union leapt ahead of America in the space race, Glenn gave his countrymen a badly needed lift in 1962 when he orbited the planet. His 1984 presidential campaign fell flat in part because of his down-to-earth personality. "If you were driving through New Concord, Ohio, and you needed directions," remembers Jonathan Dorfman, who ran Glenn's New York state campaign, "he was the guy who would get in his car and say, 'Hey, follow me.'"

Glenn ultimately got his wish to serve his country yet one more time. On October 29, 1998, the 77-year-old returned to space as a payload specialist on space shuttle Discovery.

John Glenn would have turned 100 this month, a month that saw billionaires Richard Branson and Jeff Bezos flaunt their galactic wealth and double-galactic egos to travel to the edge of space. Their trips, which earned them the media attention they crave, marked a new frontier in self-promotion. This was quite a contrast with Glenn, the small-town boy who took self-effacing national service to new heights.

"Glenn lived the life that Ronald Reagan played in the movies," observes Dorfman. As the country searches its soul and wrestles with the meaning of patriotism, we could do worse than to reflect a bit on American patriot John Glenn on his 100th birthday.

Sweet and Spineless: Ben and Jerry's Caves to the Anti-Israel Mob

August 3, 2021

The announcement that Vermont ice cream maker Ben & Jerry's was terminating its relationship with its longtime Israeli distributor because it sold ice cream on the West Bank may have been nutty, but it was a sign of the times. It was also a feather in the cap of Vermonters for Justice in Palestine, which makes no secret of its desire to eliminate Israel altogether, and which boasts — understandably — that it required only 614 anti-Israel emails to Ben & Jerry's CEO in order to get the two old lefties to cave.

The rejoicing, however, was short-lived. First, Ben & Jerry's parent Unilever rejected its subsidiary's demand that it stop doing business with Israel altogether. Unilever's announcement that it was "fully committed to our presence in Israel, where we have invested in our people, brands and business for several decades" was greeted with outrage by Ben & Jerry's board chair, Anuradha Mittal, who accused it of "deceit" for not agreeing to boycott the Jewish state. It then emerged that Mittal, who publicly opposed a congressional resolution condemning antisemitism ("I am not antisemitic," she insists), is the founder of an institute that has repeatedly defended Hezbollah and Hamas.

Nor did it take long for the odor of hypocrisy to attach itself to both Unilever and Ben & Jerry's, an odor that routinely shrouds the Israel boycotters and that opens them up to charges of bias, which — let's face it — are not without basis. Unilever is pleased to do business with Russia, China, Iran, Syria, Yemen and Saudi Arabia, the world's most notorious human rights violators. Do Ben and Jerry criticize their parent company, let alone disassociate themselves from it in any way? You bet your chocolate mocha chip they don't.

As for Ben, Jerry and their team, they opened a store in Malaysia in 2019, the very year our State Department issued a report finding that the Malaysian government was guilty of arbitrary detention and extrajudicial killings; restrictions of free expression; rampant interference with freedom of assembly, association and religion; and the criminalization of homosexuality. This did not trouble Ben & Jerry's one lick; it proudly announced on social media that "Malaysia's Top Ben & Jerry's Flavors of 2019" were Strawberry Cheesecake, Half Baked and Sweet Cream and Cookies.

Meanwhile, the efforts by those who hope these boycotts will make Israel disappear continue to fail. Israel's Arab neighbors are normalizing relations with Israel at a pace that no doubt frustrates the boycotters. Bahrain, Morocco, Sudan and the United Arab Emirates have joined Egypt and Jordan in establishing formal relationships with Israel. Much of the rest of the Arab world engages in economic, diplomatic and security cooperation with Israel off the radar screen.

The mob may be losing, but it is not for lack of intellectual dishonesty. The little matter of how Israel came to occupy the West Bank in the first place — through defending itself against a Jordanian attack that was part of a multienemy effort to annihilate it — matters, of course, not at all. Ditto the fact that Israel offered virtually all of the West Bank, all of Gaza and part of East Jerusalem in return for peace: This was rejected by Palestinian leaders, who much preferred the status quo to a two-state solution.

As for the thousands of Hamas rockets fired from Gaza at Israeli civilians over and over, effectively consigning Israelis and Palestinians alike to fear, injury and death, this has not made a single scoop of difference to those who would be hard-pressed to specify the difference between the Gaza Strip and the Louisiana Purchase.

The more those who claim to care about peace give those who reject it a pass, the more remote the prospects for peace become. This is obvious, but evidently not obvious enough. It requires spine to stand up to mindless fashion rather than simply cave in to it. Ben and Jerry are sweet fellows. Courageous they are not.

Pandemic Perpetuators: The Enablers of the Coronavirus's Spread Keep On Enabling

August 10, 2021

In her new book, "The Enablers: How Team Trump Flunked the Pandemic and Failed America," Barbara Kellerman examines the role former President Donald Trump's political and media acolytes played in enabling what may be the most disastrous presidential performance in American history. "By every objective measure," observes Kellerman, who has written widely on leadership, "during the first half of 2020 and beyond under the leadership of President Trump, the federal government's management of the pandemic was woefully, humiliatingly bad."

It is true that the rot spread from the fish's head, as it so often does. Apart from the historic mendacity that Trump displayed virtually hourly as the pandemic quickly mushroomed, infecting and killing first thousands, then tens of thousands and finally hundreds of thousands of Americans, the President's performance as the crisis took root and deepened was part Herbert Hoover, part Bozo the Clown.

But Kellerman focuses on the role that Trump's ever-loyal allies played in downplaying the pandemic, mocking the public health experts who called for measures to curtail its spread and belittling those measures. "No matter what Trump did or said as it pertained to the new coronavirus," Kellerman writes, "no matter how mistaken, misguided or misleading his leadership, no matter how bad the pandemic during the first half of 2020, they continued to give him their undiminished, unconditional support."

With the average number of new COVID-19 cases in the United States surging to 100,000 a day, Kellerman reminds us how we got here in the first place and of the role that a class of dolts and charlatans played in perpetuating the disease. Almost half of eligible Americans are still not fully vaccinated, despite the rock-solid evidence that the vaccine is extraordinarily effective against the disease and that it is almost only the unvaccinated who require hospitalization, and who die. Many millions of these unvaccinated Americans are instructed by political phonies and media crackpots that they should regard the call to be vaccinated as an affront to their Americanism. But it is the opposite that is true. Those who buy their hooey are jeopardizing their own lives and those of their family and community. And they are very badly weakening their country.

The ridicule visited by some on the Biden administration's exhortations to get vaccinated is precisely the same sort of ridicule that flowed from Trump groupies from the start, and that kept right on flowing as over 600,000 Americans died. The production and wearing of masks, the imposition of social distancing, the prevention of truly dumb virus-spreading events — all of the saving of lives that this facilitated was impeded, and even thwarted, by the sorts of geniuses who now mock the administration's efforts to protect public health and speed the nation's recovery.

"The coronavirus is the common cold, folks," intoned the late Rush Limbaugh knowledgeably. "The short-term crisis may have passed," opined Fox News superstar Tucker Carlson, who offered the similarly brilliant opinion that Dr. Anthony Fauci, the public health expert widely respected by the compos mentis on both sides of the aisle, was "the chief buffoon of the professional class." Carlson will not be inducted into the Credibility Hall of Fame anytime soon. "The virus," he informed us in April 2020, about a half million American deaths ago, "just isn't nearly as deadly as we thought it was." Fox colleague Sean Hannity was equally on target. Warnings about the coronavirus, he smirked, were nothing more than "mass hysteria" peddled by "panic pushers."

Meanwhile, the tragic idiocy rages on along with the resurgent virus. In Florida, where hospitalizations have soared above the state's previous high and where the Florida Hospital Association expects 60% of the state's hospitals to face a "critical staffing shortage" this week, governor and Trump wannabe Ron DeSantis promotes himself as a champion of individual rights as he blocks vaccination mandates that would save Floridians' lives.

The former president is no longer in power. The perpetuation of the pandemic by the enablers, however, continues.

First Under Fire: Freedom of Speech Gets Squeezed From Both Sides

August 17, 2021

"When I was a kid, I was shy," Ira Glasser, the longtime head of the American Civil Liberties Union, told a Canton, Massachusetts, audience last week. It seemed hard to believe. A nonlawyer and proud of it, Glasser led the ACLU from 1978 until 2001 and is credited by the organization for having transformed it "from a mom-and-pop style operation concentrated mainly in a few large cities to a nationwide civil liberties powerhouse."

"The first time I had to speak in public," Glasser said, "was teaching kids calculus. It taught me how to explain complicated subjects to people who were really not interested. All of that ended up being good training for talking to people about the Bill of Rights."

The right to free speech is perhaps the best known of the First Amendment rights; it is also perhaps the most controversial. Disrespected in some quarters, distorted in others, the right to speak freely occupied much of Glasser's career as he fought contentious battles to ensure that it is both preserved and protected from hijacking by those wishing to undermine democracy.

On university campuses, where once administrators wielded their power to block speech about civil rights or ending the war in Vietnam, now self-styled "progressive" students wield theirs to attempt to block speech that they believe deviates from what they have decreed is politically acceptable. First Amendment legend Floyd Abrams has said that the greatest threat to American free speech comes presently not from government but from within academia, principally from "a minority of students who strenuously and, I think it is fair to say, contemptuously disapprove of the views of speakers whose view of the world is different from theirs, and who seek to prevent those views from being heard."

Glasser, as indefatigable a fighter for social justice as any other American over the last half-century, is similarly concerned. "I was surprised," he wrote last year about a law school appearance, "to learn that many in the audience self-identified as 'progressives' and believed that it was both desirable and constitutional to ban what they called 'hate speech'."

Over in Trumpland, the former president has invoked the First Amendment as a defense against lawsuits seeking to hold him liable for his role in the Jan. 6 attack on the U.S. Capitol that left 140 Capitol Police injured and resulted in several deaths. One of the pending claims is that he conspired with others to use force, intimidation and/or threats to prevent federal officials — Congress — from carrying out their duties: certifying the 2020 presidential election. This claim would appear to be not only straightforward, but obvious: The express, and expressed, point of the defendants' fiery exhortations was to drive the mob down to the Capitol for that very purpose.

Trump and his defense team argue, however, that holding them liable would penalize the exercise of First Amendment rights. This concern for the right of free speech is very rich indeed coming from a former president who fired every federal official he could for speaking out about misconduct in his administration, but hypocrisy ranks so low on the list of Trump's affronts that it hardly seems worthy of mention.

Those who directed the mob to attack Congress have a problem much bigger than hypocrisy. The Supreme Court ruled decades ago that there is no First Amendment protection for speech that is "directed to inciting or promoting lawless action and is highly likely to incite or produce such action." Not for the first time, the shy math student who wasn't a born public speaker puts it best. "Just because you use words when you're doing something violent doesn't give you the protection of the First Amendment," says Glasser.

The First Amendment may be caught in a crossfire, but if we have more than a fighting chance of keeping it robust, it is in no small part thanks to American heroes like Ira Glasser, who pushed and prodded and pressed so that it would neither be eroded nor taken for granted.

Snark Attack: The Afghanistan Blame Game Obscures an Urgent Need to Restore American Credibility

August 24, 2021

In the spring of 1999, when the government of Serbian President Slobodan Milosevic had killed tens of thousands of citizens of the former Yugoslavia and forcibly expelled hundreds of thousands more, the Western European democracies turned to America to order NATO to use its armed forces, principally those of the United States, to stop him. This might have been regarded as "Europe's problem," occurring on European soil. With the United Nations even more neutered than usual and their own governments either incapable of acting or politically unwilling to do so, Europe asked President Bill Clinton to put an end to what Clinton rightfully called "deliberate, systematic efforts at ethnic cleansing and genocide."

Our allies were unenthusiastic about alienating the protesters who lined the streets of European capitals to protest what the left called American "aggression." Since it was the Americans who were intervening to halt a humanitarian disaster, the intervention was inherently suspect. One comfortable academic at a Geneva cocktail party that spring had our motivations all figured out. "This is about expanding American markets," she sniffed, leaving her interlocutor puzzled about the extent of American exports to Kosovo.

The grim, humiliating footage of America's withdrawal from Afghanistan has triggered the familiar melange of superciliousness and schadenfreude overseas. America is blamed for what it does, blamed for what it does not do.

It is blamed for what it cannot do, even though no one else can do it either. It is blamed for intervening and for not intervening. It is blamed for invading, and it is blamed for withdrawing.

The collapse of Afghanistan is a political boon for Republicans, who get to claim that the scenes on the ground have undermined America's ability to project strength. They are right: They do.

But to say that Republicans are ill-positioned to point blame for the erosion of American credibility is the understatement of the millennium. It was their own Dear Leader who left no cringeworthy proclamation behind in sucking up unsuccessfully to North Korean dictator Kim Jong Un. "He wrote me beautiful letters, and they're great letters," swooned former President Donald Trump about his Kiss the Posterior campaign to woo the butcher of Pyongyang. "We fell in love."

It was Trump who gave Saudi Arabia a pass for the murder of Washington Post journalist Jamal Khashoggi. It was Trump who, at the bidding of Turkish strongman Recep Tayyip Erdogan, sold out our Kurdish allies, who fought the Islamic State group so courageously. It was Trump who so debased our country by coddling Russian autocrat Vladimir Putin despite the latter's declaration of war against our democracy.

And it was Trump who, as conservative Republican Rep. Liz Cheney put it, negotiated a "surrender agreement" with the Taliban, bringing about the release of 5,000 Taliban prisoners and otherwise acceding to the terrorist group's con job.

But President Joe Biden's declaration that "America is back" seems open to ridicule. This is so even if the fundamentals of his decision to withdraw from Afghanistan have been confirmed by the rapid disintegration of the Afghan government, which was unworthy of further investment after over a trillion dollars' worth of American support. There is no sugarcoating it: Asking the Taliban if it would pretty-please permit Americans to get to the airport so they could escape is miserable in substance and miserable optically. The images of Afghans who risked their lives placing their trust in the United States, only to have to plead not to be abandoned, are likewise miserable, all but gutting the new administration's efforts to revive American credibility after a four-year clown show. And we are in for more, including the mass brutalization of Afghan women and the likely resurgence of the Islamic State group, al-Qaida or some witches' brew of jihadi spinoffs.

The finger-pointing is predictable and useless. The importance to our national security of an America that projects strength, credibility and, yes, power, is real. It's time for the adults remaining in the room to focus on putting those pieces back together, and quickly.

Duet: Boston's Catholic and Jewish Communities Reunite to Welcome Afghan Refugees

August 31, 2021

"The work that we're going to do now is the work that we've always done," says Marjean Perhot, Catholic Charities Boston's Director of Refugee and Immigration Services, about preparations to welcome Greater Boston's share of Afghan refugees en route to their new homes in America. "Pretty much whenever there's been a refugee crisis, Catholic Charities has been there."

It's no lie. Over the last 40 years alone, the organization's refugee relief arm has helped provide housing, food, legal representation and more to refugees from the world's war-torn regions — Vietnam, the Balkans and Africa among them — doing so, as it says, with "compassion, understanding, and positive reassurance."

They are ready again as tens of thousands of Afghans fleeing their homeland's bloodshed make their way in this direction, just as tens of millions like them have over the course of American history. "These are people who have been persecuted in their countries, and they need homes, their kids need to get into schools, they need to find work," Bill Canny, Executive Director of Migration and Refugee Services of the U.S. Conference of Catholic Bishops, told Catholic News Service. "We're grateful for the opportunity to help. We don't consider 'we're saving these people,' who are in effect saving us by giving us the opportunity to help. This is what our Church does, and it's founded in the Gospel."

In Boston, an old partnership of faith-based communities is reuniting to harness shared values to welcome these refugees. In 2017, with refugees and immigrants under siege, Barry Shrage, then the head of Combined Jewish Philanthropies, contacted long-time friend the Rev. Bryan Hehir of the Archdiocese of Boston. The result was a joint program to fund free legal assistance for those recently upon our shores. It was the latest chapter in a beautiful friendship, and it was a successful one. "We had no idea if we would raise ten dollars," remembers Sarah Abramson, CJP's Senior Vice President for Strategy and Impact. But within three weeks $640,000 was donated, and the fund would go on to attract thousands of donors.

"We know how aligned we are with Catholic Charities on these issues," says Abramson. As in the Catholic Church, helping "the other" is at the core of Jewish identity. For Jews, she says, it is grounded in "the historical trauma of knowing what it feels like when people have not opened their doors to us." The Jewish commitment to those in danger, to those fleeing, to those who are excluded or forgotten, says Abramson, "is rooted in Jewish values."

Unsurprisingly, Catholic Charities and CJP were of the same mind as the prospect of a flood of Afghan refugees took shape. "Our feeling was 'What can we do together again?'" Perhot says.

The result was the formation of the Fund for Afghan Immigrants and Refugees, or FAIR, a fund established to help Catholic Charities and the Jewish Vocational Services resettle refugees safely, quickly and with the two faith communities' trademark warmheartedness. "I could not think of a better partner to work with," says Abramson of Catholic Charities.

The two organizations are blessed with a broader community that is predisposed to welcoming newcomers. Perhot points out that Boston's universities and medical institutions have long been a magnet for other parts of the world. "People have gravitated to Boston for a long time," she says.

From top to bottom, despite the finger-pointing and the heartache over American losses, the best of America has generally been on display when it comes to these refugees. "We will welcome these Afghans," President Joe Biden said the other day. "Because that's what America is."

Boston's faith communities are already there. "This feels like a moment to ensure that we are opening the doors," Abramson says. "This is the spirit of America," says Perhot, her professional twin. "We all come together."

The dispiriting end of our long involvement in Afghanistan has plenty of dark clouds associated with it. Boston's interfaith partnership to support the war's refugees, however, is a bona fide silver lining.

Backfire: Parole for Sirhan Would Be the Wrong Message at the Wrong Time

September 7, 2021

Last week's recommendation by two California parole officials that the man who murdered Robert F. Kennedy should be released from prison was quirky, even by California standards. Over the decades, 15 separate parole boards have considered Sirhan Sirhan's claim that "justice" required that he be set free. Each rejected it, most recently in 2016. Though there is no public record of last week's hearing, which produced a sharp reversal on the supposed basis that something unspecified had changed, reports of disjointed ruminations by the two officials did not inspire confidence in their recommendation.

There was plenty of reason for head-scratching. The man who staked out Los Angeles' Ambassador Hotel to find the ideal vantage spot from which to put a bullet in Kennedy's brain knew exactly what he should say to the parole officials. He told them that he had been attending tai chi, Alcoholics Anonymous and — wait for it — anger management classes. The parole officials pronounced themselves impressed.

And not only that, Sirhan gave them his word that he had changed. "You have my pledge," he assured them. "I will always look to safety and peace and non-violence."

Now in his late 70s, it is reasonable to conclude that, for purely statistical reasons, Sirhan is unlikely to murder anyone else. But that doesn't end the analysis any more than do broad statements about the virtue of forgiveness.

In June 1968, with the one-year anniversary of the Six Day War triggered by the imminent invasion of Israel by neighbors pledged to her destruction just days away, the Palestinian-born Jordanian citizen decided to assassinate Kennedy to make a political statement. "Robert F. Kennedy must be assassinated before June 5, 1968," Sirhan wrote in his journal. "My determination to eliminate RFK is becoming more and more of an unshakable obsession." After first practicing the murder at a firing range, he shot Kennedy and five other innocent people in the hotel kitchen, and it took a group of men standing next to Kennedy to pry the murder weapon from Sirhan as Kennedy lay on the floor holding a rosary placed in his hands by a busser, blood seeping out of his head. Asked during his trial whether he had killed Kennedy, Sirhan said "Yes." Asked later why, Sirhan knew precisely. "I can explain it," he said. "I did it for my country."

Over the years, however, the supposedly profoundly remorseful Sirhan, whom we are told takes "responsibility" for the murder, has hedged, dodged and weaved with the best of them, arousing no skepticism at all on the part of the two parole officials. In 2016, asked by an official to state what he had done, here was Sirhan's acceptance of responsibility: "I was there, and I supposedly shot a gun," he said.

"I am asking you to tell me what you're responsible for," pressed the official.

"It's a good question," said Mr. Remorse. "Legally speaking, I'm not guilty of anything."

Sirhan's evasive formulations fall somewhat short of convincing acceptance of moral responsibility for murder, and for the pain inflicted on Kennedy's family and the American people. His latest: he regrets that the killing occurred, "if I did in fact do that."

It is one thing to forgive, and another to be jobbed. While it's true that any murder is an atrocity, this one was particularly atrocious. And at a time when America's historical revulsion at political violence has eroded and the dangers of that erosion are real, the cavalier release of the killer who decided to eliminate a leader with whom he disagreed seems sloppy and ill-advised. "Let there be no mistake," wrote Joseph P. Kennedy II, Robert Kennedy's eldest son. "(Sirhan's) release will be celebrated by those who believe that political disagreements can be solved by a gun."

The recommendation to set Sirhan free is worse than careless. It is exactly the wrong message to send to America at exactly the wrong time.

Foul Spirit: George W. Bush Mourns 9/11 and Warns of Our Jihadis Within

September 14, 2021

The president whose fate it was to summon the best of America after al-Qaida's murderous attack on us 20 years ago delivered a powerful warning on Saturday about the menace posed by the worst of America. "We have seen growing evidence," former President George W. Bush noted at the Shanksville, Pennsylvania, memorial to the heroes of United Flight 93, "that the dangers to our country can come not only across borders, but from violence that gathers within. There is little cultural overlap between violent extremists abroad and violent extremists at home, but in their disdain for pluralism, in their disregard for human life, in their determination to befoul national symbols, they are children of the same foul spirit, and it is our continuing duty to confront them."

The marking of the 20th anniversary of 9/11 was a painful, apt moment seized by Bush to speak pointedly about the peril in which some of our own countrymen have placed our country, a peril every bit as real as that which we face from enemies overseas. His remarks were especially resonant coming from a Republican president, the son of another Republican president, addressing the poisoned and the poisonous within the Republican Party, who threaten our future in ways as worrisome as Middle Eastern jihadis.

Indeed, many of them are themselves jihadis of a fashion: insurrectionists, white supremacists, ultra-right-wing fanatics and just plain nut cases. A tiny fraction of their number stormed the Capitol on Jan. 6 bent on overthrowing a democratic election and keeping an American Mussolini in power. But hundreds of criminals do not represent the breadth or the depth of the problem: These individuals are supported or embraced by millions of our fellow citizens.

The leaders of both political parties readily agreed that the catastrophe of Sept. 11, 2001, required a bipartisan investigation into the circumstances surrounding the attack. Supported by Bush, Congress established the 9/11 Commission to answer these questions: Who organized the attacks and who carried them out? What security failures and what intelligence-gathering inadequacies contributed to the success of these attacks? What had to be done to guard against future attacks? The importance of ascertaining the facts was a no-brainer.

Either America has changed a great deal in the 20 years since both parties sought answers to questions about an assault on our homeland, or a massive rock has been lifted, revealing a whole lot of ugly underneath. It turns out that it isn't merely a fringe that is prepared to indulge a homegrown neo-fascist mob, but a substantial slice of the country. The rise of the same kind of domestic extremism that we have watched consume other countries threatens to consume ours. So it is that a bipartisan investigation into the Jan. 6 assault on the Capitol, every bit as much of a no-brainer as the 9/11 Commission, was blocked by an overwhelming majority of Congressional Republicans, who had themselves supported nullifying the election in order to keep then-President Donald Trump in office.

Just hours before we commemorated 9/11, the information requested by the House Committee appointed by Speaker Nancy Pelosi to investigate Jan. 6 began to arrive on Capitol Hill. The Committee seeks evidence from government agencies, certain individuals in Trump's inner orbit and social media companies in order to shed light on how the attack came about, who instigated it, who facilitated it and who failed to stop it. A political party that truly cared about American values would want the answers. The Republican Party, however, isn't and doesn't. House Minority Leader Kevin McCarthy's threat to retaliate against those who provide the information sought by the Committee is a sober reminder that the GOP is more nearly the party of Don Corleone than of Lincoln.

Bush's speech in Shanksville will no doubt stoke the hatred of the American jihadis that he warned us about. But honoring the heroism of those who did America proud on Sept. 11 was just the moment to remind us that we face not only grave external threats, but also grave domestic ones.

Reckless Disregard: Senate Hearings Showcase the FBI's Doltish Indifference to Predatory Molestation of Gymnasts

September 21, 2021

Last week's Senate Judiciary Committee hearings into the sexual molestation of dozens of young female gymnasts combined the unfamiliar appearance of congressional bipartisanship with the sobering story of an FBI whose gross indifference to a physician's rampant abuse of his patients fully warranted Committee Chair Dick Durbin's verdict. The shoddiness, the insensitivity, the disinterest and the bureaucratic buffoonery displayed by the world's preeminent law enforcement agency in the face of evidence that Dr. Larry Nassar had subjected minor athletes to sexual assault was, Durbin said, "a stain on the Bureau."

The case of Nassar and his large-scale sexual abuse of young gymnasts under his professional care became national news in 2016. Nassar, an employee of Michigan State University, was also USA Gymnastics' National Medical Coordinator and responsible for treating young athletes. In July 2015, the president of USA Gymnastics, located in Indianapolis, brought the results of an internal investigation documenting Nassar's serial sexual abuse of children to the FBI's Indianapolis field office.

What happened then is detailed by the inspector general of the Justice Department, who this summer issued a withering report. The FBI waited six weeks before conducting a single telephonic interview of one of the athletes and failed to document either its meeting with USA Gymnastics or its interview with the victim. On the basis of this poor excuse for an investigation, it concluded that there was no basis for federal prosecution and declined to notify any state or local authority that would clearly have jurisdiction to prosecute or to take any steps to protect the gymnasts entrusted to Nassar's purported care. Because Nassar treated the gymnasts at Michigan State, the Indianapolis United States Attorney's office advised the FBI to transfer the matter to its Lansing, Michigan, field office. The FBI told USA Gymnastics that it was doing so — and then didn't.

After eight months in which nothing happened, USA Gymnastics contacted the FBI's Los Angeles office. That office inquired with its

Indianapolis counterpart — which falsely represented that they had transferred the matter to Lansing. The Los Angeles office thereupon opened an investigation, but like Indianapolis did nothing to move against Nassar, or notify any state or local law enforcement agencies that they could do so, or do anything at all to protect Nassar's victims, many of whom were being subjected to ongoing victimization while the FBI dithered.

It wasn't until September 2016 that anyone acted to stop Nassar from abusing children, no thanks to the FBI. A separate complaint was filed with the relatively lowly Michigan State University Police Department, then dozens. It was the MSUPD that executed a search warrant at Nassar's residence, leading finally to his arrest. In between the time that the FBI was provided with detailed and wholly accurate evidence of Nassar's crimes in July 2015 and his arrest in September 2016, an estimated 70 young women were subjected to life-scarring abuse at his hands.

The inspector general found not only gross negligence on the FBI's part in handling — or mishandling — the Nassar case, but corruption as well. It is not a pretty picture: falsification of official documents, lying aplenty and a particularly tawdry account of the head of the Indianapolis FBI office meeting with the head of USA Gymnastics about a potential job, discussing the latter's concerns about the public image of USA Gymnastics while burying the case.

At last week's Senate hearing, gymnast McKayla Maroney described the lone telephonic interview conducted by the FBI, in which she recounted "all of my molestations in extreme detail." She went on: "I cried and there was just silence on the part of the agent." It would be over a year before anyone did anything about that molestation or the molestations of so many others.

Among the obvious questions left by the inspector general's report and the Senate hearings is this one: If this was the response of the FBI to evidence of sexual abuse, what do we suppose is the response of state and local law enforcement when victims come forward?

It's the Bullying, Stupid: The Anti-Israel Lobby Targets Jewish Kids on Campus

September 28, 2021

With a new academic year underway, Jewish college students across America are in receipt of yet more empirical evidence that the anxiety they are experiencing is not a figment of their imaginations. A poll released last week by the Louis D. Brandeis Center for Human Rights Under Law found that more than 65% of Jewish college kids have felt unsafe on campus because of verbal, social media or physical attacks. Approximately 50% find it necessary to hide their Jewish identity. Almost 70% either personally experienced some form of anti-Jewish assault in the recent past or were familiar with one.

These findings, said Kenneth Marcus, the former assistant secretary of education for civil rights who chairs the Center, "reveal that students for whom being Jewish is a central or important aspect of their identity are feeling increasingly unsafe visibly expressing their Judaism for fear of harassment, social bullying and other anti-Semitic attacks." This, says Marcus, "is driving more and more students to hide their support for Israel."

This is exactly what is intended by those leading the harassment campaign, who hope that by making pro-Israel kids afraid they will make them silent. Some who wouldn't be caught dead declaring war on non-Jews' civil rights do so enthusiastically when it comes to kids who identify as Jewish and who care about the Jewish state. Bari Weiss summarized the current vogue perfectly. "Bullying in theory is wrong," she wrote of the fashion on the left. "The bullying of the right people is not just okay. It is a virtue."

In the Middle East, the normalizing of relations between Israel and her Arab neighbors has accelerated with last year's Abraham Accords. The exchange of diplomatic credentials and news of increased trade between Israel and Arab countries seems like a weekly affair. A new and historically diverse Israeli government is taking pains to revive the outreach to Palestinians characteristic of the pre-Netanyahu era. But on American college campuses, the efforts by the anti-Israel lobby to overwhelm Jewish students with cries of "Nazi" and "apartheid" and "white privilege" are not only persisting but intensifying. The boycott, divestment and sanctions, or BDS, movement, whose purpose is to render Israel and the Jews who care about her pariahs, is the vehicle, and it features untethered rhetoric which more than makes up in intimidation what it frequently lacks in intellectual honesty.

The Brandeis Center's new poll arrived the same week as a flare-up in Congress over funding for Iron Dome, the purely defensive antimissile system on which Israel relies to try to intercept the thousands of Hamas rockets targeting Israeli civilians that the Gaza-based terrorist group launches every few years. In May, Hamas fired about 4,500 of them, which depleted the Israeli capacity to fend them off. Mensa-level genius is not required to discern that Iron Dome saves Jewish, Christian and Muslim lives in Israel; without it, Israel would be defenseless, and that is how a tiny handful in Congress, half consisting of the group of congresswomen known as "The Squad", would like to have it. The system also saves the lives of Gazans; if Israelis have to conduct air strikes against Hamas rocketeers to stop them, innocent Palestinians will get hurt or killed, and that is how Hamas, for its part, would like to have it.

The anti-Israel crowd flopped badly in opposing funding for Iron Dome, mustering only nine votes in Congress in opposition, with 420 votes in favor. This followed what was for them a discouraging summer, in which the cities of Cambridge, Massachusetts, and Burlington, Vermont, rejected BDS measures. If Cambridge and Burlington are not buying BDS, it is not clear who is.

But for Jewish students hoping simply to navigate their college years free of venom and scorn, these positive developments offer minuscule comfort. They have lives to live. The trouble is that there are others who, managing to believe when they look in the mirror that they are bona fide progressives, are attempting to make those lives as difficult as possible.

Circular Firing Squad: The Democrats' Internal Warfare Threatens to Send Them Back to the Wilderness

October 5, 2021

If they are not awfully careful, the Democrats' reversion to their time-honored penchant for turning on one another may make their control of both ends of Pennsylvania Avenue short-lived. President Joe Biden's approval ratings are plunging, evidently because he withdrew American troops from Afghanistan in accord with his predecessor's deal with the Taliban and because almost half of Americans eligible for a vaccination that would save them from severe illness or death decline to get one. A razor-thin Democratic majority in the House of Representatives appears very likely to be washed away in next year's midterms, and the country has House Speaker Kevin McCarthy to look forward to. And the party's ability to keep control of the Senate by the grace of a tiebreaking vote by Vice President Kamala Harris is likewise in grave doubt.

You might imagine that this prognosis would be sufficiently sobering that Democrats would wise up and get unified. You'd be wrong. On the contrary, they have resumed doing what they do best: Fighting with one another over whether they can get half a loaf, three-quarters of a loaf or the whole loaf of bread. The internal fight over how much of America's badly decayed infrastructure and tattered social fabric can be repaired and how quickly threatens to tank Democrats' electoral prospects and pave the way for the Republicans to return to power.

The tensions between congressional Democrats self-classifying as "progressives" and those self-classifying as "moderates" have variously simmered, cooled and resumed simmering ever since candidate Biden sewed up the Democratic presidential nomination last spring. With Biden's domestic agenda on the line in Congress, Democrats have seized the opportunity to put his presidency in jeopardy by permitting their disagreements to obscure their common goals: addressing the historic damage both caused and exposed by the pandemic that former President Donald Trump maintained was a hoax. The House Democratic caucus, split between members and nonmembers of the Congressional Progressive Caucus, spawns claims and counterclaims that it is the other side's position on Biden's spending bills that is eviscerating the president's credibility.

Progressive stalwart Rep. Ilhan Omar of Minnesota contends that progressives are the ones who are "trying to make sure that the president has a success." Rep. Josh Gottheimer of New Jersey counters that "th(e) far left faction is willing to put the president's entire agenda at risk. They've put civility and bipartisan governing at risk."

Meanwhile the GOP rubs its hands together in glee at the shortsightedness and hubris of the Democrats, whose discord makes it even likelier that Republicans will retake control of at least one branch of government. That will guarantee not only that Americans will not receive the help they need for the next two years, but also that the country will be treated to nonstop congressional investigations into Hunter Biden's personal life and other urgent matters. The idea will be to gut any hope Biden has of winning reelection, assuming that the 46th president, who will be 82 in 2024, decides to run.

Even in the best case, Democrats' challenges in 2024 will be daunting. The odds are that they will face a Republican Party unified behind Mar-a-Lago's answer to Don Corleone. Democrats have soothed themselves with the fiction that they handily defeated our country's Mussolini wannabe, but they didn't. Had a mere 22,000 Biden voters spread strategically among Wisconsin, Arizona and Georgia voted for Trump, American democracy would be on the ropes, hanging on for dear life. The truth is that a narcissistic clown who bungled the pandemic and thereby tanked the American economy increased his support in 2020 among women as well as Hispanic, Black and other voters in comparison to 2016.

Against this backdrop, a small squadron of progressive Democrats ardently believes that if their party only moves left it will improve its electoral prospects rather than torpedo them. Moderates are growing openly contemptuous of this analysis, and it shows. If the two sides cannot find a way to keep the big picture in mind, the picture that is going to emerge, first in 2022 and then in 2024, won't be a pretty one.

Soul Erosion: Americans Confront a Nation They Never Knew

October 12, 2021

Fiona Hill knows something about how democracies die, and she worries that ours may be in critical condition. The working-class girl from an English mining town immigrated to America and became a Russia expert, advising Republican and Democratic presidents alike. Hill rose to prominence during the 2019 investigation into The Former Guy's attempt to extort Ukraine into announcing an "investigation" into President Joe Biden in exchange for the unfreezing of military aid.

She has had time to reflect on what has become of her chosen homeland, and she is worried. "I feel like we're at a really critical and very dangerous inflection point in our society," she told Politico recently. "I have a lot of friends who are immigrants like myself who have been here for a long time, who came from many, many different places. And they say, 'This is not the America I came to. This is not the America we chose to come to.'"

The Trump presidency may be over for now, but the Trump years are not. The stew of race-based hatred, white nationalism and domestic extremism that spilled out from under a rock over the past six years is very much with us. A mark of the jeopardy we are in is that the anger and the misinformation exploited and fomented during that period is now directed at those to whom we owe the most — our teachers and health care providers.

A surge in threats against educators because of public health measures enacted to protect students and teachers alike from COVID-19 led the National School Board Association to appeal to Biden on Sept. 29. "America's public schools and its education leaders are under an immediate threat," it wrote, asking for federal assistance "to protect our students, school board members and educators who are susceptible to acts of violence ... because of threats to their districts, families and personal safety." News of online hatred and outright assaults in response to protocols aimed simply at preventing the spread of highly contagious, potentially deadly illness reaches us on a regular basis.

In Ohio, one school board member was warned: "We are coming after you and all the members of the (Board of Education). You are forcing (students) to wear masks for no reason in the world other than control. And for that you will pay dearly." In Tennessee, a student who recounted that his grandmother, a teacher, had died of COVID-19 and who called for masks in schools was mocked by a sneering audience. Citing "an increase in harassment, intimidation and threats of violence against school board members, teachers and workers in our nation's public schools," the Department of Justice announced the formation of a task force to combat the growing problem. As for the collapse of decency that underpins this conduct, there is no task force capable of remedying that.

Our health care providers, physically and emotionally ravaged by COVID-19, are being subjected to similar mistreatment. Fury at masking or testing requirements, restrictions on visitations due to the virus and long waits in emergency rooms thanks to the pandemic's toll has resulted in what Deb Bailey of Northeast Georgia Health Systems calls "a huge increase in violence against our health care workers." Hospital workers "have been cursed at, screamed at, threatened with bodily harm and even had knives pulled on them," Jane McCurley of Texas' Methodist Healthcare System told the Texas Tribune. "It is escalating. It's just a handful at each facility who have been extremely abusive. But there is definitely an increasing number of occurrences every day." At one Missouri hospital, where assaults have tripled since COVID-19's onset, hundreds of staff have been given panic buttons to bring security officers running in the event of an attack.

Biden has both preached civility and practiced it. But he is all but powerless to reverse America's slide into incivility and its descent into civic decay, which are at the root of what is playing out in schools, hospitals and elsewhere. For that, for better or worse, we're dependent on one another.

Jail Bait: Steve Bannon Bets That His Middle Finger to Congress Won't Land Him in the Slammer

October 19, 2021

Steve Bannon has been one lucky con man, and he is betting that his luck will hold. This week the House Committee investigating the Jan. 6 assault on the Capitol aimed at torpedoing last November's election will vote to hold Bannon in contempt of Congress. The reason: The Committee subpoenaed Bannon to appear and answer questions about what he knew about the assault, and he blew them off. This places him in defiance of a Congressional subpoena, which places him in violation of federal law. Should the Justice Department indict and convict him, Bannon could land in jail for a year.

Bannon, a genuinely bizarre character on a good day, has been a Donald Trump whisperer since he became CEO of Trump's 2016 presidential campaign. He worked in the White House briefly as the then-president's "chief strategist" before being banished and then re-embraced by the famously erratic Trump. In August 2020 he was arrested and charged with a series of felonies, including money laundering and conspiracy to commit fraud. According to the federal indictment, Bannon duped donors into contributing money to build that border wall with Mexico — the one Mexico was going to pay for — and then walked off with about $1 million of their money, lending fresh meaning to "Stop the Steal."

A funny thing happened on the way to Fort Leavenworth, however: Bannon got kissed by a large, orange leprechaun. On Jan. 20, 2021, Trump's last day in office, he pardoned Bannon, undoubtedly because justice required it.

Now Congress wants to know what Bannon knows about Jan. 6, including Trump's role in it. This doesn't seem exactly like a "fishing expedition." Bannon apparently spoke to Trump on Dec. 30, urging him to focus his effort to remain in office despite being voted out of it on stopping Congress from certifying the electoral votes, a certification scheduled to occur on Jan. 6. On Jan. 5, perhaps blessed by a sudden surge of clairvoyance, Bannon told listeners to his podcast "War Room" that "All hell is going to break loose tomorrow."

Bannon's justification for his contempt of Congress was presaged by an interview he gave in 2018. "The real opposition is the media," Bannon explained about journalists' nasty exposure of the manure dispensary that was the Trump White House. "And the way to deal with them is to flood the zone with (expletive)." Bannon's lawyer's letter extending the middle finger to the Committee confirmed that Bannon has retained his flair for (expletive).

Bannon won't answer questions, his lawyer says, because Trump has instructed him not to, referring to Trump's invocation of "executive privilege," one that is patently bogus. The executive privilege doctrine can only be asserted by a sitting president. Even if things appear differently at Mar-a-Lago, here on Planet Earth, Trump isn't one. It only applies to advice given to the president by government officials. At the time of these events, Bannon had been out of government for over three years. The doctrine is only intended to apply to the safeguarding of military, diplomatic or national security secrets. Discussions about orchestrating a coup against the country do not protect Trump's conversations here.

Still, Bannon has reason to believe he will skate, as he has skated before. The Republicans are likely to take back the House. If they do, they will disband the select committee faster than you can say "Hang Mike Pence," nullifying the subpoena served on Bannon. Meanwhile, Bannon will tie up Congress and the Justice Department in court, arguing that he was only following Trump's orders, a kind of Breitbart-meets-Nuremberg defense.

The Supreme Court held long ago that it is all citizens' "unremitting obligation to respond to subpoenas, to respect the dignity of Congress and its committees and to testify fully" when Congress investigates. Bannon has given Congress and the Justice Department no choice but to pursue criminal charges against him, not only to get the truth about Jan. 6 but to attempt to repair the considerable damage Bannon, his compatriots and their master have done to the rule of law.

Burned at Both Ends: A Good President Finds Himself Torpedoed by the Right and Sniped at by the Left

October 26, 2021

    The immutable laws of politics and of human nature make one thing clear: It's easier to be angry than it is to be rational, and it's more satisfying. Leaders to whom citizens owe a great deal are often punished, undone by undercurrents of "What have you done for me lately?"

    Just two months after he had finished rescuing his nation from the brink of national obliteration, winning a once-impossible-seeming victory over Nazi Germany, Winston Churchill was overwhelmingly voted out of the prime minister's chair. Churchill's countrymen chose Labor Party head Clement Attlee to replace him in Britain's 1945 election, persuaded that Attlee was the one who could deliver competence in government.

    In 1946, American voters rejected the Democratic party of President Franklin Roosevelt, who had delivered them from a Great Depression spawned by Republican policies under Republican presidents and who had defeated the Axis coalition in the World War just recently ended. Defections from within the Democratic party contributed mightily to massive Republican gains, resulting in Republican control over Congress for the first time since 1932.

    In 2016, the fact that President Barack Obama had rescued America from financial collapse and expanded health care for tens of millions of Americans, presiding over an administration that was clean as the proverbial whistle, did not inoculate him from the white-hot white rage that catapulted Donald Trump into an Oval Office in which he most assuredly did not belong.

    So, it isn't surprising that the laws of politics and human nature have combined to batter President Joe Biden's approval ratings. A president who has done an admirable job of lifting America out of an abyss has been subjected to a frenzied whipsaw by both the Right and the Left.

    Biden assumed the presidency of a country riven by divisions not seen since the Civil War, whose economy had been decimated by a global pandemic that was taking 43,000 American lives a month. His administration has battled through dumb and dishonest misinformation campaigns in order to orchestrate the delivery of at least one dose of COVID-19 vaccine to 220 million Americans. Within weeks of being inaugurated he enacted a $1.9 trillion stimulus package for a country on the ropes, and he has nudged historic infrastructure and social safety net bills down the field, positioning them for passage in some meaningful form in the near future.

But half of Americans reside in a world of angry fantasy, lapping up the fiction that Biden lost an election that he won, and that Trump won an election that he lost. They cheer what for them is the somehow excellent news that the president is unable to wave a magic wand and make a global pandemic disappear. Meanwhile, Fox News personalities deride vaccinations, discouraging Americans from receiving them, thereby fostering illness and delaying our recovery. By mocking vaccinations, Fox's entertainers encourage their viewers not to take simple measures that will save their lives — even as the entertainers make sure to get themselves vaccinated, and even as Fox itself demands that they do so.

For their part, progressive Democrats squat in The Land of Make Believe. They make believe that Democrats hold a majority of the Senate, rather than merely 50 votes. They make believe Sens. Joe Manchin and Kyrsten Sinema do not exist. They make believe that Democrats have something more than a razor-thin majority in the House, one likely to be erased next year. They make believe that if Biden simply stamps his feet, the political realities that make it impossible for them — and him — to achieve all they wish to achieve will be replaced by different, more favorable realities.

And so they take to the airwaves and social media to criticize the president in terms that are unfair, inviting others to join them in The Land of Make Believe.

Caught in a vise between the unhinged and the irrational, Biden has his work cut out for him. As history has shown, a good and admirable job leading a country is no guarantee that his countrymen will judge him fairly.

Fresh Air: The New Boston Takes Charge
November 2, 2021

In late 1980, a white law student in Boston was on the phone with his friend in Washington, D.C., the Black son of a Virginia Baptist minister. The minister's son was himself in law school, after graduating with an Ivy League degree. "When are you getting up here to visit?" the white student asked his Black friend. "Boston, huh," mused the friend with a skeptical chuckle. "I'm not so sure that's such a good idea."

After a federal judge found an ongoing pattern of racial discrimination in the city's school system in 1974, the Court's plan to remedy the discrimination through busing was met with resistance, including violent resistance, by some in Boston's white community. An estimated 40 riots took place in Boston between 1974 and 1976. The white rage, exemplified by an anti-desegregation group called Restore Our Alienated Rights, or ROAR, became the distinctly unattractive face of Boston in the consciousness of people of color, in Boston and across the country, for years to come.

As elsewhere, there have been some big changes in Boston. In 1950, approximately 95% of Boston's residents were white. Now, just over 50% are. Founded in 1630 as a haven for immigrants and blessed ever since with infusions of newcomers whose talent and spirit have fueled the city's growth, Boston has recently seen a surge of immigrants from Africa, Asia and Latin America that has dramatically altered the city's racial and ethnic composition. When Boston Mayor Marty Walsh was appointed secretary of labor by President Joe Biden earlier this year, the President of Boston's City Council, Kim Janey, became Beantown's first Black, and first female, acting mayor. In September's primary election, the five major candidates vying to succeed Walsh were all individuals of color — four women and one man.

Tuesday's general election will determine which of those candidates — City Councilor Michelle Wu or City Councilor Annissa Essaibi George — will become mayor. Two weeks thereafter, one of them will take the helm of a city internationally acclaimed for its intellectual capital, its medical institutions, its universities and, yes, its sports teams. Both women are not only individuals of color; they are each the children of immigrants. They each know the stigma and the obstacles of being the "other." Both have succeeded in corridors of power historically dominated by whites and by men, succeeding through intelligence and grit. Each has busted barriers and defied expectations along the way.

Whoever wins the election, one thing is clear: Boston will never be the same. Janey pointed out that being Boston's first Black, first female acting mayor "doesn't mean that racism magically disappears. It doesn't mean that sexism magically disappears." But Janey's tenure as acting mayor, followed immediately by the mayoralty of another woman of color, does mean for starters that Boston's children are never going to see their possibilities, their potential, their opportunities in quite the same way again.

And it means more than that. Even before COVID-19 slammed into us, exacerbating the gaps between white communities and those of color, the gaps in Boston were pronounced. The poverty rate among white Bostonians was 11% in 2020. The poverty rate for Blacks was 22%, and for Hispanics and Asian Americans it was 29%. Seventy-one percent of white Bostonians had college degrees; 20% of Blacks and 23% of Hispanics had them. In Boston, the median net worth of a white family was just under $250,000; that of a Black family was all of eight dollars. The distance between the affluent Back Bay section of Boston and largely Black Roxbury is less than 4 miles, but there is a 30-year difference in life expectancy between the two communities.

The good news is that Boston is about to see new leadership by someone who "sees" the inequities without having to be schooled in them. She will have hundreds of millions of dollars in new federal funding provided precisely so that these inequities — in homeownership, in business creation, in education, in transportation and elsewhere — can be attacked. And she will have a City Hall staffed by fresh faces, eager to make big changes.

No doubt about it. It's an exciting time for Boston.

Sour Smell of Success: A President Under Attack for Doing What He Was Elected to Do

November 9, 2021

For a guy who seems to be doing exactly what he was elected to do, President Joe Biden finds himself under bitter attack. Most of the attacks are from people who simply want him to fail, but as last week's poor performance by Democratic candidates showed, not all of them are. The president's approval ratings are curiously low inasmuch as, since taking office, his administration has substantially lifted the country out of the ditch it was in on Inauguration Day.

On Friday morning, the Department of Labor reported that the economy had added 531,000 jobs in October, bringing the number of jobs created during the first nine months of the Biden administration to 5.6 million. The unemployment rate, which had been 6.3% in January 2021, is now down to 4.6%. Biden's American Rescue Plan, enacted in March, kept America afloat while his team pushed, pressed and prodded Americans to get vaccinated against the virus that has killed 775,000 Americans and severely damaged our economy. Despite the sneering and disinformation from the predictable quarters, the number of Americans who are fully vaccinated is fast approaching 200 million.

Late Friday, Congress passed Biden's $1 trillion infrastructure package, a long-overdue public works program that is the largest of its kind since the Eisenhower presidency. It will likely soon be followed by a massive, historic bill that will address the dire need for clean energy, provide for universal preschool and expand efforts to combat child poverty.

You wouldn't know this by listening to the thunder on the Right, which has produced the customary inanity.

Folks who demand that the government dictate that women must give birth against their wills denounce policies requiring COVID-19 vaccinations, invoking a heretofore unrecognized constitutional right to infect others with a deadly, incurable disease. Those born too late to sue George Washington to block him from ordering his troops to be inoculated against smallpox are trying to make up for it: Despite a long history of requiring Americans to be immunized before participating in certain activities, these newcomers to civil rights causes maintain that requiring Americans to protect their fellow Americans from a lethal virus is un-American.

Over in the Senate, noted civil libertarian Ted Cruz, positioning himself to capture the Third Reich revivalist wing of the 2024 Republican presidential primary vote, lectured Attorney General Merrick Garland that it is everyone's God-given constitutional right to give the Nazi salute at school board meetings.

Then there are the cries that the president is to blame for disruptions in the global supply chain. These cries are mindless, but no matter: mindlessness in defense of the conning of people is no vice. The factories that manufacture many of our products are located in countries that have been particularly hard-hit by the pandemic, and many have been shuttered or limited in their output. Shipping containers have been scarce. Blaming this on Biden is preposterous, but not any more preposterous than blaming it on Transportation Secretary Pete Buttigieg, who had the nerve to take a short period of time away from the office to look after his newborn twins. Fox News personality Tucker Carlson, always good for sixth-grade-level wit, did not disappoint, mocking Buttigieg, who adopted the twins with his husband Chasten, for being gay. "Paternity leave, they call it?" Carlson smirked. "Trying to figure out how to breastfeed. No word on how that went." Meanwhile, one of those infants just returned home after three weeks of urgent medical treatment, including time on a ventilator. No word on whether Carlson felt a moment's remorse for his stupidity, or even grasped it.

The snarkiness has not been from the Right alone. "Many who were sick of Trump chaos and ineptitude are now sick of Biden chaos and ineptitude," grumped New York Times snarkmeister Maureen Dowd shortly before Friday's jobs report and passage of Biden's infrastructure bill. But if what has been achieved since Biden took office qualifies as chaos and ineptitude, here's to more of it.

Just a Little Treason: Trump and Co. Play Hide-the-Putsch

November 16, 2021

In "Demagogue: The Life and Long Shadow of Senator Joe McCarthy," biographer Larry Tye recounts what one newspaper had to say about the man who until relatively recently held the award for the most dangerous despot in American history. "The simple truth," editorialized the Washington Post while the boozing con artist from Wisconsin was taking a wrecking ball to our democratic institutions, "is that what Ponzi was to finance and what fortune-telling is to science, Joseph McCarthy is to politics."

Former President Donald Trump has rewritten our national story in more ways than one. In his clinically notable dishonesty and in the threat he has posed and still poses to America's democracy and soul, Trump makes McCarthy look like Woodrow Wilson by comparison. The frantic attempt by Mar-a-Lago's answer to Mussolini to prevent Congress from learning about his role in the attempted coup d'etat on Jan. 6 illustrates the point.

Over the furious opposition of House Republican leader Kevin McCarthy (no relation) and other Trump dependents, Congress established a committee to investigate the Jan. 6 attack on the Capitol, including its "facts, circumstances and causes." Here's a shocker: Trump and company really, really don't want the "facts, circumstances and causes" to be investigated. You don't need to be Albert Einstein, or even Alfred E. Neuman, to know why not.

So, when Congress began subpoenaing witnesses close to Trump who had knowledge of those facts, circumstances and causes, Trump did what you would expect: He directed them to disregard the subpoenas. Trump confidant and apparent putsch-plotter Steve Bannon was indicted last week for contempt of Congress for giving the middle finger to the committee. Former Trump chief of staff Mark Meadows, who also refused to comply, appears next aboard the Arraignment Express, and the committee's issuance of more subpoenas to assorted Trump courtiers seems likely to keep the grand jury plenty busy.

Meanwhile, Trump sued to block the National Archives from turning over to the committee records belonging to the federal government, requested because they bear directly on who did what to organize the mob attempting to overturn the presidential election, and who did what, or nothing, to stop the mob once the attack began. Trump's lawsuit is frivolous, eviscerated by a long line of Supreme Court precedent, but no matter. The idea is to bog the committee down in a lengthy judicial process that will stretch until January 2023, when the GOP is likely to take back control of the House of Representatives. Should that happen, presto! No more committee. No more investigation. No more subpoena. And no disclosure of the facts, circumstances and causes of the coup attempt.

Unsurprisingly, Trump lost the first round in the courts. And federal judge Tanya Chutkan lost no time conveying her disregard for Trump's argument that Congress lacked the authority to investigate Jan. 6, and that as a former president he had the right to hide his records from the public "in perpetuity." She informed Trump briskly that she was not buying what he was selling. "On January 6, 2021," she began her decision, "hundreds of rioters converged on the U.S. Capitol. They scaled walls, demolished barricades and smashed windows in a violent attempt to gain control of the building and stop the certification of the 2020 presidential election results." As for Trump World's risible hooey that this was just a little tourist visit, the judge begged to differ. "This unprecedented attempt to prevent the lawful transfer of power from one administration to the next caused property damage, injuries and death, and for the first time since the election of 1860, the transfer of executive power was distinctly not peaceful."

"Presidents are not kings, and (Trump) is not President," Judge Chutkan wrote. The problem is that roughly half the country thinks Trump actually is president and would happily have him as king. There is, in short, trouble in River City. Whether the would-be dictator gets away with hiding the truth will say a lot about just how bad that trouble gets.

Debasement (Continued): The GOP Descends to Lower and Lower Levels

November 23, 2021

Republican Sen. John Kennedy of Louisiana is no dimwit, but you'd never have known it watching him question Saule Omarova, President Joe Biden's pick to serve as comptroller of the currency, about her childhood in the former Soviet Union. Omarova, a Cornell University law professor who advised President George W. Bush's administration on regulatory policy, emigrated to America 30 years ago and has been an American citizen since 2005.

Kennedy, who studied at Oxford, may be presumed to have read somewhere along the way that in the Soviet Union, where Omarova was born in 1966, students were not exactly free to repudiate the Communist Party. Everyone was required to sign up; it wasn't a matter of choice.

Which is why comparisons with Joe McCarthy's cruel and dishonest bullying flowed so naturally when Kennedy smeared Omarova as a "communist" at a Senate hearing last week, demanding to know about her "membership" in a communist youth organization that he knew she was not free not to join.

"You used to be a member of a group called The Young Communists, didn't you?" sneered Kennedy.

"Senator, are you referring to my membership in the youth communist organization when I was growing up in the Soviet Union?" asked Omarova.

"I don't know, I just wanted to ask you that question," replied Kennedy.

"Senator, I was born and grew up in the Soviet Union... " she began, but he interrupted her. "But were you a member of that organization?" Kennedy demanded.

She explained that as a youngster of a certain age, she had no choice but to be a member. Kennedy asked whether she had ever submitted a formal letter of resignation, which is just what young Americans do when they age out of Little League.

"I don't know whether to call you Professor or Comrade," he said mockingly, pleased with his cleverness.

"I am not a Communist," the former Bush administration official was forced to state, trembling at the humiliation. "I could not choose where I was born. I grew up without knowing half of my family. My grandmother twice escaped death under the Stalinist regime. I am proud to be an American."

Nationally renowned immigrant rights attorney Susan Cohen, whose career representing refugees fleeing persecution is chronicled in her new book, "Journeys from There to Here," gave Kennedy more credit than due. "His insensitivity and uneducated comments belie his ignorance and lack of appreciation of the valiant journeys of so many naturalized Americans precisely to flee Communist regimes," Cohen says. But there is a more cynical take: Kennedy, who repeatedly ran for office as a Democrat before switching parties to catch Louisiana's red wave, takes his opportunities to burnish his bona fides with the xenophobic set because it helps him politically.

But Kennedy is The Great American Statesman himself compared to fellow Republican Paul Gosar, Congressman from Arizona by way of Pluto. Gosar was censured by the House of Representatives last week for creating and circulating a video cartoon featuring himself murdering Democratic Rep. Alexandria Ocasio-Cortez. An even minimally compos mentis Republican caucus would have joined Democrats in censuring Gosar because, well, glorifying the homicide of a House colleague doesn't seem quite right. But not this Republican caucus, infected by a kind of disease for which there isn't a vaccine.

Gosar's siblings were less sympathetic to their brother, the Lee Harvey Oswald wannabe, than his fellow House Republicans, suggesting that Gosar belonged perhaps not so much in Congress as he does in the evaluation unit of the Arizona Home for the Criminally Insane. Gosar's brother opined that Gosar shouldn't merely be censured by Congress but expelled from it, and thereafter prosecuted. It's going to be an interesting time at the Gosar family Thanksgiving, and not because of any fighting over who gets the drumsticks.

Kennedy and Gosar are just two members of the once-Grand Old Party who soil our American flag. And they have plenty of comrades who have dirt on their hands as well.

Untruth And Consequences: The Hamas Caucus Gets It Wrong on Gaza

November 30, 2021

In his new book on last May's chapter of Hamas' long-running war against Israel, "Gaza Conflict 2021," Middle East scholar Jonathan Schanzer points out this anomaly: Even as the historic conflict between Israel and her Arab neighbors shrinks, with new diplomatic relations expanding monthly, Iran's proxy war against Israel is intensifying. Schanzer, senior vice president of research at the Foundation for Defense of Democracies, details the threats posed to Israel by Hamas on its southern border and by Hezbollah on its northern one. The estimated 4,350 rockets fired at Israeli civilian centers from the Gaza Strip in May were substantially all funded or fabricated by Iran. Hamas may have as many as 30,000 more, waiting to be used when it chooses. On the Lebanese border in the north, Hezbollah, a de facto unit of the Tehran government, has stockpiled 150,000 rockets, paid for and supplied by Iran which, like Hamas and Hezbollah, is pledged to Israel's annihilation.

Another anomaly is that each time Hamas or Hezbollah fires barrages of rockets into Israel and Israel tries to defend itself from them, it is Israel that many American progressives condemn. When it comes to the Left, the Jewish state finds itself caught in a vise between gullibility and hatred. The gullibility is old. The hatred is older. Though Schanzer doesn't put it quite this way, there are some on the Left who do not know the Gaza Strip from the Isle of Wight or Hamas from Greenpeace. But bank on this: If Israeli civilians are under siege and their government tries to protect them, in these quarters it is Israel that will be denounced.

The May conflict began with the first of thousands of rockets being fired by Hamas at Israeli civilians and ended with some on the Left lamenting that Israel had defensive systems in place to try to intercept them, which kept Israelis from being torn to pieces. This was no one-off. Hamas did the same thing in 2008, 2012 and 2014. "The 2021 conflict was the fourth war," Schanzer writes. "There will be a fifth."

Of course there will. Each time Hamas tries to shred Israelis, it will be Israel that takes a political hit — in Europe, in academia and now in progressive circles, where the inanity when it comes to Israel grows more eye-rolling with each conflict.

To be sure, the Israel-as-human-rights-violator narrative has hit some speed bumps in the form of observations by experts who never got the memo. After the 2014 installment of the conflict, when Israel absorbed 5,000 Hamas rockets, Gen. Martin Dempsey, then-President Barack Obama's Chairman of the Joint Chiefs of Staff, spoke at the Carnegie Council for Ethics in International Affairs. "I actually do think that Israel went to extraordinary lengths to limit collateral damage and civilian casualties," said Dempsey. "The Israel Defense Forces (are) not interested in creating civilian casualties. They're interested in stopping the shooting of rockets and missiles out of the Gaza Strip and into Israel."

The Gaza-based head of the United Nations' Palestinian refugee relief agency got himself into trouble in May when he praised Israel for the "precision" with which it managed to target Hamas military sites deliberately embedded within civilian areas, limiting harm to innocents. This displeased Hamas, and he was forced to high-tail it out of Gaza for "consultations."

A small but strident cohort within the Democratic Party insisted that it was Israel's fault for trying to keep its civilians from being set on fire. "We oppose our money going to fund militarized policy, occupation and systems of violent oppression and trauma," proclaimed Missouri Rep. Cori Bush, presumably referring to the Iron Dome interception system, which exists solely to prevent Hamas rockets from murdering innocent people.

The triumph of political fashion over reason is a storyline of the times. But the indulgence of Hamas and the demonization of Israel by progressives is in a head-scratcher category of its own.

Beginnings and an Ending: For Better and Worse, New Winds Change Massachusetts' Landscape

December 7, 2021

"The more things change, the more they stay the same," wrote a French essayist in 1849, and the expression has become part of our common parlance. But it isn't always true, and recent events have demonstrated that if the saying once applied to the norms of Massachusetts political life, it no longer does.

Ranked 15th among the states in population, the Bay State always punches well beyond its weight on the scale of national impact, which is why its political doings receive outsize attention. This makes sense: What happens in Massachusetts doesn't always stay in Massachusetts, politically speaking. Four of America's 46 presidents were born here, and seven others studied here. In the last nine presidential elections, three major party nominees — Michael Dukakis, John Kerry and Mitt Romney — were Massachusetts politicians. In 2020 alone, five candidates for the Democratic presidential nomination — Elizabeth Warren, Deval Patrick, Michael Bloomberg, Seth Moulton and Bill de Blasio — were either Massachusetts officeholders or were raised in Massachusetts.

Then there are the armies of campaign operatives and public-policy types that hail from the state. The result: Massachusetts politics is not only a local blood sport but an ongoing national spectacle. Just as a now-defunct financial services company's advertisements once proclaimed, "When E. F. Hutton talks, people listen," so too do political professionals ascribe tea leaf qualities to what happens here.

Two recent developments have generated national attention. The election of 36-year-old City Councilor Michelle Wu as Boston's new mayor has excited young Bostonians and communities of color, punctuating their ascendancy. The daughter of Taiwanese immigrants, Wu's election has made it clear that the days when white men ruled Boston's roost are over. "The old Boston is gone," Democratic strategist Mary Anne Marsh told the Washington Post last month, "and there's a new Boston in terms of political power."

Census figures tell part of the story. In 1970, 79.8% of Boston's population was comprised of non-Hispanic whites. Now it is 44.6%. Only 2.6% of Bostonians were Hispanic; now it is 18.7%. Asian Americans numbered only 1.3% of the city's population 50 years ago. Their proportional representation has increased almost tenfold since then.

Wu's election has electrified Bostonians. Whip-smart and seemingly limitless in her energy, the mother of two small children has been everywhere since winning the mayoralty four weeks ago. She doesn't appear to have much choice in the matter: Every group in every neighborhood in the city has been clamoring for her appearance at every ceremony that Boston's robust holiday season has to offer, and there are a lot of them. This goes beyond the normal "Wouldn't it be nice to have the mayor come?"; there is a slightly frenzied "Do you think we can get Michelle?" aspect that has taken hold. Nor is this simply a testament to Wu's personal vibrancy. Her push for free public transportation, cost containment for renters and environmental protection has resonated widely.

Also marking the end of a political era was Republican Gov. Charlie Baker's announcement that he would not seek reelection. Baker is the latest in a long series of moderate Republicans who have won the governorship in dark-blue Massachusetts over the past century, and he may be the last. Since his election in 2014, Baker has been one of the country's most popular governors, not merely projecting but displaying a steady hand, decency and thoughtfulness. These qualities have not endeared him to his own state party, which, like the Republican Party generally, is now dominated by election-deniers and other whistlers of looney tunes. The odds that Baker would have lost his own party's nomination for a third term were likely a big factor in driving a good man from public service.

In Massachusetts, the Gods of Good Governance have both given and taken away, all in the same month. One way or the other, it's plain that politics here has actually changed and also not stayed the same.

Bright Spot: Adam Schiff Reminds Us There's Daylight After Midnight

December 14, 2021

The putsch-pushers and lawbreakers that comprise Trump World despise U.S. Rep. Adam Schiff, showering him with fourth-grade, fourth-rate epithets and seeing to it that he will live in perpetual concern for his safety and that of his family. Historians, however, will hold Schiff in high esteem, a bright spot in an unusually dark chapter in American history. The veteran California congressman, chairman of the House Permanent Select Committee on Intelligence, led Congress' 2019 inquiry into Trump's attempt to extort Ukraine into announcing a phony "investigation" into Democratic frontrunner Joe Biden in order to sully Biden's reputation and thereby help Trump win reelection. The quid pro quo went like this: If Ukraine announced some sort of investigation into Biden, then and only then would Trump unfreeze the military aid Congress appropriated so that a desperate Ukraine could defend itself against Trump ally Vladimir Putin, who is waging war against the Ukrainians. If Ukraine didn't agree to help Trump, well, then, enjoy the Russian army.

The extortion plot or, as then National Security Advisor John Bolton put it, the "drug deal," was loathsome enough. But it was made even more loathsome by Trump's stonewalling of Congress' subpoenas in order to obstruct its inquiry — the well-nigh unmistakable indicium of guilt —- and by Trump's retaliation against the brave public servants like former Ambassador Marie Yovanovich and National Security Council aide Alexander Vindman, who refused to be Trump's co-extortionists.

Perhaps no one understands the danger to America posed by the witches' brew of demagogues and toadies that comprise the Trump Party better than Adam Schiff. He has spent the past five years sounding the alarm about it, and his recently published book, "Midnight in Washington: How We Almost Lost Our Democracy and Still Could," is a gripping, sobering account of how close we are to waving goodbye to the land our forebears sacrificed so much to reach.

When the House of Representatives voted to impeach Trump for his extortion and obstruction, it was Schiff who led the presentation of the evidence that supported Trump's conviction and removal from office. It was,

Schiff told an audience on Saturday, a presentation intended more for the American people and posterity than for the Senate in whose chamber it was delivered, as Republican senators, either loyal to Trump or terrified of him, would not have voted to convict Trump had he, say, murdered someone in the middle of New York's Fifth Avenue in broad daylight. Schiff's closing argument at the end of the impeachment trial rang with steely clarity. "You know you can't trust the president to do what's right for this country," he said. "You can trust he will do what's right for Donald Trump. He'll do it now. He's done it before. He'll do it in the election if he's allowed to."

Schiff has earned the right to begin every paragraph he utters for the rest of his career with the words "I told you so." Trump's "big lie" that the election he lost was stolen from him; his felonious phone call to Georgia's secretary of state to "find" fake votes so that he could pretend he won in Georgia; the plotting to block certification of Biden's election; the incitement of the mob that did Trump's bidding and stormed the Capitol on Jan. 6 to prevent the peaceful, democratic transition of power that is our national hallmark — Schiff warned the nation that this is precisely the kind of totalitarian conduct Trump would engage in if he were not removed from office. And Schiff was right.

It is not only Trump who is to blame for our national crisis, of course. "There is a dangerous vein of autocratic thought running through one of America's two great parties," Schiff writes, "and it poses an existential danger to the country."

But Schiff refuses to write America off. "Midnight is the darkest moment of the day," he says. "But it is also the most hopeful, because everything that comes after holds the promise of light. America has a genius for reinvention, and we must use it."

Guilty Party: Big Don's Cosa Nostra Takes The Fifth

December 21, 2021

Some say that former President Donald Trump lacks principles, but that's unfair. If there's one precept that guides the large bamboozler, it is that Jimmy Hoffa's body will see the light of day before Trump's tax returns do.

Last week's decision by a federal judge rejecting Trump's bid to block the Treasury Department from turning his tax returns over to the House Ways and Means Committee was unsurprising in all but one respect. Faced with a law providing that the Department "shall" furnish the returns if requested by the committee, Trump's lawyers threw everything, including the kitchen sink, against the wall, hoping that some argument — any argument — would stick. For example: Congress was politically motivated; Congress had overstepped its subpoena power; Congress lacked a valid legislative purpose — all of these arguments were trotted out, along with the argument that the moon wasn't in the seventh house and Jupiter wasn't aligned with Mars.

The judge wasn't buying any of them, and issued a lengthy, meticulous decision explaining why, as he put it, Trump was "wrong on the law." The surprise: the judge, Trevor McFadden, is a Trump appointee. By placing the rule of law over politics and whatever residual appreciation he feels to the man who put him on the bench, McFadden made clear that he was adhering to "a faithful application of binding (judicial) precedent," not partisanship.

Trump will doubtless appeal the decision until the end of time. His strategy is to keep the appellate process going until the 2022 midterms, when the Republicans will likely retake the House and the committee's request for Trump's tax returns will be withdrawn faster than you can say "tax evasion." But whatever the ultimate outcome, the ruling represented a welcome statement that not everyone associated with The Donald lacks a moral compass. And it came during a week in which the House Select Committee to Investigate the January 6th Attack on the United States Capitol was shedding considerable light on the confederacy of American neo-fascists, democracy-subverters and dunces who worked overtime to stage a coup d'etat.

Some of those who schemed with Trump to overturn the election that President Joe Biden won in order to keep Trump in power seem unenthusiastic about assisting in the light-shedding. Steve Bannon, the Trump strategist who was indicted for embezzling money before being pardoned by Trump, blew off the committee's subpoena. He has been indicted for contempt of Congress. Former chief of staff Mark Meadows delivered a trove of documents appearing to show that various Republican congressmen and staffers were part of the putsch festivities, and then joined Bannon in lifting his middle finger to the committee. The House has referred him to the Justice Department for indictment.

Then there are the Trump stalwarts who refused to answer the committee's questions about Jan. 6 on the grounds that doing so would tend to incriminate them.

Go figure.

John Eastman, the attorney who pushed a plan to pressure former Vice President Mike Pence to block the constitutionally mandated certification of the election results, is one. Another is Jeffrey Clark, the former Justice Department official who tried to con his colleagues into backing Trump's efforts to steal the election. Then there is Roger Stone who, let's face it, should never, ever answer any questions under oath on any subject, including parking violations. Stone, convicted in 2019 of lying to Congress, claims "(he) had no advance knowledge of the events that took place at the Capitol." It's just that if he told the truth about that, he is afraid he might go to jail.

None of this has left our 45th president in good spirits. "The January 6 Unselect Committee," he said in a characteristically clever statement on Saturday night, "is a cover-up for what took place on November 3rd and the people of our Country won't stand for it!" But it's not looking as though it is the committee that is the one with anything to cover up.

Merchant of Death: Public Health Be Damned, Fox News Goes for the Money

December 28, 2021

      The race for ratings at Fox News has officially entered the derangement zone, with Fox fixtures competing with one another over who can get more attention by hurling unhinged invective at Dr. Anthony Fauci, who has directed the National Institute of Allergy and Infectious Diseases since the Reagan administration. For decades, Fauci has been widely admired by everyone playing with a full deck for his efforts to combat pandemics. "Playing with a full deck," however, has been the limiting factor. While You-Know-Who was attempting to con Americans with his fraudulent flimflam that COVID-19 was a "hoax" that would quickly "disappear," Fauci had the nerve to say publicly that it wasn't and it wouldn't. Ever since, he has been a bogeyman for the crazies, rewarded for his work to save lives with a flood of death threats by the mob that has seized hold of America's right wing. The coronavirus isn't the only virus that plagues America, evidently.

      Fox superstar Tucker Carlson has accused Fauci of having "created COVID" and of "deciding to unilaterally end Christmas." This is demagogic claptrap, of course, but it causes cash registers in Fox's corporate boardroom to chime, which makes Carlson a hot corporate commodity. It is this kind of hooey that has fueled Carlson's career. Never mind the rock-solid scientific and medical evidence confirmed by data drawn from hundreds of millions of vaccinations around the world; the guy with the Bachelor of Arts degree knows better. "Maybe (the push for COVID-19 vaccination) is about social control," offers Carlson. "Maybe it doesn't work and they're just not telling you that."

      Other Fox personalities have fallen over themselves to mock vaccination as a Leninist plot, all the while doubtless getting themselves vaccinated as quickly as possible. After all, it's the increase-the-click shtick that counts, not peoples' lives. "They're going to knock on your door," says Fox host Brian Kilmeade about the Biden administration's exhortation to Americans to protect themselves and their loved ones. "They're going to demand that you take it. The focus of this administration on vaccination is mind-boggling." Fox's Laura Ingraham chirps, "The Biden administration is about to take their pressure campaign to your doorstep," deriding the public education campaign as "vaccine evangelization." Fox contributor Charlie Kirk likens the Biden White House to "the Taliban."

With some 815,000 Americans now dead from COVID-19, over 150,000 new cases daily and the overwhelming percentage of those who are dying individuals who are unvaccinated, Fox's Jesse Watters has decided to amp up the venom, using pointedly violent language to urge right-wing die-hards to forcefully confront Fauci. In terms designed to win him raves from Nut Land and corresponding huzzahs from Fox management, Watters egged on a gathering of conservatives last week to "ambush" Fauci with questions that Watters chose to call "the kill shot." Illustrating how this might work, Watters cried, "Boom! He is dead! He is dead! He is done!"

Predictably enough, Fox pronounced Watters innocent even of bad taste, let alone incitement. Watters, Fox said, was only using "a metaphor."

Sarah Palin, as good an exemplar of determined dimwittedness as America has to offer, picked up the paramilitary theme, bestowing her own battle cry on the anti-vaccination activists. She proclaimed that she would get vaccinated "over my dead body." Given our death toll, Palin's line would be funny if it wasn't so unfunny. In a less painful time we would have placed it right up there with Yogi Berra's complaint to the restaurant that told him it could not seat him for another hour. "No wonder nobody comes here," he groused "It's too crowded."

There's good news amidst the grim. There is a vaccine for all Americans who choose to get it that is virtually certain to keep them from getting very sick. The bad news: there's a cult that rages against public health mandates that aim to protect the public's health. And they're doing our nation a whole lot of damage.

Unhappy Anniversary: Marking the Deplorables' Opening Act

January 4, 2022

This week's anniversary of the Jan. 6, 2021, attempt by former President Donald Trump's loyalists to overthrow an election is a grim reminder of the razor's edge on which American democracy sits. The multifaceted schemes to nullify President Joe Biden's victory brought us dangerously close to a coup d'etat. As three retired Army generals warned in a recent op-ed, "We are chilled to our bones at the thought of a coup succeeding next time."

As well they should be, as should the rest of us. What was supposed to be the celebration of our enduring democracy — the constitutionally mandated tabulation of electoral votes — became its desecration. The insurrection will stand out either as a historic blinking red light about the fragility of America's democratic norms or the beginning of their end.

As a House committee investigates the circumstances of the Jan. 6 putsch attempt, Olympic-level stonewalling is underway by those who know what they did, and who hope to prevent their countrymen from finding it out. Trump has asked the Supreme Court to block the committee from obtaining public records that document what he did that day. The records were paid for by the taxpayers and are owned by the American people. Trump, however, is unenthusiastic about letting us know what they say.

Trump's lawsuit is frivolous and has already been rejected by two federal courts. But his hope is that the justices whom he appointed will stoop to turning the Supreme Court into a kind of Trump Protection Tribunal. Last week, a group of former top lawyers from Republican administrations filed a friend-of-the-court brief urging that Trump's Hail Mary-style move to hide the evidence be rejected a third time.

Trump isn't the only one frantic about keeping the committee from learning the truth about Jan. 6. Twice-indicted Trump strategist Steve Bannon has refused to obey a committee subpoena. Former chief of staff Mark Meadows produced damning documents, and then reversed himself, refusing to answer questions about them, thereby earning himself a criminal referral to the Justice Department.

Last week Rudy Giuliani protege Bernard Kerik delivered a trove of documents but produced a list of documents he was withholding as "attorney work product." Kerik is not an attorney. He did, on the other hand, spend time in jail for fraud, ethics violations and criminal false statements. He is withholding a document heartwarmingly entitled "Draft Letter from POTUS to Seize Evidence in the Interest of National Security in the 2020 Election." It is dated Dec. 17, 2020, the day before Trump met in the Oval Office with disgraced former National Security Advisor Michael Flynn to discuss seizing election equipment in states whose election results Trump sought to overturn. Kerik, a convicted felon, was hired by Giuliani, who is under federal criminal investigation, on behalf of Trump, double-impeached and under investigation in at least two jurisdictions. Flynn is a convicted felon.

A regular Brady Bunch.

As the committee begins holding public hearings to present the evidence it has amassed about the insurrection's decidedly un-immaculate conception, Americans are forced to confront the unpleasant similarities between how the German National Socialist Party took power in the early 1930s and how Trump's Republican Party tried between November 2020 and January 2021 to keep it. Comparisons between Adolf Hitler and Donald Trump are frowned upon, and with very good reason.

But let's be honest.

The willingness to use violence to advance political objectives, the circumvention of democratic procedures and the systematic trashing of democratic institutions that exist to guard against totalitarianism that characterized the Nazis' seizure of power can no longer be said to be foreign to the American experience. Last year's machinations to stop the counting of votes or to "find" phony ones, the fraudulent claims of election fraud and the attempts to bulldoze local officials into overriding voters, culminating in the storming of the Capitol, bear a terrible resemblance to the Nazi Party's putsch. To think it, to say it, to write it, seems inconceivable. What it does not seem, however, is off-base.

Shaken Faith: Failed by the System, Baby Rehma's Parents Try to Change It

January 11, 2022

Nada Siddiqui and Sameer Sabir would have celebrated their daughter Rehma's 10th birthday this week. The Massachusetts couple should have had all the smiles and hugs and laughter and joy that children bring to parents. And Rehma should have had her life.

But they were cheated.

Nine years ago this week, Rehma was entrusted to the care of her Irish nanny, Aisling Brady McCarthy. When Nada came home from work Rehma was non-responsive. It would emerge that a neighbor had heard her screaming and had pounded on their door. No one answered.

Rehma was rushed to the hospital, where physicians found severe bleeding inside her skull, massive swelling of the brain and cranial bruises. Police found Rehma's blood on baby wipes throughout the home. A piece of drywall was dislodged from behind her changing table, "consistent with being damaged by forceful contact with the corner" of the table, according to police.

Rehma was pronounced brain-dead 48 hours later.

A state-employed medical examiner found that Rehma's death was caused by "blunt force trauma," ruling it a homicide. The murder charges against McCarthy made international news. McCarthy, who was unable to provide any explanation for the evidence to the police, maintained her innocence but was held as a flight risk.

Her defense team did what lawyers do, engaging a bevy of doctors to offer an even bigger bevy of contradictory theories about what might have explained Rehma's death. All were refuted by Rehma's pediatrician and by Dr. Alice Newton, the child abuse specialist who examined Rehma's case while she lay in a coma.

Shortly before trial, the medical examiner who had issued Rehma's autopsy report altered it, changing the cause of death from "homicide" to "undetermined." The district attorney, who dropped all charges against McCarthy, first assured Rehma's parents that there would be an independent medical review, and then reneged. McCarthy went back to Ireland. And Siddiqui and Sabir, who had suffered the grievous death of their baby and then could not get an answer to how the overwhelming evidence against McCarthy could count for nothing, had yet more pain to come: messages insulting their faith or their national origin and cruel, misogynistic comments about mothers of young children who go back to work.

The story was recently profiled by CNN's chief medical correspondent, Sanjay Gupta. His series, "Justice for Rehma," examined the established science behind shaken baby syndrome, also known as abusive head trauma, and the band of physicians who deride the diagnosis as "fake." Child abuse specialists disagree. "Pseudo experts have falsely claimed that a debate is raging in the medical community about whether abusive head trauma is a real diagnosis," Dr. Newton says. "Let me be clear. There is no controversy."

A bill sits in the Massachusetts Legislature that would reduce the chances that politics, pressure or questionable competence will prevent parents from learning the truth about their young children's deaths. The Office of the Massachusetts Medical Examiner's website states that it exists to "investigate the cause and manner of deaths that occur under violent, suspicious or unexplained circumstances." The bill simply requires that where the deaths of children under 2 are involved, autopsy findings must be reviewed and approved by the chief medical examiner. This way, the staff physicians know that their findings about such deaths will be reviewed by the head of their office.

This seems like Accountability 101. The Massachusetts chapter of the American Academy of Pediatricians endorses the bill, stating that "(r)equiring a formal review process will lead to more confidence from parents, community and society in general." But the Chief Medical Examiner herself, paid a mere $420,000 a year, opposes it on grounds that may be summarized thusly: "I'd rather not have to do it."

Rehma's parents are not waiting around for bureaucrats to act against type. In 2014 they established The Rehma Fund for Children to support care for sick children. In that way they are ensuring that their daughter's memory, as the Jewish expression puts it, "is for a blessing."

Birds of a Feather: For Both the Far Left and the Far Right, Antisemitism's the Thing

January 18, 2022

In his new book on extremism in America, Anti-Defamation League CEO Jonathan Greenblatt quotes Voltaire to help explain the hatreds that threaten to destroy the country we love. "Anyone who can make you believe absurdities," wrote the French philosopher, "can make you commit atrocities." Saturday's hostage-taking at a Texas synagogue by a gunman calling for the release from prison of an antisemitic terrorist highlights the spread of absurdities and the upsurge in atrocities Greenblatt warns about in "It Could Happen Here: Why America Is Tipping from Hate to the Unthinkable."

Malik Faisal Akram seized worshippers in a synagogue near the prison where Aafia Siddiqui, convicted of attempting to murder U.S. personnel in Afghanistan, is serving an 86-year sentence that includes a "terror enhancement." Educated at Brandeis University and MIT, Siddiqui is known as "Lady al-Qaida." A poster woman for vicious antisemitism, Siddiqui proclaimed post-conviction: "This is a verdict coming from Israel and not America. That's where the anger belongs." She had instructed the judge that she wanted Jews excluded from the jury "if they have a Zionist or Israeli background," adding "I have a feeling everyone here is them, subject to genetic testing."

Akram wasn't the only one who called for Siddiqui's release. The Islamic State group (ISIS) did so, and the Council on American-Islamic Relations, a powerful group regularly afforded kid-glove treatment by a media often intimidated or wearing rose-colored glasses, has been actively demanding it. Siddiqui's conviction, CAIR maintains, is "one of the greatest examples of injustice in U.S. history."

CAIR is among those culpable in what Greenblatt says is "a dangerous and dramatic surge in anti-Jewish hate." In November CAIR official Zahra Billoo attacked the Anti-Defamation League, Jewish communal organizations, "Hillel chapters on our campuses" and "Zionist synagogues" as "enemies." "I want us to pay attention to polite Zionists," Billoo told a gathering in a speech defended by CAIR. "The ones that say, 'Let's just break bread together.' They are not your friends." On Saturday night, as a brilliant team of law enforcement officers ended Akram's siege, CAIR frantically released a statement condemning the attack on the synagogue. But one could be forgiven for regarding this as an attempt to self-deodorize.

Greenblatt, an Obama administration alumnus, minces no words about the Left's share of guilt for the recent swell in antisemitism, pointing to the fact-challenged demonization that followed Israel's attempt to defend itself against Hamas rockets fired from Gaza last spring. "So-called activists around the world all too often deployed rhetorical violence against the Jewish state and its supporters, by equating Israel and Zionists with Nazis, calling for Israel to be eliminated and directing anti-Israel messaging at synagogues and other Jewish institutions," writes Greenblatt. "That rhetoric, in turn, helped trigger a frightening spike in real world violence against Jewish people in the United States and around the world."

On the far Right, the Justice Department's indictment of a collection of Trumpist insurrectionists for seditious conspiracy again illustrated the threat that a metastasizing witches' brew of white nationalists, neo-Nazis and associated vermin poses to America. The mob chants of "Jews will not replace us" during their march in Charlottesville and the "Camp Auschwitz" sweatshirt proudly worn by Capitol rioter Robert Keith Packer last Jan. 6 exemplify the fascist threat that binds the Proud Boys, QAnon and the other pillars of the "Make America Great Again" movement, which is more untethered than ever. "It's hard to underestimate the organizational boost that white supremacists, anti-immigrant groups, neo-Nazis, white nationalists and others received during the Trump years," writes Greenblatt, "when their ideology was tolerated and sometimes openly encouraged by officials at the highest levels."

Like antisemitism, vitriol and violence against Black people, Muslims, Asian Americans and members of the LGBT community are rising, not abating. The FBI reports a 25% increase in the number of hate crimes over the last five years, and given what goes unreported, that is almost surely the tip of the iceberg. "Over time," writes Greenblatt, "it becomes increasingly entrenched and normalized." And that, very plainly, has already happened here.

Flimflam: Biden's Critics Take Chutzpah to New Levels

January 25, 2022

The classic embodiment of chutzpah known by every lawyer on the planet is the teenager who murders his parents and then asks for leniency on the ground he's an orphan. GOP critics of President Joe Biden are starting to sound an awful lot like that teenager, leveling criticisms that are starting to sound every bit as laughable.

The characters who have denied COVID-19's existence, encouraged behavior that spread it, dissed public health advice, derided vaccinations and attempted to block vaccination programs have contributed to the virus' devastating impacts, making it more difficult to mitigate them. Asked in late January 2020 whether there was reason to worry about COVID-19, Mar-a-Lago's answer to Einstein replied, "No. Not at all. We have it totally under control. It's one person coming in from China and we have it under control. It's going to be just fine."

Battling the Right's guerilla warfare against public health efforts, Biden's administration has succeeded in getting 210 million Americans fully vaccinated, and about 83 million of those boosted. Biden's critics, many of whom have done their best to impede this progress, gloat that Biden has not "managed" to prevent a virus from mutating, as though he were in a position to do so or they were in a position to speak.

For four years, then-President Donald Trump kissed parts of Russian President Vladimir Putin's anatomy that really should be off-limits, actively encouraging the former KGB agent to conclude that he could have his way with the United States, doing his best to weaken NATO. Trump humiliated Ukraine and withheld military aid that it desperately needed to defend itself against Russian aggression, all so that he could extort a phony announcement of a phony "investigation" into Biden and use it to win an election he knew he would otherwise lose.

Now, Trump stalwarts accuse Biden of being soft on Russia and weak on Ukraine.

When Biden took office, Trump's "there's no-virus-here" genius had tanked the American economy, leaving us in DEFCON 1. In Biden's first year 6.4 million jobs were added, more than in any president's first year.

Unemployment that was at 6.3% when Trump slinked off to Florida was at 3.9% a year later. Average hourly pay was 4.7% higher at the end of 2021 than it had been when Trump left office. And even adjusted for inflation, Americans' disposable incomes were higher than they were in 2019 and 2020.

But Biden's critics claim that his economic policies have "failed."

The narrative peddled by some and swallowed whole by others that Biden's first year has been a failure defies the facts — but then, fact-defiance has become a thing.

Perhaps most amusing is the Republicans' line that Biden has "failed to unify" America. This is nothing if not rich coming from those who, all in lockstep, some in goosestep, have refused to join Biden's effort to make legislation aimed at healing an ailing country bipartisan. Having resolved to block the Biden administration at every turn, they charge him with failing to bring the nation together. Only the truly gullible would buy that flimflam, but we have a lot of those.

Despite it all, Biden managed within 60 days of becoming president to enact the American Rescue Plan, a $1.9 trillion relief package that helped keep state and local governments functioning, paid for a massive vaccination program that has saved uncountable American lives, kept millions of renters living under a roof and put food on the table for millions whose household earners were out of work and either on the ropes or not far from it.

He navigated into law a $1.2 trillion infrastructure and jobs package which, as the Brookings Institute put it, "touches every sector of infrastructure, from transportation and water to energy, broadband and the resilience and rehabilitation of our nation's natural resources." It is, says Brookings, "a longer-term patient approach to rebuilding American competitiveness."

Not bad for 12 months on the job. It ought to make Americans pause, think, reject the chutzpah and give credit where credit is due.

Badge of Honor: Police Killings Remind Us What We Owe the Blue

February 1, 2022

Last week two New York police officers, Jason Rivera and Wilbert Mora, responded to a 911 call from an apartment where a domestic dispute was raging. A man with a semi-autonomic handgun equipped with 40 rounds of ammunition opened fire, fatally wounding both.

First to die was Mora, a 27-year-old Dominican American, one of the 30% of New York City's police force of Hispanic origin. He had gotten his bachelor's degree in 2018. "It was such a good family," a neighbor told the New York Times. "I cried, I tell you. It's such a loss."

Rivera died a few days later. The 22-year-old son of Dominican immigrants, Rivera had dreamed of becoming a police officer since childhood. His widow doubtless spoke for hundreds of thousands of law enforcement families across America, where the number of killings of police officers is higher than it has been since 1995. "We are not safe anymore," she said. Rivera and Mora were the third and fourth police officers shot in New York City in a 72-hour period.

Rivera's older brother remembered the way Jason had instinctively cared for others during his short life. "My brother was dedication," he said. "He was the definition of integrity. He was joy."

The increase in shootings of police officers comes as we ask them to respond to an increase in violent crime in many American cities. More than two-thirds of the country's 40 most populous cities reported more homicides in 2021 than in 2020, and 10 of those cities reported more homicides than in any year on record. "When homicides go up, more shootings go up, and it contributes to an overall increase in violence, and police officers find themselves in the middle of that environment," Chuck Wexler, executive director of the Police Executive Research Forum, told CNN.

The scenes of thousands of police officers filling Fifth Avenue outside St. Patrick's Cathedral to honor their fallen colleagues served as a stiff reminder that the glib, facile blanket condemnations of police so fashionable in certain privileged progressive circles are just that — glib and facile. The wholesale hostility visited upon law enforcement as a profession, an obligatory feature of far-left rhetoric, is simply unfair. It also repels the overwhelming majority of Americans — including the majority that is simultaneously repelled by the evidence that injustices perpetrated by police against Americans of color are sufficiently pervasive to qualify as systemic.

The murder of George Floyd by a Minneapolis police officer in May 2020 punctuated a series of videotaped, utterly indefensible police shootings of Black Americans over the last several years. Unsurprising to Black citizens, these incidents penetrated White Americans' consciousness in a new way. Floyd's murder followed on the heels of the March 2020 killing of Breonna Taylor in Louisville, Kentucky, by police looking for her boyfriend. In April 2020, a police officer shot Duarte Wright in his car after pulling the 20-year-old over for expired registration tags. Then in August, police shot Jacob Blake seven times in Kenosha, Wisconsin, leaving him paralyzed.

While the charge that America suffers from systemic racism has been a difficult pill for White Americans to swallow, the evidence speaks for itself. That Black people are at risk driving while Black, jogging while Black and breathing while Black just can't be denied. Outrage at that fact is not only understandable. It is called for.

But this doesn't translate into a basis for deriding police, let alone disrespecting the terrible burdens borne by police officers and their families. And Americans know it. A Pew Research survey conducted last October found that only 15% of adults believe that funding for police should be cut. Only 24% of Black adults, and only 16% of Hispanic adults, believe this.

Shrill and sweeping denunciations of police and disregard for our debt to them are no more rational than denials that America suffers from persistent, pernicious racism. Both are thoughtless. Both are foolish. Both are divisive. Those with a sense of humanity who care about the precarious state that America is in can do better.

Sheep And Black Sheep: The GOP Goes Full Hezbollah

February 8, 2022

There should be nothing surprising about this past Friday's official defense by the Republican National Committee of the Jan. 6, 2021, assault on the United States Capitol, one aimed at preventing the constitutionally mandated transfer of power central to our democracy from taking place. The GOP's proclamation that the assault constituted "ordinary citizens engaged in legitimate political discourse" was almost ho-hum for a party that has become America's Hezbollah, the militant Islamist party that subjugates Lebanon. Hezbollah means "Party of God" in Arabic. Substitute "former President Donald Trump" for "God" and you've got today's Republicans.

The mob's vicious, deadly attack on Capitol Police; its cries to hang a vice president who declined to declare that someone who had lost the election should be president; the seditious plotting of a paramilitary operation to seize power; and the felony- and fraud-filled scheme to keep Trump in power — all of this was the stuff of fascists. Yet the GOP has been worse than merely too cowardly to stand against this. Overwhelmingly, Republicans have embraced it.

"The Republican Party is so off the deep end that they are describing an attempted coup and a deadly insurrection as political expression," observed Rep. Jamie Raskin, a member of the House committee investigating the multifaceted putsch attempt organized by Trump and his kitchen cabinet of Mussolini-wannabes and simple wackadoodles. But, really, what else is new? The party of Ronald Reagan has turned itself toxic out of fealty to Trump and fear of him, even though he is the kind of crooked despot that Americans have always flattered ourselves into believing could never come to power here.

We were badly mistaken.

"From my front row seat, I did not see a lot of legitimate political discourse," remarked Marc Short, former Vice President Mike Pence's chief of staff. Pence was slated to be hanged from gallows pre-constructed by a mob that wanted him killed for refusing to declare Trump "still the president" even though the American people had voted otherwise. The good news: Only those suffering from "Trump-as-Fuehrer syndrome" believe this was "legitimate political discourse." The bad news: This syndrome has taken root more broadly than we once thought thinkable.

The occasion for Friday's declaration by the GOP was its vote to censure conservative Republican Reps. Liz Cheney and Adam Kinzinger, for whom conservatism does not mean defending sedition. The vote came just days after Trump excoriated Pence for refusing to "overturn the election" and after he indicated fairly clearly that if elected in 2024, he would pardon the insurrectionists. Cheney and Kinzinger have had the guts to face down their GOP colleagues, first by voting to impeach Trump for his role in the Jan. 6 coup attempt and then by agreeing to serve on the House committee seeking to ascertain the complete set of facts surrounding it. The censure vote was intended to punish them.

Neither Cheney nor Kinzinger is backing down an inch. "I do not recognize those in my party who have abandoned the Constitution to embrace Donald Trump," Cheney said. "History will be their judge." Kinzinger was equally resolute. "I have no regrets about my decision to uphold my oath of office and the Constitution," he said.

Pence has at long last summoned the fortitude to publicly criticize Trump, a mere 13 months after being threatened with a lynching by Trump's troops. "I had no right to overturn the election," Pence told the Federalist Society, a group of conservative legal scholars for whom this was presumably not news. "The presidency belongs to the American people. And frankly, there is no idea more un-American than the notion that any one person could choose the American president."

This should fall comfortably in the realm of Captain Obvious. But the GOP is now certifiably morally bankrupt, a stain on America's reputation abroad and a threat to her security at home. Not mincing words about it may not make a bit of difference. But mincing words is increasingly difficult to do.

Royal Flush: More Hidden Document Tricks from the Shredder-In-Chief

February 15, 2022

Until last week the most uproarious explanation ever offered for the disappearance of evidence in the possession of an American president involved the erasure of 18 1/2 minutes of Richard Nixon's tape recording of a key White House meeting he had about the Watergate break-in just after it took place. The tape of Nixon's meeting about the break-in was subpoenaed, which led to the darndest discovery: a large portion of the tape was missing, and Nixon had no explanation for what in the heck had happened to it.

His longtime secretary, Rose Mary Woods, loyally volunteered to offer reporters a theory of how she might have accidentally destroyed a portion of the tape. While reviewing the tape at Nixon's request, she speculated, she might have inadvertently placed her foot on a pedal that erased the tape while keeping her foot there for an extended period of time, stretching the rest of her body several feet in the opposite direction to answer the phone. While attempting to demonstrate this, however, what she demonstrated was that no circus performer on earth could have kept foot and torso virtually in separate rooms for 10 seconds, let alone the length of time she professed. Woods' claim of truly superhuman elasticity led the late Rep. Al Lowenstein to dub her "Miss Glue-Shoes The Contortionist" and, indeed, her valiant attempt to take the fall for Somebody Else was later found by forensic testing to be impossible.

Last week's revelations about plumbing problems at 1600 Pennsylvania Ave. trumped the Rose Mary Woods Stretch in more ways than one. So very much about former President Donald Trump was so very clearly amiss that his fixation on problematic toilet-flushing was far down a long list of concerns about him. "People are flushing toilets 10 times, 15 times, as opposed to one," the leader of the free world proclaimed from the Roosevelt Room. "Ten times, right, 10 times," he told a rally. "Not me, of course, not me. But you," he said, no doubt mystifying a crowd of Make America Greaters. "I won't talk about the fact that people have to flush their toilets 15 times," Trump assured another crowd, thereby talking about it.

It seemed fair even at the time to wonder what in God's name would lead the president of the United States to publicly mention even once his concerns about having to flush a toilet multiple times before dispatching whatever was in the bowl, let alone to return to the subject repeatedly. The explanation for why flushing troubles were so often top of Trump's mind may have arrived with news that journalist Maggie Haberman's forthcoming book reports that White House staff would find wads of printed paper clogging a toilet used by Trump and concluded that he flushed government documents therein. Trump denies this, trotting out the usual "fake news" line, but he does not enjoy a great deal of credibility on any subject, much less on subjects involving himself.

Trump's credibility was not helped by a Washington Post report that he regularly tore up briefing materials, letters and memos, or by a former White House staffer's on-the-record disclosure that Trump "loved to tear up those documents" and that she observed him eat the pieces of documents he had just ripped up.

And Trump's attempts to destroy or otherwise make unavailable government documents appear to have been wholesale rather than merely retail. Late last week the National Archives and Records Administration said that it had retrieved 15 boxes of White House records that were supposed to have been transferred to the National Archives when Trump left office, but that instead were taken to Mar-a-Lago. Like the flushing, the ripping and the eating of documents, this is more than a fetish or a penchant for hiding information that the former guy doesn't want anyone to see. It's an apparent violation of federal law.

"Lock her up," Donald Trump would cry about Hillary Clinton's improper handling of government emails.

Just sayin'.

Testing, Testing: Putin Bets the West Will Wobble

February 22, 2022

Russian President Vladimir Putin has been feeling his oats in recent years, and with reason. Asked in 2012 what would lead him to use military force to stop Syria's regime from slaughtering Syrians, President Barack Obama replied that using chemical weapons would constitute a "red line." When Syria murdered hundreds of its civilians with chemical weapons in 2013, the West melted. Our allies jumped ship. Obama punted to Congress, which made clear that it would not support anything more than mere words in response to Syrian war crimes. The American people were similarly unsupportive. The West was bailed out by Russia, whose removal of its client state's chemical weapons permitted America to save a measure of face.

When Russia invaded Crimea in 2014, the Obama administration and congressional Republicans alike signaled that it wasn't our business.

In 2016 when Putin directed a sophisticated cyber campaign against American institutions to tilt the outcome of the presidential election in order to install the president of Putin's choosing, he did so without any adverse consequences.

For the next four years the Kremlin's preferred president did his best to undermine NATO, which has successfully constrained Soviet aggression in Europe since its creation in 1949. This put a smile on Putin's face, as he raged about the former Warsaw Pact countries and former Soviet republics that had joined NATO seeking refuge from Russia and protection against it.

Putin has had cause to believe that the United States was too feeble, too riven to organize a united international response to the moves he is making on Ukraine. Despite his success leading Americans through the pandemic he inherited and bringing their economy back from the brink, President Joe Biden's approval ratings have gone south, battered by a Fox News hooey machine that has been largely uncountered. If Americans are too weak-kneed and too susceptible to nut-job conspiracy theories to don masks and vaccinate themselves against a deadly virus, Putin must figure, they won't give much of a hoot if he forcibly subjugates 40 million Ukrainians and won't be willing to do anything about it.

And if Biden is under political pressure because Americans' gas prices are at four dollars a gallon, Putin calculates, Biden will never impose the sanctions on Russia which, while hurting Russians badly, will turn those four dollars into five.

On the American Right, Putin can count on his very own amen corner to belittle America's president for trying to prevent Europe from becoming a free-fire zone for well-armed bullies. J.D. Vance, a Republican candidate for Senate in Ohio, exemplified the useful idiots in the pro-Putin wing of the GOP. "I got to be honest with you," Vance said last week. "I really don't care what happens to Ukraine one way or the other."

Then there's the Ben & Jerry's wing of the Democratic Party, which occupies its own ozone layer, believing that the way to stop tyrants and murderers around the world is to sing "Imagine" by John Lennon. "We call on President Biden to de-escalate tensions and work for peace rather than prepare for war," tweeted the Chunky Monkey Mavens mindlessly, ignoring reality. "Sending thousands more US troops to Europe in response to Russia's threats against Ukraine only fans the flames of war."

Putin has misjudged Biden, who has painstakingly constructed a program to expose, isolate and punish Putin for his aggression against Ukraine that seems likely to inflict economic and political consequences on Russia costlier than Putin had expected. It is a program that serves America's national interests and does honor to its name. And it calls to mind the methodical diplomatic spadework done by President George H. W. Bush in 1991, assembling a complex coalition of states in response to Saddam Hussein's invasion of Kuwait.

Hussein and Putin have more than a little in common. As for Biden, Moscow has underestimated him. And he is doing the job that Americans elected him to do.

Tools: Putin's Useful Idiots Find a New Way to Degrade Democracy

March 1, 2022

The term "fifth column," coined during the fascist attacks on democracy in the last century, has historically denoted groups and individuals who seek to subvert their nation, generally in order to aid an enemy government. The phrase usually describes those who operate clandestinely to undermine national solidarity, frequently by spouting the propaganda of enemies.

While Russian President Vladimir Putin certainly has people operating within the United States to promote his interests clandestinely, he has plenty of characters who do so perfectly openly. On Sunday, Republican Sen. Mitt Romney called Americans who support Putin "almost treasonous," and he is not wrong. But the specter of Americans siding with a murderous tyrant commanding a police state that has invaded a democracy, committing war crimes against civilians in service of his personal desire to subjugate them, is unfortunately not new. In his book "Hitler's American Friends: The Third Reich's Supporters in the United States," historian Bradley Hart recounts that the extent of American support for Adolf Hitler both before our entry into World War II and afterward was greater than we like to acknowledge.

That former President Donald Trump and acolytes enthusiastically embrace the KGB agent whose brutal assault on Ukrainians in order to conquer them fits neatly into the "no surprise" category. As president Trump missed no opportunity to take Putin's side against America, welcoming the Kremlin's efforts to tamper with an election for his benefit and then denying it occurred, picking Putin over the United States. While Putin nodded and laughed, Trump withheld military aid Congress had appropriated to enable Ukraine to defend itself from Russia, adding extortion of an ally in favor of an enemy to the long list of actions that left America humiliated, weakened and turned into a global laughingstock.

It was unsurprising, therefore, to see Putin-run Russian television play and replay Trump's fawning over Russia's invasion of Ukraine. Putin, Trump declared in the wake of an invasion that has disgusted the world, is a "genius" and his invasion was "wonderful."

Putin made similar use of others who chose the Russian totalitarian over the brave people of Ukraine, who fashioned homemade Molotov cocktails out of wine bottles to try to stop Russian tanks from overrunning their cities. "Why would we take Ukraine's side?" sneered Tucker Carlson, Fox News' favorite and highly profitable bro. "Why wouldn't we take Russia's side? I'm so confused." Would that he were confused. "Why shouldn't I root for Russia, as I do?" demanded Carlson. Here was conservative podcaster Joe Oltmann: "I'll stand on the side of Russia right now."

As for the choice between the president of the United States and a Russian totalitarian, for America's fifth column it was a no-brainer, in more ways than one. Dinesh D'Souza, right wing commentator, convicted felon and recipient of a presidential pardon from guess who, tweeted that President Joe Biden "poses a far greater threat to our freedom and safety than Putin. He's the lesser evil." Lauren Witzke, Republican candidate for the Senate in Delaware, proclaimed "I identify more with Putin's Christian values than I do with Biden."

On a mission to prove the prevalence of crazy, talk show host Candace Owens declared that "Ukrainians are dying because of the Biden family's criminal connections and insistence on stoking conflict in the region." At the Conservative Political Action Conference last week, the founder of Papa John's Pizza, self-evidently qualified to opine on such matters, offered that Biden had "caused" Putin to invade Ukraine "to create a great smokescreen to create a distraction from all the real issues affecting America."

In recruiting American propagandists to do his bidding, Putin has plenty to work with. A Yahoo News/YouGov poll reaffirmed Republicans' admiration for him, with 62% of GOP voters saying that he was a "stronger leader" than the democratically elected president who has spearheaded international opposition to Russia's invasion.

Recent days have showcased the breathtaking courage of the Ukrainian people. But they have highlighted the real disease within America that somehow Americans will have to find a way to cure.

Patriotic Interlude: In a Rare Moment of Consensus, the GOP Gathers 'Round the Flag

March 8, 2022

There was good news at last week's State of the Union: Only two Republican congressmen interrupted the president of the United States when he was speaking about his son's death from cancer in order to scream insults at him. It was difficult to know whether the GOP's Lunatic Caucus has shrunk or if it was simply that, at a time when democracy is under the most vicious assault it has faced since the Nazis, their colleagues had chosen to boycott the speech.

But that wasn't all.

President Joe Biden reminded a country confronting antidemocratic forces of its own of our responsibility to defeat tyranny. Russian President Vladimir Putin, Biden said, "sought to shake the very foundation of the free world, thinking he could make it bend to his menacing ways. Instead, he met a wall of strength he never anticipated or imagined. He met the Ukrainian people."

Something remarkable happened. Republicans rose and applauded. And when the president asked everyone to stand to honor the Ukrainian ambassador in order to "send an unmistakable signal to the world and Ukraine," they stood, and they cheered.

Sen. Mitt Romney, who as the Republican presidential nominee in 2012 identified Russia as the single greatest threat to our national security only to be mocked by President Barack Obama and the Democrats, had the grace to praise Biden's leadership in galvanizing the world against Putin. Mobilizing our European allies to follow America's lead on anything is much more difficult than herding cats, particularly when imposing sanctions on Russia will mean economic pain for Europeans.

Americans seem to appreciate what Biden has achieved. A new NPR-PBS poll found that 52% approved of the president's handling of the Ukraine crisis, up from 34%. Eighty-three percent of Americans said they supported sanctioning Russia, and that was before some of the worst evidence yet of Russia's deliberate murder of Ukrainian civilians en masse.

A GOP that spent four years kissing Putin's ring and deriding NATO has now done a screeching reversal, and Romney explained why. "A lot of these people are changing their stripes as they are seeing the response of the world and the political response in the United States," he said.

He's clearly right. "There's no room in this party for apologists for Putin," former Vice President Mike Pence told Republican donors last weekend. This was quite a switch for the vice president who had staunchly defended then-President Donald Trump every time he had curried favor with the former KGB agent. "To those who argue that NATO expansion is somehow responsible for the Russian invasion of Ukraine, ask yourself: where would our friends in Eastern Europe be today if they were not in NATO?" This was more welcome stripe-changing from someone who nodded approvingly every time his former boss undermined NATO.

Trump himself tried a nifty two-step. Right after Putin's invasion of Ukraine, Trump called the invasion "pretty savvy" and "genius." Days later Trump called it a "holocaust." Evidently, he viewed it as a pretty savvy holocaust.

Even Tucker Carlson, who appears on reels of tape proudly proclaiming that he supports Russia over Ukraine, found himself so at odds with America that he claimed that he had never said what he was on tape saying. It's no fun being an isolated isolationist.

No one should be naive about where this is headed, however. The inevitable cost to Americans of imposing sanctions on Russia in order to stop its slaughter of Ukrainians is that we will pay more at the gas pump, more in the supermarket and more elsewhere.

Count on Republican pundits and politicians to profess that they are all for sanctioning Russia, but that Biden has "failed" because of higher gas prices and delays in deliveries from Amazon. This will be hypocritical and shameful, but you can bank on it. It will be up to ordinary Americans to toughen up, do their part to stop Putin and show what they are made of.

Bad Bet: Putin Confronts an America That Has Edged Closer Together

March 15, 2022

President Joe Biden is fond of saying "it's never been a good bet to bet against America," and even those of us who thank the good Lord he's president have rolled our eyes at this old chestnut. It sounds like sweet, outdated wishful thinking, naive cheerleading with a twist of fuddy-duddyitis.

But given the bipartisan support for the Biden administration's moves to pour weapons into Ukraine and put the screws to Russia's financial institutions, Biden's claim has some basis. Our raw partisan divisions must have encouraged Russian President Vladimir Putin to conclude that we would roll over rather than punish him for his barbarism against Ukraine.

But to a remarkable degree, Americans agree that Russia's wholesale slaughter of Ukrainians, its naked attempt to conquer a sovereign state and its obliteration of Ukrainian cities and towns just can't be accepted — and that both morality and self-interest dictate that we help Ukraine beat Russia and remain free.

A new CBS poll shows that broad American support for sanctions on Russia's energy sectors is overwhelming. Eighty-four percent of Democrats support such sanctions, as do 76% each of independents and Republicans. Three-quarters of Americans support a United States military response if Russia attacks a NATO country — and over half of Americans believe we have not responded to Putin strongly enough.

With polls showing that Americans' collective stomach has turned witnessing images of Russian war crimes, the GOP may be moving away from being the party of Putin poodles, a position it claimed during the administration of former President Donald Trump. When Fox News' Bill O'Reilly allowed that "Putin is a killer," the Republicans' Master wouldn't have it. "There are a lot of killers," Trump replied. "We have a lot of killers. You think our country is so innocent?"

No photo captured Trump's intimate relationship with Putin better than the one of him yukking it up with Putin's top henchmen — in the Oval Office. Trump had just fired FBI Director James Comey for refusing to terminate the Bureau's investigation into links between Trump's 2016 campaign and Moscow. "I faced great pressure because of Russia," he gloated to Russia's visiting foreign minister and ambassador to the U.S. "That's taken off."

The GOP fervently embraced the Trump-Putin embrace.

On the Democratic side, the obstacles to unity have come from the party's far Left, which insists on remaining disconnected from reality. Two days after Putin invaded Ukraine, the Democratic Socialists of America blamed the invasion on the United States and NATO, a bit of idiocy that must have brought not merely smiles but snickers to the Kremlin. It called "for the U.S. to withdraw from NATO and to end the imperialist expansionism that set the stage for the conflict." NATO, of course, exists solely and precisely to deter Russian invasions like the one that has resulted in the mass annihilation of Ukrainians.

Then there was a tweet from Ben & Jerry's that has aged less well than a pint of ice cream left for a month on an Equatorial Guinean sidewalk. "We call on President Biden to deescalate tensions and work for peace rather than prepare for war," proclaimed the frozen-treat mavens in late February. "Sending thousands more US troops to Europe in response to Russia's threats against Ukraine only fans the flame of war." Many shook their heads at this childishness, but there was some speculation that it was a clever marketing move to roll out the new Ben & Jerry's flavor, "Dumb Nuts."

We're in for days that will test our new bipartisan spirit. How will the president's oft-repeated statement that we will not directly confront Russia work if Russia bombs the Polish or Romanian borders with Ukraine, where refugees are escaping and arms desperately needed by the Ukrainians are flowing in? What is the "severe price" that Russia will actually pay if it deploys chemical weapons?

All we can do is recommit ourselves to American unity and to demonstrating to Putin that he has made a bad bet by betting against us.

Ukrainian Takeaway: A Strong National Defense and American Leadership Are as Needed as Ever

March 22, 2022

The first month of Russia's barbaric campaign to conquer Ukraine and the Ukrainians' inspiring resistance has reminded Americans of a fact that has gotten obscured in recent years: It's crucial that the United States maintain an overwhelmingly strong national defense and stay prepared to lead on the world stage.

The proposition that America must have a first-in-class military, and that it has to make the investments necessary to guarantee that we have it, has been derided in the Left-most sectors of the Democratic Party, where a certain obliviousness to the world and what occurs if America is unprepared to lead it holds sway. Cliches to the effect that we "cannot be the world's policeman" go only so far; the need for a military fully ready to defend America and help defend its allies has not seemed so obvious since the late 1940s. The Russian slaughter of Ukrainians and its threats to do unto other former Soviet republics what it is doing unto Ukraine has not placed the traditional progressive nostrums about defense preparedness in an especially favorable light.

Directly or indirectly, Ukrainians look to America for sophisticated military hardware so that they can save themselves from the Russian onslaught. In order to provide it we need to have it; in order to have it we need to pay for it. Our allies in eastern, central and even western Europe rely on America to partner with them in protecting themselves against Russia, and wishing that it weren't that way doesn't do much good.

That means that the United States simply must have the capacity to project military force. If some have mocked the notion of "peace through strength," the Ukrainians' experience has made the notion seem quite a bit less mockable.

And it isn't only Russia that we need to be sufficiently well-armed to deter. It is China, which threatens Taiwan. It is North Korea, which threatens South Korea at a minimum. And it is Iran, long designated by our State Department as the world's foremost state sponsor of terrorism, racing to acquire nuclear weapons and winning that race, which threatens the entire Middle East and beyond.

This doesn't mean toadying to the defense industry and its lobbyists or succumbing to contractors' con jobs about weapons systems that aren't needed, or that don't work or that aren't worth the money. But it does mean drawing the lesson that the Russian aggression against Ukraine has retaught the world: Democracies cannot invite aggression and must be prepared to stop it.

Fortunately, even a Congress split right down the middle along party lines and afflicted by historically vitriolic partisanship sees eye to eye on the need to preserve, and even improve, American strength. "While the voices calling for America to cut back on defense may have loud bullhorns," wrote Thomas Spoehr of the Heritage Center last December, "they are in the distinct minority." Spoehr was referring to lopsided votes in both houses of Congress in favor of the 2022 National Defense Authorization Act. The Senate approved it by 88 to 11 after the House did so by 363 to 70. And this was two months before Russia invaded Ukraine.

Americans have also been reminded of what it means when we lead the free world. By his dignity, his respect for our allies and his willingness to do diplomacy's difficult work patiently and out of public view, President Joe Biden has helped restore at least a measure of our lost credibility — and self-respect.

But a prerequisite for leading is deserving to lead. That will mean sidelining embarrassing fruitcakes like Rep. Marjorie Taylor Greene and dangerous demagogues like Prince Bone Spurs of Mar-a-Lago. It will mean holding those responsible for the attempted Jan. 6, 2021, coup d'etat fully and publicly accountable, and more.

It is at once a terrible time and, in some respects, a strangely hopeful one. For America, it is a time to summon whatever is necessary to rise to the occasion.

With Malice Toward Some: Violent, Frontal or Merely Sly, the Assaults on Jewry Keep Coming

March 29, 2022

Of the world's 7.8 billion inhabitants, barely 15 million are Jewish, a minuscule percentage. Yet there seems no limit either to the volume or the variety of malice that the Jewish people are required to fend off. Some of it is violent, some of it frontal, and some of it merely sly. Over the past several generations the malice has manifested itself in hostage takings, shootings, bombings — and outright genocide.

Then there are the attacks that are not physical but rather intended to degrade and delegitimize. This past month has seen some notable ones.

In early March, the American director of Amnesty International, Paul O'Brien, told a Democratic group that Amnesty is "opposed to the idea" that Jews should be permitted a national homeland in Israel. Amnesty's pronouncement, unsurprising to those who have followed its insouciance about the murder of Israelis by genuinely loathsome groups, came 75 years after the United Nations voted to create the Jewish state. That vote, in turn, came shortly after the Nazis had exterminated six million Jews, hoping to erase the Jewish people from the face of the earth altogether. O'Brien, born in Ireland, offered that his "gut" told him that Amnesty's position mirrored what "Jewish people in this country believe," an invention both stunningly arrogant and wildly inaccurate.

A week later, Tufts University's chapter of Students for Justice in Palestine issued a demand that all students sign a pledge to avoid any campus group or program that has anything to do with Israel. This would include all Jewish groups, all Jewish studies classes, all Jewish cultural programs and the campus Hillel. This was perfectly in line with SJP's raison d'etre: bullying and isolating Jewish kids on campus. The Anti-Defamation League's Robert Trestan had it right, calling upon Tufts to reject this latest form of harassment. "Creating lists of students who either support or, by omission, don't support the anti-Israel agenda," Trestan wrote, "effectively shuns Jewish students, who will be forced to either hide their personal views or risk being ostracized and excluded from campus life."

Cut to Amsterdam, where a move to cash in on Anne Frank's memory while placing the blame for her deportation to a Nazi death camp on the city's

Jewish community gained real commercial traction before being debunked. Relying on what was claimed to be a "cold case team," a Canadian author published a book called "The Betrayal of Anne Frank," arguing that circumstantial evidence suggested that a Dutch Jewish notary named Arnold van den Bergh had reported the Frank family's Amsterdam hiding place to Nazi authorities in order to save his own family. The book deal had a lot going for it: the painful story of the Jewish teenager killed in the Holocaust has enduring popularity worldwide, and the sales appeal of blaming her death on a fellow Jew made it a no-brainer.

A hiccup occurred last week, when five prominent historians released a 69-page report eviscerating the book's credibility, leading the Dutch publisher to announce that it was immediately ceasing publication. The historians scrutinized the totem pole of assumptions on which the book's theory hung. The results weren't pretty. Using phrases like "remarkably contrived," "absurd," "unfounded" and "speculative fantasy," the scholars deemed the book's thesis "very weak," plagued by "an erroneous reading of the sources" and reliant on "fabrications."

The book's selling point that Anne Frank was betrayed by a Jewish person, says Evelyn Markus, a Dutch-born antisemitism expert, "not only is false, but also fuels anti-Semitism: the Jews as traitors, the Jews as having brought the Holocaust onto themselves, and the Jews as the Nazis." The first two, Markus notes, are favorite tropes of far-right white supremacists, while the latter is preferred by the far Left.

The Dutch publisher has apologized for the book. But the American publisher, HarperCollins, has dollar signs in its corporate eyes, and still plans to publish the book in more than 20 languages. Business, after all, is business.

Heroes And Crooks: Ukraine Teaches Americans a Thing or Two and More

April 5, 2022

Ukrainian President Volodymyr Zelenskyy's rebuff of the suggestion that he be evacuated from his besieged city of Kyiv is already immortal, and rightly so. "I need ammunition, not a ride," he snapped, even as the Russian army was poised to decimate Ukraine's capital and annihilate its residents, including him.

These words take their place next to colonist Patrick Henry's famous call for a militia to take up arms against King George III in 1775, only Henry's proclamation came long before there were cruise missiles.

The scenes of Russia's butchery have only reinforced the world's awe at the Ukrainian people, whose courage in the face of attempted genocide is historic. There can be no silver lining here, but one hopes that the vast, sickening scope of Russia's atrocities will keep the American people unified for the long-term commitment required to defeat Russian President Vladimir Putin.

In his speech in Warsaw in late March, President Joe Biden spoke for hundreds of millions of people around the world when he stated the obvious: genocidal murderers should not run countries. The words "For God's sake, this man cannot remain in power" stoked several days' worth of tsk-tsking from Biden's GOP opponents, who just spent five years kissing Putin's posterior. They now ricochet back and forth between attacking Biden for not giving Ukraine fighter jets to battle Putin's air force and whining that he should avoid saying anything that hurts Putin's feelings.

The posterior-kissing has largely come to an end, other than on Tucker Carlson's nightly show on Fox, which positively cleans up in the wackadoodle demographic. This is likely because Americans now overwhelmingly line up with Ukraine and against Russia. A Pew poll taken days ago found that 72% of Americans have a favorable opinion of Zelenskyy, compared to 6% who have one of Putin, and you really have to wonder about that 6%.

There was another notable passage in Biden's Warsaw speech, but it received scant attention. "All of us, including here in Poland, must do the hard work of democracy each and every day," said the president, adding, "my country as well." It was a purposeful note of humility by Biden, whose credibility abroad contrasts with the global consensus that his predecessor was a narcissistic buffoon, a view with which it is difficult to quarrel. Biden's standing abroad has played a pivotal role in the forging of a unified NATO response to Putin.

That Biden has been instrumental in reinvigorating America's capacity to lead is hardly speculative. There's been "a major shift in the global image of American leadership after the election of Joe Biden," Pew determined in a recent report. "Majorities in each of the 16 (countries) surveyed expressed confidence in Biden. In all countries where there is a recorded trend available, there was an increase of at least 40 percentage points in confidence in the U.S. president after Biden took office."

"My country as well" was a humble acknowledgement to the world of the cleanup work we need to do here, and a gentle reminder to the American people, who have got to do it. Late last week a federal judge reviewing only a discrete sliver of the evidence that is extant of former President Donald Trump's law-breaking found that it was "more likely than not" that Trump "corruptly attempted to obstruct the joint session of Congress on January 6, 2021," and that he had "dishonestly conspired to obstruct" those proceedings. More likely than not, in short, that Trump committed federal crimes. More likely than not that he belongs in a federal penitentiary.

Oh, and not just that. The federal judge found unequivocally that Trump "launched a campaign to overturn a democratic election, an action unprecedented in American history. It was a coup in search of a legal theory."

A lot of work for us to do here indeed. And plenty to learn from the Ukrainians.

High Achievers: America's Diplomats Do Us Proud on Ukraine

April 12, 2022

The best line about low expectations for diplomacy belonged to Adlai Stevenson, President John F. Kennedy's ambassador to the United Nations. Diplomacy and the reproductive lives of elephants, Stevenson observed, have this in common: there's a great deal of commotion, all of it occurring at very high levels, and then you have to wait two years before anything happens.

Last week's 93-24 vote of the U.N. General Assembly to boot Russia out of the U.N. Human Rights Council for its barbarism against Ukrainians was welcome, with a wrinkle. Jurists may be obliged to insert the word "alleged" before "war crimes," but the rest of us have no need to mince words: Russia is guilty of war crimes. Friday's missile strike on a train station in the Ukrainian city of Kramatorsk where thousands of civilians were waiting to escape to safety killed more than 50 civilians, including 5 children, and maimed 100 more. The Russians had painted "For The Children" on the missile they aimed at the train station, well-known as a safe passage point for civilians.

This was simply the latest act of genuine evil committed by Russia since it invaded Ukraine in February, and more come daily. For Russia to be permitted in a human rights organization whose stated purpose is to "uphold the highest standards in the promotion and protection of human rights" is, as U.S. Ambassador to the United Nations Linda Thomas-Greenfield put it, "a farce." Indeed, that Russia should remain on the U.N. Security Council is just as farcical.

The wrinkle is that the Human Rights Council is itself a farce, a body historically dominated by totalitarians and autocrats whose governments are themselves egregious human rights violators that could not tell the difference between due process of law and a pina colada. Votes on toothless resolutions that virtually no one reads and even fewer care about are bought by governments whose focus is on keeping themselves from being scrutinized.

Mostly what the Council does is condemn Israel for... whatever. Over the past week or so, Israelis, including Israeli Arabs, have been murdered in cold blood by anti-Jewish fanatics, egged on by the rhetoric of the Palestinian Authority and Hamas, promises of posthumous payments to their families and the prospect of celebrations honoring them in the Gaza Strip and the West Bank, complete with the distribution of candy for all, to mark their heroism and the happy occasion of Israeli deaths. The Human Rights Council will say nothing about these massacres of innocent Israeli souls. It never does. It isn't that the Council is indifferent to the murder of Israelis. It's just that it couldn't care less.

But the overwhelming vote in the General Assembly to expel Russia from a body that is eye-rolling doesn't make it less of a good thing. The Biden administration's leadership in making Russia a pariah state is just one part of its multifaceted achievement in mobilizing much of the international community against Russia, capitalizing on the credibility it has in part because it isn't the Trump administration and in part by dint of the Biden team's experience and skill. Across the globe, often underneath the radar, Americans working for the State Department, the Defense Department, the CIA and other agencies have been working for months on turning the screws to the Russian economy, engineering boycotts of Russia, isolating Russia diplomatically and delivering weapons, weapons systems and intelligence to the Ukrainians. For Biden and his administration, this is not the stuff of self-congratulatory tweeting, unlike for some people. Their efforts frequently go unreported and are woefully under-praised. But they are having a huge impact.

The level of appreciation that Americans have for our countrymen serving overseas runs the gamut from scant to nonexistent. They work in circumstances that are exhausting, emotionally draining, obstacle-filled and dangerous. It helps that they have an administration to be proud of. It would help even more if they were given the credit they are due.

On the Edge: Democracy in the Balance, Here and Elsewhere

April 19, 2022

With heartbreaking videos of mass graves filled with Ukrainian victims of Russian genocide, civilians mowed down by sadistic Russian soldiers and apartment buildings pulverized by Russian missiles, there hasn't been much occasion for mirth. But you can count on Trump World to provide some comic relief.

Turns out North Carolina election officials removed former Trump chief of staff Mark Meadows from the state's voter rolls after it emerged that Meadows had voted absentee from a North Carolina residence where he had never resided. He not only listed a false address on his absentee ballot application, but his civic-mindedness in exercising his franchise was so fervent that he had registered to vote in two states at the same time.

It was Meadows who teamed up with his former boss to try to pressure Georgia's secretary of state to nullify Georgia's 2020 election results and induce him to fraudulently proclaim that a state that Joe Biden had won had been won by Donald Trump. Meadows is among the esteemed band of Trump aides who, subpoenaed to testify about the Jan. 6, 2021, coup attempt, either refused to honor the subpoena or invoked their Fifth Amendment right to avoid self-incrimination. He's been referred to the Justice Department for criminal charges for contempt of Congress. But the nation owes Meadows a real debt of gratitude for reminding us that the only apparent voter fraud in the 2020 election was committed by Trump's chief of staff.

Witlessness isn't a crime, but it does seem plain that Meadows is no Einstein. Fumbling to come up with something, anything, that would provide a molecule of support for Trump's fraudulent claim of election fraud, Meadows had this exchange with CNN's Jake Tapper at one point: "Do you realize how inaccurate the voter rolls are?" he asked the host without any sheepishness on account of his own voter fraud. When Tapper replied that there was no evidence of widespread voter fraud, Meadows was ready. "There's no evidence that there's not, either," he said. "That's the definition of fraud, Jake."

With Trump and many of his closest advisers either under criminal investigation, indicted, referred to the Justice Department for criminal prosecution or already convicted, the prospect of a return to power by the former president and the party that swears fealty to him should concentrate Americans' minds in a most serious way. It is a real prospect. The thanks accorded Biden for steering America through the national COVID-19 disaster bequeathed him by Trump, record economic growth, an unemployment rate of 3.6% and a historic response to Russian President Vladimir Putin's invasion of Ukraine is a 39% approval rating. Fifty-five percent of Americans say they disapprove of Biden's job performance.

Just what we need right about now is a Putin loyalist in the White House. Let's face it: As far as Russia's president is concerned, assuming Belarusian dictator Alexander Lukashenko is unavailable to take up residence at 1600 Pennsylvania Avenue, Trump would be the obvious next best choice.

Things don't look promising for democracy either here or abroad if the Party of Trump regains power. "I think NATO is obsolete," pronounced the Sage of Mar-a-Lago about the alliance of European democracies that holds a nuclear Russia at bay and is enabling Ukraine to defend itself. Former Trump national security adviser John Bolton believes Trump would have withdrawn from NATO in a second term. "And I think Putin was waiting for that," Bolton says.

More than 60 congressional Republicans recently voted against a resolution expressing support for NATO. Trump is seeking to bolster the bloc of Republicans happy to sell Ukraine down the river. Last weekend he endorsed Ohio Republican J.D. Vance for the Senate, not long after Vance bragged to former chief Trump strategist and twice-indicted podcast host Steve Bannon, "I gotta be honest with you, I don't really care what happens to Ukraine."

In this season of holidays, as we emerge from pandemic-induced hibernation, it's painful to consider that democracy is on the edge. The next months may determine whether and where it survives.

Two Steps Backward: Discrimination against Asian Americans Spikes, and Spikes Again

April 26, 2022

When newly elected Boston Mayor Michelle Wu announced last December that those entering certain indoor spaces would have to show that they had been vaccinated against COVID-19, there were some who believed it was simply outrageous for the mayor of Boston to try to protect Bostonians from a demonstrably deadly, highly transmissible virus. And no wonder they were outraged.

After all, only 1.6 million Massachusetts residents had contracted the virus, 175,000 of them in Boston. How Boston's mayor could have concluded that it would be sensible to impede the spread of the disease by taking steps to protect the public health was anyone's guess.

Many of the apoplectic expressed their disapproval of the policy measure in notably highbrow fashion. "Communist Wu needs to go back to China," one demanded of Wu, whose parents emigrated to America from Taiwan, not the Communist-run People's Republic of China. But, hey! Is being an ill-informed racist truly that much worse than being a plain old racist? "Another oriental in a governmental position," commented another. "Is it me or are there more oriental people within all facets and levels of influence?"

Some clever souls showered epithets on Mayor Wu of a sort that raises questions about whether their affliction is racism or simply remaining stuck in the fourth grade. Popular examples are "Michelle Wuhan" and "Mayor Wuhan". Get it?

Wu has impressed her city with sober, nuts-and-bolts governing; swift action to implement promises to relieve the pressures on communities particularly badly battered by the pandemic; and her upbeat persona. This hardly immunizes her from the haters. If anything, being an Asian American woman who is succeeding in a high-profile public position guarantees that she will find herself plagued by Lilliputians.

The vitriol that a small but ardent band of haters directs at her meshes with the data indicating that anti-Asian American bias, which surged in 2020, continues to climb, only at steeper and steeper rates. A report recently issued by the Center for the Study of Hate and Extremism at California State

University found that anti-Asian American hate crimes in America increased by 339% in 2021 over 2020. This is just the latest increase in a sharp upward trend; anti-Asian hate crimes had already spiked 124% in 2020 over 2019.

These statistics were consistent with last year's survey by the Anti-Defamation League, finding that harassment of Asian-Americans was on the rise. According to the ADL report, 17% of Asian-Americans experienced threats, insults or other forms of harassment. That figure is almost certainly conservative. "After a year where national figures, including the president himself, routinely scapegoated Chinese people for spreading the coronavirus," said ADL head Jonathan Greenblatt at the time, "Asian-Americans experienced heightened levels of harassment online, just as they did offline."

Greenblatt was alluding to former President Donald Trump's sneering references to COVID-19 as "the Chinese virus" or "Kung Flu," references intended to rouse his base to new lows of hatred, and often successfully so. But the data suggests that the poison released in 2020 is spreading, not receding. Gregg Orton, director of the National Council of Asian Pacific Americans, put it thus: "It's easy to dismiss racism when it doesn't impact you," Orton told ABC News. "This is people's safety and it's affecting their lives."

This week, Northeastern University School of Law is convening the first in a two-part series of programs on discrimination against Asian-Americans. Professor Margaret Woo, who is moderating one of the programs, says "Every single Asian-American I have talked to has had some experience with discrimination — every single one." It is, she says, "non-stop."

But the program's organizers, says Woo, "don't want this to be a victim's story." She points to the growth in Asian-American activism that has accompanied the sheer numerical growth in the percentage of Americans of Asian origin. "We won't be invisible anymore," says Woo. Keeping the spotlight on what Asian-Americans are subjected to can only help.

Honoring Albright: Making Certain the Ukrainians Win

May 3, 2022

At Madeleine Albright's funeral last week, former President Bill Clinton recalled one of his last conversations with the former secretary of state. A refugee first from the Nazis and then from Soviet tyranny who arrived on America's shores as an 11-year-old, Albright was a forceful advocate for the defense of democracy at home and freedom abroad, and she was plenty worried about both. Asked about her health, Albright told Clinton, "Let's don't waste any time on that. The only thing that really matters is what kind of world we're going to leave our grandchildren."

In his eulogy of Albright, President Joe Biden once again purposefully described America's circumstances as an "inflection point," and he is dead right about that. He finds himself called upon to steer America through three overlapping existential challenges, all occurring simultaneously, each making the others more difficult and more dangerous.

One is a still-unsolved pandemic that has killed one million Americans in a little over two years and has turned American society and the American economy upside down. Another is the growing strength of antidemocratic and even neo-fascist forces within our own country, more vast and more open than America has ever experienced, coddled and actually embraced by a Republican Party supported by half of Americans. The last is the invasion of a European ally by a nuclear-armed Russia guilty of crimes against humanity on a scale not seen in Europe since Adolf Hitler's last moments in a Bavarian bunker, led by a power-hungry dictator who threatens the world with nuclear war if he doesn't get to conquer a sovereign nation.

While keeping America's recovery from COVID-19 on track and reminding a divided America what being a democracy means, Biden's burden is to ensure that America doesn't succumb to weariness or a wandering attention span when it comes to Ukraine, and that our commitment to do what it takes to help Ukrainians defeat Russia doesn't flag.

The president's announcement of a new $33 billion military and economic aid package for Ukraine served multiple purposes. First and foremost, the Ukrainians desperately need it: Defending themselves against Russia's onslaught consumes huge amounts of weaponry, while the invasion has destroyed their infrastructure and their economy. American support determines whether the Ukrainians are overrun or not. Second, the aid package is a crucial message to Russia that America will stand by Ukraine's side for as long as it takes. Third, it spurs our European allies to do more of what we, and they, have been doing: keeping the arms and the financial assistance pouring into Ukraine, and reinforcing both the aid itself and the message to Moscow.

Biden put it plainly. "The cost of the fight is not cheap," he said in announcing his request for additional funding. "But caving to aggression is going to be costly if we allow it to happen. We either back the Ukrainian people as they defend their country, or we stand by as the Russians continue their atrocities and aggression in Ukraine."

The challenges that Biden faces rank right up there with those faced by Abraham Lincoln and Franklin Roosevelt. Like them, Biden is hectored by pundits and partisans who will be remembered for being demagogues or fruitcakes, or not remembered at all. Like Lincoln and Roosevelt, for all the venom directed Biden's way, he is meeting the challenges with steadiness and the warranted sense of the grave responsibility he bears.

Madeleine Albright, may she rest in peace, could not have put it any better than Biden did last week. Vladimir Putin's attempts to split the European allies, split America from Europe and split Americans in order to achieve his designs in Ukraine haven't worked thus far. There's no better way to honor Albright's legacy than to make sure they never do.

White Knight: The Producer Who Brought 'The Music Man' to Life

May 10, 2022

In his memoir "But He Doesn't Know the Territory," theatrical journeyman Meredith Willson recalls the eight long years he spent writing his homage to early 20th century life in the small-town Iowa of his youth. There were 30 revisions. There were 40 songs. And there were endless efforts to interest someone, anyone, in taking his play about the fictional town of River City, Iowa, and putting it on stage. Willson's rewrites, his pitch meetings, his attempts to buttonhole potential producers, were earnest, dogged — and unsuccessful.

Until the night of Dec. 19, 1956, when Willson and his wife visited Broadway producer Kermit Bloomgarden in his New York apartment, sat in front of a piano in the Bloomgarden family's living room and performed every line and song in the play. Bloomgarden's young sons John and David were there, and listened to the story of Professor Harold Hill, the charming if fraudulent musical instrument salesman who traveled the territory swindling the locals out of their money before moving on to new victims in unsuspecting pastures. Wilson introduced the Bloomgardens to songs that would go on to become American classics, like "(Ya Got) Trouble," "76 Trombones" and "Till There Was You."

Exactly one year later, on Dec. 19, 1957, "The Music Man" opened on Broadway. Bloomgarden, the son of Polish immigrants, was a product of New York public schools who began his career as an accountant before deciding that "the theater was for me." When he agreed to meet with Meredith Willson, he had already produced dramas like Arthur Miller's "Death of A Salesman" and "The Crucible." Bloomgarden's son David remembers Miller and his wife, Marilyn Monroe, coming to see his father at their apartment. It's a vivid memory: Monroe would play with him on his bedroom floor while Miller and his father talked business.

Kermit Bloomgarden loved the Willsons' husband-and-wife rendition of "(Ya Got) Trouble," and quickly told the couple he would produce it — even though he was in the middle of producing another Broadway play, "The Diary of Anne Frank." Unable to believe the good news, Willson asked one of Bloomgarden's competitors whether he should believe him. The competitor vouched for Bloomgarden's reputation as a straight shooter. "If he said he'll do it," said Bloomgarden's rival, "he'll do it."

Bloomgarden did. The story of Harold Hill's extended stopover in River City was one of small-town America: the good, the bad, the closed-minded and the kindly, the ugly and the sweet. The songs brought audiences to their feet. The show ran for three years, became a hit movie and has spawned several revivals. The number of high school, college and community theater productions of "The Music Man" since Kermit Bloomgarden first brought it to life roughly approximates the number of cornfields in Iowa, and it's no wonder. The show is cynic-proof; you would have to be the Unabomber not to love it.

Three years ago, a new revival was announced, scheduled to open in 2020, with Broadway megastars Hugh Jackman and Sutton Foster set to lead the big parade. A not-so-funny thing happened on the way to the opening, however: COVID-19 shut Broadway down for two years. The revival finally opened in February.

Kermit Bloomgarden died in 1976, leaving behind a rich theatrical legacy. Earlier this month, his son David, a retired physician now in his 70s, visited the show with his wife Jane. The experience left him drained: by the show's exuberance and by the emotional memory of accompanying his father to the theater at age 10 as the great American musical took shape. When it was over, and 1,500 theatergoers had finished a standing ovation, David Bloomgarden was brought backstage so that he could pay his respects to Jackman and Foster, and they to him and, through him, to his father. The two stars were warm, even tender, leaving Bloomgarden in tears, sure that his father would be as well.

In the Belly of the Beast: An Israeli Hero Goes to Harvard

May 17, 2022

"If you're not a socialist before you're 25," goes the expression, "you've got no heart. And if you're a socialist after 25, you've got no head." Retired Israeli Air Force Gen. Amos Yadlin wryly recalls the line in his office at Harvard University's Kennedy School, where he is wrapping up a semester as a senior fellow. Once an ace fighter pilot, Yadlin rose to deputy commander of the Israeli Air Force and since retirement has become one of his country's most widely respected defense experts.

Naturally, he was treated to weekly protests by a handful of Harvard students who screamed the customary "war criminal" and "colonialist, imperialist, apartheid-monger" epithets at him. As someone who flew over 250 combat missions, Yadlin is not intimidated. He is, he told one interviewer, proud "to defend Israel from those who wish to destroy it."

The ferocious efforts of those who want Israel to disappear and who are prepared to say anything at all about it are intended to drive students, faculty and administrators into silence, or complicity, and it often works.

Last month the student editors who presently run the Harvard Crimson acceded to the fashionable blather. Praising the "spirited activism" of those calling for Israel's elimination, the students published an editorial endorsing the boycott, divestment and sanctions, or BDS, movement, founded by characters who wish to wipe Israel off the map, designed to attempt to do just that. Of course, just two years ago, in 2020, the Crimson formally opposed BDS, criticizing narratives "that paint either (side of the Palestinian-Israel conflict) as 'the evil one'."

The current editors now say that they "regret and reject" the position they espoused just 24 months ago.

So much for stare decisis.

As usual, the Crimson editors and those to whom they caved offered no indication that they knew or cared to know about the Palestinian leadership's repeated spurning of the very Palestinian state that would end the occupation that they claim, falsely, the conflict is all about.

The death of Palestinian journalist Shireen Abu Akleh generated more of this. After a recent spate of murders of Israelis — murders in which the

Crimson displayed no interest — Israeli soldiers went into a West Bank town to try to apprehend those responsible. Palestinians fired automatic weapons at them from streets, alleyways and rooftops. The Israelis fired back. Abu Akleh was hit in the crossfire.

There's literally no basis for accusing Israel of deliberately killing her. Indeed, it's presently unclear whether she was accidentally struck by a Palestinian bullet or an Israeli one. Palestinian medical officials overseeing the autopsy stated they could not tell. The Israelis asked the Palestinians to cooperate in a joint investigation, so that the fatal bullet could be jointly analyzed.

No dice.

One can guess why the Palestinians refuse a joint investigation. Meanwhile, charges that Israel "murdered" Abu Akleh are simply rubbish. This, however, is what titans of intellectual rigor and fair-mindedness like Rep. Ayanna Pressley and Cori Bush have peddled. But they were positively Solomonic compared with forensic expert Susan Sarandon, who tweeted (all caps) that Israel had "EXECUTED" Abu Akleh.

The Israeli government contributed its own stupidity to the mix, bungling the journalist's funeral by attacking individuals next to her casket in response to rock-throwing for which it should have been prepared, and then claiming that the chanting of anti-Israel slogans partly justified their response. Shouting "How good it is to murder Jews!" is horrific. But attacking mourners is more horrific.

The BDS campaign, notes Yadlin, is composed of two groups. One includes those who simply want Israel dead. "These people are antisemites," he says. "Whatever you say to them will do nothing. The others, whom I respect, have criticisms of the policies of the Israeli government. For these, I'm happy to engage in dialogue. I tell them when I agree and when I disagree."

Seems sensible. But there's no surplus of sensibility at Harvard as long as the loudest voices succeed in causing sensible ones to run for cover.

Senator Scrappy: New Hampshire's Maggie Hassan Tells Mitch McConnell to Bring It On

May 24, 2022

Every politician alive claims they aren't afraid of a tough fight. Sometimes it's true, and sometimes it isn't. New Hampshire's Sen. Maggie Hassan doesn't flaunt it — or, for that matter, anything else — but where a willingness to take on fights is concerned, she's got some bragging rights.

The junior United States senator from the Granite State began her political career by challenging an incumbent state legislator in 2002, losing, and then getting right back up and challenging him in 2004, this time successfully. She served three terms in the state legislature — until that same former opponent came back to defeat her.

Unfazed, she launched a bid for governor, won, and then won reelection. Concentrating on governing's nuts and bolts, she balanced the state's budgets even while expanding the state's Medicaid coverage, freezing tuition at New Hampshire's state universities and lowering it at community colleges. In 2016 Hassan took on well-regarded Sen. Kelly Ayotte and defeated her by only about 1,000 votes.

Unsurprisingly, as Hassan runs for reelection she has been targeted by the National Republican Senatorial Committee and Senate Minority Leader Mitch McConnell, who are pouring anti-Hassan money into New Hampshire in hopes of defeating her. The fire hose of attack ads flows as though the control of the United States Senate depends on it, which it very well may. With the Senate equally divided between Democrats and Republicans and the House of Representatives likely to pass to Republican control, Hassan's defeat would formalize gridlock in Washington, with the Democrats controlling the White House, Republicans controlling both houses of Congress, and nothing, but nothing, achievable in our nation's capital for the ensuing two years.

Knocking Hassan off won't be easy. One of the reasons that Democrats risk being clobbered in November's midterms is the caricature made of them, a caricature in part of their own making: punctiliously "woke," dutifully singing from the "No-One-Has-Ever-Been-More-Progressive-Than-Me" hymnal. The big problem for national Republicans who need Hassan to lose won't be finding enough money for television ads, but rather Hassan's reputation as an independent in a state that honors independence.

Earlier this month the nonpartisan Lugar Center at Georgetown University, founded by the late Richard Lugar, the Republican senator from Indiana revered for his decades of bipartisan work with Democrats, ranked Hassan the most bipartisan member of the Senate. The Center issues a Bipartisan Index measuring how often members of Congress work productively with the other party. It noted that in 2021 Hassan had obtained a Republican co-sponsor for each of the 48 pieces of legislation she introduced.

This included legislation enacted into law on cybersecurity protection, targeted tax cuts for new businesses and support for mental health. She joined with Republican Sen. Bill Cassidy, R-La., to pass a law ending surprise medical billing, the so-called No Surprises Act, which protects patients from having to pay out-of-network costs for a range of services. She worked with Republicans to strengthen health care benefits for veterans. And she was one of the original Senate negotiators who crafted the bipartisan infrastructure law enacted last August.

This may not be bread-and-butter stuff for the Democratic Socialists of America, but it is for American families, including New Hampshire families. Hassan's ability to work with those across the dreaded divide has gained the attention of those idealistic few who still believe that bipartisanship in America, however ailing, isn't quite dead. "In 2021, Sen. Hassan not only had the highest Bipartisan Index score in the Senate," said Dan Diller, the Lugar Center's Policy Director, "she posted the highest score by a Democratic senator in the 29 years for which we have data. In doing so, she demonstrated an exceptional commitment to bipartisanship that sets the standard for other senators."

Not bad for a first-term senator. It's part of the reason McConnell and company know they have their work cut out for them.

Sorry State: Texas Massacre Highlights America's Gun Disease

May 31, 2022

Those whose goal in life seems to be keeping America in constant fear of mass shootings have an endless capacity for mindless, and dishonest, sloganeering. Years ago, former New York Rep. Al Lowenstein was napping in the front seat of an aide's car while being ferried to an event. In front of them was a car with a bumper sticker featuring the National Rifle Association's favorite rallying cry: "If they outlaw guns, only outlaws will have guns."

Lowenstein woke from his nap for a split second, saw the bumper sticker and murmured to no one in particular: "And if they outlaw marriage, only outlaws will have in-laws," before falling back asleep.

Distinguishing the gun lobby's mindlessness from its dishonesty can be a challenge. No one is suggesting that guns be "outlawed." But what has so obviously been so badly needed for so long are restrictions that reduce the frequency with which those too dangerous to be permitted to obtain guns nevertheless obtain them, and laws which keep weapons of mass destruction whose very purpose is to slaughter people off the streets — so that the number of instances in which those slaughters occur is reduced.

The preeminent conservative jurist of his time, the late Supreme Court Justice Antonin Scalia, authored a seminal Supreme Court decision holding that the Second Amendment's right to bear arms is "not unlimited." Nothing, Scalia wrote in that 2008 decision, should "cast doubt on longstanding prohibitions on the possession of firearms by felons and the mentally ill, or laws forbidding the carrying of firearms in sensitive places such as schools and government buildings, or laws imposing conditions and qualifications on the commercial sale of arms." Further, Scalia wrote, government is entitled to prohibit "dangerous and unusual weapons." Assault rifles manufactured for use in war are such weapons.

You might think that after the massacres of children at Columbine High School, Sandy Hook Elementary School, Parkland High School and now Uvalde, Texas' Robb Elementary School, among others, those responsible for blocking measures aimed at saving children's lives would at least show some sheepishness. Think again. The response to Uvalde by politicians leading the charge for firearms proliferation has been a veritable festival of inanities.

"I'm EMBARRASSED. Texas #2 in nation for gun purchases, behind CALIFORNIA. Let's pick up the pace Texans," tweeted then gubernatorial candidate Greg Abbott in 2015, when the number of gun purchases by his fellow Texans had already exceeded one million that year alone. After 19 schoolchildren and two teachers were blown to pieces last week by yet one more 18-year-old toting an assault rifle, Abbott informed the nation that "It could have been worse." Then this falsehood: "The reason it was not worse is because law enforcement officials did what they do. They showed amazing courage by running toward gunfire for the singular purpose of trying to save lives."

They did nothing of the sort. Instead, they waited passively outside the classroom while a teenager with a war machine that gun control advocates have long tried to ban ripped 21 souls to shreds — passively, quite likely, because they feared that their ordinary guns were no match for the murderer's assault weapon.

Texas Sen. Ted Cruz, long in the gun industry's pocket, chimed in with clever deflections. The way to prevent school massacres, he claimed with a straight face, was to make sure the back doors to school buildings were kept closed. As for gun massacres generally, says Cruz, why, that's because of "declining church attendance," "broken families" and "video games."

After they experienced massacres of the kind we experience regularly, democracies like the United Kingdom, Canada, Australia, Norway and New Zealand imposed new gun restrictions. The gosh-darndest thing then happened: their rates of gun violence plummeted.

There's a reason that America's rate of gun violence is so many times higher than elsewhere, and it isn't because we have more video games, don't go to church enough or do a poor job locking the back doors of our school buildings.

Weak Knees and Atrocity Fatigue: Putin Pins His Hopes on a Wavering West

June 7, 2022

As Vladimir Putin's missiles continued to reduce Ukrainian churches, homes and shelters to rubble, and as Russian artillery continued to pulverize Ukrainian communities with impunity, Ukraine's first lady implored Americans not to abandon the Ukrainian people out of weak knees and atrocity fatigue. "Don't get used to our pain," Olena Zelenska, wife of President Volodymyr Zelensky, pleaded in an interview with ABC News last week.

It's been 100 days since Russian forces invaded Ukraine because they could, in order to brutally subjugate a free nation whose people had the temerity to wish to remain free. Although Ukraine has resisted the Russian military with epic courage, its civilians remain largely defenseless against Russian barbarity. In European capitals, pro-Ukrainian rallies have disappeared. In America, rather than blame Putin for the rising energy and food costs spurred by the invasion, many blame President Joe Biden, suggesting that the inevitable escalating costs tied to the most significant European conflict since 1945 reflect on his "competence." This is a perception effectively peddled by Fox and friends; in truth, Biden has led the world's military, economic and diplomatic response to Russia with a steadiness that history will record with admiration.

Putin has reason to be encouraged, reinforced in his conviction that the West lacks the discipline, the staying power and the will to stand up for Ukraine if it means economic and political sacrifice. There is a stream of evidence that international resolve to stick with Ukraine has gone wobbly and attention on the consequences of a Putin victory has wavered.

French President Emmanuel Macron, who admits that he has spent 100 hours uselessly beseeching Putin to please respect Ukraine's sovereignty, proclaims that the world should make sure not to hurt his feelings. It is essential, Macron asserts, "not to humiliate Russia" in seeking to discourage it from slaughtering innocent Ukrainians. German Chancellor Olaf Scholz, professing when convenient to be Ukraine's staunch friend, has slow-walked German military assistance to the besieged Ukrainians. The Swiss just vetoed

Denmark's request to send Swiss-made armored vehicles to Ukraine, citing "neutrality."

At home, 11 Republican senators and 57 Republican members of Congress opposed the recent Ukrainian aid package. And the New York Times editorial board, which had published a ringing editorial in March pronouncing it America's sacred responsibility to signal to Putin that we would support Ukraine whatever it takes, triggered a wave of high-fives in the Kremlin by flip-flopping just 10 weeks later. It was, the Times intoned just 10 days after the Russians invaded, "imperative that the world continue to coalesce around the same message to Ukrainians and Russians alike: no matter how long it takes, Ukrainians will be free."

On May 17, after proclaiming that it was "imperative" that we send an unequivocal message to Russia that we stand with Ukraine, the geostrategic mavens of midtown Manhattan determined that it was now "imperative" that we make clear that we will not provide Ukraine with unequivocal support. The Times has ascertained that war is "messy" and "complicated," so Biden must "make clear to Zelenskyy that there is a limit to how far the United States and NATO will go to confront Russia, and limits to the arms, money and political support they can muster."

You guessed it: "It is imperative," the Times now tells the Ukrainians, "that the Ukrainian government's decisions be based on a realistic assessment of its means and how much more destruction Ukraine can sustain."

It was a gelatinous display by the Times, a message of vacillation dispiriting to brave Ukrainians battling to survive without the creature comforts enjoyed by editorialists and oxygenating to Putin and company. The Ukrainians can only hope that Americans will understand that their battle is our battle, and that we owe them all the support they need for as long as they need it, for their sake and ours.

High Crime in Prime Time: The Jan. 6 Committee Lays a Corrupt President Bare

June 14, 2022

In 1954, at a time when Sen. Joe McCarthy was still the most dangerous demagogue America had ever experienced, it was a courtly Boston lawyer named Joseph Welch whose words finally broke the grip on much of the country held by the thuggish senator from Wisconsin. "Have you no sense of decency, sir?" was the entirely rhetorical question posed by Welch that somehow exposed the morally bankrupt McCarthy for what he was during the Army-McCarthy hearings, jump-starting his political collapse. It's the line from the McCarthy era that history remembers most vividly.

If it turns out that the alarming fever that is Trumpism finally breaks and the nation that has more than flirted with Donald Trump now repudiates him, it may be Rep. Liz Cheney's message to her Republican colleagues last week that history remembers in the same way it remembers Welch's takedown. Cheney, a profile in political courage if America ever has had one, is the Republican vice chair of the congressional committee charged with investigating the former president's fraudulent, felonious attempts to remain in power despite being voted out of office by the American people. She has sacrificed her leadership position in the GOP, and will probably lose her seat in Congress altogether, because she has refused to go along with Trump's colossal con that he won an election he lost.

Lepers have been treated better than Cheney's fellow Republicans have treated her, because she, unlike they, refused to be intimidated by Mar-a-Lago's answer to Mussolini. "I say this to my Republican colleagues who are defending the indefensible," Cheney said during the committee's first night of hearings, "there will come a day when Donald Trump is gone, but your dishonor will remain."

The opening session was a tale of two women's courage. Joining Cheney in the history books was Capitol Police officer Caroline Edwards, granddaughter of a Korean War veteran who, like his granddaughter, was seriously wounded defending America. Edwards told a rapt nation about trying to hold the police line on Jan. 6 as the MAGA mob rushed the Capitol, bashing her brain in and leaving her with injuries from which she may never fully recover. Battered to the ground, she got back up to join her overwhelmed fellow police officers, slipping on their blood, catching them as the horde exhorted by Trump to stop the counting of electoral votes knocked them over.

"What I saw was a war scene," was how Edwards described Jan. 6. Here is how the most brazen liar in American history described it. "The love — the love in the air," Trump told Fox News. "I have never seen anything like it."

The Proud Boys and the Oath Keepers, the white supremacist paramilitary squads and Trump loyalists extraordinaire whose leaders have recently been indicted for seditious conspiracy, were literally front and center in the Jan. 6. assault, summoned to Washington by Trump, who exhorted them to "Be There. Will Be Wild!" The Proud Boys and the Oath Keepers are to Trump what the Iranian Revolutionary Guard is to the ayatollahs, and they rampaged through the Capitol looking to kidnap House Speaker Nancy Pelosi and Vice President Mike Pence.

Like everyone else who stormed the Capitol, they believed the lie that Trump trumpeted that he had won the 2020 election. This, as Trump's own attorney general told him, was pure "BS." A deeply dishonest Trump told his countrymen otherwise.

The committee expects to address other aspects of Trump's attempt to hold onto power any way he could, including discussions among certain of his Cabinet members about whether he should be removed from office immediately. It's never ideal when a president's own appointees are chatting about whether the man who appointed them is a criminal, insane or criminally insane. But America is in a dangerous place, and the Jan. 6 committee is doing its best to demonstrate just how dangerous that place is.

Prelude to a Perp Walk: 'Team Normal' Takes the Stand

June 21, 2022

    Those who had hoped that the public hearings of the congressional committee investigating former President Donald Trump's attempted coup d'etat would land with a thud must be disappointed by the wall-to-wall coverage of the evidence of the former president's effort to stay in office after being voted out of it. Every network has covered them except Fox, which would have run Roto-Rooter commercials rather than facilitate the viewing of the testimony.

    Some 20 million Americans watched the committee's opening session in prime time, and that doesn't count those who watched excerpts on social media or cable. An ABC/Ipsos poll conducted last weekend found that 60% of Americans feel the committee is conducting a fair, impartial investigation. Worse yet for Trump World, it found that 58% believe that Trump should be indicted.

    The committee meticulously laid out its case through the live and videotaped testimony of witnesses from Trump's inner circle: his attorney general, his deputy attorney general, White House counsel, his campaign manager and even his daughter. Their testimony demonstrated that Trump knew he'd lost the election, knew that the only fraud was his own fraudulent claim of election fraud, knew that Vice President Mike Pence had no authority to reject the electoral ballots from states President Joe Biden had won and knew that when Trump demanded that Pence reject them anyway, he was demanding that Pence violate the Constitution and federal law. That testimony was augmented by that of Pence's chief counsel and of iconic conservative jurist J. Michael Luttig, both of whom advised Pence that what Trump was demanding was illegal.

    Trump's campaign manager, Bill Stepien, described those in the Trump White House who tried weakly to persuade the president of the United States to obey the law rather than break it as "Team Normal." But this was only relative to the dominant team in the White House, "Team Wack Job," captained by the leader of the free world, which came within a hair of ending American democracy. It might have been nice had "Team Normal" spoken up before Jan. 6 instead of 18 months afterward, and also nice had they told the truth without the threat of congressional subpoenas requiring them to answer questions honestly or face perjury charges.

The committee has not messed around merely demonstrating Trump's disregard for his country, his dereliction of duty or his historic lack of moral compass. There's no longer any point to that.

It has focused instead on laying out the case that Trump is criminally culpable — quite simply, a crook. It is demonstrating that the evidence that he committed federal crimes isn't merely substantial, and that it is not just evidence beyond a reasonable doubt, but evidence that comfortably exceeds that high standard. And it is tailoring its presentation to two federal criminal statutes in particular. One makes it a crime to corruptly attempt to obstruct, impede or influence an official proceeding like the constitutionally mandated counting of electoral votes. The other makes it a crime to conspire to defraud the United States by obstructing an official proceeding by dishonest or deceitful means.

The committee is not exactly shooting in the dark here. Indeed, a federal judge who had occasion to review barely a sliver of the evidence of Trump's culpability has already ruled that he "more likely than not" was guilty of these two crimes, if not others. That judge hadn't even seen the mountain of evidence that the committee possesses inculpating Trump.

Ominously for Trump, the Justice Department has asked the committee to turn over copies of all of the transcripts and documents it has obtained during its investigation. Attorney General Merrick Garland has the unenviable task of deciding whether to seek to indict Trump, which will further inflame our national divisions, or decline to indict him, which will ruin America's right to regard itself as a nation of laws.

At Mar-a-Lago, Trump and his loyalists aren't just riding around in golf carts. They are chewing their fingernails.

Bum Rap: Slimed by the Right, Sniped at by the Left, Joe Biden Presses On

June 28, 2022

If you follow Fox News, the big story of the week wasn't about the former American president who urged his supporters to murder his vice president so that he could stay in office after being voted out of it. It was that President Joe Biden who, according to a wingnut-driven narrative was elected by election machines manipulated by Martians, fell off a bicycle. This was really significant for acolytes of a certain former leader who — let's put it this way — is not exactly notable for his athleticism, and it was just the evidence Biden's detractors were looking for that he "is not up to the job." It seemed a wee bit like wishful thinking by supporters of someone who encouraged his countrymen to self-inject cleaning fluid to avoid contracting COVID-19, but there you are.

Americans suffer from short memories, which works decidedly to Biden's disadvantage. When he took office, the country was in economic, social and political free fall. A pandemic that Biden's predecessor had brilliantly dismissed as a "hoax" had ravaged Americans, leaving millions of them suddenly out of work. Instead of pulling together in a crisis, Americans targeted one another. And a former president who legitimately qualified as a fascist had undermined the institutions on which American democracy rests.

Biden began by managing to persuade Americans to vaccinate themselves and their families against COVID-19, overcoming the right-wing influencers who belittled the vaccine while making sure that they received it. Over 67% of us are now fully vaccinated, to huge beneficial effect.

The aid packages orchestrated by Biden did what they were intended to do. The first year of Biden's presidency saw record economic growth and record job creation. Unemployment, which stood at 6.7%, now stands at 3.6%.

Biden's critics blame him for our high inflation rate. This makes no sense. Michael Klein, professor of international economic affairs at the Fletcher School at Tufts University and founder of the economic analysis website Econofact, puts it succinctly: "Inflation is a problem all over the world." A recent Deutsche Bank report shows that America's year over year inflation rate is near the median among the 111 countries surveyed. Our 8.6%

rate is lower than that of the United Kingdom (9.1%), the Netherlands (8.8%) and Spain (8.7%), and only slightly higher than that of the Eurozone as a whole (8.1%).

Biden has nothing to do with the problem. Asked what role a president has in inflation, Klein replies, "Virtually none." And to the extent that COVID-19 aid packages so vital to our recovery contributed to inflation at the margins, Klein makes the necessary point with an analogy. "During COVID," he says, "we were on the precipice of an abyss. It's very hard when you're putting out a fire to avoid water damage."

Then there's the little matter of Ukraine, a country that people of conscience understand needs to be defended against Russia, a country that people of conscience understand needs to be defeated. The spikes in energy and food prices caused by Russian aggression should be laid not at Biden's feet but those of Vladimir Putin, whom the not-so-Grand Old Party coddled for four long, humiliating years.

The Left's carping at Biden makes no more sense than that of the Right. If the president does not cancel all student debt upon the demand of Rep. Alexandria Ocasio-Cortez and Sen. Elizabeth Warren, he is denounced by the same crowd who helped hand the country over to former President Donald Trump in the first place. They seem prepared to do it again. The Squad gets to tweet. Biden has to run the country and lead what is left of the free world.

Bulletin: tweeting is easier.

With Roe v. Wade demolished, we remember the geniuses who refused to support Hillary Clinton because there wasn't much difference between Clinton and Trump. We have them to thank for three Supreme Court justices and an end to constitutional protection of women's right to choose.

Thanks, guys. Job well done.

Courting Dissolution: An Unprincipled Gang of Justices Threatens to Take America Down

July 5, 2022

In December 2000, then-Rep. Edward Markey was at a charity dinner in Boston, and the conversation turned to the court battle over the disputed Florida election that would determine whether Vice President Al Gore or Texas Gov. George W. Bush would win Florida and be declared the next president. Bush was leading by just over 500 votes in an election marred by rampant irregularities, and the Florida Supreme Court had ruled that state law required that there be a recount.

Bush asked the U.S. Supreme Court to overrule the Florida court and order that the Florida recount then underway be stopped, meaning that he would win the presidency.

Not long before, the staunchly conservative chief justice of the Supreme Court, William Rehnquist, had raised eyebrows by having four gold stripes placed on the sleeves of his black judicial robe, channeling the costume of the all-powerful Lord Chancellor in the Gilbert and Sullivan operetta "Iolanthe." Rehnquist debuted his new gold stripes while presiding over the Senate impeachment trial of President Bill Clinton. The stripes seemed somewhat peculiar, and perhaps even worse than that.

As the nation awaited the Supreme Court's decision, Markey asked the lawyers at his table whether they thought it would review the Florida state court's ruling holding that Florida law required that the votes cast in Florida's election be recounted.

Absolutely not, came the unanimous reply. After all, conservative Supreme Court justices had been forever adamant that federal courts had no business interfering with state law on state matters such as state election procedure. Accepting the Florida case for review would violate long-cherished conservative jurisprudence, or at least what conservatives had long claimed was long-cherished conservative jurisprudence.

"I disagree," said Markey. "Anyone who puts gold stripes on his sleeve is going to take the case."

Markey was right. The majority of the Supreme Court, loyal Republicans all, were delighted to disregard the precedent they had said was sacrosanct, and not only review the Florida decision but reverse it, stopping the recount and ensuring that Bush, not Gore, became president. It had nothing to do with exalted-sounding legal principles. It had everything to do with politics.

Even before the Supreme Court officially overturned 50 years of its own precedent by nullifying Roe v. Wade, a Gallup poll found that confidence in the court had fallen to an all-time low, with only 25% of Americans expressing confidence in America's highest court. That places it lower than body shop cost estimators and insurance adjusters, and with good reason.

The conservative justices who decided that a woman's constitutional right to bodily privacy no longer existed had earned their own stripes insisting that government has limited power to dictate to citizens how to live their lives. So much for that hooey: the court has now ruled that government is entitled to demand that women give birth against their will on pains of being criminally prosecuted. Justices like Neil Gorsuch and Brett Kavanaugh, who gravely assured United States senators of their profound respect for stare decisis — the doctrine that courts should consider themselves bound by judicial precedent — played the Senate for suckers, and it worked. They knew full well that when given the opportunity to eliminate women's right to choose whether to give birth by jettisoning the 1972 Roe decision they would do so — and that's exactly what they did.

We're all suckers now, and there's more to come. Last Thursday the court announced it would consider adopting the "independent state legislature theory," a heretofore fringe argument that would permit state legislatures to determine not only voting rights but whether Republican-controlled legislatures can disregard actual presidential election results and certify their own phony presidential electors without review by state courts or election officials. Four of the conservative justices have already expressed support for this theory.

Twenty-two years ago, Ed Markey observed that things ain't all on the level at the Supreme Court. The question now is whether America will pay the supreme price.

Political Asylum: The Jan. 6 Committee Spotlights America's Crazy Problem

July 12, 2022

It was just over a week ago that 100 members of the white nationalist group Patriot Front descended on Boston and marched along the city's iconic Freedom Trail holding a banner reading "Reclaim America." The group, which spearheaded two of the largest white supremacist rallies in the country last year, is described by the Southern Poverty Law Center as "one of the most prominent white supremacist groups in the United States" and openly embraces Nazism.

Boston Mayor Michelle Wu called the group's march "disgusting." She is right, of course, but it was also unsurprising. The Front boasts chapters in 40 states, and actively recruits on college campuses, in the military and elsewhere. Along with the Proud Boys, the Oath Keepers, QAnon and a witches' brew of organized, semi-organized and loosely organized right-wing groups, it represents a steadily metastasizing American cancer that in an all-too-real sense threatens America's survival.

Sociologist Pete Simi, co-author of "American Swastika: Inside the White Power Movement's Hidden Spaces of Hate," notes that many of those guilty of the mass murders that get passed off as the product of plain vanilla "mental illness" have taken the teachings of these lunatics to heart. "We are dealing with a massive movement," Simi says. "We saw it manifest itself in terms of the January 6th insurrection. We saw it in Charlottesville at the deadly rally there. We're seeing it with these single actor attacks all over the country: Buffalo, El Paso and Pittsburgh. Time and time again we're seeing these incidents of violence kind of written off as a single lone deranged actor instead of an actual movement that's promoting this kind of violence."

Indeed, many of those guilty of the massacres to which professor Simi alludes share a common adherence to "replacement theory," a racist doctrine endorsed by Fox personalities Tucker Carlson and Laura Ingraham and spread by them to their viewers.

The House committee investigating former President Donald Trump's attempt to overturn an election and keep himself in power will hold two more hearings this week. California Rep. Zoe Lofgren, a committee member, told

CNN that she expected them to "connect the dots" for Americans on the symbiotic relationship between the former president and America's dregs.

Lofgren was being not merely discreet but generous. Anyone who still needs to have the dots connected for them wouldn't acknowledge a dot if it jumped onto the kitchen table and began performing the "Macarena." The relationship between Trump and white supremacists isn't only a mutuality of interests. It is a two-way love fest.

Trump, who defended the "very fine people" among the white nationalists, neo-Nazis and klansmen chanting racist and antisemitic slogans at Charlottesville, Virginia, was heartily endorsed by former Ku Klux Klan leader David Duke in 2016 and again in 2020, though Duke did urge Trump to replace Vice President Mike Pence on the ticket with Tucker Carlson. Patriot Front leader Thomas Rousseau, arrested recently for conspiracy to attack an LGBTQ event, is another huge Trump booster.

After The Donald urged his supporters to travel to Washington, D.C., on Jan. 6 to pressure Congress to block the transfer of power to President Joe Biden and promised them a "wild" time, his biggest fans showed up in force and with weapons. The neo-fascist Proud Boys, identified by the Southern Poverty Law Center as an "alt-right fight club," came ready to do what was needed to keep their man Trump in office. Ditto for the Oath Keepers, whom the FBI has called a "paramilitary organization" and the Anti-Defamation League calls "heavily armed extremists with a conspiratorial mindset." The leaders of both groups have been indicted by a federal grand jury for conspiring to overthrow the government of the United States by force, which used to be considered a bad look.

Yes, there will be some fairly straightforward connecting of the dots this week. One would have to be inordinately resistant to dot-connecting to miss the connections.

But in the America in which we find ourselves, we have plenty of that kind of resistance.

Family Visits: Biden's Mideast Trip Starts Warm, Ends Chilly

July 19, 2022

President Joe Biden's recently completed trip to Israel and Saudi Arabia was a tale of two family visits. But these were two very different families.

The warmth that Biden received and returned in Israel was obvious, and unsurprising. Beginning with his arrival at Tel Aviv's Ben Gurion Airport, he seemed among kin, and he was greeted that way. Noting that it was his 10th visit to Israel, Biden remarked that it was "like returning home." Israeli President Isaac Herzog welcomed him as "our brother Joseph," and the top officials in the American delegation mingled with their Israeli counterparts with smiles, embraces and back pats that had the appearance of a college reunion.

Biden, who entered the Oval Office with more experience in the mind-splitting complexities of the Middle East than any of his predecessors, wasted no time standing up once again to Democratic leftists who've been irreversibly snookered by a fundamentally antisemitic BDS (boycott, divestment and sanctions) movement. Asked by an Israeli interviewer about the slice of Democrats who have supported sanctions against Israel and voted against funding a defensive anti-missile system deployed to protect Israeli civilians from rockets intended to murder them, Biden pulled no punches. "There are a few of them," Biden replied. "I think they're wrong. I think they're mistaken."

The runup to Biden's trip to Israel was attended by knowledgeable-sounding reports that his schedule would have to be curtailed so he could rest after a long flight. The president then proceeded to do what seemed like 137 separate events over his two days in-country: here conferring with Prime Minister Yair Lapid, there sitting with elderly American Holocaust survivors, here meeting with Herzog, there cheering on 1,400 American athletes participating in an international sporting competition.

Biden's display must have disappointed Republicans, who feverishly treat any word misread off the presidential teleprompter as evidence that Biden is not "up to the job," but whose once and future hero passed his four years in the White House clicking the television remote and riding in golf carts. Biden, who keeps himself admirably fit, looked positively like an Olympic swimmer standing next to 86-year-old Palestinian Authority President Mahmoud Abbas, now in the 17th year of a four-year term. It's a wonder that former President Donald Trump never felt a stronger affinity for Abbas, who proves year after year that it is indeed possible to stay in office long after the law says you have to leave it.

Then it was on to a meeting with Arab leaders in Jeddah, which began with the fist bump scrutinized 'round the world between Biden and Crown Prince Mohammed bin Salman, the de facto head of the Saudi royal family. MBS, assessed by American intelligence to have ordered the murder of journalist Jamal Khashoggi, is the loathsome face of a loathsome regime. Trouble is, on everything from energy costs burdening American families to the burgeoning malign alliance between Russia and Iran, Saudi Arabia is positioned to be helpful. Presidents, alas, cannot ignore facts like this. Editorial writers can, and that Biden's trip to Saudi Arabia was criticized by Sen. Rand Paul on one side and Sen. Bernie Sanders on the other is prima facie evidence that under the circumstances the trip made sense.

As for the much-ballyhooed fist bump, from the breathless media coverage afforded it one might suppose it signified "Great to see you again, old buddy!" rather than "I had to come here and I had to do something, and I ain't shaking his hand." If there's ever been a more unsmiling state visit than this one, it doesn't come to mind.

For his part, former President Barack Obama sent not only greetings but tens of billions of dollars in sanctions relief to Iran's god-awful leaders. As for Trump, think "love letters" to North Korean madman Kim Jong-un and four years of posterior-kissing of Vladimir Putin, the slaughterer then and now of thousands of Ukrainians.

For Biden, it's now back to America, and more fun at home.

Symptoms of a Different Kind: Biden's May Be Mild, but the Former Guy's Aren't

July 26, 2022

On Thursday morning the news broke that President Joe Biden had tested positive for COVID-19, two and a half years after its outbreak. His symptoms were mild. Turns out the vaccine actually helps. Go figure.

But by Thursday night, with the close of the Jan. 6 committee's first set of hearings into former President Donald Trump's attempted coup d'etat, if anything was clear it was that the former president has symptoms of a different variety, and the last thing they are is mild. Just as Trump lied to Americans that COVID-19 was a nothingburger, that it was a media contrivance and that his administration had it "under control," he lied to Americans that he had won an election he lost.

It didn't matter that he knew he had lost — he didn't want to stop being president, poor thing. So, he tried to bully election officials and state legislators into violating the law on his behalf. And when that didn't work, he tried to bully his vice president into violating not only the law but the Constitution on his behalf.

When that didn't work either he decided to summon a mob of crazies to storm the U.S. Capitol, watching in glee for three hours as his mob ransacked the Capitol, mauled and beat 100 police officers and, oh yes, threatened to hang the vice president who had refused to be bullied.

Along the way, Trump met with some truly certifiable advisers, off their rockers one and all, about seizing America's voting machines and ordering an election do-over in battleground states he had lost. The proffered justification? Well, what else: that the voting machines had been manipulated by a deceased Venezuelan, or maybe by Italians, or perhaps space aliens. He came close to appointing the barking mad attorney Sidney Powell to the newly created position "special counsel," deputized by Trump to bring charges against, well, anyone he wanted her to bring charges against. And considering that 81 million Americans chose Biden over Trump, that could have been a whole lot of charges.

For good measure he attempted to appoint an emergency attorney general who pledged to proclaim that the 2020 election was fraudulent because Trump lost it. Trump backed off only when informed that the Department of Justice would basically resign en masse if he did.

On Jan. 6 Trump watched the mayhem he had created with satisfaction, rejecting the pleas of the compos mentis around him to tell his supporters to stop the violence and go home. He told people that his mob's calls to hang the vice president were OK by him. And when he finally told the storm troopers who reported to him to stand down, it was only when it was plain they wouldn't succeed in overturning the election and keeping him in power.

Yes, Donald Trump has symptoms, all right, and we're not talking about a runny nose. When the committee showed outtakes from his reluctant taping of a video address to the nation on Jan. 7, the country saw a faker, forced by his daughter to disavow the previous day's attack, but refusing to say that the election was actually over. And for someone whose supporters quiver with excitement every time Joe Biden stumbles over a word, the outtakes weren't pretty. Trump had trouble with simple words. "'Yesterday' is a hard word for me," lamented Trump, who ordered his staff to remove the complex expression from the teleprompter.

There have been signs that lightbulbs that have stayed dark for inexplicably long have flickered on here and there. Focus groups of Trump voters in Wisconsin and Arizona announced that they wanted him criminally prosecuted. One dares to hope that if they believe he should be in prison they wouldn't vote for him, but, hey, who knows?

This past weekend the two newspapers most loyal to Trump, The Wall Street Journal and the New York Post, both published editorials stating that he was unfit to be president. Which brought one word to mind above others: Duh.

Damned Either Way: Merrick Garland Weighs the Mother of All Indictments

August 2, 2022

In October 1974, President Gerald Ford appeared before Congress to provide his rationale for pardoning former President Richard Nixon after Nixon had resigned from office. Ford's purpose in absolving Nixon of criminal prosecution for crimes including obstructing the investigation into the Watergate break-in, he said, was "to change our national focus." We would, he argued, "needlessly be diverted from meeting (our) challenges if we as a people were to remain sharply divided over whether to indict, bring to trial and punish a former president, who already is condemned to suffer long and deeply in the shame and disgrace brought upon the office he held."

To recall Ford's preemptive get-out-of-jail-free card, issued to America's first certifiably felonious president, is to wonder whether Ford paved the way for our second. Was former President Donald Trump emboldened by the precedent of letting off a criminal ex-president scot-free in order to spare the nation "division"? Was he encouraged to regard himself as free to commit crimes while in office by the legal opinion issued by Nixon's Department of Justice in September 1973 — while Nixon's criminality was being exposed but before he was forced to resign — that a sitting president couldn't be indicted?

We'll never know. But we do know that Ford's rationale for letting Nixon skate doesn't apply to the decision Attorney General Merrick Garland must make whether to ask a grand jury to indict Trump.

For starters, Nixon's obstruction of the investigation into the White House's role in Watergate may have been profoundly criminal, but it amounted to jaywalking compared with Trump's attempt and conspiracy to obstruct the constitutionally mandated counting of electoral votes governing the democratic transfer of power — let alone the crime of conspiracy to commit sedition. As serious as Nixon's crimes were, they pale beside the evidence of a criminal coup d'etat, and there is quite a mountain of such evidence already in the public record.

Here is one question: if a former president is not prosecuted for attempting a criminal coup to keep himself in power against the expressed will of the American people, when would he or she ever be prosecuted? Here's another: how can we look at ourselves in the mirror if someone guilty of that crime is simply allowed to walk?

The answer to the first question: never. The answer to the second: we can't.

It isn't only the magnitude of criminality that differentiates Trump from Nixon. Trump has defrauded America every time it suited him and cheated it when he couldn't defraud it. When he couldn't do either, he simply disgraced it, and in so doing disgraced all of us.

Nixon at least slunk away with a modicum of acknowledgement that he had sullied the presidency. Trump, who wouldn't recognize "sully" if it jumped up and played "On Top of Old Smoky," is not merely remorseless but defiant, eager to pick up where he left off.

Still, the critical issue is whether the Justice Department has sufficient evidence to establish Trump's guilt of a statutory crime beyond a reasonable doubt. If it doesn't, that's the end of it. If it does, then indictment is the necessary, if painful, course.

What happens if Trump is indicted? What happens if Trump is indicted but acquitted, remembering that all his criminal defense lawyers have to do is persuade one juror not to vote to convict? What happens if he is convicted? Will the Supreme Court dominated by justices Trump appointed really permit him to report to a federal prison?

For wisdom, Garland may want to consider other democracies that took a deep breath and prosecuted former leaders for various crimes of corruption. France, Italy and Israel are among them, and their democracies were strengthened, not weakened, for their having done so. They judged that the cost of prosecuting dishonest leaders was lower than that of looking the other way. Whether the United States makes the same judgment is in Merrick Garland's hands.

J Street Blues: The Group That Wants to Be AIPAC

August 9, 2022

The lobbying group J Street, which markets itself as "the pro-Israel, pro-peace" organization, wants you to know this: it, uniquely, is "pro-peace," and if you beg to differ with some of its stranger pronouncements on the Middle East, you aren't.

But there's more.

If you believe that some of what J Street asserts is wrong, and you desire to say so publicly — including, say, by supporting political candidates that J Street doesn't — it wishes to inform you that you are a "dark" force that is improperly "intervening" in American democracy.

That's the takeaway thus far from the Democratic primary season, in which J Street has locked arms with some of the most egregiously antisemitic operators around, blasting the American Israel Public Affairs Committee, the group it both despises and seeks to emulate. AIPAC has long been the boogeyman for anti-Jewish conspiracy theorists on the extreme Right and the extreme Left, who contend that Jews control Congress, the media and Major League Baseball's wild card races. J Street has taken to attacking AIPAC in terms right out of "Antisemitism for Dummies."

But its attacks aren't merely increasingly ugly. They are unabashedly hypocritical.

J Street was launched in 2008, boosted by massive cash infusions from the not-exactly-Israel-friendly George Soros, a mysterious Pittsburgh businessman and an even more mysterious character from — where else? — Happy Valley, Hong Kong. It flourished thanks to the frosty relationship between President Barack Obama and Israeli Prime Minister Benjamin Netanyahu. During the Trump years it benefited from the hubris of some in the traditional pro-Israel community, including AIPAC, who ignored the fact that President Donald Trump's embrace of Israel functioned as a poison kiss, causing Democratic constituencies to run for the exits where Israel was concerned.

By 2020, J Street boasted that it was funneling over $9 million to candidates it supported and "had emerged as one of the top bundlers in

Democratic politics." There was nothing "dark" about its own money — just that of others.

The election of a staunchly pro-Israel Democratic president in Joe Biden left J Street on shaky footing. Trump's defeat and Netanyahu's replacement with a moderate Israeli government encompassing a wide left-to-right coalition of parliamentarians left J Street without a foil.

Except AIPAC.

The more mainstream of the two organizations, AIPAC was never the Monopoly card caricature Israel-haters had portrayed it to be — the fat cat with the cigar hanging out of his mouth and cash hanging out of his pockets. With 1.8 million members across America and with national conferences that drew as many as 20,000 Americans to Capitol Hill, it has always surpassed J Street in all metrics.

To make matters worse, last year AIPAC announced that it was forming its own political action committee, and a super PAC to boot. It decided to support Democratic primary candidates it believed understood Mideast realities, and to oppose those it believed did not. Virtually all of the candidates it supported were people of color, women or both. And so far, of the nine Democratic primaries in which it has engaged, AIPAC's choices have won seven times. Washington, D.C. is a town that notices this sort of thing.

J Street lost those seven races despite spending tons of money of its own on them. It is displeased. "This aggressive intervention in Democratic primaries to promote an unpopular agenda is harmful to the Democratic Party and ultimately to the State of Israel," it proclaimed graciously after losing another race last week.

When J Street pours millions of dollars into campaigns it cares about, is it "dark" money? When Emily's List supports women, is it "aggressively intervening" in politics? When the American Federation of Teachers or the International Brotherhood of Electrical Workers, among the top PAC contributors in recent elections, supports candidates that share their views, is it harmful to democracy according to J Street or the Democratic Left?

Spoiler alert: it isn't. Which raises real questions not about AIPAC but about those expending so much effort demonizing it.

Rap Sheet: If It's Friday, It Must Be the Espionage Act

August 16, 2022

Some week last week.

On Wednesday, former President Donald Trump, already under criminal investigation for conspiring to obstruct the Senate's counting of the electoral votes that made Joe Biden president (federal grand jury), election fraud (Georgia grand jury) and tax and bank fraud (Manhattan district attorney), refused to answer 440 questions directed to him during a civil deposition that he'd been ordered to attend, invoking his Fifth Amendment right not to incriminate himself. "The Mob takes the Fifth," Trump sneered at a 2016 rally. "If you're innocent, why are you taking the Fifth Amendment?"

Uh-oh!

New York's Attorney General had compelled Trump to show up to answer questions about whether he had defrauded tax authorities, financial institutions and God knows who else in connection with false tax filings and loan applications. The Former Guy's refusal to do anything but decline to answer for four hours qualified him for induction into The Fifth Amendment Hall of Fame. But though invoking the Fifth can't be held against the invoker in a criminal case, it sure can in a civil case like the one he and his company face in New York. This means that they are likely to lose that case and pay stiff financial penalties as a consequence.

Which isn't to say that Trump's decision to clam up wasn't the right move given the alternative. It was. In the virtually inconceivable event that Trump actually told the truth at the deposition about his tax filings and financial statements, he would revive the Manhattan district attorney's criminal probe, presently dormant. And in the virtually certain event that Trump lied in the deposition, he would generate yet one more set of criminal charges against him for — you guessed it! — perjury.

By Friday, however, Wednesday's news that the former president of the United States had taken the Fifth about whether he had committed a whole lot of fraud seemed like the stuff of an almost idyllic past, sort of the good old days. By Friday it was possible to feel almost nostalgic about Wednesday.

Because on Friday it emerged that the FBI, the Justice Department and a federal judge all agreed that there was probable cause to conclude that Trump had committed three additional federal crimes — crimes that hadn't been on anyone's radar screen. Trump had chosen to announce that the FBI had executed a search warrant, duly authorized by the federal judge, at Trump's home at Mar-a-Lago. He had spent the week purporting to angrily demand that the search warrant and the list of items seized by the FBI be released to the public — even though he had these documents in hand and simply had to press "send" on his computer if he actually wanted Americans to see them.

He really didn't. The warrant, released after Attorney General Merrick Garland called Trump's bluff by asking the judge to disclose it, reflected a judicial finding of probable cause to believe that Trump had willfully and unlawfully concealed, removed or destroyed government records, knowingly destroyed or concealed documents with the intent to obstruct a federal investigation and, for the cherry on top, violated the Espionage Act.

Yes, the Espionage Act. Among the documents that Trump removed from the White House, then withheld in defiance of a subpoena, then apparently hid from the government, were highly classified materials, reportedly including documents relating to nuclear secrets.

You'd need a software program at this point to keep track of the evidence of Trump's criminality. It's all beginning to look like a first-year law student's criminal law exam: Here is the fact pattern. How many different crimes has this individual committed?

And who can forget the 10 separate federal crimes of obstruction of justice detailed in Special Counsel Robert Mueller's 2019 report that, it turns out, were just the hors d'oeuvres?

A great American, No. 45. Making America great, one crime at a time.

Armed and Dangerous: Domestic Extremism Grows, and the GOP Goes Along for the Ride

August 23, 2022

It takes a serious case of denial to dismiss the threat to America posed by domestic extremism and to pretend that it isn't a metastasizing civic cancer. But MAGA World isn't merely denying the threat. They're doing their very best to stoke it.

Financial Times editor Edward Luce recently tweeted, "I've covered extremism and violent ideologies around the world over my career. Have never come across a political force more nihilistic, dangerous and contemptible than today's Republicans. Nothing close." Gen. Michael Hayden, George W. Bush's CIA director, replied simply, "I agree."

If there were ever a time that we could really do without a nihilistic, dangerous and contemptible Republican Party, this is it. FBI Director Christopher Wray, appointed by former President Donald Trump ("He is an impeccably qualified individual," said Trump), told the Senate Judiciary Committee earlier this month that the threat of violent domestic extremism "has really surged" since 2020. "We put (it) into the category of anti-government, anti-authority, violent extremism," said Wray. "That includes everything from militant violent extremism all the way to anarchist violent extremism. What they all have in common is a focus on institutions of government and law enforcement as their likely target."

This stuff is often infused with a few extra shots of racially motivated extremism, dominated by white supremacy. Then there is the online radicalization spawned by squadrons of conspiracy theorists. And it's all topped off by the come-on-down availability of weapons of mass destruction.

So, it's an excellent moment for the GOP to hurl attacks against federal law enforcement. Sure, the attacks may be mindless and defamatory, but they are catnip for the mob. Following the execution of a search warrant at Trump's home after probable cause that he committed three federal crimes was found by a federal magistrate, the FBI and the Department of Homeland Security issued a warning that law enforcement and other government agencies were facing "increased threats." Online calls for "civil war" and "armed rebellion" have been proliferating, as have messages like "(Attorney General Merrick) Garland needs to be assassinated" and "Kill all feds."

Threats against the federal magistrate who signed the search warrant for Mar-a-Lago have necessitated the court in which he works taking special precautions to protect him.

In Pennsylvania, federal authorities arrested a man who allegedly posted: "Every single piece of (expletive) who works for the FBI in any capacity, from the director down to the janitor who cleans their (expletive) toilets deserves to die" and "My only goal is to kill more of them before I drop." In Phoenix, a group of pro-Trump protesters openly wielding automatic weapons (yes, it's legal there) converged on the FBI field office. In Cincinnati, a man with an assault rifle tried to break into the FBI office before exchanging gunfire with law enforcement, losing the exchange. He had posted messages on Trump's Truth Social platform calling on "patriots" to kill federal law enforcement agents. "I am proposing war," he is reported by The New York Times to have posted.

Republican luminaries are doing their best to fuel this kind of thing. Republican Sen. Chuck Grassley went on "Fox & Friends" to warn that IRS agents are "going to have a strike force that goes in with AK-15s already loaded, ready to shoot... middle class and small businesspeople." Sen. Ted Cruz, whose remarkable lack of moral compass will be of clinical interest to historians for years to come, tweeted that it was "obvious that (the Mar-a-Lago search) is nothing more than a blatant political persecution." Republican candidates for Congress across the country called for the defunding of the FBI. Trump's favorite nutjob, Georgia Rep. Marjorie Taylor Greene, took to selling "Defund the FBI" merchandise for her political campaign committee, WinRed.

Former Vice President Mike Pence was notable in condemning attacks on law enforcement. But he stood out. The GOP, once purportedly the law-and-order party, just looks like a party of lawbreakers.

I Spy: A Former Guy with the Look of a Crook
August 30, 2022

By the end of last week, it wasn't only that our former president was under criminal investigation for conspiracy to obstruct the counting of electoral votes so that he could illegally remain president after losing the 2020 election. It wasn't merely that a Georgia grand jury was investigating whether he had conspired to commit election fraud by demanding that the Georgia secretary of state "find" him 11,800 phony votes so that he could claim to have won an election he lost.

It wasn't simply that he had invoked his Fifth Amendment right not to incriminate himself in order to avoid answering 440 questions about whether he committed bank and tax fraud. And it wasn't just that his direct report at the Trump Organization, the company's chief financial officer, admitted committing 15 separate felonies while reporting to him.

No, by the end of last week we had entered a new realm altogether, in which a federal magistrate had found probable cause to conclude that former President Donald Trump had committed three more federal crimes, including violating the Espionage Act, and in which it was disclosed that he had decided to take hundreds of pages of "Confidential," "Secret" and "Top Secret" documents with him when he left the White House and kept them at Mar-a-Lago.

The documents classified as "Confidential" are ones that "could reasonably result in damage to (America's) national security." Those marked "Secret" "could reasonably result in serious damage to the national security." And those marked "Top Secret" are ones that "could reasonably result in exceptionally grave damage to the national security."

But it turns out to be even worse than that.

Because after the United States government pursued the documents that belonged to it but that Trump had wrongfully taken, and had retrieved 15 boxes of them, it emerged that Trump had kept others, and had not told the government. Then, when a grand jury served a subpoena for the remaining classified documents that Trump had taken, Trump turned over some, and his lawyer falsely certified that he didn't have any more.

This will come as a shocker, but that was a lie.

Trump had kept still more classified documents, which he kept secret from the Justice Department.

Which is why, apparently based on evidence presented to the FBI by witnesses inside Mar-a-Lago and others with knowledge of the matter, the Justice Department applied for and received a search warrant to search for yet more classified documents that Trump had taken, withheld and hid at his home.

And when the FBI searched Mar-a-Lago, guess what? It found them.

Which leaves Trump in some deep legal trouble. And which leaves the rest of us wondering: What did he intend to do with intelligence information derived from the monitoring of foreign communications and from clandestine human sources located in foreign countries? What was the benefit he sought to obtain from having information obtained under the Foreign Intelligence Surveillance Act?

Trump loyalists, who bleat about their devotion to America's national security, were ready with a potpourri of excuses, each more inane than the last.

Trump lawyer and hair dye aficionado Rudy Giuliani insisted that by stealing classified information his former client was just trying to "protect" it. GOP Rep. Mike Turner suggested that Trump, ever the student of history, simply wanted the documents to write his memoirs. Rep. Dan Crenshaw argued that no one had ever requested return of the documents, apparently not regarding a grand jury subpoena as a sort of request. And New Hampshire Gov. Chris Sununu told CNN that if there were anything to the investigation the Justice Department would publish the Top Secret documents so that everyone in the world could see them, offering his own special brand of intelligence failure.

But the best was from Trump lawyer Evan Corcoran, who admonished the attorney general in a letter that he should take no action against Trump. "Public trust in the government is low," he wrote.

Good thing that chutzpah isn't a federal crime.

Fall Awakening: As Alarm About the GOP Rises, the Red Wave Recedes

September 6, 2022

Republican strategists have rarely seemed more chipper in recent times than when supplies of a certain brand of baby formula ran short and gas prices ran high. Voters were buying what the GOP was selling: Joe Biden's presidency was a "failure," the overwhelming evidence to the contrary notwithstanding.

Biden had steered the country through and out the other end of the COVID-19 crisis, had managed to pass several blockbuster legislative packages that provided desperately needed financial relief through a gridlocked Congress and had presided over historic levels of job creation. He had skillfully unified Western democracies in defense of Ukraine, ensuring that, against all reasonable expectations, that brave country was able to repel Russian aggression.

Still Biden's poll numbers have remained low for the better part of the last year, even as the Republicans' case against him remained pretty darn thin. Their central pitch, duly and loudly amplified by house organs like Fox News, was that Biden was "not up to the job." The pitch consisted largely of the fact that Biden, who has a bad back, walks stiffly and, even more disqualifying, once got his foot caught on a bike pedal while coming to a stop and — wait for it — the bicycle tipped over.

For the longest time it did not much matter that the Republican Party, a veritable study in pathology, is dominated by crackpots and controlled not just by your run-of-the-mill felon but a felon on multiple counts. Democrats' prospects in this fall's midterms seemed foreordained, and not in a positive way. Buoyed by historical precedent, Biden's low approval ratings and the Democrats' time-honored penchant for internecine warfare, Republicans seemed poised to sweep into control of both houses of Congress with the greatest of ease.

A funny thing happened on the way to the Republican wave, and it began with the conservative Supreme Court's reversal of Roe v. Wade in June. Though it had been a fait accompli for months, the snatching away of a woman's constitutional right to choose what to do with her own body by those professing to oppose governmental overreach was a "Holy smokes!"

moment for America — though with something other than "smokes!" in mind. In early August voters in the deep red state of Kansas defeated a constitutional amendment that would have eliminated abortion rights by a landslide 60% to 40% margin. With a clear majority of Americans identifying as pro-choice, Kansas was an indication that women, independents and young voters who had been unmotivated about the midterms would make their voices heard about GOP politicians who followed their party's orthodoxy on choice — and virtually all of them do.

It wasn't only choice that roused anti-Republican sentiment. The massacres of schoolchildren in Uvalde, Texas, and shoppers in a Buffalo, New York, grocery once again shone a spotlight on the vapidness of the Republican line on proliferating weapons of mass destruction on American streets, which, succinctly put, amounts to "It's a doggone shame people kill other people."

In recent weeks, Republicans' spirits have fallen faster than prices at the gas pump. On Aug. 23 a Democrat defeated a Republican in a swing congressional district in upstate New York. Last Tuesday a Democrat won a special election in Alaska — Alaska! — defeating former President Donald Trump mini-me Sarah Palin in a state that Trump carried by 10 points in 2020. Republican Senate candidates in Georgia, Pennsylvania, Ohio and Wisconsin, once considered likely winners, trail their Democratic opponents in the polls. Democratic senators in Arizona and New Hampshire, once regarded as highly vulnerable, are suddenly on solid footing.

In the meantime, a fresh round of legislative victories like the Inflation Reduction Act and the CHIPS Act underscore the emptiness of claims that Biden has "failed" as president.

There are 10 weeks to go before the midterms, which is to say 10 lifetimes. But at the moment Republicans are struggling to find a rationale for supporting them that doesn't include the words "bike pedal" in it.

Special Privileges: The Judge Granting Trump a Special Master Handed Him a Special Deal

September 13, 2022

Former President Donald Trump's lawsuit demanding that the Justice Department's investigation into his purloining and concealing of classified documents be frozen and taken over by a "special master" was a shrewd maneuver for this reason: He doesn't seem to have any actual defense to the criminal charges headed his way — unless he was entitled to repurpose the documents as stocking stuffers.

Despite The Former Guy's untethered cries that the FBI consists of "monsters" and "wolves," Trump and his lawyers know that if he is indicted, his goose is very likely cooked.

Which is why Trump's lawsuit, filed in a particular Florida courthouse so that a particular judge appointed by Trump drew the case, was so clever. Delay is terrific for any prospective criminal defendant, and it is especially terrific if it appears you're going to the slammer should a criminal case be brought. Judge Aileen Cannon's ruling stopping the investigation into Trump in its tracks and inserting whomever she selects into a position to give thumbs up or thumbs down to the investigators' work brought early strains of "It's Beginning to Look a Lot Like Christmas" to Mar-a-Lago's halls.

Trump's legal arguments were heavy on rhetoric, light on the law. His yearlong game of "hide the ball," with classified documents playing the part of the ball, was nothing more than a silly matter akin to "an overdue library book." The search of a former president's home was "unprecedented" — quite true, but so is a former president pilfering classified documents and then obstructing a Justice Department investigation into said pilfering.

Cannon wasted no time showing that in filing the lawsuit with her, Trump's lawyers had come to the right place. Promptly after receiving Trump's request for a special master, the judge announced that she intended to grant it — before even doing the Justice Department the courtesy of receiving its opposition. This was a somewhat ostentatious display of injudiciousness.

But it was just the beginning. Trump's lawyers are preparing to claim that the classified documents taken by him are covered by "executive privilege," supposedly exempting him from prosecution. His executive privilege claim is baseless for at least four reasons. The documents do not belong to him. There is no authority giving a former president a claim to executive privilege. The current president has stated the documents are not covered by executive privilege. And the Supreme Court held in the case involving President Richard Nixon's tapes that even where the executive privilege exists, it is overridden by the interests of the criminal justice system — which obviously apply here.

No matter. Cannon simply breezed past the inconvenient law, ruling that a special master would be appointed to review 13,000 documents for executive privilege — a privilege that has no place here.

The handwriting on the wall was on display during the hearing on the matter, when the judge had to repeatedly remind Trump's lawyers that they were claiming executive privilege. When they stated that they based their argument solely on a need to have a special master review documents for attorney-client privilege, the judge stepped in to help them, pointedly asking: "Are you asserting any other privileges beyond the attorney-client privilege?"

Not really, Trump's lawyers responded.

Wrong answer, but the judge was there to correct them, again.

"I just want to be clear, there were some references in the papers to executive privilege," Cannon nudged them.

Trump's attorney finally got it. "Absolutely. Thank you, Your Honor," he replied. "Yes, executive privilege is in play, as well."

There was no evidence that the Justice Department had done anything wrong, or that it could be expected to. There was no evidence that a special master was necessary.

The judge appointed one anyway, out of concern for the "stigma" that an investigation into whether Trump had violated the Espionage Act would cause him. She did not explain how a special master would or could lessen any "stigma," let alone one inflicted on Trump by Trump himself.

For the moment, however, score one for Trump.

Frozen Hearts Club: The DeSantis Human Trafficking Show Lays an Egg

September 20, 2022

In July 2014, then-Massachusetts Gov. Deval Patrick defied angry opposition from certain quarters by offering two Massachusetts military bases as temporary shelter for 1,000 children who had entered America illegally from Mexico. "I believe that we will one day have to answer for our actions — or our inaction," Patrick said at a news conference, flanked by Cardinal Sean O'Malley, Boston's archbishop, and other religious leaders. "Every major faith tradition on the planet charges its followers to treat others as we ourselves wish to be treated," he said. "I don't know what good there is in faith if we can't and won't turn to it in moments of human need."

Unfortunately, as has been true so often throughout our history, those who profess most loudly and most piously to be devoted to Christian values are the ones who make it their practice to sully them. "In God we trust" is the motto not only of the United States but of the state of Florida, but what Florida Gov. Ron DeSantis actually worships are the basest instincts of his particular Almighty, the MAGA base that will determine the 2024 Republican presidential nominee. He convincingly demonstrated that point again last week, this time by concocting and implementing a human-trafficking scheme comprised of cruel lies and just plain cruelty intended to set him apart from other aspiring Republican contenders in the "Who can be the biggest bully?" primary.

Not exactly what they teach in Bible class.

It was, however, an excellent window into DeSantis' character and that of those who cheered on his scheme with lusty approval: taxpayers' money burned to pay fraudulent operators to lie to unsuspecting Venezuelan refugees from a tyrannical regime, duping them with false promises and then flying them to the Massachusetts island of Martha's Vineyard and dumping them there — without so much as giving Massachusetts authorities proper notice so that they could prepare. All so DeSantis could boast that he was sticking it to a blue state by rounding up vulnerable human beings and shipping them there.

Right out of Sunday school.

But in his zeal to set himself apart as the candidate in the GOP field with the most swagger, DeSantis may have miscalculated.

First, if he thought that dropping two planeloads of migrants on Martha's Vineyard would punish the island's residents, he thought wrong. The island community responded with a moving humanitarian display, with citizens falling over themselves to provide food, shelter, medical attention, clothing — and human warmth. Gov. Charlie Baker followed suit. The response drew international media attention, contrasting DeSantis, on one hand, with a functioning moral value system, on the other, with DeSantis and his "Attaboy!" chorus looking like the smirking schoolyard bullies we all remember from elementary school.

Second, former President Donald Trump's Florida wannabe mini-me may have bought himself a federal investigation into potential human trafficking crimes. While there may be a GOP constituency for such conduct, Americans more broadly may regard DeSantis' blend of fraud and exploitation with distaste.

Finally, over 200,000 Americans of Venezuelan origin live in Florida, and there are millions more there of Latin American heritage. They may not love seeing their brothers and sisters treated as chattel in order to serve as props for DeSantis' presidential ambitions. This could hit the fan in November, when DeSantis faces a surprisingly stiff challenge from Democrat Charlie Crist. An AARP Florida poll last week showed DeSantis with only a 3% lead over Crist. And DeSantis soulmate Florida Sen. Marco Rubio faces a similarly robust challenge from Democrat Val Demings, who a series of polls shows in a statistical dead heat with Rubio.

"He's carting them around like cattle from state to state, starving them all day and dropping them off with excuses (and) lies that they were going to get jobs and housing," Venezuelan activist Juan Correa Villalonga told a Miami television station last week. Which is about the size of it. DeSantis had better hope that no one sends their kids to Sunday school anymore.

Safe Space for Bigots: The University of Vermont Gets the Federal Investigation It Deserves

September 27, 2022

The facts at the core of the current antisemitism scandal at the University of Vermont don't seem especially disputable, and the University hasn't really disputed them. A University teaching assistant, feeling perhaps correctly that the University offered a safe space for antisemites, wasn't content to merely bully Jewish students who identified with Israel. She boasted about it publicly, chortling on social media about her threats to reduce the grades of Jewish kids for whom Israel has personal meaning.

"Is it unethical for me, a TA, to not give Zionists credit for participation???" she tweeted. "I'm trying to be lowkey on social media for Ramadan and it's going okay so far but (name redacted) keeps sending me Instagram posts from UVM Zionist Instagram accounts and I get the indelible urge to cyberbully and religion goes out the window." And "serotonin rush of bullying Zionists on the public domain."

When an Israeli flag was stolen from an off-campus student house, the TA heartily praised the vandalism. "Who stole the Israeli flag," she tweeted, "I just wanna talk and tell you how cool and special and loved you are... may the wind always be at your back." And later "at this stage in the game I don't even want to know who stole it anymore I just want to defend their honor. They are like the spider-man of Burlington, anonymously doing good."

She appears to fit in nicely at UVM, where the harassment, ostracism and belittling of Jewish identity is, well, as the lady puts it, cool, part of the campus fabric. Jewish students have decried the "vulgar anti-Semitism that Jewish students are experiencing online from student accounts at UVM... Jewish students have every right to be Jewish in their own way and not attacked and have their lived experiences minimized for their religious beliefs, personal practice or connection to Israel."

Others on campus did not see it quite the same way. Last year, UVM students organized a group called "UVM Empowering Survivors" to support victims of sexual harassment. When Hillel, the Jewish student organization, posted a statement of solidarity, the anti-sexual harassment group rejected it. They would, its leaders proclaimed, "follow the same policy with Zionists that we follow with those who troll or harass others: blocked." When the Jewish kids reached out to convey the pain that the oppressive exclusion of Jews on campus was causing, they were met with the kind of "Jews Not Welcome" stuff associated with 1930s Germany, not necessarily the purportedly progressive, supposedly civil rights-oriented college quads of Burlington, Vermont. The group would have nothing to do with Jewish kids, it stated; it would instead "hold our peers accountable for their pro-Israel or Zionist stances."

Then there was the targeting of the Hillel building, increasingly commonplace on American campuses. A group of students spent some 40 minutes throwing rocks at the building's windows. The University insisted that there was nothing anti-Jewish about an attack on the Jewish students' campus center, a proposition that tended to be undercut ever so slightly by the evidence that one of the vandals shouted, "Are you Jewish?" while throwing the rocks.

In response to a quite detailed complaint filed by the Louis D. Brandeis Center for Human Rights Under Law, the U.S. Department of Education has opened a formal investigation into whether UVM has fostered or permitted a hostile environment for Jewish students, in violation of the federal civil rights laws. Instead of acknowledging "Burlington, we've got a problem," UVM's president responded with a statement at once inane and threatening, warning darkly that the investigation would hurt Jewish students. "You'll be sorry," he seemed to be telling them. Twenty Jewish organizations denounced UVM's president for a response that was insensitive, offensive and just plain dumb.

It was Justice Louis Brandeis himself who observed that frequently sunlight is the best disinfectant. Based on what we know so far, UVM could stand some disinfecting, by one means or another.

Loose Cannon: Trump's Mar-A-Lago Judge Says 'You've Got a Friend in Me'

October 4, 2022

When we last left U.S. District Judge Aileen Cannon, the former President Donald Trump appointee to the federal bench had bestowed upon the man to whom she owed her judgeship a most welcome gift. To recap: A federal magistrate reviewing a detailed FBI affidavit had found probable cause to conclude that Trump had violated the Espionage Act and committed obstruction of justice. He had thereupon authorized an FBI search of Trump's Mar-a-Lago home.

That search did not exactly come up empty: The FBI found some 100 classified documents that The Former Guy had unlawfully taken, unlawfully retained, unlawfully concealed and, evidently, unlawfully lied about. This was over and above the approximately 200 similarly classified documents the government had previously learned Trump took with him when he left office.

This did not put Trump in an advantageous position, legally speaking.

Cannon, however, proved ready to do her part. Trump's lawyers scored a perfect 10 in the judge-shopping competition, filing a lawsuit in Cannon's court, asking that she block the Justice Department's criminal investigation by prohibiting it from using the classified documents — that is, the evidence of criminality — until a "special master" had first reviewed the 11,000 documents taken from Trump's residence.

The purpose? To have the special master spend weeks, perhaps months, assessing whether the classified documents were indeed classified, and to determine whether any document could be withheld from the investigators on the ground that it was subject to "executive privilege."

Cannon was quick to oblige — very quick. Without even waiting for the Justice Department's response to the request, she announced that she was inclined to grant it, and grant it she did.

This was a head-scratcher.

For one thing, the classified documents were marked "classified," and, unless the Classification Fairy had put the markings there, they were, well, classified. Trump's lawyers had literally no contrary evidence, and the former president's claim that he had declassified them by waving a magic wand between bites of a double cheeseburger ("Mirror, mirror, on the wall: who's the biggest declassifier of them all?") was not the sort of thing customarily credited by federal judges.

As for any claim of "executive privilege," Trump's team likewise declined to offer any factual or legal basis that would shield a single piece of paper taken from Trump's home. They may as well have demanded that a special master evaluate whether Trump was entitled to the Bugs Bunny Privilege.

No matter. A special master was appointed, and the investigation was put on ice.

Not for long. The special master, a highly respected federal judge appointed by President Ronald Reagan, put the Trump lawyers on notice that he wasn't tolerating any song-and-dance. He asked whether Trump had any evidence that the classified documents were somehow not classified.

We'll get back to you, they replied.

They were spared the trouble. Because before you could say "What was she thinking?" a three-judge federal appellate panel including two Trump appointees ruled that Cannon's decision was so fundamentally contrary to the law as to constitute an abuse of her discretion. It reversed her order blocking the Justice Department from using the retrieved classified documents as it saw fit.

But the matter isn't over. The special master is under orders from Cannon to determine whether Trump is entitled to invoke the Bugs Bunny, er, executive privilege as to any of the remaining 11,000 documents. The special master will likely rule that Trump is not and recommend that Cannon rule the same way. Lord knows what she will do, and what delays, the Holy Grail of potential criminal defendants, will ensue.

The Justice Department has asked the appellate court to reverse the rest of Cannon's order, whose effect and likely purpose is to make federal prosecutors slog through quicksand. It hopes that if the appellate court tells Cannon a second time that she was wrong, she will be too embarrassed to continue running interference for Trump.

One can only hope.

Reckless Disinterest: Iranians Get Oppressed as Their Regime Gets Coddled

October 11, 2022

Nineteenth-century French politician Alexandre Auguste Ledru-Rollin is remembered for only one thing, but that's more than will be said for most of us. "There go my people," history records that he mused at one point. "I must find out where they are going so I can lead them."

This was called to mind by Rep. Ilhan Omar's sudden flurry of newfound criticism of the Iranian regime, a regime that has been fundamentally, pervasively oppressive for decades but has not seemed to interest Omar or her colleagues on America's far Left until recently. "There is no morality in oppressing women," Omar tweeted as Iranians took to their streets to protest the murder of young Iranians by their government and were murdered in turn. "There is no morality in forcing people to participate in a religion they don't want to."

The killing of 22-year-old Mahsa Amini, who died in the custody of Tehran's morality police after being arrested for not covering her hair with the traditional Islamic hijab, has spawned protests across Iran by young people demanding an end to a regime that has largely been coddled by the American Left, even though its systemic human rights atrocities have long been obvious to the entire world.

Last year's annual State Department report on the condition of human rights in Iran is a repeat of what has been reported year after year. Iran is guilty of "unlawful or arbitrary killings" and "torture or cruel, inhuman or degrading treatment" by its government or its agents, "severe restrictions on free expression" and "serious restrictions on internet freedom." The government commits "violence against ethnic minorities," criminalizes consensual same-sex sexual conduct, imposes "significant restrictions on workers' freedom of association" and fosters "the worst forms of child labor."

Other than that, it is a model of progressivism.

And, oh, yes, it has been deemed by our State Department the world's foremost state sponsor of terror, responsible for brutalizing innocents throughout the Middle East and beyond. This includes tens of thousands of Syrian civilians butchered by the Assad regime, bankrolled by Tehran, and the terrorized citizens of Lebanon, forcibly occupied by Hezbollah, an Iranian proxy.

One might have hoped that progressives would have emitted a mild criticism of Iran every now and again. But until the recent profusion of social media coverage of brave Iranians protesting their government and being brutally repressed as a consequence, stirring some on the Left to feel as though they really should go on record, there was virtual silence on the Left when it came to Iran.

On the contrary, the Left — and not only the far Left — was often pleased to deride those who warned about the tens of billions of dollars in sanctions relief handed over to Iran as part of the 2015 nuclear deal as "neocons" or "warmongers." This, sad to say, was the dishonest and ugly line one heard from some in the Obama administration at the time.

And there were those who, like the National Iranian American Council, criticized by some as an apologist for the Iranian government and a darling of Team Obama, repeatedly demanded an end to sanctions on Iran — sanctions intended to help spur and support the in-country opposition now on display. Omar has been one such person, repeatedly calling for the repeal of sanctions. Such sanctions, Omar proclaimed in 2019, "have simultaneously strengthened the Iranian regime's credibility at home and united human rights activists and the Iranian leadership." In 2020, Omar joined fellow Squad members Reps. Alexandria Ocasio-Cortez, Ayanna Pressley and Rashida Tlaib in urging an end to sanctions on Iran — even as they endorsed imposing them on Israel.

Now that support for Iranian dissenters has erupted across the globe, Omar and friends are scrambling to create the impression that they have been interested in Iranian oppression all along. They haven't. But it's better late than never.

Letter From Sing Sing: Trump's Subpoena Response Sounds Like He's Already in Solitary

October 18, 2022

The House Committee investigating former President Donald Trump's assorted efforts to overthrow the 2020 election and remain in power wrapped up its hearings last Thursday, capping a mountain of evidence that the former president, knowing he'd lost, tried everything but the kitchen sink to torpedo American democracy — and then tried the kitchen sink as well. The committee put a bow on things by voting to subpoena Trump to testify under oath about the wannabe Mussolini's coup attempt, daring him to answer questions under oath about the open-and-shut case that he and he alone is the one who tried to steal an election.

It's not that there's a fat chance that Trump will comply with the subpoena. It's more like there's no chance. Before Trump comes in to answer questions under oath, not only will pigs fly; they will circumnavigate the globe. Trump already has pleaded the Fifth more times than Jimmy Hoffa, and he's just getting started.

That Trump will no more appear in the House Committee's hearing room than he will visit Pluto was reinforced by the screed he released hours after the committee voted to subpoena him, complete with the usual whack-job razzmatazz eaten up by the QAnon set. This consisted of the customary fraud-filled oldies-but-goodies, right down to the untethered (and incorrectly used) capital letters. These increasingly make Trump look like he is a prison inmate writing from solitary confinement after corrections officers found he posed a danger to himself or others. "Despite very poor television ratings, the Unselect Committee has perpetrated a Show Trial the likes of which this Country has never seen before," Trump proclaimed in a letter on his website. The committee, according to him, was comprised of "highly partisan political Hacks and Thugs, whose sole function is to destroy the lives of hard-working American Patriots." The sixty-plus judges, including Trump appointees, who determined that Trump's allegations that he won the election were every bit as legitimate as sightings of the Loch Ness monster had conspired against him to commit "the Crime of the Century," and so forth.

These were the ravings of someone for whom walls are closing in, facing very substantial evidence that he has committed multiple violations of the Espionage Act, obstruction of justice, election fraud in Georgia and a conspiracy to impede the counting of electoral votes. If pigs do indeed grow wings and he testifies before the committee, he will generate charges of lying to Congress so numerous as to approach the number of grains of sand on the seashore. If he disregards the subpoena, Congress may refer him to the Justice Department for indictment for contempt of Congress. This would place him in the same boat as his longtime advisers, Steve Bannon and Roger Stone, each the very model of good citizenship if there ever were one.

He has taken the Fifth 440 times in response to questions about whether he committed bank fraud. His former chief financial officer at the Trump Organization has pleaded guilty to 15 crimes, and his company itself goes on trial shortly. He is being sued for $250 million by the New York State attorney general. A judge has ordered him to testify this week in a deposition brought by a woman who alleges he raped her. Mayhem appears to reign among his lawyers, many of whom have been obliged to hire lawyers of their own thanks to their involvement with him. This has led to circulation of the joke that "MAGA" actually means "Making Attorneys Get Attorneys," which is funnier if you're not one of the lawyers who needs one.

But, hey! What a grand choice for the 2024 Republican nominee for president if you're the Grand Old Party, the party of Abraham Lincoln. Trump doesn't have a very great deal in common with Lincoln. He does, however, sound like he's got a great deal in common these days with someone in solitary confinement at Sing Sing.

Land Of Oz: America Barrels Toward a Crossroads

October 25, 2022

The tea leaves suggest that next month's midterms will fall somewhere between a Republican wavelet and a wave, with the GOP virtually certain to win control of the House and given a strong shot at taking the Senate. This will set off a tsunami of finger-pointing within Democratic circles, complete with the recriminations that are their extra-special specialty. Calls for President Joe Biden to stand down from reelection will dominate media coverage and may well force Biden, an enormously successful president in an enormously difficult time, to do just that.

Of course, even casual students of American history know that the "seesaw effect" is a fixture in our electoral tradition. In the 1982 midterms, thanks to a recession and then-President Ronald Reagan's consequent unpopularity, Democrats picked up 26 House seats. Two years later, Reagan demolished Democratic nominee Walter Mondale, taking 535 electoral votes and 59% of the popular vote.

In 1994, brutalized for having the temerity to seek increased health care coverage for Americans, President Bill Clinton's party lost eight Senate seats and a whopping 52 House seats, catapulting Newt Gingrich into the speakership and punctuating what was deemed a Republican Revolution. Two years later, Clinton handily won reelection.

In 2010, then-President Barack Obama paid a price for his own health care heresy. The Republicans tore him apart over the Affordable Care Act, now a piece of health care protection that most Americans want to maintain. The GOP won 7 Senate seats and fully 63 House seats, the largest shift in the lower chamber since 1948. That didn't stop Obama from winning 332 electoral votes, including those of traditional red states like Florida, Ohio and Iowa.

What is likely coming down the pike this November, therefore, is hardly a harbinger for 2024.

Still, it is difficult to gainsay the chaos that these midterms are likely to trigger, or the genuinely dire threat that they will pose to the already shredded, slender and fragile reed by which American democracy as we had known it now hangs. For starters, the next speaker of the House will probably be

Republican Rep. Kevin McCarthy of California, a man who is clinically amoral on an extremely good day. That makes him preferable to the next most likely speaker, Rep. Jim Jordan of Ohio, for whom amorality would be an improvement. In this regard it's a little bit like rooting for Spanish fascist Francisco Franco over Italian fascist Benito Mussolini: it's tough to root for one over the other.

Anyone wondering what Congress will look like under Republican control had only to watch serial criminal Steve Bannon on "Tucker Carlson Tonight" the night Bannon was sentenced to prison. The two commiserated about what it meant for our sorry state that Bannon could actually be prosecuted for willfully flouting a congressional subpoena to tell the truth about a coup d'etat about which Bannon had personal knowledge. Their takeaway: it's the Justice Department, rather than Bannon, that disrespects the rule of law.

It's not just those two who will be thrilled at a GOP takeover. Saudi Arabia's Mohammed bin Salman and Russia's Vladimir Putin will see it as the first step toward reinstalling former President Donald Trump, and in the meantime the consignment of Biden to lame-duck status.

And speaking of ducks, over in Pennsylvania a multimillionaire quack physician named Mehmet Oz, resident of anywhere but Pennsylvania, may well be the Keystone State's next senator. A veteran of the Turkish Army and a promoter of faith healing and other branches of pseudo-medicine, Oz earned his MAGA stripes going on Fox to advocate for the use of quack COVID-19 cure hydroxychloroquine. On the other hand, unlike Republican Senate candidate Herschel Walker, Oz never held a gun to his wife's head and threatened to blow her brains out.

So, there's still time to look on the bright side as America confronts what's in store for it. But it's going to require some effort.

Bloody Hands and Guilty Parties: Just Another Tourist Visit to the Pelosi Home

November 1, 2022

Though they spent much of the afternoon of Jan. 6, 2021, hiding in undisclosed locations and running for cover, most congressional Republicans have spent the past 22 months treating former President Donald Trump's attempted coup d'etat and his bloody insurrection at the Capitol as a nothingburger, too much ado about pretty much zero. "Watching the TV footage of those who entered the Capitol showed people in an orderly fashion staying between the stanchions and ropes taking videos and pictures," said Republican Rep. Andrew Clyde about the unhinged mob that beat the daylights out of the Capitol Police in order to try to prevent electoral votes from being counted. "If you didn't know the TV footage was a video from January the 6th, you would actually think it was a normal tourist visit."

Since then, the Republican Party has left little doubt that it is controlled by a base that doesn't merely indulge political violence. It embraces it. It encourages it. It incites it, all the while claiming to want to make America great again. And it is given air cover by political leaders too petrified of MAGA World and its demagogic leader to give a hoot about the wrecking ball they are administering to the country.

We now have more evidence of this, not that we needed it. A drifter consumed like so many of his countrymen with the madness of Trumpism broke into the home of House Speaker Nancy Pelosi in the middle of the night looking to assassinate her. "Where is Nancy?" he demanded, bringing a hammer, zip ties and duct tape with him to do what he had been led to believe should be done. He was echoing the "Where is Nancy? We're looking for Nancy!" cry of the Trump-fueled mob on Jan. 6 as it broke into the speaker's office searching for her so they could kidnap or kill her — all part of their tourist visit.

Nancy Pelosi wasn't home, so the assailant did the next best thing. He tried to murder her 82-year-old husband Paul, smashing his head in with the hammer, cracking his skull open.

Encouraged and coddled and protected by the mocking and the snark and the moral cowardice of its enablers, MAGA World disclaims any responsibility for the attack. But they are full of it. The party that still thinks

Jan. 6 is a joke and the investigation into it a witch hunt has been inciting violence against Pelosi for years.

Republican Rep. Marjorie Taylor Greene liked a Facebook post that argued that "a bullet would be a quicker" way of eliminating Pelosi as speaker. She posted a petition she launched to impeach Pelosi for "treason," calling her a "traitor." "It's a crime punishable by death — is what treason is," Greene exclaimed. "Nancy Pelosi is guilty of treason."

A Republican candidate for senator in Arizona portrayed himself as a sheriff in a campaign ad, shooting at actors playing President Joe Biden, Arizona Sen. Mark Kelly and Pelosi. "The good people of Arizona have had enough of you," he intones, and starts shooting at the three of them.

Just last week, Republican Rep. Tom Emmer of Minnesota, chair of the National Republican Congressional Committee, posted a video of himself taking target practice with an automatic rifle with the hashtag #FirePelosi.

This sort of thing is embedded in the theology of MAGA World. When the FBI uncovered a plot to kidnap Michigan Gov. Gretchen Whitmer because she had instituted policies to save lives during the COVID-19 pandemic, the GOP was silent, or laughed it off.

Biden had it right this past weekend. "What makes us think that one party can talk about stolen elections, COVID being a hoax, it's all a bunch of lies," he asked, "and it not affect people who may not be so well-balanced?" The loser who wanted to kill Nancy Pelosi and tried to kill her husband is diseased, of course. But there are influential people among us who have spread the disease.

Officious Nonsense and Putin Apologists: Biden Bears a Cross on Ukraine

November 8, 2022

Legend has it that in 1944, bowing to traditional protocol at 10 Downing Street, British Prime Minister Winston Churchill circulated a draft of one of his speeches to civil servants in his office for their review. One bureaucrat took the perfunctory procedure somewhat overly seriously, returning the draft with a correction. The prime minister, he noted, had committed a syntactic error, ending one of his sentences with a preposition.

Churchill returned the draft to the aide with a note of his own. "This," he scribbled with some irritation, "is the sort of officious nonsense up with which I will not put."

President Joe Biden may have felt something similar on Oct. 24, when 30 Democratic members of Congress constituting the "Progressive Caucus" delivered a letter to him, duly released to the media, lecturing him on the need to pursue negotiations with Russian strongman Vladimir Putin. The representatives felt that the president could benefit from their insight, which they believed he did not already have: Putin's invasion of Ukraine was killing thousands of Ukrainians and ravaging their country, and everyone would be a lot better off if he stopped killing Ukrainians and ravaging their country. "We urge you," they wrote, "to make vigorous diplomatic efforts in support of a negotiated settlement and ceasefire, engage in direct talks with Russia (and) explore prospects for a new European security arrangement acceptable to all parties."

Here's the thing: there are fifth graders who would have known that such a letter was not only unnecessary but foolish, telling Biden nothing that he did not already know, telling Putin that support for Ukraine within Biden's own party was shaky and telling the courageous people of Ukraine that the United States may be getting ready to abandon them.

The letter made as much sense as it would have for members of Parliament to deliver and leak a letter to Churchill during World War II, urging him to please explore a peaceful resolution of Hitler's claims on Europe. It wasn't just naive, not merely childish, but obviously exactly the wrong message to send to Putin, whose fundamental calculation is that

America will lose its resolve to defend Ukraine, and then when American support fades so will that of Europe.

The backlash against the letter was swift and disgusted, whereupon the chair of the Progressive Caucus declared it withdrawn hours after it had already done its damage. "The letter," she proclaimed, offering the American public a choice between concluding that her members either were buffoons or dissemblers, "was drafted several months ago, but unfortunately was released without vetting."

But it is the Republicans whom Ukrainians really have to fear, and in whom Putin continues to place his hopes. "Under Republicans, not another penny will go to Ukraine!" Rep. Marjorie Taylor Greene proclaimed recently. Whether despite the fact that she is a nutjob or because of it, Greene is a force in the GOP caucus. Speaker-in-waiting Rep. Kevin McCarthy has announced that Ukraine had better not count on a "blank check," words that no doubt warmed whatever exists of Putin's heart.

In May, 57 House Republicans voted against an aid package for Ukraine, which passed anyway. Fox celebrity and Putin fanboy Tucker Carlson, the second most influential voice in the Republican Party, has appeared on Russian state television more than Mehmet Oz appeared on Oprah, criticizing Biden's support for Ukraine and belittling the very notion that we should come to Ukraine's defense. And a Wall Street Journal poll released last week found that 48% of registered Republicans believed America was helping Ukraine too much — up from 6% in March.

The brave Ukrainian people do not only need our support; they deserve it. The profoundly heinous Putin regime does not only deserve our determined opposition; it compels it. Of such triumphs of will or failures of it history is made. Democrats and Republicans must be one on this point if on no other.

Bad Night for Crazy: Trumpism Stalls — For Now

November 15, 2022

The first thing they teach you at Kamikaze School is: If you're going to blow yourself up, at least get the other guy. There are a whole bunch of election deniers and fraud-peddlers running for office this election cycle who appear to have missed the first day of class. Either that or they confused "kamikaze" with "hara-kiri," the ritual self-evisceration once practiced by Japanese samurai, because after the midterm results were tabulated, the battlefield was strewn with defeated Republicans whose crazy conspiracy theories had boomeranged, leaving their Democratic opponents victorious.

Americans' midterms verdict seems to have been: Inflation or no inflation, we'll take sane over crazy. That they would choose so wisely was not a foregone conclusion. For weeks pundits had been predicting a "red wave," and Republicans had crammed the cable news channels crowing about it. Now they are eating crow.

Even Arizona gubernatorial candidate Kari Lake, a cross between Evita and Cruella de Vil, was struggling at weekend's end to win an election she'd seemed certain to win. Another stable genius, Lake threatened a reporter who posed a mild, even flattering question to her about whether she would consider being former President Donald Trump's running mate in 2024. "Are you new covering this? Because we have talked about this before," she snarled. "I'm going to be your worst fricking nightmare for eight years, and we will reform the media as well. We are going to make you guys into journalists again, so get ready. It's gonna be a fun eight years. I can't wait to be working with you."

Turns out arrogance is far down the list of what's notable about Lake. Lack of principle is right down there with it. She was a registered Republican until 2006. Then she changed her registration to become an independent. Then in 2008 she became a Democrat. Then in 2012 she became a Republican again. What she lacks in gravitas, however, she more than makes up in crazy. Her gubernatorial campaign focused on the phony claim that the 2020 election was "rigged and stolen," which endeared her to you-know-who, who endorsed her, which was the point.

Across the country, Republican candidates cut from the same crazy cloth as Lake were widely defeated. These included Arizona's Republican candidate for Secretary of State, Oath Keeper and election-denier extraordinaire Mark Finchem, who marched on the Capitol on Jan. 6, and GOP Secretary of State nominees in Nevada, Michigan and Minnesota, all boasting a similar pedigree.

Michigan Gov. Gretchen Whitmer mopped the floor with Republican Tudor Dixon, who claimed that COVID-19 was part of a Democratic plot to "topple" the United States. The Republican gubernatorial candidate in Pennsylvania, Doug Mastriano, promoted QAnon social media posts, denounced the 2020 election as stolen and sought to overturn it, all among other similarly impressive qualifications for office. He was trounced even more thoroughly than Dixon.

Dr. Mehmet Oz, Donald Trump's nattily dressed hand-picked nominee for the Senate in Pennsylvania, lost to a 6-foot, 8-inch bald man with a beard and tattoos in shorts and a hoodie. New Hampshire's Dan Bolduc, another Trump favorite, endorsed The Former Guy's claim that the 2020 election was rigged, which led Trump in turn to pronounce him a "strong guy, tough guy," which is also what they said about Mussolini. Sen. Maggie Hassan defeated Bolduc by over nine points.

Still, there's plenty of reason for caution, and none for hubris. Fully 39% of American voters have a favorable view of Trump, even after an attempted coup d'etat, 300 violations of the Espionage Act and God knows how much obstruction of justice. There were plenty of victories by Trump acolytes, including an awful lot of election deniers. Many of the races that Democrats won were won by narrow margins. And the former president is poised to announce he's running again for president, and most of the Republican Party will support him full-throatedly.

Schadenfreude Express: Democrats Should Beware of Hubris

November 22, 2022

Former Secretary of State Henry Kissinger came up with a good line about the Iran-Iraq War, the vicious conflict of attrition between Iraq's Saddam Hussein and Iran's Ayatollah Ruhollah Khomeini. "Pity," Kissinger quipped, "both sides can't lose."

Democrats elated by Republicans' poor showing in the 2022 midterms are taking similar pleasure in the Grand Old Party's suffering and, in particular, the internecine warfare that has broken out within the GOP. Rep. Kevin McCarthy, whose gelatinous spine will land him in the history books for the wrong reasons, is battling the simply crazy elements of the Republican House caucus to win election as the next House speaker. Sen. Rick Scott thought that the disastrous performance of Republican Senate candidates fielded under his tenure as head of the Republican Senatorial Committee made him a strong candidate to replace Minority Leader Mitch McConnell. His colleagues begged to differ, decisively.

At Mar-a-Lago, former President Donald Trump watched as his most buzzed-out acolytes lost their election races. His former protege, Florida Gov. Ron DeSantis, reinforced his standing as Trump's chief rival for the 2024 Republican presidential nomination. His crushing victory in his reelection campaign stood in stark contrast with the party's generally dismal performance, one for which Trump is widely blamed by Republicans and thanked by Democrats.

Hoping to wrest the spotlight from DeSantis and reposition it on himself, and to throw sand in the gears of the Justice Department's accelerating criminal investigation, Trump announced before the midterms that he would launch his campaign to retake the White House on Nov. 15. His announcement speech was a pallid affair, delivered to a ballroom full of hangers-on and sad cases by a candidate who sounded like a carnival barker on Librium.

The reaction from those whom one expected to serve as Trump's Hallelujah Chorus was worse than tepid. Some of those who attended grew so bored so quickly that they headed for the ballroom's exits — or tried to. Those who sought an early getaway were prevented by security guards from leaving. Once reliably fawning sycophants like former Vice President Mike Pence and former Secretary of State Mike Pompeo, hoping to run for president themselves, issued carefully worded, cautious statements intended to signal some distance — but not too much — from The Big Guy.

Rupert Murdoch dissed Trump with gusto. Fox News declared DeSantis the new leader of the GOP, and the New York Post ostentatiously buried its dismissive "coverage" of Trump's speech, placing the words "Florida Man Makes Announcement — page 26" at the bottom of its front page the morning after Trump's campaign kickoff.

Still, Democrats would do well to keep their chortling to a minimum. There was plenty about the midterms for them to worry about.

For starters, despite oft-expressed hopes that they were poised to turn from red to blue, electoral vote-rich Ohio, Texas and Florida just aren't. Instead, the midterms showed that they are hard locks for the Republicans in 2024.

Despite the hoopla about Democratic victories in Nevada and Arizona, those victories were razor thin. Kari Lake, nut cake par excellence, lost the Arizona gubernatorial race by only 17,000 votes. Democratic Sen. Catherine Cortez Masto defeated election denier Adam Laxalt by only 9,000. In Georgia, Democrat Stacey Abrams lost her return match with Gov. Brian Kemp by 300,000 votes. And Republican Senate candidate Herschel Walker, a virtual rap sheet on two legs, trailed Georgia Sen. Raphael Warnock by barely 35,000 votes out of 3.9 million cast as the two headed to a runoff that could just as easily go Republican as Democrat. In Wisconsin, another battleground state, the largely untethered incumbent, Sen. Ron Johnson, won reelection to the Senate, even if just by the skin of his teeth.

The good news for Democrats is that the Republicans' "case," such as it is, continues to be this: President Joe Biden got his foot caught on a bicycle pedal, and not only that, but his son also once had drug problems. It's pretty thin gruel. But thin gruel is a Republican specialty, and Democrats had better beware of hubris.

Murder, Then Sweets: The Palestinians Reelect Benjamin Netanyahu

November 29, 2022

Neither the savage attacks on Israelis over the past two weeks nor the sadistic celebrations of them in Palestinian quarters was anything new. For Israelis, the killings of their innocents took on a dreadful familiarity long ago, and the same is true of the scenes of Palestinians rejoicing in those deaths by honking horns and handing out candy.

In Jerusalem, bombs packed with nails and ball bearings so as to shred Israeli flesh to the maximum extent possible were detonated at two bus stops, murdering a 15-year-old boy and a 50-year-old Ethiopian immigrant and maiming over 20 others. A police official described the death tools as "two high quality, powerful devices (capable of) a high level of damage," and a high level of damage is what they did. Just ask the victims' families. This came just days after a Palestinian stabbed some eight Israelis in an industrial zone, killing three.

There has been a wave of these sorts of murders in recent months, and for Israelis they evoke the period from 2000 to 2005 when, encouraged by Palestinian leaders, bombings carried out on buses and in cafes killed almost 1,100 Israelis and wounded about 8,300 more. That's the proportional equivalent of about 40,000 Americans killed and 320,000 wounded.

Guess how Americans would feel if that had happened on our streets. That's exactly how Israelis feel.

Which leads to the lamentations greeting the return to power of right-wing Israeli leader Benjamin Netanyahu and, in particular, the hard Right coalition the incoming prime minister is putting together to form a parliamentary majority. The critical problems with the lamentations are twofold. First, Netanyahu won in a free, fair and typically robust democratically conducted election in a country that takes its democratic elections very seriously indeed. Second, those doing all the lamenting have Palestinian attacks to thank for the choice made by the Israeli electorate, which above all wants to be kept safe and which lacks the confidence that their centrist parties, let alone their left-leaning ones, can do the job.

Israel's relations with many of its Arab neighbors have openly warmed, and its ties to others have expanded, even if less openly. But the

Palestinian-Israeli conflict remains stuck in gridlock. On the West Bank, the supposedly governing Palestinian Authority is a hot mess. In the Gaza Strip, Hamas continues to hold Palestinians hostage. No two-state solution, and no fundamental progress at all, is possible until that siege lifts.

Stalemate, however, is no license for hubris, let alone arrogance. Some in Israel's political right wing seem to think that whatever the Israeli government does or doesn't do has little bearing on American popular support for their country. They are wrong. During the period from 2009 to 2021, when Netanyahu last served as prime minister, support for Israel among Democratic constituencies — younger voters, women, voters of color and self-described progressives — hemorrhaged. The damage was serious, and yet some in Israel's governing circles, as well as in certain segments of America's pro-Israel communities, comforted themselves with denials or shrugs.

It remains to be seen whether Netanyahu's new government will embrace the old hubris or learn from it. If Netanyahu uses his return to office to sidestep or override the judicial processes underway to determine whether he is guilty of crimes, the stain on the country he loves will be next to impossible to remove. Settler violence against Palestinians is going to have to be prosecuted, not coddled. If fanatics and racists with whom Netanyahu has bonded for the purpose of forming his new government are permitted to subvert Israel's democratic values, the price paid by Israel among Americans who care about those values will be very high.

Few countries face a greater assortment of profound challenges than Israel. Add to those challenges the need to reinforce the underpinnings of bipartisan support for America's only genuine ally in the Middle East, a need one hopes Benjamin Netanyahu and his new government take seriously.

Dog Days for Donald: Migraines Mount for the Former President

December 6, 2022

When the cookie crumbles it really crumbles, and since his somnolescent announcement that he sought to reclaim the presidency other than by an insurrection, former President Donald Trump has looked like one crumbling cookie. Just before Thanksgiving Trump hosted antisemite extraordinaire Kanye West, now Ye, for dinner. Wouldn't you know it? Who else should join the party at the table of the former president of the United States but Ye's good buddy Nick Fuentes, not only an antisemite but an avowed white supremacist? It was just sheer good luck that Hermann Goering and Bull Connor had previous commitments.

Trump saw nothing wrong with hosting two of the most repugnant individuals in America not presently in solitary confinement, which surprised nobody. But it must have stung when some of his most prominent acolytes actually permitted themselves a few public murmurings of disapproval, as though this were somehow a deviation from the Prince of Mar-a-Lago's character. Trump does seem to be trolling the bottom of America's barrel with even more abandon than usual, and in West and Fuentes he has certainly found it.

Last week saw a series of unfavorable legal developments for Trump who, as he put it in Don Corleone-inspired fashion about former Ambassador Maria Yovanovitch, is going to go through some things. The Supreme Court, dominated by conservative justices on whom Trump thought he could rely, cleared the way for the IRS to turn his tax returns over to the Democratic-controlled House Ways and Means Committee. The returns have now been delivered, meaning that financial information that Trump has tried every trick in the book to keep hidden may see the dreaded light of day.

Next came the conviction of five leaders of the Jan. 6 assault on the Capitol, on charges of seditious conspiracy and obstruction of the counting of electoral votes. This was a setback for MAGA diehards who maintain with a straight face that an attempted coup d'etat was a barely boisterous tourist visit, rather like a middle-school trip to Disney World. The conviction demonstrated that the Justice Department isn't firing blanks. Since the physical attack at the Capitol end of Pennsylvania Avenue was likely not spontaneously conceived, those involved in summoning the mob to Washington by promising them a "wild" time now have yet more reason to purchase headache medicine.

Last Thursday brought the evisceration of Team Trump's effort to throw sand in the gears of the investigation of The Donald's apparent pilfering of over 300 classified documents, a little frolic that may cost him an indictment under the Espionage Act and for obstruction of justice. Trump's lawyers had found a Florida judge appointed by their client to the federal bench not merely willing to help her benefactor but seemingly eager to do so. She had obliged by erecting roadblocks for prosecutors. Three Republican appellate judges issued a decision not only dismantling the roadblocks but dismissing Trump's lawsuit altogether.

The Jan. 6 Committee is about to release a massive report detailing reams of evidence of the former president's wrongdoing, also known to his supporters as "fake news." This ought to keep journalists busy for weeks and keep Republican members of Congress hustling through the Capitol to avoid journalists' questions. The Justice Department's multi-track criminal investigation into Trump continues to advance. The team of lawyers and investigators examining whether Trump should be indicted for obstructing Congress on Jan. 6 has forced the grand jury testimony of Trump confidant Kash Patel and former White House lawyers Pat Cipollone and Patrick Philbin, presumably about Trump's various instructions and demands about staying in office after being voted out of it.

Meanwhile, a Georgia grand jury is wrapping up a criminal probe into whether Trump committed election fraud, and Trump awaits a verdict in a criminal case against his company. 'Tis not the season to be jolly for The Former Guy. It's more like a whole lot of chickens coming home to roost.

So Much For 'Dementia Joe': Biden Comes Out on Top, Again

December 13, 2022

  In commemoration of last week's anniversary of Japan's attack on Pearl Harbor, a group of World War II veterans came to the White House for a visit, invited there by the president of the United States. On walkers or in wheelchairs, a remnant of the Greatest Generation felt at ease bantering with their Commander-in-Chief, who clearly needed neither prompter nor prompting to communicate the debt their country owed them. "Because of you the rest of the world still looks to the United States," President Joe Biden told them. "I don't know you, but I love you." One by one the men stood or leaned forward to shake the president's hand. "This is the proudest moment of my life," one told Biden, saluting the president who had saluted them.

  One of the reasons that Biden has prevailed over crazed, concerted attempts to portray him as a "radical" is that he is as old fashioned as apple pie, and Americans get it. Unlike his predecessor, who thinks that the letter "D" in "D-day" stands for "Debutante," Biden knows American history, and cherishes it. That is one of the reasons that Americans, in turn, owe him a debt of gratitude. Another is that he is as decent as his predecessor is indecent. In a time dominated by demagogues and charlatans, Biden is a mensch.

  America isn't simply cynical these days. It is vicious. In those spaces where outright vitriol doesn't reign, snarkiness does. It is a fortuitous moment to have a good person as president. Before he went Full Weasel, Republican attack dog Sen. Lindsey Graham, who has now found his own safe space as former President Donald Trump's wingman, called Biden "as good a man as God ever created. He's the nicest person I've ever met in politics."

  Almost under the radar, Biden has managed to restore some of the traditional respect for an office pretty much ransacked by the guy he defeated. He's also managed to finagle through a divided Congress and into law a body of legislation unmatched by any president in his first two years of office since Franklin Roosevelt. The American Rescue Plan Act, the Infrastructure Investment and Jobs Act, the Inflation Reduction Act, the CHIPS and Science Act, the Safer Communities Act — all of these will improve Americans' lives for decades.

Meanwhile, Biden's credibility has made the difference in solidifying Western opposition to Russian barbarity in Ukraine, stiffening a cross-Atlantic alliance that had been badly degraded by Trump's buffoonery. Putin had come to expect he could have his geopolitical way, encouraged in that expectation by a former American president who was in the Russian autocrat's hip pocket. Nine months after invading Ukraine, Putin is in retreat, flailing this way and that to stanch Russia's humiliation.

Now Biden has confounded pundits from Right to Left in the midterm elections, holding Republicans to tiny gains in the House and actually picking up a Democratic seat in the Senate. The GOP is in disarray, not just pointing fingers at one another but wielding knives. Some even dare to murmur the occasional criticism of their titular leader, the Mussolini of Mar-a-Lago.

Biden can expect the Republicans to turn to this truly important issue: the former addiction problems of his surviving son. Hunter Biden suffered the deaths of his mother and sister in a car crash, the death of his brother from brain cancer and the near death of his father from two brain aneurysms. So, it seems only fitting for Republicans, giddy at their control of House committees, to use congressional investigative power to probe the depths of the younger Biden's past emotional misery, hoping that in doing so they can torment the president and damage him politically.

It is, after all, what makes the Republican Party of 2022 such an impressive enterprise. Having failed to beat Joe Biden by mocking him for an arthritic spine, the residue of a childhood stutter and a fall off a bicycle, they've got what they've got.

Dishonorable Mention: Referred for Criminal Prosecution, Trump Enters the Realm of Humpty Dumpty

December 20, 2022

Humpty Dumpty is the world's most famous egg, immortalized for sitting on a wall before suffering a very great fall. "All the king's horses and all the king's men," goes the legendary nursery rhyme, "couldn't put Humpty together again."

Former President Donald Trump is looking a lot like Humpty Dumpty these days, as the criminal investigations targeting him pile up and accelerate and his shell shows more cracks with each passing week. Last week a Wall Street Journal poll reflected Trump trailing Florida Gov. Ron DeSantis by 14% among Republicans asked to choose a favorite for the 2024 GOP presidential nomination. A USA Today poll released a day earlier had Trump trailing by 23%. Meanwhile, the former president made another stop on his "How Many Ways Can I Make a Fool of Myself?" tour by announcing that he had a "major announcement" to make. This turned out to be an announcement that he was selling trading cards featuring himself as a cartoon superhero, offered to all interested suckers for a mere $99 per set.

It has long been crystal clear that Trump made even flagrant scam artists look like George Washington by comparison, but never quite this crystal clear. Even deep-in-the-tank criminals like Steve Bannon and Michael Flynn expressed their disgust. "I can't watch it again, make it stop," said the clinically amoral Bannon about Trump's commercial. When you've lost fraudsters like Bannon and Flynn, you're in trouble.

And Trump is. This week the House committee investigating Trump's attempted coup d'etat was set to complete 18 months of work interviewing about 1,000 witnesses, including Trump's inner circle and immediate family. It prepared to recommend that the Justice Department prosecute the former president for at least three federal crimes: corruptly obstructing the constitutionally mandated tabulation of electoral votes, conspiring to defraud the United States government and assisting in an insurrection against the country and its legal system. And the recommendations, which are backed by voluminous evidence organized crime by crime, are not exactly plucked from thin air.

Indeed, one federal judge who only had a small sliver of the available evidence before him found it "more likely than not that President Trump attempted to obstruct the Joint Session of Congress on January 6, 2021." Another federal judge ruled that, based on the detailed allegations filed by 11 members of Congress and two Capitol Police officers, Trump may be civilly liable for conspiring to prevent Congress, by force, intimidation or threats, from discharging its official duties and to prevent President Joe Biden from assuming office, all in violation of — wait for it — the Ku Klux Klan Act of 1871. The committee will note that during Trump's second impeachment trial, on a single charge of incitement to insurrection, seven Republican senators joined 50 Democratic ones in voting to find Trump guilty.

The referral to the Justice Department has little substantive significance. The Department, which is not obliged to pay attention to the referral, is plowing ahead on its own with investigations of Trump not just for his attempted coup but for violation of the Espionage Act and obstruction of justice related to his wholly separate pilfering of classified documents. Still, the evidence amassed by the committee will be a treasure trove for prosecutors as they build their cases against Trump.

Trump's response to the criminal referrals was, well, just what you'd expect of a con man pitching fictitious depictions of himself as a superhero to the easily conned. "The January 6th Un-Select Committee held show trials by Never Trump politicians who are a stain on this country," proclaimed a spokesman for Trump, who chickened out of answering the committee's questions rather than assert his Fifth Amendment rights against self-incrimination several thousand times on national television.

The stains left on the country weren't left there by the committee, of course. They are there courtesy of the guy the committee was duty bound to investigate. Which is why Humpty Dumpty's horses and Humpty Dumpty's men will have a slog putting their hero back together again.

Champion for the Disabled: Jim Brett Keeps Fighting

December 27, 2022

Jim Brett has a lot of admirers, and a lot of them think about him this time of year. The longtime president and CEO of the New England Council, a powerhouse consortium of civic institutions and businesses representing the region in Washington, might otherwise be best known for modeling non-partisanship in a time of vitriol. The former Democratic state legislator from Massachusetts, who nearly became Boston's mayor in the early 1990s, has been the Council's steady hand for 26 years as Republicans and Democrats have rotated in and out of power in the nation's capital, as inscrutable about his political leanings, if any, as a guard at Buckingham Palace.

But it's a lifetime of fierce advocacy for Americans with disabilities that the thousands whose lives Brett has touched think of when they think of him. "Help someone along the way who can't repay you," Brett was instructed by a mother who emigrated here as a poor Irish farm girl in the 1920s and supported her family by washing floors in downtown Boston. "That will be your reward."

Brett has followed this instruction doggedly, if unpretentiously. Apart from his mother, no one influenced him more than his older brother Jack, born with profound intellectual disabilities. The two lived together for most of Jack's life. "Even though Jack had an IQ of 35, he became my teacher," Brett has said. "He opened my eyes and he opened my heart."

For decades now, Brett has been asked to drive the agendas of high-level groups established to press for dignity for the disabled. This past May President Joe Biden asked him to once again serve as Chair of the President's Committee for People with Intellectual Disabilities. He had previously been asked by Presidents George W. Bush and Barack Obama to serve. He's also vice chair of the National Council on Disability. Year after year, Brett is everywhere, hammering away at the barriers that isolate and exclude the disabled.

None do more damage than the barriers to acceptable health care. "People with intellectual disabilities are the most medically underserved people in the world, including the US," says Dr. Steven Perlman, a professor of Pediatric Dentistry at Boston University's School of Dental Medicine, nationally recognized for his work providing and promoting treatment of both children and adults with intellectual disabilities. Brett and Perlman are close collaborators in the battle to induce medical societies, medical schools and Congress to do right by the disabled. Brett calls Perlman his "mentor." Perlman calls Brett a "true American hero for people with intellectual disabilities." When it comes to access to medical care, says Perlman, a legend in the effort to provide dental care for the intellectually disabled, disabled Americans are "invisible."

The two are disinterested in well-meaning chatter: there are concrete ways of changing this. Physicians receive little to no training in treating the disabled, medical facilities are not incentivized to provide care for this population, and reimbursement systems are maintained that not only do not encourage the treatment of those with intellectual disabilities but affirmatively discourage it. Group homes and assisted living facilities face staggering shortages in personal care personnel — shortages that could be reduced by targeted changes in immigration policies and increased funding. "Why are the wages so low for the people taking care of our loved ones?" asks Brett. "Some of them have to work two or three jobs. Some are on food stamps. It's a disgrace."

There's been some progress. Brett, Perlman and others have forced American dental schools to train dentists to provide dental care for the intellectually disabled, who have suffered dearly for lack of it. Legislation is pending that would require the federal government more broadly to provide more favorable reimbursement rates for providers to the disabled and significantly upgrade care. But it hasn't been enacted.

Jim Brett carries with him a picture of his brother Jack everywhere he goes. The fight for the disabled is a long one, he knows. "But it's what keeps me going," he says.

Art of the Con: On Trumpism's Wings, Mr. Santos Goes to Washington

January 3, 2023

By the time former President Donald Trump scooted out of Washington on Jan. 20, 2021, The Washington Post had counted a mere 30,573 false or misleading claims by The Great Swamp Drainer during his time in office. Even that was an undercount, because the Post decided early on that it would only count one falsehood per topic for each speech, tweet or interview, lest its computer crash under the sheer volume of fabrications. Thus, for example, if in any given speech Trump uttered multiple lies, say, about his taxes or supposed payment thereof, or about how COVID-19 was a hoax and was scheduled to shortly disappear, or about how people kept telling him he was a genius, the Post only marked him down for a single falsehood.

Even with that limitation, however, Trump did not only set the world record for lies for any figure, public or private, indicted or unindicted. When it comes to dishonesty, he is in a galaxy unto himself.

But that isn't all he has achieved. He has inspired numberless others in the Republican Party to emulate him — by repeating his fraudulent nonsense that the 2020 election was "stolen" or "rigged," for instance, or that President Joe Biden is "corrupt," or all manner of other hogwash. It once was that those holding themselves out as moral adhered to the adage "Thou shalt not lie." In the Republican Party that Trump created in his image, it's now "Thou shalt not lie unless thou hope that no one knoweth the truth."

For all the dishonest election deniers and other genuine-gold-watch-for-only-one-dollar hucksters that rule the party of Trump, no one quite embodies the depths to which the Grand Old Party has sunk more than one George Santos, the Trump acolyte and titanically brazen fraudster who flipped to red a traditionally blue congressional district on Long Island by lying his and everyone else's socks off.

Santos claimed to have attended the prestigious Horace Mann School in the Bronx. He didn't. He claimed to have graduated from Baruch College. Nope. He claimed to have worked for Citigroup and Goldman Sachs. News to them.

He claimed to be a "proud American Jew" and "Jewish." He actually isn't, so he now claims that he meant that he was "Jew-ish' — whatever that means. He claimed his mother's family were Holocaust survivors. They weren't. He claimed he had a family-owned real estate portfolio of 13 properties. He was off by 13 properties.

He claimed that he founded a major animal rescue charity. Sounds great, but the IRS has no record of it. He claimed that his company "lost 4 employees" at the June 2016 Pulse nightclub massacre in Orlando, Florida, but a New York Times review of the obituaries of the 49 actual victims of that massacre does not support this.

It turns out that Santos admitted using stolen checks and a phony name to steal money from a store in Brazil, where he lived at the time. Though he denies this, there's the little matter of that admission. And there are question marks in his financial reporting larger than Trump Tower. He has stopped offering even the most pathetic responses to journalists' questions, because there appear to be no responses, and because someone wise has apparently told him that lying about lies is risky business.

Santos finds himself under state and federal investigation, but that seems unlikely to stop the Republican congressional leadership from welcoming him into your House of Representatives. This should surprise no one: the GOP, after all, is the party of Reps. Marjorie Taylor Greene, Lauren Boebert, Matt Gaetz and the party's lead elephant, Donald Trump himself.

George Santos gives every indication of being a sociopath, but let's not mince words: the party that he supports and that supports him is dominated by sociopath enablers and sociopath defenders. There are still decent people throughout the Republican Party, but they don't run the show. America won't turn the corner until the indecent ones are run out of town on a rail.

Hunger Pain: Jim McGovern Prods America to Get Food on Everyone's Table

January 10, 2023

The slow-motion train wreck that was last week's selection of a Republican speaker of the House almost certainly drove America's regard for Congress to new lows, assuming that's possible. Televised internecine warfare within the GOP featured battling among the crazies, the phonies and the insurrectionists, once again recalling Henry Kissinger's line about the Iran-Iraq War: "It's a pity that one side had to win."

Amidst the dispiriting display it was easy to forget that there are plenty of gems in Congress who've spent careers fighting fights of real significance, often unheralded. Massachusetts Rep. James McGovern, now leaving his powerful post as chair of the House Rules Committee, combines an insider's knowledge of House procedures with an outsider's passion for the excluded. His signature issue during his 13 terms in Congress has been ending hunger in America, which decade in and decade out remains the cause of suffering for staggering numbers of Americans, consigned to third-class status in the planet's wealthiest nation.

According to the U.S. Department of Agriculture, nearly 34 million Americans, including 5 million children, lead lives of what is characterized as "food insecurity," with uncertain access to food sufficient to meet basic nutritional needs, or just flatly unable to obtain that nutrition. Asked how it is that this can be given America's historic resources, McGovern replies: "Lack of political will. We have the money, we have the food, we have the infrastructure. But without the political will, you have tens of millions of people hungry in America."

Inspired by the bipartisan example of Democratic Sen. George McGovern (no relation) and Republican Sen. Bob Dole, who spearheaded groundbreaking legislation to reduce hunger in the 1970s, Jim McGovern has partnered with numerous Republican colleagues to vitalize, reinforce, supplement, reform and expand programs to make food — and, specifically, healthy food — available to those for whom it isn't. Along the way he has buttonholed members of the executive branch, held hearings, convened conferences and inserted amendments in legislation, all in service of militating on behalf of the undernourished.

He has long been focused on getting the funding to state and local governments as well as the highly consequential nonprofit sector, convinced that they are often the best positioned to meet needs where they are located — often needs that are more complex than meet the non-expert eye. When it comes to getting food to those who don't have it and don't have the means of getting it, McGovern says, "there are good and very effective models that are springing up all over the country that government should embrace. A one size glove doesn't fit all."

For all of its vaunted status as a center of higher education, financial services, health care and high tech, Massachusetts has failed abjectly to ensure that its citizens have access to nutrition. According to the non-profit Project Bread, nearly 17% of Massachusetts households suffer from food insecurity, more than double the pre-pandemic rates. Boston Mayor Michelle Wu, whose focus on food security is steeped in both personal experience and public policy knowledge, has established two offices to fill nutritional gaps in the city. The Mayor's Office of Food Justice and GrowBoston, her office for promoting urban food production, employ a range of targeted approaches to connecting people with food and vice versa in ways that illustrate McGovern's "one size doesn't fit all" observation.

But as McGovern knows as well as anyone in Washington, eliminating the nutrition gap can't be left to the resourcefulness of localities, or be permitted to fall victim to weary rhetoric about "welfare." Food insecurity isn't only a matter of unacceptable suffering; it also saps the strength of American society. Whether or not the nutrition deficit is at long last eliminated will drive whether we succeed or fail to educate our children, whether health care costs are contained or continue to surge, and whether the country coheres or keeps on fracturing. Jim McGovern's been right about this for a long time.

Send in the Clowns: Biden's Mistakes Invite the GOP Circus

January 17, 2023

With all the outstanding questions about who packed up then-Vice President Joe Biden's files in the Obama administration's final days, who unpacked them and why documents with classified markings were unlawfully removed in the process, one fact is pretty well-established. Biden's testy response to a reporter's question about how such documents ended up next to his Corvette ("By the way, my Corvette is in a locked garage. OK? So it's not like it's sitting out in the street.") was God-awful. It may not have matched former President Donald Trump's idiocy about the COVID-19 pandemic ("Supposing we hit the body with a tremendous — whether it's ultraviolet or just very powerful light"), but it was bad.

While it remains a stretch to imagine that the departing vice president personally packed his papers, there are plenty of legitimate questions. They are questions, of course, to which the Biden White House generally can't respond publicly, for reasons that are also legitimate. It knows that the media is demanding answers to what happened when, who knew it and what the classified documents said, and that not providing them quickly subjects the president to withering criticism. That's the way that works.

But White House personnel and Biden's lawyers aren't at all in a position even to know what those answers are, let alone to state them publicly. This is because there are individuals who worked in the vice president's office, or at Biden's Washington think tank or on his personal staff who have to be questioned — and neither the White House nor Biden's own lawyers can interview them. From the outset the Justice Department and now a special counsel have been conducting an investigation, and no one can contact these people without risking being perceived as interfering with it.

And making statements that may later prove incomplete or inaccurate will generate its own political problems, if not legal ones. Remember the trouble Susan Rice got into with a Republican Congress when then-President Barack Obama's national security adviser repeated reports about the attacks on our consulate in Benghazi that turned out to be incorrect?

But this is Washington, after all, where being loudly irresponsible trumps being circumspect every time. It was hilarious to see congressional

Republicans, who were silent as a graveyard when Trump removed over 300 classified documents to Mar-a-Lago, then stonewalled requests for their return, then disobeyed a grand jury subpoena and then had an attorney lie about the ongoing concealment of top-secret materials, decide that 20 classified documents found under Biden's control was a very big deal. When pressed to explain this flagrant hypocrisy, the cat doesn't only have their tongue. It has their larynx.

Last Friday the new chairman of the House Judiciary Committee, Ohio Republican and Trump favorite Rep. Jim Jordan, demanded that Attorney General Merrick Garland turn over documents that Jordan knew could not be turned over while the investigation that he knew was ongoing was ongoing. Jordan was the Republicans' exemplary choice to head the Judiciary Committee since he isn't a lawyer and never even took the bar exam. He calls himself a lawyer "wannabe," which is just what you want to have running the Judiciary Committee. He did, however, vote to reject the electoral votes in the 2020 election, and blew off a subpoena issued by another congressional committee compelling him to answer questions under oath about the Jan. 6 coup d'etat.

Rep. James Comer, the incoming chair of the newly named Oversight and Accountability Committee, was understandably stumped when asked on Sunday why, if he was so "concerned" about the 20 classified documents found among Biden's papers, he pronounced the over 300 taken by Trump to Florida "not a priority." And Speaker Kevin ("It's about transparency!") McCarthy, who opposed an investigation into Trump's pilfering of classified material and obstruction of justice, demanded an investigation into Biden.

Here's where we stand: About the Biden document debacle we don't know much. About congressional Republicans we know all we need to.

White Wash: Ron DeSantis Will Decide What Your Children Learn About Black History

January 24, 2023

Facing History and Ourselves has a mission statement that seems not just sensible but indisputable. "To build a more just and equitable future," it posits, "we must face our history in all its complexity."

President Gerald Ford first recognized February as Black History Month, urging Americans to "honor the too-often-neglected accomplishments of Black Americans in every area of endeavor throughout our history." Of course, Black American history is not only the history of high achievement. It is the history of slavery, America's original sin, and the injustice, struggles, triumphs, movements and voices that are all part of the Black experience, and America's.

The theme of Black History Month this year is "Black Resistance." The Association for the Study of African American Life and History, Black History Month's founders, explain why. "African Americans have resisted historic and ongoing oppression in all forms, especially the racial terrorism of lynching, racial pogroms and police killings since our arrival upon these shores," ASALH writes. "These efforts have been to advocate for a dignified, self-determined life in a just democratic society in the United States." For many white Americans, words like these are difficult to hear, but also difficult to deny.

Florida Gov. Ron DeSantis is doing his best to control what students in his state learn about Black history, seeking to dictate a sanitized version of history more palatable to white conservatives' ears than, say, the real thing. He has marked Black History Month by vetoing the nonprofit College Board's proposal to give Florida students the opportunity to take an Advanced Placement course in African American Studies, ruling in terms that evoke Leonid Brezhnev: "The content of this course is inexplicably contrary to Florida law and significantly lacks educational value." If this sounds like balderdash, it's because it is: the course, developed over years by serious historians, encompasses such evidently verboten topics as slavery's legacy, systemic racism and the emergence of Black Lives Matter. That is what makes it impermissible. DeSantis, who castigates state mandates on vaccines to safeguard Floridians from lethal diseases, is pleased to mandate what they can learn about history and what they can't.

Founded in 1955, the College Board has offered Advanced Placement courses in European history, German history and Chinese history. There will not, however, be an Advanced Placement course offered in Florida in Black American history because the governor doesn't approve of the curriculum.

Deficient in their knowledge of our country's history generally, Americans are particularly ignorant of African American history, and they know it. According to a Quinnipiac University poll taken last year, only 27% of Americans say the history they were taught in school provided a full, accurate account of African Americans' role in that history. "Removed from the classroom, two-thirds of Americans look back and say they were not taught enough about the struggle and the triumphs of African Americans," Quinnipiac polling analyst Tim Malloy told the Alabama Political Reporter.

Against that backdrop, the class DeSantis has vetoed would have given qualified high school students the chance to study African American history on a university level and would have incentivized them to do so for college credit. It would have promoted continued studies in the subject at university and it would have encouraged some of those taking the class to go on and teach the subject to others. It would have stimulated middle school and high school students to open books that will remain closed on a crucial aspect of our nation's history. At its core, Christopher Tinson, Chair of African American Studies at Saint Louis University, told National Public Radio, "the reason why this is even an important area of study is because of the historical erasures from historical records in public schools of African experiences."

This is an erudite way of saying the following: White Americans know next to nothing about Black history, and Black Americans are often frozen out of meaningful opportunities to learn about their own place in America. Ron DeSantis is more than happy to have it stay that way.

Demagogues' Devil: Targeted by MAGA World, Adam Schiff Resumes Punching

January 31, 2023

It was nearly 50 years ago that Edward Markey, then the lowliest of Massachusetts state legislators, challenged the legislative old guard by pushing through judicial reform measures that ended a gravy train for ethically suspect politicos and their allies. Displeased at Markey in the extreme, the legislative leadership retaliated against him by ostentatiously stripping him of his office, forcing him to sit in the hallway.

This boomeranged. Markey took the act of revenge as a badge of honor, and so did voters. They rewarded him by electing him to Congress. Markey's television ad in his congressional race highlighted this episode, and it has become legendary in political circles here. It featured Markey standing in front of a desk placed forlornly in a State House corridor. "They may tell me where to sit," Markey says into the camera. "But they'll never tell me where to stand." After 20 terms in Congress, Markey was elected to the U.S. Senate in 2013.

California may be about to experience something similar, with the announcement of U.S. Rep. Adam Schiff, blocked by House Speaker Kevin McCarthy from resuming his seat on the House Intelligence Committee, that he is running for the Senate. That Schiff would be ousted from the committee he served so admirably once the Republicans took control of the House has been a foregone conclusion.

As the committee's chairman in 2019, Schiff led the inquiry into then-President Donald Trump's attempt to extort the Ukrainian government into announcing a patently phony "investigation" into then-candidate Joe Biden by withholding aid desperately needed by Ukraine to defend itself against Vladimir Putin's aggression. Schiff, a former federal prosecutor who knows how to run a real investigation, disregarded relentless waves of vitriol, including death threats, ensuring that the country had a record of the "drug deal," as John Bolton put it, that Trump had commandeered. In order to do so Schiff had to work around unadorned obstruction by Trump, who ordered his administration to do everything it could do to deny America the truth about what had transpired.

The country watched day after appalling day as Trump's closest allies on the committee debased themselves seeking to derail the committee's hearings, often by ad hominem attacks on Schiff. Puerile insults by Trump — "Shifty Schiff" and "Pencil Neck Schiff" were among the then-president's displays of brilliance — amped up MAGA World's social media war on the California congressman.

It was Schiff who, knowing that a GOP-controlled Senate would never vote to convict Trump regardless of the evidence against him, led the presentation of that evidence in Trump's first impeachment trial. Vainly urging Republican senators to put aside politics and attend to our democracy, Schiff methodically recounted the evidence of Trump's corruption, not merely a mountain of it but a veritable mountain range. "Can we be confident that he will not continue to try to cheat?" Schiff asked, warning a year before the 2020 election that Trump would try to torpedo the rule of law in order to stay in office. "And the short, plain, sad, incontestable answer is, no, you can't. You can't trust this president to do the right thing, not for one minute, not for one election, not for the sake of our country. You just can't. He will not change, and you know it."

Schiff could not have been more on target, as America has learned, painfully. And by being on target, he made himself one. McCarthy's desperate desire to be elected House speaker depended on favoring Trump and his acolytes by kicking Schiff off the Intelligence Committee. To be precise, you can't say that someone with no soul has sold it, but if you could, you'd be talking about McCarthy.

But turnabout, as they say, is fair play. Schiff has a good chance of being elected senator next year. And that would position him to stand up to the demagogues even more effectively than he has until now.

Grace And Disgrace: Black America Suffers Another Outrage

February 7, 2023

During his last interview before his death three years ago, U.S. congressman and civil rights hero John Lewis was asked whether he ever grew so discouraged by the persistent enormity of racial injustice in America that he felt his efforts "weren't working." Lewis, who as a civil rights activist had been falsely imprisoned and savagely beaten, said no. "I never came to that point," he said. "You get thrown in jail, maybe for a few days, and then you go to Mississippi, and you go to the state penitentiary, and you find some of your friends and your colleagues. And you get out, and you go on to the next effort. We used to say struggling is not a struggle that lasts for a few days, or a few weeks, or a few years. It is a struggle of a lifetime."

The outrageous murder of Tyre Nichols by Memphis police officers and the equally outrageous indifference to Nichols' suffering by firemen and emergency medical technicians who share guilt for his death is yet another replay of a disgrace that by now seems commonplace. It's obvious that for every murder of Tyre Nichols or George Floyd or Daunte Wright or the other souls whose names have crossed our television screens, there are others — plenty of them — whose names we will never learn. And for every police murder, there are hundreds, or thousands, of incidents in which Black Americans are bullied or mistreated or brutalized by law enforcement officers afforded guns and badges by a citizenry that is entitled to have law enforcers, not lawbreakers, acting in their name. It is naive to think otherwise.

While we are at it, the poison doesn't reside in police departments alone. There is a culture of disrespect, or even disregard, for Black Americans in too many quarters. Black Americans know it. White Americans have to work increasingly hard not to.

"For me," wrote professor Deborah Ramirez, of the Northeastern University School of Law's Center for Law, Equity and Race, "the heroine in this tragedy is RowVaughn Wells, Tyre Nichols' mom. Surely her trauma is the worst trauma I can imagine suffering. And yet, she is praying for the officers who killed her son. She believes her son is now an angel and that this was meant to happen because it will become a catalyst for change."

After Nichols' killing, his family started a fund to turn their horror into a tangible community good. "We want to build a memorial skate park for Tyre," they said, "in honor of his loves for skating and sunsets."

The latest depravity has stirred new moves in Congress to pass legislation reforming the "qualified immunity doctrine," the shield in place that benefits those accused of police misconduct and protects them from lawsuits. The rule imposes on victims of such misconduct the burden of proving that police violated "clearly established statutes or constitutional rights." In practice, it serves as an escape hatch for police departments, often enabling them to get away with murder, figuratively if not literally.

The principal argument against reducing qualified immunity shields is that doing so would encourage frivolous lawsuits. But the same was said of other legislation that vastly improved America, like the securities laws enacted during the Great Depression to protect Americans from fraud and the civil rights laws enacted in the 1960s to protect them from discrimination.

Even police reform won't do the trick, says Leslie Short, an experienced strategist in the area of Diversity, Equity and Inclusion. "I think it's fantasy to think we will restructure the police with a wave of the wand," Short says. "Until we dig deep into the systemic racial issues in every layer of (the existing) mentality, nothing changes."

With it all, America's communities of color press on, gifting resilience and grace to a nation that must sometimes seem to those communities not to deserve it.

Bulwark: University of Haifa Helps Israel Hold the Line

February 14, 2023

Winston Churchill's proposition that "democracy is the worst form of government, except for all others that have been tried" has picked up support in recent years, courtesy of two of the world's foremost democracies. The United States and Israel, which have much in common generally, have each given democracy skeptics plenty of cause for skepticism, each emerging from elections that, however democratic, produced results that were god-awful.

Our 2016 presidential election was a fair one, but America's system of disregarding the actual popular vote in favor of a questionable Electoral College resulted in the election of a narcissistic nightmare, a pathological con man, a Hindenburg Disaster on two legs. Israel's recent parliamentary election, in which the raw vote was closely divided between center-left and center-right, produced a coalition government dominated by autocrats, fanatics and homophobes, with a prime minister under criminal indictment maneuvering to rejigger Israeli democracy to avoid a trial that could land him in jail.

If the two nations have a saving grace, it lies in the nations themselves. America's judiciary and free press managed to hold the line against Donald Trump, albeit just barely. Israel has an equally free press and, for the moment, at least, an independent judiciary whose authority trumps that of the government. But what Israel also has going for it is an extraordinarily vibrant, passionate civil society, comprised of individuals and institutions whose intention in the face of a dreadful parliamentary coalition is to not go quietly.

Crowds of as many as 200,000 protesting the government have assembled in Tel Aviv on successive Saturday nights, the proportionate equivalent of about 7 million Americans. Israel benefits from a society with an abundance of commitment to strengthening the country's social fabric. If there is a country with a greater number of social justice entrepreneurs per capita, it would be surprising.

Among the institutions that serve as engines for pluralism in Israel is the University of Haifa, which serves approximately 18,000 students from every stratum of Israel's diverse society. Approximately 45% of the University's students are Arab Israelis, and this is no accident. When professor Mouna Maroun, the University's vice president and dean of research and development, began studying psychology there over 20 years ago, about 6% of the student body was Arab, and Arab Israelis doing graduate work were nowhere to be found. "When I started graduate studies in psychobiology," says Dean Maroun, "I was the only Arab student (in the department), and this was the same for other departments. No Arabs."

Maroun is pleased with what has been accomplished to promote enrollment of Arab Israelis and to boost their advancement at the university and beyond. "The (Israeli) Government understood the potential of integrating the Arab population," she says, "creat(ing) a holistic program to encourage Arabs to pursue their studies. This program started in high schools to increase awareness of the importance of higher education, to encourage them to study fields in which Arabs are underrepresented and to move on to graduate studies."

Maroun is proud of what she and her colleagues have achieved and are achieving. "For me," she says, "the greatest achievement is that the University of Haifa is integrating the highest percentage of Arab students, empowering them and creating the new middle class, one which will have equal opportunities."

University President Ron Robin reinforces Dean Maroun's point. "In addition to a well-defined academic mission," he says, "we are driven by a social mission as well. We approach education in general, and higher education in particular, as a vehicle for social mobility. We seek to expand access to the middle class by opening our doors to socially peripheral groups in Israel."

The University of Haifa is a source of pride in Israel, but it is representative of an extremely rich number and variety of social actors committed to ensuring pluralism and democratic values there. It's a reminder that, as in our own country, there's plenty to worry about, but also reason to think that this, too, shall pass.

Sly Fox: Libel Lawsuit Documents Network's Sad Embrace of Trash, for Cash

February 21, 2023

When Dominion Voting Systems filed its $1.6 billion (that's with a "b") lawsuit against Fox News Network two years ago, it alleged that Fox had intentionally and recklessly defamed it by publishing and republishing false claims that Dominion had rigged the 2020 presidential election, manipulated vote counts and paid kickbacks to government officials. News Alert: Fox is in trouble.

Last week, after using the judicial process to disgorge internal Fox documents and take the sworn testimony of Fox producers, executives and television hosts, Dominion's lawyers filed hundreds of pages of materials strongly indicating that it has the proverbial receipts, and that Fox has a headache. The conservative media powerhouse will be fortunate to avoid a jury's verdict that it lied about Dominion, that it knew it was lying and that among its principal motivations for promoting lies was its perceived need to pander to the most untethered of its viewership, which keeps Fox's bank books fat and Rupert Murdoch happy. To put it succinctly: Dominion's court filings show that Fox is perfectly happy to traffic in falsehoods in order to preserve its cash flow.

For weeks following the 2020 election, Fox hosts hawked former President Donald Trump's poisonous snake oil, fostering and repeating the fraudulent claim that Trump, not President Joe Biden, had won the election. They endorsed, regurgitated and recycled the hogwash spewed by patent nutcases like Trump lawyers Sidney Powell and Rudy Giuliani, and the entirely certifiable pillow salesman Mike Lindell, that Dominion had cooked the election in Biden's favor using "software" and "algorithms," changing Trump votes to Biden votes.

It was garbage, of course — and, of course, Fox knew it, as a ton of evidence from Fox's own internal files makes quite clear. Fox host and money machine Tucker Carlson admitted to his producer "Sidney Powell is lying," acknowledging that what she was selling on Fox "news shows" was "ludicrous," "totally off the rails" and "shockingly reckless." One Fox reporter admitted to Fox's chief political correspondent: "It's dangerously insane these conspiracy theories." A Fox producer called the accusations against Dominion "complete BS." The company's senior vice president warned that this stuff was "mind-blowingly nuts".

Fox's internal fact-checker stated simply that the allegations against Dominion were "incorrect." Asked under oath about the claims published on Fox, the network's own political editor replied, "No reasonable person would have thought that."

But that didn't stop Fox from continuing its barrage of trash — because it concluded that if it didn't, it would lose viewers, and revenue, to Newsmax, the fledgling ultra-conservative network that makes Fox look like the house organ of the Democratic National Committee. When Fox called the Arizona election for Biden on election night, the full fury of Trump World was unleashed on Fox, and Fox management panicked that its base would turn to Newsmax. "Do the executives understand how much credibility and trust we've lost with our audience?" an alarmed Carlson texted his producer. "We're playing with fire for real... an alternative like Newsmax could be devastating to us." Internal Fox documents warn of "the Newsmax surge" happening in real time, referring to Newsmax's "theft" of Fox viewers as "vandalism."

When a Fox reporter tweeted "There is no evidence that any voting system deleted or lost votes, changed votes or was in any way compromised," Carlson was furious. "Please get her fired. Seriously." he texted colleague Sean Hannity. "It needs to stop immediately, like tonight. It's measurably hurting the company. The stock price is down. Not a joke." A Fox executive agreed. "She has serious nerve doing this," he responded about the reporter-gone-rogue, "and if this gets picked up, viewers are going to be further disgusted."

The next day, the reporter deleted her tweet.

"We can't make people think we've turned against Trump," one Fox executive admonished. Carlson's producer made the same point, only slightly differently. "Many viewers were upset tonight that we didn't cover election fraud," he warned. "It's all our viewers care about right now." Turns out that the only fraud was that which Fox was promoting — for profit.

Hacks and Heroes: The Fight Against Putin Highlights the Good, the Great and the Ugly

February 28, 2023

President Joe Biden's dramatic train trip through a war zone to stand with Ukrainian President Volodymyr Zelenskyy in Kiev inspired most of the world, but not everyone. Vladimir Putin's Kremlin hacks, who ardently wish not to join the thousands of Russians thrown into jail for opposing the former KGB agent's corrupt autocracy, did not applaud Biden's trip. Neither did America's MAGA set, led by Putin fanboy Tucker Carlson and others who are either looney or have lost their way. But most Americans saw Biden's unprotected trip through an area vulnerable to Russian missile attacks at any moment as a brave, historic move, one intended to physically demonstrate our solidarity with the Ukrainian people, who are suffering mass death and horrific hardship in order to resist subjugation by a brutal Russian regime.

Biden was greeted in Kiev by the man who exemplifies Ukrainian courage in the face of relentless Russian war crimes. When the Russians invaded Ukraine a year ago, no one bet on Zelenskyy remaining alive, let alone walking the streets of his country's capital. It is in no small measure thanks to Zelenskyy's ability to inspire Ukrainians and non-Ukrainians alike that his country was able to repel Russia's designs in Kiev and is holding the line against brutal assaults in the east. And he has exposed Putin as a tyrant, a war criminal and a crook.

But as for exposing Putin, someone else got there first, and he sits, deteriorating and perhaps dying, in a Russian cell, condemned to spend what may be the rest of his life there as a consequence of his own courage. Indeed, it isn't easy to imagine anyone more courageous than Alexei Navalny, the Russian anti-corruption activist and opposition leader whose condemnation of Putin's corruption and resourceful organizing against Putin's kleptocracy resulted in sham criminal convictions and confinement in harsh conditions that will not end as long as Putin is in power.

Navalny, whose criticisms of Putin focused undesired attention on the embezzlement-prone despot, made a documentary exposing Putin's rip-off of his people, entitled "Putin's Palace." After previous attempts to assassinate Navalny failed, agents of Putin's Federal Security Service poisoned him in Siberia in August 2020. Navalny nearly died, and the Kremlin was extremely displeased that he did not. Instead, a German charity spirited the dissident, near death, to Berlin, where he was miraculously nursed back to health.

While in Germany, Navalny had the notion that he could get one of the Russian agents who had poisoned him to admit that he had done so. It worked — and Navalny played the tape containing the admissions to an international audience.

But that wasn't all. Knowing that he would be arrested upon his arrival and sent to prison, Navalny nevertheless then boarded a flight home to Moscow — where he was arrested upon his arrival and sent to prison. That is where he sits, and that is where he may very well die.

HBO and CNN teamed up to produce a documentary about all of this, called "Navalny," in which one can watch as, with minimal effort, Navalny induces a Russian goon to confess the poisoning, and as he then returns to Moscow on his mission to draw attention to Putin's tyranny. "Navalny" is up for an Academy Award on March 13. As his daughter told The New York Times' Nicholas Kristof last week, Navalny's family and supporters hope the documentary is his "get out of death card," one which will garner so much attention that Putin will feel obliged to keep her father alive rather than slowly kill him.

Back in America, the likes of Ted Cruz mock support for Ukraine. "A Ukrainian flag has become like a COVID mask," Cruz said last week. "It's a sign to show your virtue." Some become heroes. Some become hacks. History has a way of judging these things.

Lucky Hank, Lucky Us: An American Hero Leaves Behind a Gift

March 7, 2023

In October 1942, 20-year-old Jacob Henry (Hank) Goldman, the grandson of Russian Jewish immigrants, walked into a Navy recruiting center in Philadelphia, hoping to enlist. It was 10 months since the Japanese had attacked Pearl Harbor.

Goldman was attending the University of Pennsylvania's Wharton School at the time, studying to become an accountant. But as far as he was concerned, that could wait. There was a country to help defend.

For reasons that were forever a mystery, the Navy turned him down. So, Hank Goldman shrugged and walked down the street to the Army Air Corps office, where he asked to enlist in that branch, which would later become the United States Air Force. "There was no question in his mind that he wanted to fight for his country," says Nancy Taicher, Goldman's daughter.

The Army Air Corps accepted Goldman, which proved a smart move and a lucky one for the country. After ranking No. 2 out of 150 students in navigators' school, Lt. Goldman was assigned to a bomb group in the South Pacific. He and the other young men from every corner of the country, strangers at first then bonded for life, were tasked with eliminating Japanese fortifications on islands whose names once gripped the nation's attention as it anxiously waited to see which way the war would go. The names are now obscure to Americans, whose knowledge of the bravery and grit of those that preceded them has also largely evaporated with time.

Goldman's job was to guide bomber pilots to their target while reducing the likelihood that they would be blown out of the sky, helping them hit their targets and then, somehow, getting them back to their base. His skill and judgment kept American crews alive and their planes in one piece during 25 bombing missions, leading to a series of promotions: first to flight leader, then squadron leader and then bomb group leader by the time the Japanese surrendered. He received two presidential citations: for the role his group played cutting Japanese supply lines and for leading a successful attack on a key Japanese position in the Philippines.

This, however, doesn't capture the overarching fact for Hank Goldman and approximately one million others who saw active combat in

World War II and came back home alive: Their survival was often by the sheer grace of God. Goldman's plane was hit by enemy fire twice and forced down. He survived crash landings and near misses, when only quick thinking and serendipity enabled his crew to avoid being taken prisoner or shot to pieces. It is small wonder that when he was 88 and published a short memoir of his time at war, he called it "Lucky Hank." It's his story, but it's more broadly the story of a country able to summon the patriotism of its finest young people to fend off the global designs of fascists.

Turns out, that isn't all Hank left behind. Shortly before he died last summer six weeks before his 100th birthday, his nurse at the Vitas Hospice in Delray Beach, Florida, telephoned his daughter Nancy. The nurse, a Ukrainian immigrant named Elena Leo, who was watching as her own homeland resisted totalitarianism, said excitedly, "I didn't know your father was a war hero!"

Taicher asked how she knew. "I googled Jacob H. Goldman last night," she replied, informing Goldman's daughter that, unbeknownst to his family, there were 23 YouTube interviews with Goldman about his time in the South Pacific.

Seems the Central Florida World War II Museum had interviewed Goldman late in his life and posted the interviews online. "Without Elena," says Nancy Taicher, "we never would have known they existed."

As of this year, only 167,000 of the 16 million Americans who served in World War II are still alive. Each month their number shrinks. In their absence, accounts like that of Hank Goldman will have to suffice to remind us of how much their country owes them.

Indecent Exposure: The Rot That Is the Republican Party Reclaims Center Stage

March 14, 2023

Former Vice President Mike Pence made news last Saturday by saying something that shouldn't have been news at all, but rather self-evident pablum right out of the mouth of Captain Obvious. Twenty-six months after an insurrectionist mob attempting a putsch stormed the Capitol on Jan. 6, 2021, beating the daylights out of police and seeking to overthrow an election so that Donald Trump could remain in power, Pence was ready to make a momentous announcement. "Make no mistake about it," he told attendees at the Gridiron Club's no-cameras-allowed dinner, where no video could be taken of the big declaration, "what happened that day was a disgrace, and it mocks decency to portray it any other way."

To Pence's credit, confirming what everyone playing with a full deck could see with their own eyes is political suicide for anyone harboring a modicum of hope of winning the Republican presidential nomination in 2024, and somehow or other Pence harbors half a modicum. His speech was a direct challenge to the MAGA base's second favorite tool, Fox's Tucker Carlson, who has amped up his Off-The-Deep-End Tour by stitching together snippets of Jan. 6 footage to make it look like nothing happened that day. This is an especially curious choice for Carlson, whose internal communications to colleagues at Fox expressing his contempt for The Donald while publicly praising him do bring the word "fraudster" to mind.

And while we are "making no mistake," if it isn't nice to fool Mother Nature, it isn't smart to contradict Tucker Carlson if you happen to want to avoid enraging Trump World. A man could get hanged. Rep. Jamie Raskin observed that the Republican Party is the party of "dangerous nihilism." That it surely is. An Associated Press-Ipsos poll taken last year found that about two-thirds of Republicans still believe that the 2020 election was stolen from Trump, even after lawsuit upon lawsuit, audit upon audit, recount upon recount determined that this is hogwash. And 55% of Republicans believe that whatever violence they are actually prepared to concede occurred on Jan. 6 was organized by left-wing activists trying to make Trump look bad. More hogwash.

So, give Mike Pence his due, and more. Not only were his actions on Jan. 6 patriotic, brave and democracy-saving, but he seems to be at peace with this: his bid to win the 2024 Republican presidential nomination isn't merely a long shot. It is The Voyage of the Damned.

With Republicans in control of the House of Representatives and Speaker Kevin McCarthy owned lock, stock and barrel by the most thoroughly unhinged among the Party's pro-Trump loyalists, finding evidence of moral rot within the Party does not exactly require Sherlock Holmes. Despite warnings from the Capitol Police that release of the full footage of events within the Capitol complex on Jan. 6 could expose security vulnerabilities there, McCarthy turned over 40,000 hours of security camera videos to Carlson. This was in order to facilitate Carlson's excision of footage of violence and presentation of footage without violence so that he could claim that it was all a nothingburger.

GOP lawmakers have launched an investigation into the House Select Committee investigating Jan. 6 — because, after all, it wasn't the attack that was the problem, but instead the investigation into the attack. Over in the House Judiciary Committee, Republicans were accusing the Biden administration of failing to comply with subpoenas. Of course, Rep. Jim Jordan, the Committee's chairman, gave the middle finger to the subpoena he received from the Select Committee last year, refusing its request that he turn over the evidence of what he knew about the insurrection.

As for former president Trump, he was — what else? — at the Conservative Political Action Conference, vowing vengeance against those who, all things considered, prefer a democracy over a fascism-tinged autocracy. "For those who have been wronged and betrayed, I am your retribution," said the leader of the Republican Party, sounding just like a certain failed Austrian-born painter mesmerizing Germans in the early 1930s. American democracy is in for another ride.

Arresting Developments: Donald Trump Prepares to Face the Music

March 21, 2023

    Sir Walter Scott's famous line about what a tangled web it is that we weave when first we practice to deceive was written in 1808, but the poet might as well have prophesied former President Donald Trump's ill-fated one-night stand with Stormy Daniels when he wrote it.

    The "affair," let's call it, was suffused with dishonesty at every stage, and it is that dishonesty that may soon result in the most famous mug shot in history.

    The sexual liaison between the real estate mogul and the porn star occurred in Lake Tahoe, while Trump's wife Melania was back home with their newborn son. Not a great start to the story for Trump. He had numerous conferences in 2015 and 2016 about how to keep that adulterous tryst and at least one other one hidden. When the public disclosure of the Access Hollywood tape threatened to torpedo his chances of winning the 2016 election just before the voting began and the additional risk that the revelation of his decidedly non-business meeting with Daniels would end his candidacy, Trump decided to pay Daniels $130,000 to silence her. His agreement to pay her came days before Election Day and falsified the names of the parties to the agreement in order to ensure that the arrangement remained concealed.

    Trump's hush money payment to Daniels was laundered through his trusted fixer, Michael Cohen. Trump personally repaid Cohen through a series of smaller checks, which added up to $130,000, falsely labeling the payments as being for "legal services." Trump has repeatedly lied about the affair. He has also lied about knowing of Cohen's payments — lies that have not held up well given the reimbursement checks to Cohen signed by him. Quite apart from all of this, it seems like a gratuitous insult to Ms. Daniels to characterize the services she provided to Trump as "legal services," but that's a separate issue.

    Things have moved beyond a mere miasma of dishonesty and sleaze. The former president, who wanted to buy Daniels' silence using his company's money rather than his own, faces imminent indictment under New York law for falsifying business records with the intent to commit an additional crime — here, a violation of the campaign finance law. The charge is hardly a slam dunk for prosecutors, who are relying on an untested legal theory and the testimony of Cohen, who served prison time in part for perjury. But Cohen also went to jail for his role in this scheme. That fact, coupled with the substantial volume and variety of evidence corroborating his account of the purpose of the payoff, places Trump in serious jeopardy of being convicted by a jury if the indictment survives legal challenge.

And the indictment expected this week is likely the beginning of Trump's confrontations with the criminal justice system, not the end. Any day now a Georgia grand jury will indict him for election fraud. Then there's the federal grand jury that will be asked to decide whether to indict him for obstruction of justice in connection with the purloining of classified documents, and whether he obstructed the counting of electoral votes.

Ever the statesman, Trump announced that he was about to be arrested, and called upon his most ardent supporters to take to the streets on his behalf. He is banking on a witch's brew of as-yet unjailed Proud Boys and other fine specimens to interfere with the rule of law as loyally, and as blindly, as they did on Jan. 6.

Making this still more challenging for Trump is this: The number of lawyers both equipped to handle the prosecutorial onslaught and willing to associate with him is starting to dwindle. Between grand jury subpoenas served on them and cellphones seized from them, Trump's lawyers are dropping like flies. Anyone contemplating representing Donald Trump at this point has to keep one hand on his wallet and the other on his law license. With indictments dropping and lawyers scattering, we are entering very uncharted waters indeed.

At The Ramparts: Under Siege from Autocrats and Crooks, Fighters for Democracy Hang Tough

March 28, 2023

The fight to preserve democracy around the world has come to resemble Whac-A-Mole, with autocrats wielding power or chasing it emerging on the global scene only to be faced down, then to emerge again. The biggest battle of them all is playing out in Ukraine, where a conscience-less war criminal unrepentant about committing mass murder has sought to lay waste to civilians indiscriminately, and where a historically brave population is showing the world, quite simply, what it means to fight and die for freedom.

In Iran, tens of thousands of citizens protesting in the wake of the killing of Mahsa Amini, a young Iranian-Kurdish woman who died in the custody of that regime's "morality police," have been detained. According to Human Rights Activists in Iran, an organization that tracks the government's repression of dissidents, at least 530 demonstrators have been killed by the mullahs' goons. That is likely an underestimation and does not include those summarily executed by the government — show executions that swiftly followed show trials.

Iran is the U.S. State Department's No. 1 state sponsor of terror and is currently illustrating why by providing drones to help Vladimir Putin annihilate Ukrainian civilians, using cash handed to it by the Obama administration to do so. Its rulers have been ruthless and efficient in suppressing dissent, but it hasn't been able to still dissent entirely. The day when Iranians will give the boot to the tyrants who rule them, just as they booted out the Shah, is on its way.

Here at home, we are trying to put democracy's near-death experience with a would-be Mussolini in our rear-view mirror, but he will not fade from view. It doesn't seem that our national flirtation with autocracy is over. The likelihood is that the Mussolini wannabe in question will be the 2024 Republican presidential nominee, and polls show a country evenly split between a narcissistic Caesar and a temperate, humane leader who has tried to get us to choose the rule of law over mob rule.

Among the most dramatic scenes of pro-democracy forces battling antidemocratic ones are those in Israel, pitting Israelis of every stripe and variety against an unseemly junta. Prime Minister Benjamin Netanyahu has permanently stained his legacy and the good name of his country by a gambit aimed at shielding himself from being held accountable for corruption charges, placing his own interests over the character, security and even survival of his country. He presides over a coalition government composed of crooks, sleazebags and fanatics that he has summoned in order to retake power. It is a government that each day alienates not only his countrymen but Israel's friends around the world, handing Israel's enemies a gift that was beyond their imagination just months ago.

The positive news amidst the dreadful is the massive demonstration of democratic fervor spawned by the Israeli government's attempt to squelch democracy. It comes as no surprise to anyone who knows anything about Israel, but it is impressive nonetheless. This weekend some 500,000 Israelis took to the streets to protest their government's bid to subjugate Israel's judiciary. That's over 5% of Israel's population, or the proportional equivalent of about 17 million Americans.

All across Israeli society, Israelis are publicly condemning their leaders and demanding they change course. Diplomats are resigning from the Foreign Ministry; military reservists, the backbone of Israel's defense, are announcing that they will not serve a government that has lost its way. The die-hards who defend the current Israeli government angrily insist that what that government does is none of our business. They are very wrong. Assaults on democracy are everybody's business, thanks very much, and those who have been outspoken about the torpedoing of American democracy or democracy anywhere do not intend to be silent when the torpedoing occurs in Jerusalem.

In Ukraine, in Iran, in America and in Israel, the world watches to see who will lose and who will win. The good news is that the good guys aren't going down without a fight.

Multiple Bookings: Mr. 'Lock Her Up' Ponders a Lockup

April 4, 2023

If there's anyone who embraces the strategy "The best defense is a good offense" more fiercely and more relentlessly than former President Donald Trump, it would be surprising. After news broke of his extortionate telephone call to Ukrainian President Volodymyr Zelenskyy conditioning American release of congressionally mandated military assistance to our embattled ally on a phony announcement of a phony investigation into Joe Biden, Trump boasted that his was "a perfect call."

When it was revealed that after losing Georgia in the 2020 presidential election Trump telephoned Georgia's Secretary of State and exhorted him to commit election fraud on his behalf, Trump insisted that this, too, was "a perfect call."

So, after Trump is arraigned on Tuesday on approximately 30 criminal charges arising from his attempts to launder $130,000 in hush money payments to Stormy Daniels, expect him to tell the media throng outside the New York Supreme Court that he is being unfairly persecuted for making the perfect porn star hush money payment. Also, that the grand jury indictment is yet another "witch hunt" in a long series of them, past and future.

The former president finds himself in a whole lot of legal trouble, and nobody's cousin Vinny is going to rescue him from it very readily. The New York indictment is very likely only the first of several that will drop on him over the weeks and months to come. Next up, in all probability, is an indictment by a Georgia grand jury for election fraud, and perhaps racketeering. Trump is being pursued as well by a formidable special counsel, Jack Smith, who has won court orders compelling former Vice President Mike Pence, former Trump chief of staff Mark Meadows and other top aides, and Trump lawyer Evan Corcoran to testify about what The Donald said to them.

Trump will be lucky to escape indictment for obstructing justice in connection with his willful and seemingly felonious retention of classified documents at Mar-a-Lago. And Smith appears to be steaming toward the conclusion of his investigation into whether Trump conspired to obstruct the counting of electoral votes on Jan. 6, 2021. If all of this comes to pass, Trump is going to reminisce nostalgically about the days when all he was grappling with was a mere indictment by a Manhattan grand jury about hush money to a porn star.

Indeed, Manhattan District Attorney Alvin Bragg is going to have his hands full convicting Trump on the most serious charges approved by the grand jury, even in New York, where those who have known Trump the longest loathe him the most. It's far from clear that the courts will permit a felony prosecution where the falsification of business records (a violation of state law) is said to have been for the purpose of violating the federal campaign finance laws. And if they do, Trump's lawyers only need to persuade one juror out of 12 that there is "reasonable doubt" about Trump's motivation for concealing his payments to a woman who claimed to have had an affair with him. They'll argue, moreover, that the prosecution's case is dependent upon the credibility of convicted felon and longtime liar Michael Cohen, as inviting a punching bag for a cross-examiner as has ever taken the witness stand.

Prosecutors will correct this, pointing out over and over (and over) that their case doesn't depend on Cohen's credibility at all, since they have documents, audiotapes and corroboration from other witnesses showing that in this particular case Cohen is telling the truth. But all it will take is just one juror out of 12 to believe that this case against Trump really does depend on Cohen ("If you don't trust Michael Cohen a whit, you must acquit") and Trump wins, at least on the felony charges against him.

Still, Bragg's office has doubtless taken all this into consideration. As for Trump, whose lifetime of evading the law is colliding with a future full of criminal indictments, the party appears to be over.

Smell Test Alert: The Embarrassing Case of Clarence Thomas Gets More Embarrassing

April 11, 2023

When President George H.W. Bush chose Clarence Thomas to replace Thurgood Marshall on the U.S. Supreme Court in 1991, he called Thomas "the best man for the job on the merits." This claim was preposterous, and over the course of the 32 years since Thomas was nominated his appointment has been a national embarrassment.

His confirmation was marred by a sweeping under the rug of compelling evidence that while he was head of the Equal Employment Opportunity Commission, Thomas had engaged in repeated acts of crude sexual harassment. On the nation's highest court for almost one-third of a century, his lack of anything resembling intellectual engagement has been the only notable thing about him. Even to call Thomas an ideologue would seem to elevate him, because the term presupposes that his votes are the thoughtful product of ideology rather than the rapid determination of which political "team" the parties to any case before the Court seem to be on.

However, it's one thing for a Supreme Court justice to be intellectually languid and reflexively, implacably partisan. It's another to emit the strong appearance of a conflict of interest and then to affirmatively worsen it.

Thomas' wife Ginni, a longtime and, one may fairly say, rabidly right-wing lobbyist both for a living and as an avocation, was as unhinged a proponent of former President Donald Trump's "the election was a hoax" hoax as anyone not under federal indictment. The Jan. 6 Committee unearthed some 21 texts from her to Trump chief of staff Mark Meadows exhorting Team Trump to overturn Joe Biden's election to keep Trump in power. "Help The Great President stand firm, Mark!!!" she implored Meadows after everyone playing with a full deck had acknowledged that Biden had won. "You are the leader, with him, who is standing for America's constitutional governance at the precipice," she wrote in another text. "The majority knows Biden and the left is (sic) attempting the greatest Heist of our History."

Referring to disgraced and disciplined crackpot Trump lawyer Sidney Powell, Thomas wrote: "Sounds like Sidney and her team are getting inundated with evidence of fraud. Make a plan. Release the Kraken and save us from the left taking America down." She also emailed Arizona state legislators urging them to impanel a phony pro-Trump slate of electors after Biden carried the state.

Justice Thomas was legally required to recuse himself from any proceeding in which his impartiality might reasonably be questioned, or if he knew his wife had "an interest (in the proceeding) that could be substantially affected by (its) actions." But in February 2021, when the Supreme Court voted to refuse to hear Trump's challenge to the 2020 presidential election, Thomas not only refused to recuse himself from voting. He dissented, criticizing his colleagues' decision as "befuddling."

Now it emerges that Thomas has accepted (along with his wife) hundreds of thousands of dollars' worth of lavish trips on private planes and yachts from conservative megadonor Harlan Crow, and failed to disclose any of this, year after lucky year, for over 20 years, in violation of Supreme Court rules. Crow has been a board member of the American Enterprise Institute since 1996, during which time the Institute has frequently filed friend-of-the-court briefs with the Court on which Crow's friend Clarence Thomas sits. Just to make things more optically appealing, Crow turns out to be an avid collector of Nazi memorabilia, including a signed copy of Adolf Hitler's manifesto, "Mein Kampf." For his part, Thomas assures us that he consulted with unnamed associates who in turn assured him that violating the express terms of Supreme Court ethics rules was OK.

It seems pointless to have Supreme Court Chief Justice John Roberts investigate a member of his own Court. But the rules seem to have been flouted in a way which further damages the Court's credibility. One hates to add another investigation to Attorney General Merrick Garland's plate. But looking the other way once again when it comes to Clarence Thomas doesn't seem like an option.

Unjaded: Celebrating the Irish, Joe Biden Celebrates America

April 18, 2023

The late Irish poet Eavan Boland paid famous homage to the daughters and sons of Ireland who, beginning in the early part of the 19th century, endured the trauma of uprooting themselves from their homeland and traveling to the strange, forbidding land that was America. "What they survived we could not even live," she wrote in her poem "The Emigrant Irish." "Now it is time to imagine how they stood there, what they stood with. Their hardships parceled in them. Patience. Fortitude. Long-suffering in the bruise-colored dusk of the New World."

"And all the old songs. And nothing to lose."

The bond between America and Ireland is a powerful one. It has been forged in part by the vibrant role Irish Americans have played in the building of this country, and also by the profound connection the 32 million Americans of Irish descent feel in their hearts for the land of their forebears, a connection that has not withered even approaching two centuries since the Irish started arriving in America in large numbers.

Anyone who visits Ireland and fails to feel the magic of the Irish is made of stone, and President Joe Biden's trip there last week placed Ireland's magic on display. "Joe Biden's big day out in Dublin was a joy," wrote Miriam Lord, longtime columnist for The Irish Times. And the joyousness appeared to go in both directions. The Irish were thrilled to see one of their own. Twenty-seven thousand of them showed up to greet Biden outside St. Muredach's Cathedral in Ballina, a town of 10,000 inhabitants. After all, Biden's great-great-great-grandfather set sail from Ireland to America in 1851. And that Ireland is dear to the president's heart is not a secret.

Biden himself does not present as a joyous person, the successful politician's broad grin to the contrary. It's not that he's morose, or a pessimist. But he has suffered a whole lot of loss. And he seems to feel that loss and the loss experienced by others much too keenly to ever look as though the shadows are very far off.

In Ireland, however, the president seemed rejuvenated, as though he were at home. Even the trip's painful aspects seem cathartic. His visit to the Knock Shrine, the famous Roman Catholic pilgrimage site in County Mayo, was buoyed by an unplanned, emotional reunion with the local priest, who while assigned to the Walter Reed Hospital in Washington, D.C., administered last rites to Biden's son Beau before he died of brain cancer in 2015. From there he went to a hospice he had dedicated when he was last in the country, where a plaque has been laid in memory of his late son.

Biden's joy may have been in his homecoming and the obvious warmth the Irish have for him. But he took repeated opportunities to emphasize that America is itself the product of the industriousness and the perseverance, the spirit and the drive, of immigrants — of those who have left their homes all over the world to come here. They have given their all — including their children and grandchildren — to the continuing American experiment. From Africa, from Asia, from South and Central America, from Europe, immigrants refresh and refuel our country on an hourly basis. America's not-so-secret weapon is the people who come here from other places.

"Just as I imagine their life in County Mayo," the president said of the Irishmen who braved the frightening journey to America, "I can only imagine how hard it must have been to leave it all behind, to leave the only place they ever called home. They became the untiring backbone of America's progress as a nation, even as they endured the discrimination and they were denied opportunity."

This immigrant story of America is not one to be sugarcoated. But it does remain one to be honored. It is yet something else that redounds to Joe Biden's credit that he understands this, and understands it to his core.

Unhidden Gem: Mouna Maroun Leads Israeli Arabs Down the Path She's Blazing

April 25, 2023

What separates humans from other species, the late William F. Buckley Jr. once told an interviewer, is "the ability to make distinctions." Not every human has that ability, of course, and certain issues are so susceptible to distortion that even those with the ability to make distinctions don't necessarily make them.

Israel is one issue on which a combination of ingrained hatreds and an addiction to cant frequently blurs facts and encourages fictions. Sixteen straight weeks of massive pro-democracy demonstrations on Israeli streets have spotlighted the noxious coalition government that presently prevails, one dominated by some truly repugnant figures and led by a prime minister willing to sacrifice Israeli democracy to save his own skin.

As usual, however, when it comes to Israel, distinctions are often disfavored. The scope and size of the protests are evidence of Israel's essential character, evidence that is unwelcome for those determined to despise it. The same holds for its multicultural, pluralistic society, which does not produce a citizenry in lockstep. It is a society, moreover, that is densely packed with social justice warriors.

A case in point is Mouna Maroun, professor of neurobiology, vice president and dean of research and development at the University of Haifa. A dynamic woman with a ready smile, Maroun grew up in an Arab village just outside of Haifa, a city known for its heterogeneity. Her father's family came from Lebanon, and Maroun recalls with a laugh that while her childhood friends dreamed of becoming pop stars, she dreamed of becoming Israel's Ambassador to Lebanon.

Neither of Maroun's parents even finished elementary school. "But I was lucky," she says, "because they both believed that their four daughters should get higher education, and they did everything they could to make it happen." Her father was able to provide the barest basics by running a small grocery store, and once a month bartered groceries so that Maroun, an avid reader from the outset, could get French lessons. She passed the University of Haifa campus every morning going from her village to her school, "dreaming that one day I would be one of its students."

Maroun had no money and knew no Hebrew. "But the University provided us, the Arab students, with academic support that enabled me and many other Arabs to keep from dropping out," she recalled, "and to be able to continue our studies and succeed."

Succeed she has. Fascinated by the brain, she proceeded to earn a bachelor's degree, master's degree and Ph.D. from the University of Haifa, all in psychology. Her appointment as head of the Neurosciences Department made her the first Arab woman to head a university science department in Israel.

But her influence extends much further. Her emphasis on promoting Israeli Arabs in academia and in the sciences in particular is one of the reasons that the University has become an exemplar of diversity. Nearly half of its students are Israeli Arabs. Maroun's awareness of how well-positioned she is to showcase opportunities and to help provide them is keen. "I am a minority within minorities," she says. "I am an Israeli, an Arab, a Christian, a Catholic Maronite and a woman."

She helps lead a number of national commissions formed to lift Israeli Arabs further up the academic ladder. She is a ubiquitous presence in Israeli Arab communities, where she mentors, lectures, exhorts, pushes and prods. Once named among Israel's 50 most influential women, she organizes partnerships with the Ministry of Education, the European Union and philanthropic foundations devoted to elevating those on the periphery.

"I was blessed to be born in Israel," she says. "Israel is facing difficult times these days. But the University of Haifa is an island of sanity. It represents a real shared society, with a mosaic of different ethnic groups, which represents Israeli society."

Maroun's life is notable in more than one respect. Only one of them is as a reminder that things are rarely as simple as they are portrayed.

A Question of Rape: Donald Trump Goes on Trial

May 2, 2023

As former President Donald Trump solidifies his support among Republicans for their party's 2024 presidential nomination, a civil trial underway in federal court in Manhattan will adjudicate whether next year's presumptive Republican presidential nominee is a rapist.

Writer E. Jean Carroll has sued Trump for battery and defamation. The battery claim is based on Carroll's charge that Trump sexually assaulted her; the alleged defamation arises from Trump's accusations that she is lying. There is really only one question that the jury, which began hearing testimony last week, will have to answer: did Trump rape Carroll or didn't he?

Carroll provided a highly detailed account of what she maintains Trump did: where she was, what transpired in the minutes preceding the alleged assault and precisely what she contends occurred in a dressing room in the lingerie department of a fashionable New York department store.

Trump's lawyers have a few arrows in their quiver. An event as shocking and traumatic as the one Carroll describes, they argue, would be sufficiently memorable that the victim would remember when it occurred — if not the date, then at least the week, if not the week, then at least the month, and if not the month, then at least the year. Carroll cannot do this, and there will be jurors for whom that's a problem.

Then there's the evidence of the potential motivations for Carroll's allegation, which Trump's team hopes will make jurors doubt her. Carroll has made few bones about despising Trump and opposing his presidential candidacies. But it isn't hard to imagine why the victim of a violent sexual assault might have a misgiving or two about electing the man who committed the assault the leader of the free world.

Then there's Carroll's admission that she hoped that her charge that Trump raped her would help her sell her book. Her comeback that it unfortunately did not turn out that way didn't exactly dilute the point.

Trump argues that it's odd that Carroll would stay silent as long as she did about the assault she asserts took place. His problem is that it isn't. There are obvious reasons for sexual assault victims to stay silent for decades, if not a lifetime, and it happens all the time. And where the man on the other end is tremendously wealthy, with battalions of lawyers at his disposal regularly deployed by him to file frivolous lawsuits for sport, why Carroll would have chosen to keep private what occurred is not difficult to understand.

If Carroll's lawyers have some minor headaches, Trump's have migraines, beginning with their client's refusal even to show up to tell the jury that he denies Carroll's testimony. This isn't a case of "She said, he said," so much as one of "She said, and he headed for the hills." It is reasonable for jurors to infer that if Trump isn't willing to appear to deny Carroll's claim, there's a reason, and not one that reflects favorably on his case.

The cross-examination of Trump would have been a bloodbath, and the bloodletting would have gone on for quite a long while. For starters, jurors will be shown the infamous 2005 Access Hollywood tape, wherein a decade after Carroll claims Trump decided he could do whatever he wanted to do to her, Trump bragged that that is what he had always done, and he was damned proud of it. This is Trump himself on Trump assaulting women as he pleased: "I don't even wait. And when you're a star, they let you do it. You can do anything... Grab 'em by the (private parts). You can do anything."

There's a Latin term that every first-year law student learns about evidence that is self-explanatory: "Res ipsa loquitur," or "The thing speaks for itself." Coupled with Carroll's testimony and Trump's absence from the courtroom in which he might have been expected to defend himself if Carroll's charge was untrue, Trump's own braggadocio seems likely to speak for itself. And if it does, the former president is headed for an unpleasant verdict.

Tuesdays With Charlie: A Golden Retriever Goes to College

May 9, 2023

Charlie is a 7-year-old Golden Retriever who knows there's something different about Tuesdays. For starters, her dog walker comes earlier than usual, and deposits Charlie back home by early afternoon. A bag appears out of the closet, and Charlie's favorite stuffed animal is placed in it, along with a sandwich bag full of dog treats and an empty water bowl. Charlie knows something's up and knows what that something is. When her owner calls her name, Charlie is on her feet, barreling down the stairs, out the front door and toward the car, which she remembers will transport her an hour south on the highway to a parking lot two blocks from the political science department of a New England university.

She knows the drill. There is a university security guy who must have had a Golden as a boy, because he waits for her every week, and before the hatchback is open, he is out of his car and heading over, calling, "Charlie! I missed you!" The fellow just turned 50, but you'd never know it by the way he gets on the ground in the parking lot, his face glued to the dog's until order can be restored.

Down the sidewalk Charlie goes with her tail wagging over the familiarity of it all, students streaming over to ask if they can pet her. Charlie makes it clear not only that they can but that they'd better, mushing her head between the legs of everyone who stops, besotted with everyone as everyone is besotted with her. It takes some time to get down the street. When she finally does, Charlie recognizes the receptionists in the lobby of the political science department and, weeping with emotion, takes her leash in her mouth as the sidewalk scene is repeated.

Here is what the faculty and the students in the department know by now: some dogs are wary, some prone to agitation, some diffident. Charlie is a lover, and she loves every human being who so much as makes a move in her direction, unreservedly and, frankly, indiscriminately. And if you don't make a move in her direction, she will assume it was an oversight.

Charlie proceeds to "office-surf," trotting down the hall to visit every faculty member who happened to leave their office door open. It's clear from the tail movement that she expects her arrival to be the best thing that could have happened to everyone concerned.

On to class. If the idea is that Charlie's presence can help create a warm setting, Charlie embraces the mission with gusto. She makes the rounds of the students before picking a (seemingly) random spot on the floor, usually on someone's feet, and eventually falls into a deep sleep, the stuffed animal stuffed between her paws and in her mouth. Every once in a while, someone will get up and come over to stroke her. This seems to please Charlie, but it is equally possible that by this point she's oblivious. Two and a half hours later, dog and friends say their goodbyes until the following week.

Last week U.S. Surgeon General Vivek Murthy issued an "Advisory on Our Epidemic of Loneliness and Isolation," reporting that even before COVID-19, 50% of American adults experienced significant feelings of loneliness. There is, he said, "an underappreciated public health crisis that has harmed individual and societal health." According to Murthy, more than one in five adults are living with mental illness — and more than one-third of all young adults do.

As if there were much doubt about it, study after study has shown that interacting with animals decreases stress, lowers blood pressure, reduces loneliness, increases feelings of social support and just simply improves moods. From the National Institutes of Health to the American Psychiatric Association, the data is clear.

Charlie is not what you'd call "data-driven." But she knows who she likes, and that's everyone. They don't call them man's best friend for nothing.

Discredited Suisse: Congress Spotlights a Bank's Attempt to Obscure Its Nazi Links

May 16, 2023

Until lately, America's longstanding tradition of bipartisan congressional investigations had been robust, recognized even by partisans as an essential feature of Congress performing the job Americans need it to do. The tradition has taken hits recently, falling victim to extreme, vitriol-infused polarization and the erosion of what had been assumed to be sturdy civic norms.

But it got a boost last month, when a subpoena issued jointly by Senate Budget Committee Chairman Sheldon Whitehouse, D-R.I., and Ranking Member Chuck Grassley, R-Iowa, forced into daylight a transparent attempt by banking giant Credit Suisse to abruptly terminate an investigation that was in the process of reinforcing its reputation for scandal. The investigation had already uncovered new evidence that Credit Suisse had actively, ardently serviced high-ranking Nazi leaders while Hitler was in power, facilitated the Nazis' retention of assets plundered from their victims and helped Nazis escape prosecution after the war.

Thanks to Whitehouse and Grassley, the Budget Committee issued its first subpoena since 1991, compelling the handover of a report prepared by two prominent investigators hired by Credit Suisse in 2021 in order to placate its critics. Those investigators were suddenly axed last year, when they unearthed additional evidence that the bank, long known to have been a FON (Friend of the Nazis), was even worse than previously understood. The bank not only sacked the two investigators, former federal prosecutor Neil Barofsky and former U.S. Special Envoy for Monitoring and Combating Anti-Semitism Ira Forman, but also blocked the report they had prepared before being fired from being published.

Because of the congressional subpoena, that document, entitled "Report of the Independent Ombudsman and Independent Advisor to Credit Suisse," was turned over and has now been made public. It is yet another indictment of Credit Suisse, not just because of the new disclosures of its hand-in-glove relationship with Hitler's murderers during the war and long afterward but for the patently obstructionist moves it made to prevent those disclosures from seeing daylight.

Credit Suisse had professed to come clean about its role facilitating Nazi war crimes after a number of investigations in the 1990s shined light on its historic guilt. As the report now made public despite the bank's best efforts to suppress it states, those investigations, while limited, incomplete and impeded in various ways, "uncovered significant bodies of information about how some Swiss banks, especially that era's large banks, including Credit Suisse, assisted in exploiting the victims of the Holocaust; retained assets belonging to Holocaust victims and their heirs, and supported the economic foundations of the Nazi regime."

Several years ago, however, the Simon Wiesenthal Center, a human rights organization named after the famed Holocaust survivor who devoted decades to documenting the Holocaust's atrocities and the actions of those who committed or enabled them, presented Credit Suisse with information that the bank had not in fact engaged in a complete reckoning — either to itself or to the world. The Center informed the bank that there was significant additional evidence that it had financially supported Nazis in their escape to Argentina after 1945, and safeguarded the funds of such individuals, and benefited from the accounts of other Nazis whose identities it had not previously disclosed. There was evidence of what the report's authors euphemistically call "lack of candor" on the bank's part.

This "lack of candor" paled next to the bank's termination of the investigation it had agreed to undertake after the Wiesenthal Center produced its evidence. Its new management claimed that there was no need for the investigators to complete their work. There is a distinct, and distinctly unpleasant, odor to Credit Suisse's reversal. To their credit, Senators Whitehouse and Grassley have not only forced the disclosure of the report the bank sought to hide but extracted promises to follow up on the investigators' work.

It remains to be seen whether Credit Suisse will act honorably. If it does, it will be a refreshing departure from its historical record.

Sauce for the Goose: Democrats Scramble to Whitewash a Scandal of Their Own

May 23, 2023

From national security adviser Michael Flynn to Rep. George Santos, former President Donald Trump has promoted, deployed and spawned an epic parade of dishonest lawbreakers in his own mold. Democrats have had a justifiable field day pointing out what can euphemistically be called the "unsuitability" of Trump's acolytes for public office.

Now it is the Republicans' turn for a field day. Hours before the release of reports by the Justice Department's inspector general and the U.S. Office of Special Counsel detailing her arrogant spree of rule-breaking and law-breaking, United States Attorney for the District of Massachusetts Rachael Rollins announced that she would be resigning. The reports documented a series of violations of the Hatch Act — the federal criminal statute prohibiting one in Rollins' position from using her office for partisan political purposes — as well as ethical rules and the law making it a federal crime to knowingly make false statements under oath. Rollins had committed them all, and with a sense of privilege that made her a poster child for what a federal prosecutor should not be.

It's the Republicans' turn to spotlight a disgrace, and the Democrats' turn, evidently, to attempt to whitewash it. Republican Sen. Tom Cotton of Oklahoma had loudly warned about President Joe Biden's nomination of Rollins to the powerful U.S. Attorney post, pointing out that she demonstrably lacked the temperament and judgment to wield federal prosecutorial power. She had credibly been alleged to have used her position as a local district attorney to bully a motorist and had threatened a reporter who'd had the temerity to ask her about it. "Get out of here!" she reportedly snarled. "You know what I'll do? I'll call the police on you and make an allegation. Rantings of a white woman. I swear to God, I'm dead serious. I will find your name. I will have you arrested."

In his letter to Biden transmitting his report on Rollins' leaking of confidential Justice Department information in order to help her friend defeat a public official Rollins wanted defeated as well as her insistence on attending a Democratic National Committee fundraiser she had been advised not to attend, the Special Counsel called Rollins' conduct "among the most egregious transgressions of the (Hatch) Act" his office had ever seen. He described Rollins' practice of secretly leaking Justice Department information to service her own personal agenda "an extraordinary abuse of her authority, (one which) threatens to erode public confidence in the integrity of federal law enforcement actions."

But that wasn't all. When the inspector general interviewed Rollins about what she had done, she lied. Under oath. Repeatedly.

Rollins has splattered egg all over the faces of prominent Democrats who, like everyone else in the progressive establishment, swooned over her, too intimidated by her backers to acknowledge she was unfit to be U.S. Attorney. "She has the values, the vision and the courage," gushed Sen. Elizabeth Warren at the self-congratulatory, "pay-attention-to-me" extravaganza Rollins threw for herself for her swearing-in. Sen. Ed Markey, Rollins' other sponsor, blamed the debacle on the president. "We sent the names over to the Biden White House for them to do the vetting," backpedaled Markey last week, "so we were reliant upon the White House vetting."

Nor has the Justice Department covered itself in glory. The inspector general referred his findings that Rollins had deliberately lied under oath to the Department in order for it to consider criminal charges. It did so on Dec. 16, 2022. By Jan. 7, 2023, the Department had already declined prosecution. That's all of 18 days of careful consideration, including Christmas, New Year's and weekends.

Congressional Republicans will use L'affaire Rollins to blacken those who demand that Trump and his felonious friends be prosecuted, invoking the kid-gloves treatment of Rollins. They will say that "what's sauce for the goose is sauce for the gander." This will come precisely when the Justice Department will need all of the credibility and public confidence it can muster to prosecute Trump, the most dangerous domestic threat to our democracy the country has ever faced.

Sociopath Versus Sycophants: The GOP's Field of Contenders Takes Shape

May 30, 2023

"If you can't admire Joe Biden as a person," Republican Sen. Lindsey Graham once said, "you've got a problem. You need to do some self-evaluation, because what's not to like? He's as good a man as God ever created."

That was back when Graham had credibility. Those were also the days when he described Donald Trump, succinctly and precisely, as a "nut job," "a loser as a person" and "ill-suited to be president."

Graham was of course right about both Biden and Trump. But that was before his sad servility to Trump and his desperate desire to ingratiate himself to the man he knew to be a sociopath led him to assist Trump in trying to overthrow the 2020 Georgia election — assistance which may lead him to be indicted this August.

Graham is far from the only national Republican to continue to cower before Trump, too intimidated by Mar-a-Lago's Classified Document Collector-in-Chief to cross him and risk being insulted. As the 2024 election season gets underway, and the Republican case against Biden is that he has an arthritic spine, an occasional stutter and a son with a former addiction problem, the GOP nomination appears to be the indicted insurrectionist's to lose. His challengers have nether the courage nor the inclination to speak plainly about what a threat Trump is to our democracy and, indeed, to the country's ability to survive as we have known it.

After due consideration of the nature of Republican primary voters, Florida Gov. Ron DeSantis settled on this for his campaign message: "You want crazy? I'll give you crazy." What he is selling is snarling attacks on marginalized American communities, like communities of color and the LGBTQ community, which want to explore and celebrate their identities and want others in this diverse nation we're privileged to live in to have the opportunity to do the same.

Then there are the snarling attacks on books, on learning, on science and on tolerance itself. It is a particular quality of vileness that many Americans thought we had put in our rear-view mirror. But that isn't so, and it is the essence of DeSantis' campaign.

DeSantis' calculation that what Republicans want in their standard-bearer is a crude, swaggering bully of the sort we all remember from schoolyards may be loathsome, but it isn't wrong. What is questionable is his thesis that Republicans would prefer a crude, swaggering bully who isn't a felon. The truth is that the Republican base is so off base that Trump's very criminality is seen as a virtue by a sizable segment of Republicans.

And the Republican contenders for president know it. No candidate with a likelihood of obtaining the GOP nomination will be caught saying what would have been a sophomoric no-brainer in times past: It really would be good if the president of the United States were not a criminal, all other things being equal.

Trump's less serious challengers are little better. Former Vice President Mike Pence, who showed real principle on Jan. 6, seems to have decided that once was enough. Former South Carolina Gov. Nikki Haley, who said that Trump was "everything a governor doesn't want in a president" before happily accepting a position in his cabinet, has ricocheted between distancing herself from Trump and prostrating herself before him. "I don't think he's going to be in the picture. I don't think he can. He's fallen so far," Haley said about The Boss after Jan. 6. But nine months later, she was kissing his ring. "He'd has the ability to get strong people elected," she gushed. "He has the ability to move the ball, and I hope he continues to do that." Sen. Tim Scott, a recent entrant into the race, has blamed Democrats for inciting the violence on Jan. 6. "The one person I don't blame is President Trump," he said.

It's quite a crew the GOP has assembled. It is, however, one that is serving up what its voters want to see served up.

The Center Stirs: With a Crucial Debt Deal, Score One for the Adults

June 6, 2023

In his new book "The Watchdog: How the Truman Committee Battled Corruption and Helped Win World War Two," journalist Steve Drummond tells the little-known story of how a little-known Senate committee headed by a little-known senator from Missouri led a bipartisan battle to strengthen America by exposing self-interest and waste in our military establishment. Regarded by students of Congress as The Gold Standard of congressional investigations for its effectiveness, the investigation was conceived by Harry Truman and spearheaded by him. Formed in 1941, when the Nazis were rapidly overrunning Europe and America was utterly unprepared for what lay ahead, the Truman Committee proved to be a model of bipartisanship, as much a relic of the past as a telephone booth.

It was a time when Republicans and Democrats viewed themselves as competitors, with different ideas about getting to the same place, rather than as bitter enemies. Despite the GOP's venom toward President Franklin Roosevelt, just elected to his third term, and plenty of division about whether American should enter the European war, Americans still fundamentally rowed in the same direction.

It was, in short, a different time. Truman, a Democrat, proposed to run an investigation that would expose and publicize the failures of a Democratic administration that was trying to rally the country for eventual entry into the war. The Roosevelt administration approved the investigation and cooperated with it. The Democrat-run committee held hearings and issued reports that pointed out what a Democratic administration was doing wrong. The Republicans on the committee were treated as equals and, for their part, refrained from partisanship.

The result was an improved national defense program, one which, after delays when the attack on Pearl Harbor abruptly accelerated our need to defend ourselves, succeeded in providing the materiel needed to liberate Europe and defeat the Japanese.

America got a taste of old-fashioned bipartisanship last week, and a much-needed one at that. With our government on the brink of default on its debt and financial calamity imminent, Democrats and Republicans, led by

President Joe Biden and Speaker Kevin McCarthy, respectively, functioned as the grown-ups in the proverbial room, striking a compromise that extended the debt limit for two years and protected Social Security, Medicare, Medicaid and other vital programs while also cutting some spending. Biden and McCarthy stared down their parties' fringes to get the deal done, with 77% of House Democrats and 70% of House Republicans approving a compromise that passed by a 314 to 117 vote.

Neither Biden nor McCarthy had an easy task. Progressive Democrats were prepared to play a dangerous game of "chicken," risking a disastrous default rather than agreeing to an even modest rollback in spending. MAGA Republicans, aka the Chaos Caucus, seemed positively eager to implode the economy and the markets so that Biden could be blamed. To his credit, McCarthy opted to be the adult in the Republican conference, a particularly unenviable assignment given its composition and the frayed thread by which McCarthy's speakership hangs.

The president may have driven home the deal that saved America from economic collapse, and fresh jobs and growth reports may have sent the financial markets soaring, but the week wasn't a total loss for his detractors. The man tripped on a sandbag protruding on a stage at the Air Force Academy, giving Biden-haters the opportunity to crow because, well, the man tripped. Thus did Sandbag-Gate become an issue in the 2024 presidential campaign.

Still, it was a good week for the big girls and boys, and one that could not help but make one remember what once was and what might be — even if barely conceivably — once again. "Our teams were able to get along, get things done, were straightforward with one another, completely honest with one another," said Biden in an Oval Office address the night the compromise passed Congress. "Both sides operated in good faith. Both sides kept their word." Somewhere, maybe, Harry Truman is nodding approvingly.

Toast: A Crooked President Betrays His Country

June 13, 2023

If there's one thing worse than a crooked tyrant, it's an unpatriotic crooked tyrant, and with the unsealing of the detailed 44-page indictment handed down against him by a federal grand jury in Miami last week, one thing is clear: former President Donald Trump checks all the boxes. Trump, who began his adult life dodging the draft in order to avoid serving his country in Vietnam, has passed the rest of it dodging criminal indictments for tax fraud, mail fraud, wire fraud and fraud-fraud. He has finally hit a wall in the federal indictment-dodging department. The grand jury charged him with willfully retaining classified documents in violation of the Espionage Act, withholding classified documents, corruptly concealing classified documents and conspiring to obstruct justice, the latter of which Trump commits as casually as he consumes cheeseburgers.

It wouldn't be an indictment of Donald Trump if it did not contain at least one count of making false statements. One surmises that this is the only count that truly shocked Trump, who was assessed by The Washington Post to have made over 35,000 false statements during his presidency alone, and that only counts public ones. "Since when can you get indicted for making false statements?" Trump is rumored to have asked his attorneys upon hearing news of the indictment. "Is that really a thing?"

The tipoff that the rumor is untrue is that Trump apparently doesn't actually have any attorneys, at least in The Case of The Stolen National Security Secrets, because more or less contemporaneously with the unsealing of the indictment, the two principal lawyers representing him quit. True to sociopathic form, Trump insisted that he had fired them. But separate and apart from the fact that nothing Trump says is truthful, no rational attorney appreciates being associated with a debacle. Representing Trump in this case looks like the legal equivalent of the Hindenburg disaster.

Both the evidence and the law disfavor Trump — lopsidedly. Of the hundreds of classified documents that Trump deliberately took with him to Mar-a-Lago and deliberately withheld knowing that he could not lawfully do so, the Justice Department chose to confine itself to charging Trump on 31, marked either "secret" or "top secret." These included documents regarding

White House intelligence briefings, documents concerning our military capabilities and those of foreign countries, documents concerning our military planning, documents concerning our vulnerability to military attack — and documents concerning our nuclear weapons. "The unauthorized disclosure of these classified documents," the grand jury charged, "could put at risk the national security of the United States, foreign relations, the safety of the United States military and human sources and the continued viability of sensitive intelligence collection methods."

Trump had these sensitive documents strewn all over Mar-a-Lago — in his office, in his bathroom and in a ballroom, and actively schemed to keep representatives of the United States government from finding them. He suggested to certain of his lawyers that they lie to the FBI and the grand jury about his retention of the documents and suggested to another that he hide or destroy documents. In familiar mob boss fashion — familiar to mob bosses and familiar to Trump — he caused another of his attorneys to falsely certify that all classified documents had been turned over, knowing, of course, that that was a lie. We will never know the scope of the harm that Trump has caused the women and men of our armed forces, or to the country as a whole. All we really know, from experience, is that Donald Trump couldn't care less.

MAGA World responded with the usual risible nonsense, chalking the indictment up to retaliation by "the Biden Crime Family," and so forth. William Barr, Trump's former attorney general, was somewhat more tethered. "These documents are among the most sensitive secrets the country has," Barr told Fox News. "If even half of (the indictment) is true, then he's toast." Donald Trump may indeed be headed to prison at long last. But it is the country he falsely claims to give a damn about that's gotten burnt.

Jeff Robbins

Fast Asleep: 'Cabaret' Sounds a Wake-up Call
June 20, 2023

The Berkshire mountains of western Massachusetts are as uplifting a place as there is to find oneself in June, and hardly someplace that summons to mind the bitter battles for America's soul presently being waged. There's a kind of moral hand-to-hand combat going on within the country. Which side ultimately prevails — rededication to tolerance and truth-telling, on one hand, or venom and conspiracy theories, on the other — remains very much a jump ball.

The Berkshires are known for the explosion of performing arts during the summer months. Among the artistic institutions that attract the highest quality talent is Pittsfield's Barrington Stage Company, which chose to begin the season by staging a revival of the musical non-comedy "Cabaret," a deeply sobering portrayal of Germany's descent into Nazism during the 1930s. It centers on two characters, Clifford Bradshaw, an American who has come to Berlin to write, and Sally Bowles, an English entertainer who headlines a raunchy nightclub. It is principally through these two characters that the story of the metastasis of Jew hatred in Nazi Germany, which would lead to the extermination of six million European Jews, is told.

"Cabaret" seems to have been a purposeful choice given the "tsunami of anti-Semitism," as Anti-Defamation League head Jonathan Greenblatt has put it, convulsing America. This particular production opened contemporaneously with the criminal conviction of the neo-Nazi gunman who killed 11 worshipers in Pittsburgh's Tree of Life synagogue in 2018. That killing is just one stitch in a tapestry of anti-Jewish terror of the sort that has never been seen in America before, emanating both from White supremacists on the far Right and some of those who look into their mirrors and manage to see "progressives" on the Left.

The ADL's tracking of antisemitic incidents in the United States tells part of the story. The approximately 3,700 incidents of harassment, vandalism and assault targeting Jewish people formally reported last year represent a 36% increase over 2021. The number has steadily increased year after year. But hatred of Jews is hardly the only kind of hatred that has prospered here in recent years. According to statistics recently released by the FBI, reported incidents of hate crimes more generally increased about 12% between 2020 and 2021. Black Americans, Asian Americans, Hispanic and Latino Americans, Muslim Americans and LGBTQ+ Americans join Jewish Americans as the most popular victims.

America has been a favorable spawning ground for hatred these last years, with the inhibitions against taunting and bullying not merely lifted but shredded. Roughly half the country embraces a cult that relishes in-your-face cruelty toward the marginalized. Threats against public officials struggling to protect the public health against COVID-19 and calls for the banning of books are somehow touted as pro-American. Comparisons between 1930s Germany and present-day America, which once seemed melodramatic, no longer do.

"Sally, don't you understand that if you're not against all of this, you're for it?" Bradshaw asks Bowles toward the end of the play, but the question falls as flat as it has generally fallen when posed today. The chilling Nazi anthem "Tomorrow Belongs to Me" evokes the crazed fervor of this country's domestic extremist groups operating under rocks — but operating nonetheless — throughout our land.

The warning attributed to philosopher George Santayana that "Those who do not learn from history are doomed to repeat it" resonates as much now as ever. One leaves "Cabaret" feeling that it needs to be seen less by those middle aged and older than by younger Americans, who are so spectacularly ignorant about the extermination of 6 million Jews and about the domination of Europe by fascists a mere 80 years ago.

The Barrington Stage Company's production of "Cabaret" is simultaneously sparkling and deeply dark. "I was dancing with Sally Bowles, and we were fast asleep," laments Bradshaw as he prepares to depart the horror he has seen consume Berlin. Four generations later, in a country we all thought was comfortably safe from being overrun by hatred, the question whether America will sleep on or awaken is an open one.

Clown Show: House Republicans Censure Adam Schiff, and It's Perfect

June 27, 2023

In his 2021 book "Midnight in Washington: How We Almost Lost Our Democracy and Still Could," Rep. Adam Schiff recounts Donald Trump's attempts to sell out American interests for his own personal benefit while president, supported at every turn by a Republican Party too corrupt and too terrified to stand up to an obvious crook.

"There is now a dangerous vein of autocratic thought running through one of America's great parties, and it poses an existential danger to our country," Schiff writes. "The experience of the last four years will require constant vigilance on our part so that it does not gain another foothold in the highest office in our land."

As chairman of the House Intelligence Committee, Schiff oversaw the inquiry into Trump's gambit to extort a contrived announcement of a phony investigation into political rival Joe Biden in exchange for the release of desperately needed assistance that Congress had authorized for Ukraine's self-defense against Russia. Trump's scheme was perfectly consistent with his subsequent felonious attempts to steal the 2020 election from the American people and then to steal classified documents from them, all detailed by the Jan. 6 select committee and by a federal grand jury in Miami.

At the time Trump called his extortionate telephone call to Ukrainian President Volodymyr Zelenskyy a "perfect call." And it indeed was "perfect," exactly in the way that Trump's pilfering nuclear secrets in violation of the Espionage Act was perfect, and his request that the Georgia Secretary of State fabricate fraudulent election results was perfect, and his sexual assault on E. Jean Carroll in a Manhattan department store dressing room was perfect.

What actually was perfect was the leadership Schiff showed in exposing Trump's tawdry plot to tarnish Biden by withholding military aid to an ally, but, as these things frequently go, Schiff has paid a price. He and his family are exposed to continual threats from the same sort of patriots who beat the daylights out of Capitol Police on Jan. 6. They require constant security. Last week, on orders from a former president not only headed for the slammer but considerably beyond untethered, House Republicans, who control the lower chamber by a narrow margin, voted to censure Schiff.

In its fashion, the censure vote was perfect: a vote by small people who have marched like lemmings over a moral cliff to censure a hero who called them out for their immorality and gutlessness. One of the various dishonest pretexts for the censure was Schiff's statements of the obvious: that of course there was evidence that the 2016 Trump campaign sought and received assistance from Vladimir Putin's Kremlin to defeat Hillary Clinton and elect Trump.

Such statements were every bit as controversial as saying that the earth is round. The June 2016 Trump Tower meeting requested by Russian agents to discuss delivering dirt on Clinton, attended by Trump's son, son-in-law and campaign chairman, is a fact. Campaign chairman Paul Manafort's delivery of Trump campaign strategy materials to a Kremlin operative is a fact. Kremlin-directed hackings of Democratic National Committee and Clinton campaign computers to extract and disseminate emails for the purpose of helping Trump is a fact. Adam Schiff has been right from the start, and wrong about nothing. In MAGA World, the world that grips the Republican Party in a vise, that is precisely the problem.

In response to the censure vote, Schiff extended an elegant middle finger. "To my Republican colleagues who introduced this resolution," he said, "I thank you. You honor me with your enmity. You flatter me with your falsehood."

The GOP's bankruptcy is perfectly illustrated by the fact that it voted to censure Schiff while refusing to act against fellow Republican Rep. George Santos, the fraud spree on two legs who sits among them and helps them preserve their narrow control in the House. Never mind the 13-count federal indictment against Santos. He's their guy. And in case you were wondering, yes, Santos voted to censure Schiff.

Which is just perfect.

In The Dock: A Discredited Court May Be a Harbinger of Worse to Come

July 4, 2023

One of the things that do not seem to have been made great again by former President Donald Trump is Americans' respect for the Supreme Court. Yanked hard to the hard Right by Trump's appointment of Justices Neil Gorsuch, Brett Kavanaugh and Amy Coney Barrett, the Court has auto-plunged into public disrepute, with regard for our highest court at an all-time low. Two recent polls taken by Marquette Law School and Quinnipiac University showed identical results: 59% of Americans disapprove of the court, adding to the disrespect for the rule of law that has reached crisis levels.

The arrogance displayed by certain of the justices in insisting that they are free to violate self-evident ethical norms has not exactly burnished the court's sagging reputation. Clarence Thomas' serial acceptance of lavish vacations and other financial assistance from wealthy Republican donor Harlan Crow has strained whatever existed of his credibility, and his repeated, deliberate failures to disclose any of this speak volumes. Thomas' claim that he relied on people he declined to identify for advice he declined to describe has made him a laughingstock.

Now it emerges that conservative firebrand Samuel Alito is of the same let-them-eat-cake mindset when it comes to judicial ethics. Alito confirmed reports that he had been treated to a spectacular Alaska vacation by conservative megadonor and hedge fund titan Paul Singer, and then not only did not disclose it, but proceeded to vote on cases in which Singer's businesses were litigants before him. This was quite the display of disregard for fundamental judicial ethics, but as far as Alito was concerned, the only wrongdoers were the investigative reporters who disclosed that which he refused to. Requested by the Senate to answer questions that surely interest the American people about what, precisely, the Court's Justices perceive to be their ethical obligations, Chief Justice John Roberts declined.

It isn't only contempt for obvious ethics that has placed the court's credibility in the tank. When it came to reversing the 50-year-old precedent recognizing women's right to determine whether to terminate their own pregnancies, the Right's braying about keeping government out of citizens' lives proved to be balderdash. Americans' overwhelming disapproval of the court's reversal of Roe v. Wade further eroded its legitimacy.

Last week the court again jettisoned judicial precedent, reversing its 1978 decision permitting the use of affirmative action to admit minority students for the purpose of promoting educational diversity. It had reaffirmed that decision just 20 years ago, authorizing the "narrowly tailored use of race in admissions decisions to further a compelling interest in obtaining the educational benefits that flow from a diverse student body."

In its decision now holding that the very affirmative action that it has held for 45 years was constitutional is now unconstitutional, the court was good enough to acknowledge that the two centuries of slavery followed by the century of state-mandated segregation to which Black Americans were subjected were "regrettable." But it found that the discriminatory legacy of those three centuries was now over, which was nice of it, but also dead wrong. The baked-in, unjust and adverse effects of 200 years of slavery and then a hundred years of legalized discrimination do not simply evaporate overnight. The justices who argued that affirmative action is warranted as a means of remedying centuries of restraints — physical, legal or institutional — were correct.

The Trump Court is a gift from the Hillary-haters and the Bernie Bros who decided in 2016 either that there wasn't sufficient difference between Clinton and Trump to warrant voting — or that a Trump presidency would be "cleansing" for the country.

Some cleansing. If those who whine about how President Joe Biden doesn't agree with them on everything don't cut it out, this country is really going to be taken to the cleaners, maybe for good.

Claptrap: Israel Has Some Nerve Challenging Murder, Incorporated in Jenin

July 11, 2023

Webster's Dictionary defines "sophomoric" as "overconfident of knowledge but poorly informed." This fairly describes Israel's bitter critics who, as always, denounced Israel's most recent attempt to stop Palestinian Islamic Jihad and Hamas from murdering more of its civilians, at least for a couple of days or so.

The two heavily armed groups, recognized by the international community as Iranian-funded terrorist enterprises that have vowed to violently eliminate Israel, have carried out nearly 300 separate attacks on Israelis in the last 12 months alone. These have killed over 50 Israelis and injured hundreds more just since last July Fourth. One of the principal launching pads for these attacks is Jenin, located on the West Bank, which has become one large manufacturing facility for missiles and bombs, and a staging ground for the rocketing, shooting, bombing, stabbing and car-ramming of Israeli civilians, all intended to kill or, failing that, maim innocent souls.

One might imagine that it would be commonly understood that Israel cannot simply permit this to go on ad infinitum. But evidently there are those who do not in fact understand it. The Palestinian Authority, which professes to want an independent Palestinian state despite having repeatedly rejected one, is incapable of governing Jenin, which it nominally controls. Riven by clan warfare and rife with corruption, the Palestinian Authority is a hot mess.

That leaves Israel with two options. Option 1 is for it to do nothing to stop its civilians from being murdered at will. This is the option of choice of the terminally sophomoric, the Blame-Israel-No-Matter-What crowd, who constitute a booming if not wholly intelligible cottage industry. It is not, however, the ideal option for Israel, which, all things considered, would prefer not to have its civilians blown to bits, shot, stabbed or rammed to death.

That would appear to leave Option 2, which is to try to stop those committing murder from committing murder. This does seem like a no-brainer. But there is a certain set indisposed to use their heads when it comes to Israel. So, when Israeli troops finally entered the weapons factory that is Jenin last week to try to slow down Murder, Inc., the predictable crowd proclaimed the predictable things. Amidst all the idiocy it wasn't easy to rank the most untethered comments, but the top prize surely went to the British Broadcasting Corporation anchor who alleged that "Israeli forces are happy to kill children."

A close second was commentator Peter Beinart, whose take on Islamic Jihad and Hamas murdering innocents was that "The fundamental problem is that Palestinians lack the most basic rights." No, it isn't. It was Palestinian President Mahmoud Abbas himself who explained Palestinian leadership's rejection of a Palestinian state to The Washington Post thus: "In the West Bank we have a good reality. We are living a good life." And the attacks by these groups have nothing to do with "rights." They have to do with the express pledge to eradicate Israel, full stop. This makes Beinart something of a fraud-peddler, albeit with no shortage of customers.

The bronze went to Squad members Rep. Rashida Tlaib and Rep. Ilhan Omar, who called Israel's efforts to protect its civilians a "pogrom." Sure it is. The dismantling of missile factories, weapon storage depots and IEDs planted under civilian roads is a "pogrom."

Now, Israel's current coalition government is comprised of some miserable characters — autocrats, fanatics and charlatans. Their plan to jettison an independent judiciary deserves every bit of the opprobrium it has generated both within Israel and without.

But those who dismiss the self-defense-based entry into Jenin as the expression of right-wing ideology don't know what they are talking about. It had the backing of the entire spectrum of Israeli society, which is plenty sick of seeing their grieving countrymen at funerals. It was, as opposition leader Yair Lapid put it, "a justified operation."

Still, there are a whole lot of sophomores out there, with a whole lot of megaphones. You can only hope that at some point they will graduate to something a little bit fairer.

The Brawler: Chris Christie's Not Mincing Words

July 18, 2023

Last week's release of the second quarter's fundraising figures for the 2024 presidential candidates produced two notable news stories. One was that President Joe Biden and his associated fundraising arms raised $72 million between his late-April reelection launch and June 30. This financial haul, double what former President Donald Trump raised in the second quarter, poured 72 buckets of cold water on the "Dementia-Joe-isn't-supported-by-Democrats" narrative that had gained currency, pushed and peddled by Republicans.

And it was similarly unhelpful to wishful thinking in Republican circles that Robert F. Kennedy, Jr., the candidate from Pluto, poses a "headache" for the president. This isn't the case, except perhaps on Pluto.

The other news was that former New Jersey Gov. Chris Christie, whose uphill battle for the GOP presidential nomination was initially deemed by pundits to be destined for a rapid flameout, had already collected contributions from over 40,000 donors in the first 35 days of his candidacy. This lifted him over one of the qualifying thresholds for Republicans hoping to participate in the party's Aug. 23 presidential debate. Christie is not on the debate stage yet; he has to poll at 1% or more among Republicans in three approved polls. But with a recent Morning Consult poll showing him at 3%, he is getting there. Meanwhile, a super PAC supporting Christie, called Tell It Like It Is, seems likely to generate substantial financial backing from those who would like to see Trump flattened in the debate, and who see Christie as the only challenger capable of exposing the twice-indicted former president for the fraud that he is in prime time.

A former prosecutor, Christie has not minced words about Trump, which sets him very far apart from his fellow candidates, who are all mince, all the time. The reason for Trump's felonious pilfering of classified documents, Christie says, is because "he wants to pretend he's still president." While other Republicans have hemmed, hawed and hidden when asked whether they would pardon Trump if he's convicted and they're elected, Christie is unhesitatingly unafraid of heresy. "I would have a hard time considering any pardon," he says. As for Trump's threat to skip next month's debate, Christie is blunt about the old draft dodger's latest case of bone spurs. "If Donald Trump doesn't show up," Christie says, "he's a coward."

When it comes to Trump, Christie goes where no other Republican dares to go, which, of course, isn't necessarily saying much. When it recently emerged that the Money-Funneler-In-Chief had had one of his committees pay Melania Trump $155,000 for "event planning and consulting," Christie unloaded on them both. "Trump is shameless," he tweeted. "A billionaire using donor money to pay personal legal fees and now paying his wife more than 2x what the average American makes just to pick some tableware. There's grifting, and then there's Trump grifting. Undisputed champs."

On matters relating to Donald Trump, the Republican field runs the gamut from kneeling to groveling. To say that Christie stands out is an understatement. A "tell" that Trump doesn't relish having Christie hanging around on a prolonged basis to tell the truth about him came with Trump's attack on Christie for recommending that he appoint FBI Director Christopher Wray. "(Wray) was recommended very strongly by Chris Christie, who is, you know, a sad case," Trump told Fox's Maria Bartiromo this past weekend. Christie isn't inclined to back down. "I think Chris Wray has done a very good job," he says.

A new poll of New Hampshire Republican voters showed Christie in a tie for second place with Ron DeSantis, poised to overtake the Florida governor, who is in free-fall. Evidently tens of millions in cash on hand cannot cure a repellent personality. But an awful lot would have to happen in order for a Republican base so ill-disposed to acknowledging the truth about Trump to reward someone like Christie for telling it. In the meantime, however, Christie, a congenital brawler, seems to be all in, and is serving notice that he intends to keep on punching.

National Zoo: Under MAGA's Gavel, There's Debasement in the House

July 25, 2023

    Congress has never enjoyed stratospheric esteem among Americans, who long ago came to understand that their elected representatives include a fair share of lightweights, airheads and demagogues. "Suppose you were an idiot, and suppose you were a member of Congress," Mark Twain postulated. "But I repeat myself." "You can lead a man to Congress," observed the late philosopher Milton Berle, "but you can't make him think." In the musical "1776," John Adams decried his hapless fellow members of the Continental Congress thusly: "We piddle, twiddle and resolve; not one damned thing do we solve."

    But there's piddling, twiddling and resolving, and then there's other stuff. The debasement of Congress to which we were treated last week was something else again, not merely a national embarrassment but one that made us a global laughingstock. It was another MAGA production: Republican Rep. Marjorie Taylor Greene had blown up and then displayed for television cameras photographs of President Joe Biden's son Hunter nude, having sexual relations with various women. This was for the simple purpose of humiliating the son and inflicting pain on the rest of his family.

    Everyone knows by now that Hunter Biden, who lost his mother and sister tragically as a young boy, almost lost his father several times and then lost his brother to brain cancer, spent several years in the depths of a severe drug addiction, and went through everything that goes along with it. Millions of American families have suffered the kinds of agony the Bidens have suffered.

    Neither Greene nor her GOP colleagues who control the House of Representatives care a whit about any of that. The flimsy pretext for Greene's "presentation" of photographs of Hunter Biden having sex was a hearing of the House Oversight and Accounting Committee, on which Greene, remarkably, sits, into whether or not the younger Biden should have been charged with more serious tax crimes than the ones to which he has agreed to plead guilty.

    Never mind that it was former President Donald Trump's Justice Department that initiated and spearheaded the prosecution of the younger

Biden. Never mind that it was a Trump-appointed U.S. attorney who decided what charges were warranted. Never mind that the son's crimes have nothing to do with his father and cannot be linked to him by anyone other than the genuinely certifiable. Never mind any of that: The indecency reflected in this hearing was that of Greene. As Rep. Alexandria Ocasio-Cortez put it: "I don't care who you are in this country. No one deserves that."

Greene may be appalling, but she is no rogue operator. The Republican-controlled committee's Twitter account tweeted out her photographs.

GOP Rep. Matt Gaetz is a bird of similar feathers. In 2019, the day before Trump fixer Michael Cohen was scheduled to testify about his former boss' payoffs to a porn star, Gaetz sent him this moblike warning: "Hey @MichaelCohen212," Gaetz tweeted, "Do your wife and father-in-law know about you and your girlfriends? Maybe tonight would be a good time for a chat. I wonder if she'll be faithful when you're in prison. She's about to learn a lot." The House Ethics Committee reprimanded Gaetz for "not (meet)ing the standards by which Members of the House should govern themselves."

In 2021, Rep. Paul Gosar posted an animated video of himself murdering Ocasio-Cortez. He was censured by the House, then controlled by Democrats, with only two Republicans prepared to agree that this was conduct unbecoming of someone in Congress. The rest of the Republican conference gathered around him after the censure vote to affirm their support for him.

These are the same folks, of course, who continue to support their colleague Rep. George Santos, the indicted fraud artist soon headed for an extended vocational course in license-plate making. They have turned Congress into a national zoo, and their fellow citizens can only stop, shake their heads and point.

Boss Man: America Has a Problem, and the Problem Is Us

August 1, 2023

The only thing worse than a conspiracy to obstruct justice is a conspiracy to obstruct justice committed by criminals who aren't very good at it. If the allegations in the superseding indictment handed down by a federal jury against former President Donald Trump last week are accurate, he was at the center of a conspiracy to obstruct justice comprised of The Gang That Couldn't Shoot Straight.

After the FBI observed surveillance cameras located at Mar-a-Lago near where Trump was illegally retaining the classified documents he had illegally pilfered, the Justice Department notified Team Trump that it was subpoenaing the surveillance footage from those cameras. Trump's lawyers informed Trump in New Jersey, who promptly summoned loyal aide and co-defendant Walt Nauta for a meeting. Nauta immediately made arrangements to fly to Mar-a-Lago, texting a colleague that he was returning there on a "family emergency," using a "shushing" emoji.

No joke.

Trump's property manager at Mar-a-Lago, one newly indicted Carlos De Oliveira, told another Trump employee that Nauta was changing his plans and coming to Mar-a-Lago, but that he should not tell anyone because Nauta wanted it kept secret.

When Nauta arrived, he and De Oliveira made a cloak-and-dagger trip to the surveillance booth. De Oliveira asked how long the server retained the surveillance footage, stating that "the boss" wanted the server deleted. Told that this could not be done, De Oliveira repeated that "the boss" nevertheless wanted it done.

It is of course possible that when De Oliveira insisted that "the boss" wanted the server deleted, he was referring to Bruce Springsteen, but since Springsteen has not played a major role in Trump's various Espionage Act violations, it is likelier that this was instead a reference to Trump. And that poses a real migraine for Trump's lawyers, because if Trump didn't know that he was in illegal possession of classified documents, or if the documents he was hoarding really were just double cheeseburger order forms from the White House mess kept as a memento, there wouldn't be any need to delete surveillance footage of the documents. Jurors will not need to be Sherlock Holmes to get this.

Put another way, "shushing" emojis and "The boss wants the server deleted" are not where you want to be as a criminal defendant charged with conspiracy to obstruct justice.

Still, Trump's base remains enthralled by, and Republican leaders remain terrified of, "the boss," and therein lies the rub of the tipping point on which American democracy hinges. While Trump remains generally unpopular — a recent Pew survey found that 63% of Americans have an unfavorable opinion of him — nearly four out of 10 Americans regard him approvingly — insurrection, obstruction, Espionage Act, falsification of business records, porn stars and all. The 2024 presidential election promises to be what the Battle of the Bulge was to World War II — determinative of whether democracy prevails or something very dark does.

We aren't the only ones gripped in this battle. In Israel, the present coalition government, led by someone who, like Trump, searches desperately for a get-out-of-jail card, is supported by only half the country. But this has been enough to do grievous damage to Israeli democracy. In Italy, Prime Minister Georgia Meloni is an ardent admirer of fascist dictator Benito Mussolini. Hungary's Prime Minister, Viktor Orban, has done his best to undermine democratic norms, assaulting judicial independence and freedom of the press.

"How to combat this authoritarian ascendancy is one of the most pressing matters of our time," writes Ruth Ben-Ghiat in her book "Strongmen: Mussolini to the Present." Writing recently in The New Republic, Michael Tomasky observed that "fascism is a sensibility more than it is a political program," noting that it revolved around support for absolute state power, the notion that majority groups are racially superior and peoples' "complete obeisance" to the would-be dictator.

Whether we call it fascism or we don't, millions of our countrymen have demonstrated their "complete obeisance" to a crooked autocrat. What that tells us about ourselves isn't pretty.

Right To Lie: Trump Claims First Amendment Protection for a Coup D'etat

August 8, 2023

Former President Donald Trump has boasted that he regards being indicted as "a badge of honor." If so, he has racked up quite a pile of badges. Last week's latest federal indictment brought the total number of criminal charges against him in New York State court and federal courts in Florida and in Washington, D.C., to nearly 80, and he is about to be awarded another batch of badges by a grand jury in Georgia. So, it has been a bumper crop for Trump where badges of honor are concerned, and things are about to get bumpier.

In truth, Trump did not seem all that honored when he stopped at Reagan National Airport on Thursday to speak to reporters after being arraigned. He lashed out at trash collection in Washington before boarding his private plane, now evidently renamed "Arraignment One" for all of the shuttling back and forth between arraignments it has been doing.

That Trump was not feeling quite as honored by the new criminal indictment was strongly suggested by his furious reaction to it. "IF YOU GO AFTER ME, I'M GOING AFTER YOU" proclaimed our model citizen on his social media platform, which sounded an awful lot like a threat to potential witnesses against him, of which there is no shortage. Among those that he appears to be going after is the federal judge assigned to the new case, who has been no-nonsense when it comes to handling the criminal cases in front of her brought against Trump's Jan. 6 foot soldiers. Trump is demanding that she recuse herself.

His lawyers are also demanding that the case be transferred out of Washington, D.C., to a venue that they feel will be more hospitable to him. They seek a trial in West Virginia, and not because of the John Denver song: It is a state that voted overwhelmingly for Trump in 2016 and 2020, and Moscow is unavailable.

Trump's team is auditioning two principal defenses to the latest indictment charging him with fraudulently and corruptly attempting to block the constitutionally mandated counting of the electoral votes cast in the 2020 election won by President Joe Biden. One is that Trump's intent was innocent, because either (1) he actually won the election or (2) he honestly believed he had won it. This defense has a number of problems with it, starting with the fact that both theories are laughable. Another drawback is that for Trump to try to convince the jury that he actually believed he had won the election he would have to take the stand in his own behalf, a scenario which would call to mind Custer's Last Stand. The cross-examination of Trump by prosecutors would lend new meaning to the phrase "shooting fish in a barrel."

Trump's second defense is that any conspiracy by him to obstruct the counting of electoral votes, any effort to pressure Vice President Mike Pence into blocking the certification of those votes and any scheme to substitute phony electors for legitimate ones was protected by the First Amendment. This is also a tough one. All conspiracies to violate the law involve "speech" to some degree, which doesn't immunize them from criminal prosecution.

A 2012 Supreme Court decision illustrates the uphill battle Trump faces to wriggle out of the latest indictment on First Amendment grounds. The Court listed a number of contexts in which deceitful "speech" is criminal, including "advocacy intended and likely to incite imminent lawless action," "speech integral to criminal conduct" and lies aimed at undermining "the integrity of governmental processes." This bodes ill for Trump.

And Trump is also charged with fraud. "Where false claims are made to affect a fraud or to secure valuable consideration," the Supreme Court held, "it is well-established that the Government may restrict speech without affronting the First Amendment."

"You're too honest," Donald Trump is alleged to have admonished Mike Pence. That is one reason why Trump is in the dock, and Pence isn't.

Blowin' Smoke: Hunter's Hubris Heightens GOP Hooey

August 15, 2023

Just to compound the other serious mistakes he has made in his life, Hunter Biden made the mistake last week of overplaying his hand. Afforded the opportunity to plead guilty to tax crimes committed while addicted to crack and other drugs, the president's son held out for a commitment by the Justice Department that it would never prosecute him for anything else. This was a commitment the Department could not and would not make — and it was a commitment that any practical person mindful of his past misconduct would have known wouldn't be made.

The younger Biden's demand that the Justice Department declare that it was absolving him of any further criminal jeopardy left Department lawyers with no choice but to tell him to pound sand. And it left Attorney General Merrick Garland, whose fealty to the rule of law exceeds that of all of his congressional critics combined, with no choice but to appoint a special counsel to investigate anything and everything Hunter Biden related. And speaking of fealty to the rule of law, the man Garland appointed was David Weiss, the United States Attorney for Delaware, appointed by none other than former President Donald Trump and asked by President Joe Biden to stay on precisely so that the criminal investigation of his son could be completed by a federal prosecutor installed by his Republican predecessor, not by him. When it comes to integrity, not all presidents are created equal.

As special counsel, Weiss will not only have the unquestioned authority to follow the trail of any evidence of Hunter Biden's misconduct but also to write a report documenting that evidence. The decision by Hunter Biden and his legal team to play "chicken" with the Justice Department may bring other adverse consequences home to roost. At a minimum, it means Biden will face extended uncertainty about his legal fate, and the Department probably will feel obliged to seek jail time for charges on which it had previously offered him probation.

How dumb was that?

Very. Not only for him, but for a Biden family that has already suffered badly from the terrible choices he's made. This includes a father who, like most loving fathers would, has done everything he could to demonstrate his love for a son not only bent on self-destruction but prepared to hurt his family as well as himself. Naturally, MAGA World has made the usual untethered accusations about Biden Senior. Their hero, of course, is already facing 78 felony counts handed down against him by three separate grand juries, with a fourth grand jury set to boost that number to 85 by the end of the week.

The GOP's claim that they have "evidence" that incriminates President Biden has not withstood scrutiny, to put it mildly. House Oversight Chairman James Comer's absent "star witness" against the president, one Gal Luft, turns out to be an international fugitive. Indicted earlier this year on a slew of federal charges, Luft was arrested in Cyprus and jumped bail while awaiting extradition. He's in hiding somewhere.

A real gold-plated witness, worthy of the Republicans' gold-plated investigation.

Then there was Fox News' Peter Doocy, who confronted President Biden claiming that Hunter's former business partner had testified to Congress that the elder Biden was frequently "talking business" with his son's business associates. Except that the former partner had actually testified that he had not heard any such discussions.

The GOP response to Weiss' appointment as special counsel captures the moral quality of their Say Anything caucus. Last year 33 Republican senators wrote Garland demanding he appoint Weiss as special counsel. Sen. Ted Cruz, dubbed "Lyin' Ted" by someone who is not one to talk, now denounces Weiss as "a wildly inappropriate person to be a special counsel." Sen. Marsha Blackburn, another signatory, has gone full Stalin, denouncing Weiss as a "collaborator." Sen. Ron Johnson, very nearly certifiable, now says Weiss "is probably the least independent person that Merrick Garland could have appointed."

In other words: just another day of hooey-spewing in the Grand Old Party.

Cruel Limbo: Frozen in Uncertainty, Loyal Afghan Allies Wait for the Safety They Deserve

August 22, 2023

"America," wrote novelist Thomas Wolfe, "is a fabulous country, the only fabulous country; it is the only place where miracles not only happen, but where they happen all the time." We're having more than our share of trouble doing the fundamentally right things, let alone achieving miracles. But a properly bipartisan bill pending before Congress would at least do the fundamentally right thing for tens of thousands of Afghans, most of them women and children, whose families risked their lives helping us confront al-Qaida and the Taliban, and who now depend on us to offer them the permanent safety they deserve.

In the 20 years following Sept. 11, 2001, untold numbers of Afghans chose to help American forces attempt to ensure that the kind of mass murder visited upon us when planes smashed into lower Manhattan never happened again. They were drivers, interpreters, soldiers, nurses, social workers, cooks, construction workers and more, and they enlisted alongside our own men and women serving us in far-off Afghanistan as we tried to rid that country of a brutally repressive regime, one that threatened our own security. They wanted to believe in America, and they did believe in it, and they trusted that in return for having America's back, America would have theirs.

When the U.S. military hastily departed Afghanistan in 2021, these families faced deadly retribution by the Taliban. About 80,000 Afghans who had risked their lives on our behalf were urgently evacuated, transferred first to other countries where American military personnel screened and vetted them. They were then flown to the United States for further screening and then resettled in communities across the country.

But with a big and painful catch. Under current law, they are only permitted to stay here temporarily. Whether and when they will be forced to leave America and are left to their own meager devices is entirely up in the air, which means that they live not only in legal limbo, but under a very frightening cloud.

In a rare display of bipartisan problem-solving, congressional leaders from both sides of the aisle came to the following sensible conclusion: No. 1, this can't be right. No. 2, this has to be fixed. Democratic Sen. Amy Klobuchar and Republican Sen. Lindsey Graham, along with colleagues from both houses of Congress, have fashioned the Afghan Adjustment Act as a means of providing permanent status here for eligible Afghans who have passed screening measures and who pass additional ones. Backed by a long list of veterans organizations with particular sensitivity to what Afghans temporarily resettled or still living in Afghanistan have given to our country, the Act ensures that everyone permitted to stay here first undergoes multiple levels of rigorous scrutiny and then streamlines a path for them to start new lives in the country for which they risked their old ones.

The one impediment to the bill's passage is the effort by some to link relief to the Afghans — whose right to it merits little disagreement — to a comprehensive solution to our immigration problems — about which there is nothing but disagreement. At best, holding the Afghans hostage to the illusory hope for broad agreement on immigration anytime soon makes the perfect the enemy of the good. At worst it is cruel to those who we know deserve better.

Klobuchar, who has spearheaded the Act, has been particularly dogged about it. "It's about a covenant," she said on the Senate floor in late July. "A covenant that we have made and we must keep to those who stand with us on the battlefield. This bill does right by Afghans who worked alongside our troops, and shows the world that the United States of America, when we make a promise, we keep it."

As with virtually all of Americans' forebears, the Afghans no doubt regard it as miraculous that they have made it to this fabulous country. Now it is up to us to do the right thing by them.

Mugged: America Digests the Specter of Inmate No. PO1135809

August 29, 2023

It wasn't a midnight train to Georgia that carried the 19 criminal defendants charged by a Fulton County grand jury to that county's sheriff's office to have their mug shots taken last week, but one by one they all made the humiliating trek to the local jail to post the bond needed to avoid sitting in prison until their trials and to have the photographs snapped that would memorialize their disgrace. Those dreadfully humbled included former President Donald Trump's chief of staff, Mark Meadows; former Trump lawyers Sidney Powell, John Eastman, Ken Chesebro and Jenna Ellis; former Justice Department official Jeffrey Clark; and Trump's uber-consigliere Rudy Giuliani.

Of that sorry band, no one has been humiliated more thoroughly than Giuliani, who has gone from being America's Mayor in the aftermath of Sept. 11, 2001, to being a broke, broken and bankrupt laughingstock. Stripped of licenses to practice law, sanctioned by courts for contemptuous misconduct and reduced to begging a disdainful Trump for the legal fees necessary to defend himself against civil lawsuits and criminal cases, Giuliani stands a real chance of going to prison, which is no laughing matter. Along the way he has had his hair dye drip down his face in full public view during a fraudulent press conference held between a crematorium and a sex shop and been obliged to ask for a bail bond at Second Chance Bail Bondsmen across the street from the jail in which he may find himself residing if found guilty of the various felonies with which he is currently charged.

On Thursday night came The Mother of All Mug Shots. Flying into Atlanta on a private plane that is racking up some serious frequent flyer miles ping-ponging from arraignment to arraignment, Trump himself swept into the Fulton County jail complex in a motorcade fit for a former president, complete with flashing lights. He emerged 21 minutes later as the first former president with his very own inmate number: PO1135809.

Posing for his mug shot in the sheriff's office, the former president got off just the menacing glower he had practiced for the occasion, succeeding in projecting a sort of "Super Felon" look he knew would thrill his faithful base. And, boy, are they ever faithful. ABC anchor Kyra Phillips put her finger on what Trump's flock is worshipping: it is "defiance," and all that goes with it. But defiance of what? Of laws that prohibit every citizen, including presidents, from stealing nuclear secrets, obstructing grand jury investigations and trying to steamroll elected officials into falsifying election results so that an unsuccessful candidate for reelection can remain in office despite the will of American voters?

Apparently so.

The epic snake oil salesman has bamboozled students into paying to attend a bogus "university" named after himself, cheated charities, stiffed vendors, paid off porn stars and conned innumerable hard-working Americans into forking over hard-earned dollars to the self-professed billionaire in order to pay his criminal defense lawyers so that he could be spared having to pay his criminal defense lawyers himself. Small wonder that he had no difficulty selling 7 million dollars' worth of merchandise bearing his prison photo within hours to people who could only worship him more fervently than they already do if some grand jury somewhere indicted him yet again.

Trump's most recent indictment brings the total number of felony charges against him in the four jurisdictions in which he's a criminal defendant to 90. As if the country has not experienced enough of a chilling roller coaster ride since the morally challenged real estate mogul first announced his presidential candidacy, we are in for yet more. The months ahead will feature a daily diet of hearings held, trial dates set (and postponed), and judicial rulings issued and digested, as Americans grapple with the stone-cold realization that roughly half of us will support this guy in 2024, inmate number and all. It's increasingly clear that the wild ride we are on in the United States is very far from over.

'Ain't Rabbit No More': New Biography Highlights Dr. King's Enduring Legacy

September 5, 2023

On Aug. 26, a 21-year-old White racist left his Florida home, bringing with him his swastika-festooned assault rifle and a handgun. He headed to Edward Waters University, a historically Black university in a largely Black section of Jacksonville, then got out of his car and donned a bulletproof vest. Chased off campus by a university security guard, he drove to a Dollar General store and executed three Black people in cold blood: Angela Michelle Carr, 52, Jerrald Gallion, 29 and Anoit Joseph "AJ" Laguerre, Jr., 19. The murderer's racist writings and rants left Jacksonville Sheriff T.K. Waters with "no question" that the killings were racial. "He hated Blacks, and I think he hated just about everyone that wasn't White," said Sheriff Waters. "He made that very clear."

This latest targeted killing by White Americans of Black Americans for being Black Americans came only hours before America marked the 60th anniversary of Martin Luther King Jr.'s iconic "I Have a Dream" speech at the Lincoln Memorial in August 1963. One might say that flagrantly racist assaults by Whites against Blacks take place every day in one place or another in our country, except they occur multiple times a day in more than one place, and generally go unnoticed. Writing in the 1950s about our race problem, James Baldwin noted that "(w)hat it comes to, finally, is that this Nation has spent a large part of its time and energy looking away from one of the principal facts of its life."

Dr. King's speech to a crowd of 250,000 in Washington that day is so iconic that there's a danger his personal courage — his heroism, in fact — and his historic role in galvanizing support for civil rights will be forgotten in the passage of time, and that what he meant to this country will seem remote to those who only associate his name with a day off from work or school. Jonathan Eig, the author of the new biography "King: A Life," aims to prevent that. Subjected to beatings, firebombings, trumped-up jailings and death threats, the young minister inspired boycotts, protests, sit-ins, marches and legislation, in turn spawning countless acts of courage and belief that have not stopped reshaping America, even as events like that which occurred in Jacksonville illustrate the steepness of the remaining climb.

Setting the stage for the recounting of King's role in leading the boycott against Montgomery, Alabama's segregationist bus companies in the mid-1950s, Eig writes about the lasting legacy of slavery there. Alabama's slaves comprised about half of its population by the Civil War. "Many of those enslaved men, women and children," Eig writes, "were bought and sold in downtown Montgomery, marched through the city's streets, made to stand on auction blocks, shackled, inspected and traded for cash or animals. More than half of all enslaved families were broken up."

Rosa Parks, the quiet seamstress who in refusing to give up her seat on a Montgomery bus sparked the boycott intended to bury slavery's legacy for good, told a historian: "Treading the tight rope of Jim Crow from birth to death, from almost our first knowledge of life to our last conscious thought, is a major mental acrobatic feat."

On her 56th straight day of walking to and from her job as a domestic worker rather than riding a segregated bus, a Montgomery woman named Dealy Cooksy told an interviewer that she was indeed tired but had no intention of backing down. "I ain't begging, and I sure ain't getting back on the bus 'til Reverend King say so, and he says we ain't going back 'til they treat us right. There ain't nothing they can do but try to scare me. But we ain't rabbit no more."

The white supremacists and assorted deplorables have their moments — in Jacksonville, Charlestown and Buffalo, and elsewhere. Gone three generations now, Martin Luther King Jr.'s most enduring legacy has been motivating millions of Americans who, in Dealy Cooksy's words, "ain't rabbit no more."

Giving Irish: A Nation and a Vibrant Community Celebrate One Another

September 12, 2023

The phrase "fighting Irish" did not originate with Notre Dame's football team, but with the Irish immigrant soldiers who fought for the Union during the Civil War. It was Confederate Gen. Robert E. Lee himself who is said to have coined the term, a testament to the bravery and effectiveness of the so-called "Irish brigades" that helped save their new Nation.

When Irish statesman Eamon de Valera came to America in 1919 to generate support for the Irish cause, he naturally came first to Boston. There he told a huge rally in Fenway Park what the phrase meant. "What we actually mean when we talk about it," he explained, "is an indomitable spirit, a commitment, never tentative, always fully committed, to life itself... that's really the spirit of 'the Fighting Irish.'"

Ireland's magic is plain to anyone who visits the Emerald Isle, but it is hardly the country's physical beauty alone that furnishes the magic. Since time immemorial the Irish have been gifted at community — at nurturing and preserving communal celebration of tradition, music, humor, literature and memory. They've been gifted as well at transplanting community to the places to which painful circumstances have forced them to emigrate — and then nurturing and preserving community in those places.

America has been a blessed beneficiary of this Irish gift, and Boston has perhaps been the most blessed of the blessed. Those who have interacted with Boston — as students, as patients or as transplants themselves — have reason to know that the phrase should be "the giving Irish." The imprint of Irish Americans on Massachusetts is vast and deep. But you can see and breathe it all over Boston. There is a great deal that is generous and good here, and so much of it has an Irish American aspect.

A walking illustration of this is John Connors Jr., the justly iconic philanthropist who has done as much good for Bostonians over the last two generations as anyone, and who at 81 continues to do it. The grandson of Irish immigrants, Connors grew up in a lower-middle-class home in a humble Boston neighborhood and was the first in his family to go to college. What the Connors family lacked in discretionary income it possessed in values passed down from forebears. Connors sold peanuts at Fenway, drove a cab, served in the Army National Guard and supported his sister and her children when his sister's husband abandoned them.

A self-professed "peddler," Connors went on to found the advertising agency Hill Holliday, which under his leadership became a behemoth. There isn't much in Boston that hasn't benefited from Connors' relentless philanthropy — hospitals, shelters and treatment centers, colleges, camps for underprivileged kids, improved education for inner-city children and, of course, an uncountable number of families who have been quietly, or anonymously, uplifted by Connors' acts of kindness.

Uncomfortable talking about what he had done, Connors, who has been to Ireland 55 times, makes clear that he has been moved and motivated by his Irish heritage. His generosity to those who are disadvantaged and discriminated against is a visceral reaction to the Irish American experience of his grandparents' and parents' generations.

In Boston later this month, the Irish Cultural Center of Greater Boston, a collaboration of the Irish government and local Irish Americans, will gather to ensure that the appreciation of Irish heritage that meant much to the likes of Jack Connors and so many others stays vibrant for years to come. It will give an award named after the late U.S. Rep. Brian Donnelly, spearhead of a visa program that strengthened the America-Ireland relationship, to longtime CEO of the New England Council Jim Brett. Those in attendance will honor what center head Jerry McDermott describes as the core Irish legacy that he hopes will always flourish here: "the yearning to make things better for the next generation." It will be yet another one of those occasions when Irish Americans demonstrate that, at the end of the day, it is all about the giving.

Pulp Fiction: Bowing to Trump, the GOP Launches a Phony Impeachment Inquiry

September 19, 2023

A political gaffe, journalist Michael Kinsley once said, is what happens when a politician accidentally tells the truth. Republican Rep. Ken Buck is no doubt drawing fire from his Republican colleagues in the House for his Washington Post op-ed last week deriding his party's newly launched "impeachment inquiry" into President Joe Biden for "relying on an imagined history." But what else is new? As we Jews recite every year at Passover: "Why is today different from any other day?"

In the case of congressional Republicans, it isn't: imagined history, imagined facts, imagined rigged elections, imagined declassification of documents — this sort of thing has been the Republicans' staple since the Big Bamboozler took his famous escalator ride down Trump Tower in 2015. Buck's accurate labeling of the impeachment inquiry as suffused with fiction will surely stir unhappiness among the Proud Boy Wannabes to whom the Grand Old Party caters.

The inquiry was ordered up by former President Donald Trump, who is keen to divert attention from the 91 separate criminal charges pending against him in four separate jurisdictions, for everything from falsifying records to hide his hush money payments to a porn star, to trying to block the counting of electoral votes in order to illegally stay in office, to racketeering, to stealing classified military secrets. He claims that he is innocent of all 91 charges, but he also claimed that ingesting cleaning fluid might be a neat way of avoiding COVID-19. So, a little bit of distraction is highly desirable from his perspective, in order to interrupt the diet of the once and, he hopes, future president's rich assortment of apparent felonies.

Ergo the announcement by House Speaker Kevin McCarthy, his manhood in consignment, that the GOP-controlled House was starting impeachment proceedings into Biden. What the basis of them is, we do not know, and he could not say, but if Trump and his acolytes want an impeachment inquiry then that is what they — and the country — shall get. The gist of it all is that Hunter Biden, the president's son, whose personal life has been a self-inflicted disaster for 20 years, took advantage of his father's name in order to generate business opportunities he wouldn't otherwise have gotten.

What a bombshell! If grifting off of a famous family member's name was a crime, Donald Trump Jr., Eric Trump and Jared Kushner would be doing time in Leavenworth.

But Buck cannot find any there there that makes Joe Biden responsible for anything at all, let alone anything impeachable, having to do with his son. "What's missing," Buck wrote, "despite years of investigation, is the smoking gun that connects Joe Biden." And which connects Joe Biden to what? Republican Rep. Mike Lawler put it gingerly: "The question for me right now is, the investigations, are they producing enough facts and evidence that arranges taking it to the next step? I don't think it's there at the moment."

Of course, it isn't that GOP investigations, with the accompanying huffing and puffing about "the Biden crime family," haven't produced "enough" evidence of any wrongdoing by Joe Biden. It's that they have produced nothing — as in zero. Thus far they have recollections of a couple of handfuls of pleasantries offered by then-vice president Biden to business associates of his son, no doubt knowing that his son wanted to make himself look good, over six years before Joe Biden became president. Now there's a high crime and misdemeanor for you!

Not only do the Republicans have nothing on Joe Biden, apparently — they don't even seem to have anything on his son other than the gun and tax charges already filed against him by Biden's Justice Department, all related to his addiction. The House Oversight Committee chaired by MAGA maven Rep. James Comer keeps promising to subpoena the younger Biden but keeps backing off. "Well, he can fight the subpoena in court," stammered Comer on Fox News. "It's very difficult."

No, it's not. It's simple. What's difficult is cooking up something out of nothing, even if that happens to be a House specialty.

Difficult and Necessary: Arming Ukraine Is Costly and Also Our Only Option

September 26, 2023

In late 1940, Nazi Germany had successfully subjugated virtually all of Europe in barely a year's time, and turned its eyes to rolling over England, first by bombing it to smithereens and cutting off its shipping and then by invading it if required. Still recovering from the Great Depression and unpersuaded that Hitler's aggression was any of our business, Americans were tepid at best about lifting a finger to help the United Kingdom, out of cash and staring defeat in the face, defend itself against the Third Reich. Begging for help from its last and only hope, Prime Minister Winston Churchill implored the United States famously: "Give us the tools and we'll finish the job."

Tens of millions of Americans were unmoved and did not see that what seemed to be Europe's war threatened the entire world order, and that playing ostrich was no substitute for paying attention to history. President Franklin D. Roosevelt, who had secured a third term by promising that American sons would not fight overseas again, devised a scheme to help our ally — and a "scheme" is what it was. The Lend-Lease program served first as a "loan" of 50 destroyers to the British, followed by 50 billion dollars — the equivalent of about 700 billion of today's dollars — worth of aircraft, ships and weapons to our allies to hold off the Germans and ultimately deplete them.

The Lend-Lease legislation passed Congress on a nearly party-line vote, with Republicans bitterly opposed to it. "You can dress this measure up all you please, you can sprinkle it with perfume and pour powder on it, masquerade it in any form you please," proclaimed Republican Rep. Dewey Short of Missouri, "but it is still foul and it stinks to high heaven. It does not need a doctor, it needs an undertaker."

Republicans had the better of Roosevelt when it came to flowery, angry rhetoric. It did not take long, however, before Roosevelt was proven decisively correct, and his opponents disastrously wrong. The aid that Roosevelt's adversaries fought so hard to block was instrumental in the defeat of Hitler, Mussolini and Hirohito, and enabled the world to avoid another global conflict over the four generations since the end of World War II. "We are," argued Secretary of War Henry Stimson in urging support for Great Britain, "buying our own security," and he was right. Those who opposed the aid were wrong — very wrong.

On his trip to North America to shore up weakening support for his brave people last week, Ukrainian President Volodymyr Zelenskyy accused Russia of attempting genocide in Ukraine. Call it what you will: It is the mass slaughter of the Ukrainian people for the purpose of strangling them into submission in order to forcibly bring them under the heel of a murderous despot. "I believe you're supporting either Ukraine or Russia," said Zelenskyy. "By weakening the support of Ukraine, you're reinforcing Russia."

It really is that simple. And yet the financial costs of maintaining support for Ukraine, coupled with the toll taken by a witches' brew of pro-Putin proselytizers, MAGA madness and shortsightedness have combined to erode American resolve for doing what Americans need to do if Putin isn't to enslave Ukrainians and threaten a wider swath of Europe. A CNN poll taken last month found that 55% of Americans believe Congress should cease funding for Ukraine, with 71% of Republicans telling pollsters that America should call it quits.

It doesn't take a moment's reflection to appreciate that delivering over 100 billion of American taxpayers' dollars to a country many of us couldn't locate on a map two years ago is not politically advantageous to President Joe Biden. This is particularly true at a time when American voters disapprove of his handling of the economy, despite excellent reasons to approve of his performance. All the more proof that what Biden has done and is doing to keep Putin from flattening Ukraine is historic for its courage and leadership. Historians will recognize it as such, even if by the time that history is written many of us won't be around to read it.

Flop House: The GOP's 'Impeachment Inquiry' Lays an Egg

October 3, 2023

  The tip-off that House Republicans' cobbled-together opening of their "impeachment inquiry" into President Joe Biden was going to flop came last Wednesday, the day before the first hearing. House Ways and Means Committee Chairman Rep. Jason Smith, R.-Mo., whose unfortunate lot it was to hold a press conference announcing new "evidence" that Biden had used his public office to help his son Hunter, was utterly unable to explain how there was evidence of any such thing.

  Asked by NBC's Ryan Nobles how a document dated August 2017 could suggest that Biden had used public office to benefit his son when Biden held no office at the time, Smith sounded a very great deal like Jackie Gleason's iconic Ralph Kramden character failing miserably at answering basic questions from his wife Alice. "I'm not an expert on the timeline," Smith blathered. "I would love to have President Biden and his family to tell us all about the timelines."

  "But if he's not the president or the vice-president at the time," asked the perplexed reporter, "where's the wrongdoing? He wasn't even a candidate for president at the time."

  "Apparently you'll never believe us," came Smith's brilliant reply, as he turned to another questioner.

  The hearing itself proved to be just as much of a lead balloon as Smith's hemming, hawing and stammering presaged. It was led by House Oversight Committee Chairman James Comer, R-Ky., who has spent the last year predicting that, any decade now, there would be evidence of wrongdoing by Joe Biden or, as Comer put it on Fox News, "I sure hope so." Notable in his Committee's stellar investigation thus far was his triumphant announcement that they finally had a witness, only to have to admit that the witness had gone missing. It emerged that he hadn't gone missing so much as he turned out to be an international fugitive, indicted on a series of felony charges and hiding from law enforcement. Let's put it this way: The "investigation" into Joe Biden has not exactly yielded results.

  Comer's hearing got off to an inauspicious start and proceeded directly downhill from there. The Republicans' panel of "witnesses" commenced one by one to announce that, actually, they were unaware of any evidence of wrongdoing by President Biden. Jonathan Turkey, a former Justice Department tax attorney who up until now has been a reliably go-to lawyer for Trump World, got things rolling by volunteering that he saw no basis for claiming that Biden had committed any impeachable offense. "I do not believe that the current evidence would support articles of impeachment," he admitted. But exactly what "the current evidence" is of any wrongdoing by Joe Biden other than having won the 2020 election has remained rather elusive, or an extremely closely guarded secret by House Republicans who, after months of subpoenaing bank records and repeating the phrase "Biden crime family," still cannot tell us what it is.

At this point, one would have expected the Republicans to produce evidence of something: parking in a loading zone or an overdue library book if they cannot identify a high crime or misdemeanor. But evidently, they cannot. It isn't weak tea the House Committee was serving up. It was Kool-Aid.

Across the country in Arizona, President Biden was paying tribute to the late Sen. John McCain, a conservative Republican who, as Biden pointed out, believed with all his heart in "country first: honor, duty, decency, freedom, liberty, democracy." Biden recalled just how completely McCain, shot down while flying a Navy jet over Vietnam, put his faith in these things. "Imprisoned five and a half years," Biden noted. "Solitary confinement for two years. Given an opportunity to come home if he just said a couple things. He was beaten, bloodied, bones broken, isolated, tortured, unable to raise his arm above his shoulders again."

How sad McCain would be to see his fellow congressional Republicans now, five years after his passing. How sad all the rest of us should be.

Slaughter Incorporated: Coddled by the Left and Armed by Iran, Hamas Stages a Massacre

October 10, 2023

On Saturday morning, several thousand young Israelis were celebrating a Jewish holiday at an all-night music festival in southern Israel, a few miles from the border fence that separates Israel from the Gaza Strip. Shortly after sunrise, hundreds of Hamas operatives armed with machine guns and grenades broke through the fence and headed for the festival, murder on their minds, wielding the tools with which to carry out a massacre.

Descending on the terrified youngsters, who ran for their lives, the Hamas gunmen mowed down the children with everything they had, chasing them by car, surrounding them and blowing them to pieces. They slit these youngsters' throats. They bound the limbs of these kids, some lifeless and some barely clinging to life, and rammed their bloody bodies onto their vehicles, speeding back into Gaza, where Palestinians on the street screamed with joy, passed around celebratory sweets and once again displayed the bloodlust that so tragically has come to characterize significant segments of Palestinian society.

When Hamas' rampage at the festival was over, 260 young Israeli bodies were found. That doesn't count those wounded, kidnapped or still missing.

Meanwhile, other Hamas gunmen were invading 22 Israeli villages, going from home to home, executing the elderly, the disabled, women, husbands, children and babies at point-blank range while the victims begged for their lives. This should surprise no one: Hamas has functioned as a kind of Palestinian SS, the Nazi organization that carried out the genocidal murder of 6 million Jews, ever since its founding as a radical Islamic killing enterprise in 1987. Hamas' very raison d'etre has always been the annihilation of Israel.

After Hamas violently seized control of the Gaza Strip from the Palestinian Authority in 2007, it commenced intermittent mass rocket attacks on Israeli civilian centers, using Palestinian innocents as human shields from which to fire several tens of thousands of rockets at Israeli innocents. Each time this occurred, it was funded and equipped by Iran, long regarded by our State Department as the world's foremost state sponsor of terror, which, like Hamas, vows to wipe Israel off the face of the map.

And each time this has occurred, Israel has found itself reeling under the rocket attacks, while its armed forces were required to undertake to stop the rocketing. Each time, it took the Left but seconds to decide that it was Israel that was to blame for trying to stop its civilians from being blown to smithereens. The truth is simple: Hamas' apologists, among them The Squad in the Democratic caucus in Congress and academics in fashionable faculty lounges on elite college campuses, are not troubled by Hamas' determination to terminate Israel's existence. Progressive poseurs operating under the umbrella of groups with clever names like "Students for Justice in Palestine" work 24/7 at intimidating pro-Israel students and, indeed, at driving Jewish students underground with fear.

Since Saturday's sunrise, Hamas has not confined itself to murdering at gunpoint, slitting throats and abductions. It has fired about 5,000 more rockets into Israeli communities, smashing houses, apartment buildings and hospitals. Emboldened by the hatred of Israel that has spread like a virus on the far Left, indulged by supposed human rights advocates who do not recognize Israelis' rights to live in peace and armed to the teeth by Iran, Hamas is a chicken that has come home to roost.

By Monday afternoon, it had emerged that over 900 Israelis had been murdered by Hamas, more Jews murdered on any day since the Holocaust. Over 2,500 had been wounded. Israel's death toll is the proportional equivalent of over 32,000 Americans massacred in a single day, the equivalent of 10 times the number of those killed on Sept. 11, 2001.

If there is a meaningful distinction between Hamas and ISIS, it is not apparent. Nevertheless, Hamas has benefited from international support in malign quarters and, incredibly, from people who actually hold themselves out as progressives. Hamas has blood on its hands, and plenty of it. But it isn't the only one.

Blast-Off: Israel's Critics Depart Planet Earth
October 17, 2023

There is a famous scene in the movie classic "Annie Hall" in which protagonist Alvy Singer visits his girlfriend's family and encounters her somewhat untethered brother in a hallway. Singer listens as the brother rambles incoherently before politely taking his leave. "Right, well, I have to go now, Duane," he says, "because I'm due back on planet Earth."

"Planet Earth" came to more than one person's mind about 36 hours after the news emerged about Israelis slaughtered in cold blood, babies riddled with machine gun bullets in their cribs, hundreds of young people mowed down at a music festival, human beings decapitated, raped and abducted by Hamas. Thirteen hundred Israelis murdered. Three thousand seven hundred Israelis maimed. Over 150 terrified innocents held hostage in the terror state established in Gaza by Hamas for the purpose of annihilating Israel.

At a solidarity rally for Israel in Boston, Massachusetts Sen. Edward Markey announced that what was called for was "de-escalation" of "the conflict." He was booed by several thousand incredulous people gathered there, since "de-escalation" would mean that Israel should simply ignore the mass slaughter, move on and pray that nothing like this happened again — or at least not too soon.

Unless Israel consigns itself to simply absorbing the mass slaughter visited upon it by a neighboring terror state, it has literally no choice but to attempt to dismantle Hamas, no easy task. No nation that gives a fig about its own existence could do otherwise — and Israel has plenty of reason to be concerned about its existence, a point about which its critics could not care less.

Some concluded that Markey was simply addled, but he is addled like a fox. Once a stalwart supporter of Israel when it helped him politically, Markey, a shrewd student of raw politics, correctly adjudged that when he wished to secure and then hold the Democratic nomination for senator in Massachusetts, his best move was to prioritize locking up the support of the AOC wing of the Democratic Party. That's a wing that has adopted a "see-no-evil" policy about tens of thousands of Hamas rockets slamming into Israeli civilian centers over the past 15 years, and that ritualistically condemns Israel's attempts to defend itself as "war crimes" and "crimes against humanity."

If Markey's call for Israel to "de-escalate" after 5,000 of its citizens were murdered or maimed was mindless, others' pronouncements were risible. MSNBC commentator Peter Beinart, who has called for Israel to self-dissolve, claimed that Hamas had little choice but to be violent because Palestinians lacked a "pathway" for "ethical protest." This, of course, is drivel: Hamas was founded in the 1980s in order to obliterate Israel, and since then it has devoted itself to blocking an independent Palestinian state next to Israel. After Israel uprooted 11,000 Israelis living in Gaza in 2005 in order to pave the way for a Palestinian state, Hamas forcibly seized control of Gaza and expelled the Palestinian Authority for the purpose of scuttling the very Palestinian state that Palestinians assert they want. After Beinart delivered himself of this balderdash on national television, MSNBC host Jen Psaki thanked him for his "insight."

Israel's critics now demand that it somehow achieve the magic trick of responding to Hamas without hurting civilians, even though even those who don't know the Gaza Strip from the Louisiana Purchase know that Hamas deliberately makes that impossible, embedding its fighters and their weapons in apartment buildings, mosques and hospitals, forcibly making civilians human shields. Longtime Hamas whitewasher Rep. Ayanna Pressley conceded over the weekend that "the murder of innocent Israeli civilians at the hands of Hamas is unacceptable," but demanded that Israeli ensure that civilians are not hurt. Has she not a clue about what happens in Gaza? And if the massacre of Israeli civilians is "unacceptable," then what exactly is Israel supposed to do to avoid accepting it? Must Israeli permit it to happen again — and then again after that?

When it comes to Israel, some people have simply departed planet Earth. The challenge now is to keep others from joining them.

Hail to a Chief: The President Overrides the Kindergarten

October 24, 2023

    The narrative that President Joe Biden is too old to be president isn't holding up all that well, taking more than a few hits in recent months. Biden's arduous secret trip to Kiev to demonstrate solidarity with Ukraine while it fends off Vladimir Putin's barbarism didn't exactly advance the narrative. His visit to Israel while it is besieged by thousands of Hamas rockets, landing on Air Force One at an airport easily reached by the Iranian proxy's missiles, set the narrative back even further. If this is what it means to be too old to lead the free world, one wonders whether there is anything a younger president could do to make Americans prouder.

    Biden's personal courage was accompanied by wisdom, all displayed with the knowledge that his immediate, resolute commitment to Israel would unleash rage from the predictable quarters. The leaders of Arab countries that American taxpayers help sustain nonetheless refused to meet with Biden on his Mideast trip, fearful of being toppled by the spillover of raw Jew-hatred on the Arab street. This is not Biden's first rodeo: He tipped his cap to these leaders and stayed diplomatically mum.

    Meanwhile, in order to warn the Iranian mullahs who fund and control both Hamas and Hezbollah that we had Israel's back more than nominally, Biden moved promptly to bolster Israel's military capacity, and sent two warplane-packed aircraft carriers to Israel's coast. Thus far Biden's move has restrained Iran from directing Hezbollah to unleash its 130,000 rockets from Lebanon into Israel.

    Here at home, Biden has remained unbowed by his party's hard Left wing, which adjudges itself "progressive" while whitewashing Hamas' murder and maiming of 5,000 Israelis and while condemning Israel for having the nerve to try to prevent the slaughter, decapitation, burning alive, raping and abducting from happening yet again. From the moment news emerged on Oct. 7 of the mini-Holocaust perpetrated by the ISIS emulators who brutally rule Gaza, the president has been a forceful, unapologetic voice of moral clarity, denouncing the massacres as the massive crimes against humanity that anyone with decency can see they are. By asserting over and over that the

United States stands with Israel, he purposefully informed America and the rest of the world that one either backed Israel on this or stood for nothing.

Europe, host of the Nazis' extermination of 6 million Jews, followed Biden's lead, one hopes without too much moral difficulty. In America, Republicans and the vast majority of Democrats comprehended the obvious: If Israel cannot stop Hamas from slaughtering Israelis, then Hamas will continue to slaughter Israelis. Pretty simple.

Some in the president's party either do not grasp the obvious or are not excessively bothered by it, any more than they have been excessively bothered by the smaller bore versions of the same thing that have been happening for the last 20 years preceding this month's murder spree: tens of thousands of rockets fired by Hamas while hiding behind Palestinian innocents in order to kill Israeli innocents. The so-called Squad, Democratic Socialists of America and comfortable faculty and students on America's most fashionable campuses have been perfectly down with this for years, and nothing about this latest massacre moves the moral needle for them a centimeter.

The embrace by some of Hamas' Slaughter Inc. isn't merely tough to dislodge. It is impossible. When Palestinian Islamic Jihad fired a rocket from Gaza intended to kill Israelis, but that instead killed Palestinians in a Gaza hospital, Reps. Rashida Tlaib and Ilhan Omar and others bitterly denounced Israel for "targeting" the hospital. No matter that every intelligence service and independent analyst evaluating this concluded that Israel was innocent and Palestinian Jihad to blame. As always, facts present no obstacle: Tlaib, Omar and the usual sources in Hamas' corner continue a thoroughly dishonest refrain and, to boot, condemn Biden for declining to buy the hogwash they enthusiastically buy — and peddle.

To the president's great credit, he is not buying. And he is not pretending to do so.

Tools' Paradise: Academia Says It's Down with Mass Slaughter

October 31, 2023

As of this past weekend, Israel's Institute of Forensic Medicine reported that of the 1,400 Israelis slaughtered on Oct. 7 by Hamas gunmen shouting "God is great!", 400 bodies still could not be identified. That is because all that is left of them are fragments, if that, once part of the bodies of 400 different human beings. And that, in turn, is because the 2,500 Hamas "militants" wielding automatic rifles — built to shred flesh deliberately — methodically blew as many of those 1,400 souls to pieces as they could, tying families together and then burning them alive, decapitating and dismembering people and then continuing the process after their victims stopped breathing. Recordings recovered after the massacre showed them rejoicing, one calling his parents to brag about how many Jews he had killed. His father blessed him, saying: "God protect you."

So, what the Israelis continue to find are body parts, the humans with which those parts were once associated blown up or burned beyond recognition, such that extracting and examining DNA is impossible.

And this, of course, doesn't count the 5,800 Israelis who, maimed and mutilated on Oct. 7, are still alive. It doesn't count the 230 people — the elderly, the disabled, the frail, the wounded, the helpless, children and babies, all terrified — abducted at gunpoint and held in Hamas' tunnels, constructed under hospitals, homes and mosques so that Israel is constrained from going after them. And it doesn't count the rest of Israel's families, virtually all of whom know someone killed, maimed or held hostage by Hamas.

While Israelis were being blown or burned to unrecognizable pieces by a joyful Hamas, here in America the academic year had barely begun at colleges and universities where students pay upwards of $100,000 annually for the privilege of studying the humanities and liberal values. Comfortable faculty members were returning to the familiar, pleasant routine of attending to personal jealousies and intradepartmental rivalries. Students resumed arguing on social media about just how egregiously the disturbing prospect of knowing that a speaker had been invited to campus prepared to express a view contrary to their own would constitute a violation of their safe spaces. News that 1,400 Israelis — including many hundreds their own age — had been butchered to death and 5,800 more maimed barely piqued their interest. After all, these were Israelis — and whether Israelis were even entitled to live life free of being butchered was politically debatable.

As for the 230 souls who have been kidnapped and are forcibly held in dank Hamas tunnels, either near-dead or scared to death, among faculty members and students who fancy themselves "progressive," this has elicited a Big Yawn.

But when Israel, like any other country not only on the planet but in the history of the planet, determined that of course this could neither be tolerated nor permitted to recur, the ears of faculty and students perked up. And not only perked up. Promptly and self-confidently, they assessed that the outrage was not Hamas' slaughter of Israelis, but Israel's determination not to permit the slaughter to happen again.

So, it is now a "thing" for pious defenders of "free speech" in all contexts other than those involving Israel to rip down posters with pictures of kidnapped Israelis held in captivity, posted so that we can see their faces and hold them in our hearts.

On innumerable American campuses, in settings in which students are charged to learn that humans are to be respected, not massacred, vigils are held to honor as "martyrs" those who pulverized Israeli children — and boasted about it.

Faculty members compete to ingratiate themselves with pro-Hamas students by proclaiming themselves "exhilarated" by the killings, and "in solidarity" with the murders as acts of "resistance." Students cheer on the murders as contributions to the "cleaning" of Israel. Professors at Columbia University inform us that the slaughter of Jews demands "contextualization."

Here's where we are. When it comes to the slaughter of Jews, many in American academia are down with it. But ask them if they're antisemites?

Of course not.

Bit of Blackmail: The Hamas Lobby Tells Biden to Bend, or Else

November 7, 2023

In the stiff competition to produce the least credible members of Congress, the Republican Party's leading entrants are Reps. George Santos and Marjorie Taylor Greene, and the Democrats' top contender has to be Rep. Rashida Tlaib. The Michigan congresswoman has worked tirelessly to burnish her reputation for mendacity, doing so on a nearly 24/7 basis since Oct. 7, when several thousand Hamas gunmen invaded Israeli communities and slaughtered 1,400 civilians in their homes and while they were at a music festival, blowing some to pieces and burning others alive.

When Palestinian Islamic Jihad fired a rocket from Gaza hoping to murder Israeli civilians and instead hit a Gazan hospital, Tlaib dutifully and angrily repeated Hamas' falsehood that Israel was to blame, and continued to repeat the false claim even after international intelligence agencies and a battery of independent experts confirmed that what Hamas and Tlaib were claiming was actually a lie. Tlaib doesn't merely defend Hamas' "Killing Israelis is perfectly fine" ideology. She embraces it full-throatedly, confident, as well she should be, that a vocal segment of America's hard Left will back her all the way.

So, it was unsurprising that Tlaib would swiftly turn on President Joe Biden, who has forcefully affirmed what ought to be the obvious takeaway from Oct. 7: Israel has not only the moral right but the moral obligation not just to defend itself, but to make sure that Hamas, which has been slaughtering Israelis for years, cannot do so anymore. Tlaib and others who ardently desire that Israel accede to its own elimination have threatened Biden that if he doesn't simply sacrifice Israel to the far Left's nuzzling of Hamas, they will withhold their support from him in next year's rematch with former President Donald Trump. "Joe Biden supports the genocide of the Palestinian people," posted Tlaib a few days ago, displaying her customary penchant for sane discourse. And if Biden doesn't force Israel to stop defending itself from Hamas' death grip — a death grip that consigns Israelis and Palestinians alike to constant danger — then "don't count on us in 2024."

This is the American Left's version of taking hostages, and they are perfectly happy to take America hostage. If this means that Trump is returned to the Oval Office, so be it. As for the consequences to America of another Trump presidency, Tlaib and company have two words for America: drop dead.

At the same time that the far Left threatens to sit on its hands next year, jeopardizing Biden's reelection from one end, its embrace of butchery as "resistance" makes it look maniacal to most of America, and by extension makes the Democrats look too weak to be trusted to govern. The footage over the weekend of mobs of pro-Hamas demonstrators scaling the White House fence, smearing red paint all over the place and shouting "Allahu Akbar!" plays well among the Democratic Socialists of America and the "Where-is-the-Ayatollah-Khomeini-Now-That-We-Need-Him Society." It doesn't play well in America's heartland, and one imagines that GOP ad-makers are already cutting ads seeking to label Democrats as the party of Hamas.

It hasn't taken Republicans long to point out that the families of slaughtered Israelis have Iranian cash to thank for their losses. And Iran has the Obama administration to thank for tens of billions of dollars handed over to it courtesy of a nuclear deal that its critics warned would end up funding Hamas and Hezbollah. The former president, whose musings about the current conflict have been somewhere between muddled and meaningless, belittled those who worried about this as "neo-cons" and even unpatriotic. It's looking a good deal as though Obama was wrong about this, and that those whom he mocked and marginalized deserved to be taken seriously rather than haughtily dismissed. Acceding to the supporters of Iran's proxy in Gaza now is an invitation to undo the Biden administration's strong record of standing up to killers.

Put simply, Tlaib and crowd seek to hold up Biden at political gunpoint. If that means that they hold up America at gunpoint as well, that's fine with them.

See No Evil: On American Campuses, It's Tiki Torch Time

November 14, 2023

Lexington, Massachusetts, is a peaceful town, famous for being an ideal place to raise children. Young couples move there from everywhere so that their children can attend its public schools, which in disproportionate numbers send students to the finest universities in the land. Lexington has a robust library serving its hypereducated residents, and its own symphony. It is a community of bake sales and charity drives and back-to-school nights.

A walk into Lexington Center one recent morning revealed that heart-wrenching posters had been pasted onto a window of a vacant store. They said "Kidnapped," and featured pictures of the Israeli babies, toddlers, children, elderly and disabled, including Holocaust survivors, who had been brutalized by Hamas gunmen on Oct. 7, and then rammed — maimed, raped, bleeding, terrified — onto the backs of trucks and abducted into Gaza. These were the "lucky" ones, who were not butchered to death, blown to pieces or burned to dust by 3,000 Hamas killers who invaded Israel for the purpose of slaughtering as many Israelis as they could.

Each "kidnapped" poster had a picture of an innocent soul who is now held at gunpoint in underground Hamas tunnels. Any of them who manages to survive will live the rest of their lives as a human shell. It's hard to believe that anyone could fail to feel for them or to respect the idea of keeping them in the hearts of decent people.

Believe it.

By the next morning, the posters had been ripped down.

The ripping down of the posters of kidnapped Israelis by the grinning, the leering, the amped up and the cruel has become not just a fad but a craze among those who fancy themselves "progressive" while they cheer on anti-Jewish hate, or outright engage in it.

Ground zero for hatred-posing-as-progressivism is academia, where Jewish students and others who are disgusted by the Hamas massacre of Israelis have found themselves assaulted, bullied, surrounded, forced to run gauntlets of students screaming for the eradication of the Jewish homeland or otherwise harassed while faculty members and their fellow students stay silent, or urge it on.

At the University of Pennsylvania, one student speaker invoked the "joyful" images of beheaded and dismembered Israelis from the "glorious October 7th," and encouraged her audience to "bring it to the streets." Observed Rep. Ritchie Torres of New York, "This is not a patient at a psychiatric hospital. This is a student at an Ivy League institution."

At Harvard, a group of law and divinity students surrounded a Jewish student walking alone and attacked him. At Cornell, where a professor pronounced himself "exhilarated" by Hamas' massacre, a student made death threats against Jewish students. At Cooper Union, Jewish students had to hide in a library while anti-Israel protestors violently pounded on the door. At Tufts University, one student group issued a statement praising the "creativity" of Hamas' various methods utilized in hacking, burning and shredding Israelis to death. At Yale University, a student group hailed Hamas' slaughter, praising the group for "making history this Saturday morning."

This is intended to destroy the emotional well-being of Jewish students. And it's working. "We want to be able to go to class," one Jewish Tufts student told a reporter. "We want to (go around campus) without having somebody actively chanting for our demise."

Those holding themselves out as progressives now closely resemble the racists marching at the "Unite the Right" rally in Charlottesville, Virginia, in 2017. Those protesters were "expressing" themselves, too, marching against the removal of a statue of Confederate Gen. Robert E. Lee. They held tiki torches aloft as they chanted white supremacist slogans, the torches intended to intimidate.

Progressives who denounced the hate festival at Charlottesville are now staging hate festivals of their own. Their victims are Jews. What would never be OK if the victims were others is perfectly OK now.

They believe they are really progressives. That's what they tell themselves and each other they are. But what they really are is the new tiki torch carriers. And that is how history will remember them.

No Surrender: Lacking Other Options, Israel Needs to Finish the Job

November 21, 2023

In June 2006, U.S. Sen. Dick Durbin, D-Ill., was asked what the Democrats' plan was for addressing the threat posed by Iran, even then recognized by the international community as the world's foremost state sponsor of terrorism. "I really don't know," Durbin sighed. "With any luck Israel will take care of it, and then we can all blame Israel."

The parlor game played in Western capitals of looking privately to Israel to do necessary things and then publicly blaming it for doing so has come recently to mind, as some recite how important it is that Hamas be defeated while criticizing Israel for attempting the difficult job of defeating it. The European Parliament recently voted 500 to 21 in support of a resolution affirming "that the terrorist organization Hamas needs to be eliminated." Last week the European Union's foreign policy chief, Josep Borrell, told a Bahrain conference "Hamas cannot be in control anymore."

This, of course, is so obvious that Capt. Obvious himself would be embarrassed to say it. But here's the thing: who's going to eliminate Hamas? Who's going to ensure that Hamas isn't in control of Gaza anymore?

The answer is also obvious: it is either going to be Israel or it is going to be nobody. And with all due respect to the pablum-dispensers who go on television to mouth the mantra that "Of course, Israel has the right to defend itself, but...", Hamas will in fact remain in control of Gaza and will continue to crush Palestinians and murder Israelis unless Israel finishes the job it has started. Going on MSNBC and offering up the meaningless drivel that "Israel is going to have to find a way to eliminate Hamas that doesn't harm civilians" is the intellectual equivalent of peddling cotton candy, all fluff and no substance.

The political attacks on Israel may be inane, but there is so much inanity that it's sometimes hard to keep track of it all. One particularly vapid formulation in vogue in recent days and increasingly common among Democratic representatives fearful of being primaried from the Left next year is that there should be a ceasefire and Hamas should be gone from Gaza. It sounds great, and it is also patently ridiculous. How, precisely, is Hamas to be removed if there is a ceasefire?

Answer: It can't be, and it won't be. It takes no Einstein to comprehend that a ceasefire is a license to Hamas to reconstitute, as it has before, to continue repressing Palestinians and to continue murdering Israelis. So, you can have a ceasefire, or you can remove Hamas, but you can't have both, and those calling for both do a very fine job of looking witless.

Then there's the line that Israel should back down because otherwise it will generate "more hate." Really? On Oct. 7 Hamas sent 3,000 murderers into Israel and slaughtered 1,200 Israeli innocents, gleefully decapitating, dismembering, burning, mutilating, shredding and raping human beings while kidnapping 240 others and bringing them back into Gaza. There, Gazans paraded disfigured Israeli bodies around the street and jubilantly celebrated en masse. Is the argument that if Israel tries to prevent this from recurring, it may make Gazans hateful?

That leaves the argument that "the number of civilian deaths is unacceptable." But what exactly does that mean? Every civilian death is "unacceptable." No civilian death is "acceptable." But where Hamas purposefully operates from sophisticated tunnels underneath hospitals, mosques, apartments and schools, and from within those structures, there simply is no way of attacking Hamas without killing civilians, no matter how careful Israel is — because that, giving its middle finger to the civilized world, is how Hamas functions. If Israel's critics have some magic method of eliminating Hamas, or even protecting Israelis from another mass slaughter, without harming civilians, those critics should by all means share their wisdom with the Israel Defense Forces posthaste.

In the meantime, a ceasefire with Hamas means capitulation to Hamas. Which means that Israel has no other choice but to finish the job it has started.

The Truman Show: Another Uncool President Makes His Mark

November 28, 2023

On Dec. 26, 1972, hours after Harry Truman's death, Senator-elect Joseph Biden sent Truman's widow a condolence telegram. The 33rd American president, Biden wrote, had proved a historic leader, one who had "made his mark" for being "purposeful, smart and tough."

Truman had been bitterly attacked by Democrats and Republicans alike, belittled for his charisma-deficit and dull persona. Before the word "cool" entered our lexicon, Truman was uncool personified. Yet historians regularly rate Truman as among our finest presidents. C-SPAN's surveys of presidential historians consistently rank him as either our fifth or sixth greatest leader.

A half-century after Truman's passing, with a record of achievement that by rights should earn him considerable credit, President Joe Biden is sold short in the same way Truman was. The biggest knocks on Biden are that he is 81, has an arthritic spine and as a child had a stutter. In a TikTok world, his crime appears to be that he is all substance and no flash — all cattle, to reverse the old saying, and no hat. But just as he has skillfully led America out of COVID-19 and revitalized an economy that under his predecessor had bordered on implosion, Biden's management of multiple simultaneous global crises is evidence that the words he used to describe Truman — "purposeful, smart and tough" — can be said about him — and will be.

Thrust suddenly into a presidency for which he seemed ill-equipped, Truman implemented a strategy for containing the Soviet Union's threat to the West, furnishing crucial military, economic and political reinforcement to democracies that were profoundly at risk. To do so, Truman was required to fend off criticism from every direction, including from Democrats.

Biden was anything but ill-equipped to become president, but he has navigated challenges no less daunting than those faced by Truman. These have included deep, bitter divisions at home; the rise of dangerous domestic antidemocracy forces; an economy placed on the brink by COVID-19; and a transatlantic alliance severely weakened by his predecessor. He nevertheless forged an international coalition that has enabled Ukraine to repel Russia's initial invasion and hold Putin's armies at bay.

Biden has been similarly skillful in the wake of the Oct. 7 mass slaughter of Israelis by Hamas, a genocidal ISIS clone funded by Iran. In standing up for Israel he has had to stand up to Arab governments that, while privately hoping for Israel to eradicate Hamas once and for all, are obliged by a jihadist Arab street to blame Israel for a war it did not start. He also has had to stand up to the Democrats' left wing, which has its share of wing nuts, and to do so at a time when young voters who don't know the Gaza Strip from the Louisiana Purchase are telling pollsters that Biden's stand against mass slaughterers will actually cost him their support. This is the sort of Alice-in-Wonderland-itis with which the president has to cope.

The West is frankly fortunate that Joe Biden is president now and not Barack Obama. Certain that a policy of deterring malign state and non-state actors was the domain of "neoconservatives" and just passe, Obama projected American weakness, encouraging those actors to conclude that they could engage in aggression without consequences.

In 2013, after declaring that Syria's use of chemical weapons would be a "red line" that Syria dare not cross, Obama retreated when Syria crossed it.

In 2014, when Vladimir Putin invaded and occupied Crimea, Obama looked the other way, letting it stand.

In 2015, determined, and seemingly desperate, to conclude a nuclear deal with Iran that handed Tehran over $100 billion with which to fund Hamas, Hezbollah and the Houthis and repress Iranian democracy movements, Obama mocked those who argued we would live to regret it.

We have now lived to regret it. And it is Biden who has had to deal with it all, including Iranian support for Putin's war on Ukraine. In a season of counting blessings, one of them is that there is someone in the Oval Office who may be uncool but knows what he's doing.

Masks Off: The Hamas Defense Forces Show the Unmistakable Bigotry on the Left

December 5, 2023

In the eight weeks since 3,000 Hamas terrorists invaded Israel and slaughtered 1,200 Israelis and mutilated 5,800 others, it's become clear that Hamas' purpose was not merely genocidal. As interrogated Hamas gunmen have admitted, and as video from the gunmen themselves demonstrates, Hamas had the specific purpose of raping Israeli women before killing them, and doing it en masse.

And it went about it gleefully. Here is what one survivor of the music festival at which Hamas murdered hundreds of young Israelis recounted. "I saw this beautiful woman with the face of an angel and eight or 10 of the fighters beating and raping her," he says. "She was screaming 'Stop it! — already I'm going to die anyway from what you are doing, just kill me!' When they finished, they were laughing and the last one shot her in the head."

One might hope that progressives, especially feminists, who rightly unequivocally condemn sexual violence on an individual basis would do so when it is inflicted in large numbers. But one would be disappointed. When it came to Israeli women raped on Oct. 7, feminist leaders and organizations have either mumbled meaningless platitudes about how sexual violence is never favored or stayed silent. United Nations agencies and human rights organizations have remained mum. Pressed by CNN's Dana Bash on why she and her fellow progressives have had little to say about Hamas' abomination, Rep. Pramila Jayapal, D-Wash., backpedaled, changed the subject and then offered the inane deflection that "we have to be balanced" — whatever that means.

"Balanced" about mass rape? "I knew it wouldn't take weeks for the denial to begin," says Michal Cotler-Wunsh, the human rights lawyer appointed as Israel's special envoy to combat antisemitism, "but days."

She was right. The unmistakable fact is that when it came to slaughtered Jews, maimed Jews, raped Jews and kidnapped Jews, self-professed progressives did not waste any time in jettisoning progressive values. Never mind that Hamas' express raison d'etre is genocide, genocide is what Hamas intended on Oct. 7, and genocide is what Hamas' leaders vow to attempt again and again; it is actually Israel that is guilty of genocide, progressives claim, for trying to prevent themselves from being the victims of genocide.

"So many masks were removed on 10/7," says Cotler-Wunsh. Preeminent among them is the profession that when progressives condemned murder, rape and kidnapping of innocents, it was a condemnation that would apply as well to the murder, rape and kidnapping of Jews. But to the contrary, many who are proud to call themselves progressives, who cannot locate the Gaza Strip on a map, who know nothing about Hamas and do not feel they need to, have enlisted wholesale in the Hamas Defense Forces. This would be laughable if it were funny. As Cotler-Wunsh notes, far from being "progressive," Hamas is guilty of "the most regressive and barbaric savagery," and it takes no Ivy League education to see it.

"Hamas knew that there would be professors who would be exhilarated" at the slaughter of Israelis, says Cotler-Wunsh. And that is so even though Hamas' genocidal sadism was worse even than that of the Nazis. "As opposed to the Nazis that hid their war crimes and their crimes against humanity," she says, "these people actually livestreamed them." The video of Israeli mothers begging for their children's lives, the footage of the decapitation and the dismembering, the graphic images of families bound together and burned — throngs of people on the Left have done whatever intellectual gyrations they deemed necessary to blame the victims, or at least to avoid blaming the victimizers.

"This is a moment of reckoning," Israel's special envoy to combat antisemitism said on a recent trip to the U.S., unbowed and undiscouraged. "Where I draw the most hope is from regular Americans, maybe Americans who didn't go to elite colleges, maybe Americans who didn't go to college at all." A lot is riding on regular Americans right about now — not only the survival of Israel but the survival of our own country as we know it.

Ain't Budging: Attacked from The Left on Israel, Biden Stands His Ground

December 12, 2023

Taking the podium at an event in Boston last Tuesday, President Joe Biden wasted no time taking aim at a leading progressive's hemming and hawing when asked to condemn Hamas' mass rape of Israeli women on Oct. 7. Two days earlier, Democratic Rep. Pramila Jayapal had tried to duck journalist Dana Bash's questioning about Hamas' atrocities, which included rapes so violent that they broke women's pelvic bones before Hamas gunmen shot their victims in the genitals and the head.

Biden summoned reporters into the closed session precisely in order to broadcast his repudiation of Jayapal to the world. "Over the past weeks," he began, "survivors and witnesses of the attacks have shared the horrific accounts of unimaginable cruelty. Reports of women raped — repeatedly raped — and their bodies mutilated while still alive, of women's corpses being desecrated, Hamas' terrorists inflicting as much pain and suffering on women and girls as possible and then murdering them. It's appalling."

Calling out Jayapal while ostentatiously not mentioning her, Biden continued: "It's on all of us to forcefully condemn the sexual violence of Hamas terrorists without equivocation." Just to punctuate who and what he was talking about, Biden repeated: "Without equivocation, without exception," before turning to other subjects, point made.

For all of the facile derision of Biden that abounds, the president has repeatedly shown that he can be pretty steely. The master class he has put on since Hamas' October invasion of Israel has triggered the trigger-happy anti-Israel regulars on the Left to no end.

On Friday evening, the Biden administration stood alone in the Security Council, vetoing a resolution calling for a "ceasefire" in Gaza, a fine-sounding idea which would simply guarantee Hamas' ability to massacre Israelis again, which its leadership has pledged to do. Calls for a ceasefire are as mindless as they are fashionable. The proof, if any were necessary, is that Hamas, whose murderous rampage violated a ceasefire already in place, is demanding one. The Left's call for "Ceasefire Now!" so that a "just and peaceful solution" can be reached is sweet inanity, appealing to the unthinking and especially to those who wouldn't be greatly troubled if Israel disappeared.

But inanity is what Biden faces from a vocal slice of his party, and with some threatening political retaliation against him if he doesn't bend their way, he has politely told them "No." In response to allegations that Israel, which hardly wished to have 1,200 of its citizens slaughtered by a genocidal Hamas regime committed to the genocide of Jews, was actually the party guilty of genocide, administration spokesmen have repeatedly and forcefully snapped that this is nonsense.

Last week, the head of the Council on American-Islamic Relations (CAIR), an organization with long documented links to Hamas but long indulged by the media, praised the Oct. 7 murder of Israelis. "We condemn these shocking antisemitic statements in the strongest terms," responded a spokesman for the White House, which then removed CAIR's name from an official listing of organizations involved in a White House effort to combat hatred.

Shortly after three university presidents called to testify in Congress about the rampant intimidation of Jewish students on their campuses refused to state that calls for the genocide of Jews violated their institutions' policies, second gentleman Doug Emhoff took the opportunity at a White House ceremony to take them to task. These leaders were, Emhoff said, "unable to denounce calling for the genocide of Jews as antisemitic." They were smugly evasive, their evasions indicative of the poison indulged on their campuses and others, and the Biden administration did not simply let it go. "The lack of moral clarity is unacceptable," Emhoff said.

Some on the Left, addicted to vapid rhetoric which, if adopted, would hand Hamas a victory that would grievously harm Israelis and Palestinians alike, keep hurling political fastballs at Biden's head. They hope to pressure him into leaving Israel on its own in what amounts to a fight for more than just Israel. In a display of leadership that history will remember, the president has refused to be brushed back.

Immunity Disorder: The Man Who Would Be King Comes Out and Says So

December 19, 2023

"There's a recklessness in the air in America" was the elegant yet apt way ABC News journalist Terry Moran put it on Friday evening. Moran made the observation in the context of Rudy Giuliani's misbegotten belief that he could egregiously defame two Georgia poll workers and get away with it. He didn't. The "Say Anything" ethos Giuliani appears to have absorbed from former President Donald Trump backfired spectacularly on New York's former mayor, who was hit by a defamation verdict against him of $148 million, and that's a whole lot of hair dye.

That recklessness, that disregard for either truth or consequences, afflicts both sides of the political divide. A Harvard/Harris poll released last weekend showed that a majority of Americans aged 18-24 are sufficiently untethered to tell pollsters that it would be good and just for Hamas, an internationally acknowledged terrorist organization that slaughtered 1,200 Israelis in cold blood on Oct. 7, to displace the state of Israel. That this cohort receives its "information" from TikTok and thinks the Gaza Strip is in downtown Las Vegas is little consolation. Left and right, across the country, recklessness and ignorance have combined to form a pincer, degrading the threads of America's democratic fabric and degrading American democracy itself.

Trump has been surpassingly shrewd about America's descent and bold about exploiting it. He believes that he can assert the right to absolute power without losing votes and that, indeed, presenting as The American Strongman will actually help him regain the Oval Office. And given the recent polling showing him leading President Joe Biden, he may be right.

The Constitution, Trump declared while president on July 19, 2019, "allows me to do what I want." He doubled down on this days later. "I have an Article 2 (of the Constitution) right where I have the right to do whatever I want as president." Last year he proclaimed that the growing evidence that he committed crimes as president "allows for the termination of all rules, regulations and articles, even those found in the Constitution." Last week, offered the opportunity by Fox host and acolyte Sean Hannity to deny that he would abuse his power if he regained the White House, Trump pointedly declined. "Except for day one," he replied.

Trump has formalized his position that he was and will be above all laws applicable to lesser Americans in the criminal proceeding against him in Washington, D.C., where he has been indicted for defrauding the United States and attempting to stage an illegal coup d'etat. He maintains that he is immune from prosecution for any crimes he committed as president because, well, he was president when he committed them.

Federal judge Tanya Chutkan, who is presiding over Trump's case, has rejected Trump's immunity defense. Trump "contends that the Constitution grants him 'absolute immunity from criminal prosecution for actions performed within the outer perimeter of his official responsibility,'" Chutkan wrote in her decision. "The Constitution's text, structure and history do not support that contention. No court — or any other branch of government — has ever accepted it. (Being president) does not confer a lifelong 'get-out-of-jail-free pass.'"

Trump has appealed her decision, which he hopes will delay his criminal trial until after next year's election. Special Counsel Jack Smith has countered by asking the Supreme Court to decide whether Trump is beyond the rule of law, and to do so on an expedited basis.

In any other period of American history, a former president would be too embarrassed to claim that he was immune from criminal prosecution for crimes committed while president and to force a federal judge to cite the "widely acknowledged contrast between the President and a king." But in any other period, a twice-impeached former president facing 91 separate criminal charges in four criminal indictments would not have a 50-50 chance of being returned to the presidency.

There's a recklessness in the air in America, just as Terry Moran says. It has eroded our common sense, our fealty to facts, our capacity to separate truth from chaff. And, alarmingly, where that recklessness leads is anyone's guess.

Tunnel Vision: Congress Prepares to Investigate Taxpayer Subsidies of Hamas

December 26, 2023

It emerged over the weekend that the House Foreign Affairs Committee plans to investigate the use of American taxpayers' dollars to fund the Murder, Inc. that is Hamas. With the revelations that billions of donor dollars that were supposed to be used for humanitarian aid for Gazans have instead been diverted to construct a network of terror tunnels spanning several hundred miles, it's clear that such an investigation is long overdue. And while they complain with justification that the last year in Congress has been utterly dysfunctional, Democrats ought to join the Republicans who are initiating the investigation and make it a fully bipartisan one.

When it comes to the Mideast, U.N. agencies have modeled moral rot for decades, so investigating the U.N. looking for corruption and the abetting of terror is shooting fish in a barrel. The Committee intends to focus on UNRWA, the United Nations Relief and Works Agency, which is in charge of aiding Palestinian refugees in Gaza. In point of fact, there aren't actually any Palestinian refugees in Gaza as the word "refugee" is commonly understood. Gaza's population consists of those whose families have lived there since time immemorial, as well as the descendants of Palestinians who moved to Gaza 75 years ago to escape the fighting that followed five Arab nations' invasion of Israel in 1948 for the purpose of annihilating it.

Decade after decade, the impoverished residents of Gaza have been abandoned by petrodollar-flush Arab countries that declined to help them, even as Israel was absorbing 850,000 Jewish refugees from the Arab countries that expelled them starting in 1948. Gazans sat mired in dreadful poverty before 1948, and the same between 1948 and 1967, when they were administered by Egypt. They sat mired in poverty after 1967, when Arab countries commenced another war against Israel, ending with Gaza under Israeli control. When Israel forced 11,000 of its citizens to leave Gaza in 2005 in order to facilitate an independent Palestinian state linked to the West Bank, Hamas violently torpedoed that idea, seizing control of Gaza and pledging that it would never permit Israel to exist within any borders, period.

UNRWA is a target-rich subject for a congressional investigation if ever there were one. Americans have contributed many hundreds of millions of dollars to the billions that have been forked over to UNRWA for humanitarian aid, only to have those billions ripped off by Hamas — or handed to it. Hamas leaders have literally taken the money and ran, absconding with several billions to lavish residences in Qatar. Another 2 to 4 billion dollars has been used by Hamas to construct those tunnels, in which Hamas gunmen hide while Gazans starve.

The tunnels are located under and next to UNRWA schools, hospitals and community centers — which are used not only to store Hamas rockets but to fire them at Israeli civilians. UNRWA spokesmen claim that this is all news to them — just like the summer camps UNRWA runs which, according to the monitor group U.N. Watch, are used to "regularly call to murder Jews, glorify terrorism, encourage martyrdom (and) incite anti-Semitism." Any post-Hamas scenario in Gaza will have to include the dismantling of UNRWA and its replacement with an agency that actually helps Gazans and promotes peace.

While the Committee is at it, it can investigate Qatar. "For more than a decade," writes former national security official Richard Goldberg in Commentary Magazine, "Qatar pumped hundreds of millions of dollars into Hamas on the promise that it would moderate the group. That was a scam. Hamas used the money to build the terror tunnel networks we see today. The blood of 5,000 Israeli dead and wounded, including American citizens, is on Qatar as much as Iran." The Committee's spotlight on Qatar will not spread holiday cheer to American universities, many of which eagerly solicit and happily accept billions in Qatari donations — and are pleased to convey their appreciation.

This is an investigation not only worthy, but critical. Democrats should promptly serve notice that they stand shoulder to shoulder with their Republican colleagues in conducting it.

Genocide Jujitsu: The Hamas Lobby Flips the Facts

January 2, 2024

Nearly 80 years after the defeat of Nazi Germany, Adolf Hitler's Minister of Public Enlightenment and Propaganda remains the go-to source for how-to advice on large-scale con-artistry. "The most brilliant propagandist technique will yield no success unless one fundamental principle is borne in mind constantly," Joseph Goebbels reportedly instructed. "It must confine itself to a few points and repeat them over and over."

In other words: Keep it simple, stupid.

This rule was meant to work in tandem with another cynical Goebbels dictum: People are naturally susceptible to confident-sounding demagoguery. "You can't change the masses," Goebbels once said. "They will always be the same: dumb, gluttonous and forgetful."

This, at least, is what those who have always wanted Israel to disappear have always hoped, and since Oct. 7 they have channeled Goebbels not only with vigor but with a vengeance. On that day, Hamas, an enterprise whose very raison d'etre is the elimination of Jews, sent thousands of fighters into Israel for the purpose of slaughtering as many Jews as possible, succeeded in slaughtering or mutilating about 5,800 of them and even now pledges to return again and again to finish "the job" as best they can. "Genocide" is the deliberate killing of a large number of people from a particular nation or ethnic group with the aim of destroying that nation or group. Genocidal is what Hamas is, and genocide is what Hamas does.

But Israel doesn't merely face 40,000 or so well-trained and highly motivated (to put it mildly) Hamas slaughterers a few kilometers away in Gaza, and Hezbollah's 150,000 missiles on Israel's northern border, and now Yemen's similarly inclined Houthis launching rockets at it. All are funded by Iran, likewise resolved to annihilate Israel.

It also faces an international anti-Israel public relations war it has no capacity to win. Those who want Israel gone have many more platforms, many more voices and many more resources than Israel can ever dream of. And in America, they benefit from billions of petrodollars that have been strategically disbursed by Qatar, Saudi Arabia, Kuwait and other abhorrent nations to colleges and universities, think tanks and advocacy groups in order to buy allyship when events like Hamas' invasion of Israel take place and retaliation inevitably ensues.

Israel's enemies — and there are plenty of them — have a message so ingenious, so mendacious, that it would make Goebbels himself exclaim "Jawohl!" It is that Israel, which was after all the victim of attempted genocide by those sworn to genocide on Oct. 7, is actually the party guilty of genocide — for attempting to make sure that it does not become the victim of attempted genocide again, or at least anytime too soon. One might imagine that those genuinely concerned about genocide would take a moment's notice of what Hamas actually did on Oct. 7 and pledges to continue doing: blowing families to pieces, tying families up and burning them to death, riddling children with bullets, decapitating and dismembering innocent souls and raping women en masse, while laughing, gloating and boasting about it.

But no.

Outside restaurants owned by Jews, and where people are trying simply to celebrate Christmas, and in public squares, comes this cry from those who don't know what the facts are or know but couldn't care less: "Fill-in-the-blank, fill-in-the-blank, you can't hide, we charge you with genocide!" The propaganda is genius itself: Those who were the victims of attempted genocide are the ones guilty of it.

And, if the polls are accurate it works, at least among younger Americans. After all, it wasn't only Goebbels who understood how easily some people can be conned. "The bigger the humbug," said P.T. Barnum, until recently regarded as the most successful con artist in American history, "the better the people will like it." The Hamas lobby, which hurls the epithet "genocide" at a country that did not seek Oct. 7 but rather was shocked and brutalized by it, is nothing if not clever about humbug.

Dead Center: On America's Right and on Its Left, a Certain Madness

January 9, 2024

"Things fall apart, the center cannot hold," wrote Irish poet William Butler Yeats in 1919 as he contemplated the post-war world with dread. For anyone on the lookout for evidence that America's political center has disintegrated, 2023 was a banner year, with a bumper crop of proof that a certain madness has enveloped both the right and the left, driving what remained of the center underground.

A new Washington Post poll reflects that 36% of Americans believe that President Joe Biden assumed office thanks to an "illegitimate" election. That figure has actually increased since 2021, even as it has gone from merely crystal clear to irrefutable that Donald Trump's claim that he won the 2020 election has always been an utter fraud. Roughly half of Americans are prepared to once again make the fraud who is selling that fraud the most powerful person on the planet, nuclear codes and all.

The left has provided plenty of evidence that it has also gone mad. When several thousand genocidal jihadists invaded a sovereign country and slaughtered 1,200 Israelis at a music festival or in their bedrooms, blowing innocents to pieces, burning them to death, decapitating, dismembering and raping them as they shouted "Allahu Akbar," self-professed "progressives" decided that defending them was trendy. Feminists, social justice groups, human rights advocates, students and faculty chose silence, tortured justifications or outright praise for the murderers over solidarity with the victims. Accustomed to ascribing moral rot to MAGA World, the left exemplified it.

Enter the scandal that forced the resignation of Harvard University's president, Claudine Gay, a scandal entirely of her own making. Despite her best efforts to change the subject, Gay's resignation was not at root the fault of those on the right who doubtless wanted her gone in order to prove a point, but hers alone.

Summoned by a Republican-controlled congressional committee investigating various universities' negligence in addressing antisemitism on their campuses that has turned quite ugly, Gay declined several direct invitations to simply agree that calls for the genocide of Jews violated

Harvard's code of conduct. She declined to do so not because she was confused, ill-prepared or unintelligent, but because she is ambivalent not only about whether such calls do violate Harvard's code of conduct but whether they should.

But what did her in ultimately was her serial plagiarism or, as Harvard's Board put it in Orwellian fashion, "examples of duplicative language without appropriate attribution." But for the disclosures that she had repeatedly cheated — not once, not twice, not even three times, but over and over, by plagiarizing, or stealing others' work, before Harvard decided to make her president of the world's foremost institution of higher education, it looked as though Gay would remain in office. This kind of conduct gets students expelled from schools all over the country. President Gay apparently believed she could cheat without consequence — because that was indeed her experience.

Gay wasted no time blaming others for having the nerve to uncover what she had managed to keep hidden, playing the victim immediately and loudly. In a New York Times op-ed published the day after she resigned, Gay reframed the disclosures of her own dishonesty as an attack on — wait for it — civic virtue. "This was merely a single skirmish in a broader war to unravel public faith in pillars of American society," she actually wrote, knowing that half of America would nod their heads at the idea that the whole affair was the fault of a vast right-wing conspiracy. "Campaigns of this kind often start with attacks on education and expertise, because these are the tools that best equip communities to see through propaganda."

This was unadulterated chutzpah, since Gay's conduct has undermined public faith in one of our society's pillars — higher education in general, and Harvard in particular. But it was chutzpah that was widely swallowed whole. It is another sign that in an America comprised of two teams — my team against your team — the center has all but disappeared.

Tick Tock: As the Hostages' Lives Count Down, Hamas Has Reason to Smile

January 16, 2024

While Israeli and American hostages sit, bloody and terrified, chained, bound and caged in underground dungeons in Gaza, their kidnappers were given yet more encouragement last week. The latest helping hand to Hamas was extended by the government of South Africa, a staunch Hamas ally, which has filed a charge in the International Court of Justice accusing Israel of "genocide." If charging Israel with genocide for trying to protect itself from another genocidal attack by a Hamas regime pledged to complete a genocide against it seems like Alice-in-Wonderland-on-steroids, that's because, well, that's what it is. And for those who have long held that no matter what the facts, state and non-state actors that simply want Israel eliminated will accuse it of "war crimes" every time, there now is officially no reason to look for further proof.

For anyone who does not rely exclusively on TikTok for their information, what happened on Oct. 7 and what has happened since ought not to be obscure. Three thousand heavily armed gunmen funded and trained by Iran violated a supposed "ceasefire," invaded Israel, savagely executed 1,200 souls and mutilated 5,800 others, blowing families to pieces, executing everyone in sight, burning, dismembering and raping every human being they could — while kidnapping some 240 others. The genocide of Jews is what Hamas explicitly calls for, explicitly pledges itself to and explicitly promises to achieve.

Hamas has a sound battle plan, and some significant advantages in implementing it. By hiding in the extraordinarily sophisticated tunnels underneath apartment buildings, schools, hospitals and community centers, it dares Israel: When you come after us, you will by definition kill Palestinian civilians, and that is fine with us. Once that starts, we will accuse you of genocide. Footage of the dead civilians whose deaths we have deliberately brought about will flood the world — and the world will believe us when we say that you, not we, are responsible for it.

You will be a pariah. Useful idiots on America's left will pressure Democrats to castigate you, to call for an end to American support for Israel, to demand, "Ceasefire now!" You will be forced to capitulate to this, as you have done in the past. This will demoralize your already traumatized citizenry. Your economy will take a huge hit thanks to reserve call-ups and fearful tourists. Your country will be weakened.

And as for us, we will remain in power. As they have done in the past, our trusty international bankrollers will give us billions of dollars in "humanitarian aid." As we have done in the past, we will steal it. We will rebuild our fortifications, and we will re-arm. And then, when we are ready, we will launch another wave of attacks on Israel, more deadly than before. And the past will be repeated, just as before: rinse, and repeat.

Rep. Ritchie Torres was being polite when he addressed the claim that what Israel really ought to do now is stick its head in the sand and fold. "Those calling for a 'permanent ceasefire,'" he posted last Thursday, "are calling for something that exists only as a figment of their imagination." He might have used the phrase "willful blindness," or perhaps "intellectual mendacity." In a speech last week in Qatar, where he lives in lavish splendor while consigning Gazans to destruction, Hamas leader Ismail Haniyeh called Oct. 7 "a glorious day in the life of humanity." He urged Hamas' supporters everywhere to "hold on to the victory that took place on October 7 and build upon it." He thanked those who are "pouring weapons" onto Israel — killing Israelis.

But it's Israel that is guilty of genocide.

It requires real mindlessness not to understand that the genocide in this conflict is perpetrated by Hamas, not by the victims of that genocide, who did not want Oct. 7, and who have no choice but to try to prevent it from reoccurring.

No choice other than national suicide. Which is not a choice.

Married to the Mob: Democrats Can't Cater to the Fringe

January 23, 2024

With the presidential election in sight, pundits are breathlessly assessing just how damaged President Joe Biden supposedly is by dissatisfaction from his party's hard left over his disinclination to drink their brand of Kool Aid on the Mideast conflict. College students overdosed on TikTok and faculty whose yearning to ingratiate themselves with campus fashion has outstripped their intellectual rigor have certainly made a lot of noise. Their protests have run the gamut from laughable to cringeworthy, but they have succeeded in generating media attention. What is less clear is their impact on actual people in an actual election.

Columbia University has been a scene of considerable mirth, as self-professed progressives scream support for crazed Yemeni jihadists — funded by an Iranian regime that executes dissenters and LGBTQ community members — who are trying to blow up ships in the Red Sea to mark their hatred of infidels. "Hands off the Houthis!" and "Yemen, Yemen, make us proud, turn another ship around!" shout the children of the rich and privileged in Morningside Heights, most of whom don't know a Houthi from a jar of Hellmann's mayonnaise.

At Rutgers University, the campus chapter of Students for Justice in Palestine, on probation after having been suspended for repeatedly disrupting campus activities, held a press conference dressed like ISIS machete-wielders, their faces masked to hide their identities, issuing a set of "demands" of the university. Over at the White House, a mob of pro-Hamas demonstrators furious at the president for his "support for genocide" tried to breach the security perimeter, shrieking "F—- Biden!" at Secret Service who stood calmly behind the gates.

Last week, anti-Israel protesters demonstrated outside Manhattan's Sloan Kettering Cancer Center, hurling accusations of "genocide" against a world-renowned hospital that has helped hundreds of thousands of cancer patients and their families. Protest leader Nerdeen Kiswani exhorted the crowd to direct their shouting at pediatric patients watching from within the hospital. "Make sure they hear you, they're in the windows!" Kiswani thundered. "Shame on you, you support genocide, too!"

Though the prevailing storyline has been that disaffection among the left will hurt Biden in November, data that has flown underneath the radar indicates that were he to bend to the far left on Israel, Biden would be damaged badly, even fatally, in his race against Donald Trump. A Gallup poll released earlier this month found that 38% of Americans said Israel is getting "the right amount" of U.S. support — but 24% said it wasn't getting enough. That's the highest percentage of Americans who have told pollsters Israel wasn't receiving enough U.S. support since Gallup began asking the question in 2001.

A New York Times/Siena College poll taken in six battleground states in November found that voters believed that Trump, generally regarded as more hawkish in his support for Israel than Biden, would "do a better job" on the Israel-Hamas conflict than Biden. Of all six states, the gap was widest in Pennsylvania, a state that Biden cannot lose if he hopes to win reelection; 53% of Pennsylvanians said that Trump would do a better job on the conflict, while 37% said Biden.

White House operatives are doubtless paying attention to the reversal of political fortunes of Pennsylvania Sen. John Fetterman, who has been an extremely vocal supporter of Israel since Hamas' Oct. 7 massacre, and whose favorable net ratings are 23% higher than Biden's in the president's home state.

A recent Suffolk University poll in New Hampshire found that 49% of voters sympathized more with Israel than with Palestinians, compared with 16% the other way around. Forty-five percent of Granite State voters told pollsters that Biden's support for Israel was "about right," while 12% indicated he wasn't supportive enough. In a Biden-Trump match-up, those surveyed supported Biden over the former president by over seven percentage points.

The takeaway appears to be this: Noise-making is different from vote-winning. Indeed, it may well be that the claims made by the Hamas lobby are so repugnant to Americans' common sense that embracing those claims may burn Democrats, not help them.

Corrupt Enterprise: A Poisoned, Poisonous UN Agency in Gaza Faces the Music

January 30, 2024

It is Albert Einstein who is credited with observing that "Insanity is doing the same thing over and over expecting different results." If that is so, it is finally coming to light that those who have defended the U.N.'s special agency for Palestinians, the United Nations Relief and Works Administration (UNRWA), have been guilty of a kind of criminal insanity. It's long been obvious that UNRWA is not merely a de facto affiliate of Hamas in Gaza, but a de facto Hamas sponsor — funneling cash to the murderous group, serving as a recruitment and training vehicle for Hamas operatives, and functioning as cover for the construction of Hamas military infrastructure and a shield for the storage of Hamas weaponry and rocket attacks on Israeli civilians. Five years ago, Switzerland's foreign minister stated what even then was obvious: "UNRWA has become part of the problem. It supplies the ammunition to continue the conflict. By supporting UNRWA, we keep the conflict alive. It's a perverse logic."

UNRWA's role as an arm of Hamas in Gaza has been voluminously documented — and studiously ignored. Arab donors haven't been especially troubled. Western donors have shrugged, looked the other way and changed the subject. Meanwhile, billions of American taxpayers' dollars have been forked over to UNRWA. The Trump administration suspended American aid, but since taking office the Biden White House has restarted the fund flow, providing about a billion dollars to UNRWA in the last three years.

The jig may be up for UNRWA, a hackarama for Hamas sympathizers and, it is now clear, Hamas killers. Last Friday the United States announced that it was suspending aid to UNRWA. Within 36 hours, over 12 Western democracies followed suit. The trigger: the disclosure that UNRWA staffers in Gaza had actively participated in the Oct. 7 mass slaughter of some 1,200 Israelis and the abduction of almost 250 others. These governments pronounced themselves "shocked, shocked" to learn that UNRWA workers had invaded Israel and massacred Israelis.

But they can't possibly be surprised, let alone shocked.

Organizations like U.N. Watch and the Foundation for Defense of Democracies and numerous journalists have produced report after report, year after year, on what a cesspool of jihadism and virulent antisemitism UNRWA is. UNRWA's willful blindness about Hamas' use of its facilities to wage war against Israel is legendary. The agency's schools and summer camps consistently glorify the murder of Jews in blood-curdling terms right out of The World According to ISIS, and UNRWA's 13,000 employees in Gaza pack social media with exhortations to murder. Perfectly typical is this 2022 Facebook posting by UNRWA teacher Elham Mansour: "By Allah, anyone who can kill and slaughter any Zionist & Israeli criminal and doesn't do so doesn't deserve to live. Kill and pursue them everywhere. All Israel deserves is death."

U.N. Watch has released an analysis of a chat room for 3,000 UNRWA teachers filled with messages celebrating the Oct. 7 massacre, exulting over video and photographs of slaughtered, dismembered and raped Israelis, praying for Israel's destruction — and asking when UNRWA would pay their salaries. Released Israeli hostages report being held in the homes of UNRWA staff. There is endless evidence out of Gaza of Hamas fighters operating out of UNRWA facilities and, of course, of Hamas tunnels underneath UNRWA buildings. Asked whether UNRWA had any indication that Hamas was constructing hundreds of miles of tunnels underneath Gaza, a U.N. representative stammered: "Not to us. I mean, to think that the U.N. had any understanding of what was — any information about these operations, I think is — no, is clearly the answer to that."

Doubtful, but let's find out. It may be coincidental that the administration's announcement on Friday that it was suspending aid to UNRWA came just days before this week's scheduled hearing of the House Foreign Affairs Committee's Subcommittee on Oversight and Accountability entitled "UNRWA Exposed: Examining the Agency's Mission and Failures." The hearing promises to splatter a whole lot of egg on a whole lot of faces. Some of those faces are in Gaza. But some are in Washington, D.C.

Baked Squad: Hard-Left Democrats May Be in for a Thinning

February 6, 2024

In the Greek fable of Icarus and Daedalus, the former ignores his father's warnings about hubris and, in particular, flying too close to the sun. The rest, as they say, is mythology: Icarus flew too high, had his wings melted and fell to his demise. To put it another way: what goes up must come down.

So it may be this year with The Squad, a small knot of U.S. representatives who, since the first four of their number were elected in 2018, have been the darling of the Democratic Socialists of America and, more recently, the Hands-Off-The-Houthis set. The original four — Alexandria Ocasio-Cortez, Ilhan Omar, Rashida Tlaib and Ayanna Pressley — have since been joined in the House of Representatives by Cori Bush, Jamaal Bowman, Greg Casar and Summer Lee.

Squad members have established formidable social media star power and a knack for drawing attention. They have not necessarily been the humblest, the most deeply thoughtful or the most effectual members of the Democratic caucus, however, and are regarded warily by many of their Democratic colleagues. When it comes to the Mideast, for example, not one of them can confidently be said to know Hamas from a harmonica, the Gaza Strip from the Louisiana Purchase, and it shows. They have been nothing if not reliable: there hasn't been a murderous attack on Israeli civilians that they haven't ignored, whitewashed or defended.

There is reason to think that their ranks may be in for a thinning, and it has a lot to do with hubris.

Over the last 10 days, Bush, a two-term congresswoman from Missouri, confirmed that she's under investigation by the Justice Department after the House Sergeant at Arms announced that he had been served with a subpoena for records of her expenditures. It seems that she has funneled tens of thousands of dollars of campaign funds to her romantic partner, now her husband. Bush claims that the payments were for "security."

In the meantime, no doubt helped by concerns about Bush's sometimes bizarre conduct, her primary challenger, St. Louis County Prosecutor Wesley Bell, matched Bush's fundraising in the last quarter of 2023 and had twice as much cash on hand as she did at the beginning of 2024.

Bowman was censured by the House for falsely pulling a fire alarm in a Capitol Hill office building a few months ago, causing the building to be evacuated just when Democrats were trying to delay a floor vote. He pleaded guilty to a misdemeanor charge and was placed on probation. This may have been a move he learned from students when he was a middle school principal in New York, but it is hardly the only eye-rolling feature of his career.

Turns out Bowman once posted a poem he wrote promoting nutcase theories about Sept. 11. A building destroyed by al-Qaida, he wrote, was actually a "controlled demolition." About the planes used to attack America, he posted "Minimal damage done / minimal debris found / Hmm," embracing a wacko conspiracy theory that the U.S. faked the whole thing advanced by, well, wackos, suggesting that Osama bin Laden had been falsely "blamed" for 9/11 so that we could satisfy a craving to go war. "I was debating diving into a doctoral degree," Bowman recently explained.

As of Dec. 31, Bowman's primary opponent, Westchester County Executive George Latimer, had twice as much cash on hand as Bowman, and outraised him in the last quarter by 2-1.

Omar has had a propensity for antisemitism ("It's all about the Benjamins, baby!") and other forms of self-inflicted controversy, but she has taken it to the bank, raising $1.6 million last quarter. She is going to need it; she is facing a rematch with a primary opponent, former Minneapolis City Councilor Don Samuels, whom she just barely defeated two years ago.

The Squad members have prided themselves on not being shrinking violets. For a few of them, however, the bloom may be off the rose. November will determine whether, come the new Congress, it's the Squad's size that has shrunk a bit.

The President's Tightrope: Biden Steers Between the Necessary and the Popular

February 13, 2024

Civil War lore has it that after Gen. Ulysses S. Grant turned the Union's lackluster war performance around, his critics complained to President Abraham Lincoln about Grant's heavy drinking. "I wish some of you would tell me the brand of whiskey that Grant drinks," Lincoln replied. "I would like to send a barrel of it to my other generals."

The story comes to mind after a week in which a furor about Joe Biden's supposed lack of fitness to be president has swept the nation. An 81-year-old with an arthritic spine (the stiffness walking), gastroesophageal reflux (the frequent clearing of his throat) and the residual effects of a childhood stutter have America wondering whether he can serve. The mania deepened on Friday night, when Biden said "Mexico" rather than "Egypt" while obviously describing his discussions with the leader of the latter about trying to bring about the release of the 100-plus Israelis languishing, if not already murdered, in Hamas' tunnels in Gaza.

Biden's use of the wrong word caused a certain hyperventilation about his cognition. Never mind that his opponent, former President Donald Trump, is patently in a state of cognitive collapse, an utter mental free-fall that is evident virtually every time he takes the microphone these days, and with every posting on Truth Social.

The fly in the Biden-is-unfit-to-serve ointment, of course, is that he has been a historically successful president by objective measure after objective measure. This is all the more impressive given the implacably obstructionist political opposition he has faced, notably featuring a non-functioning House of Representatives. Given Biden's results, we might well hope that every president henceforth be in their 80s, walk gingerly, clear his throat a lot and occasionally stammer.

That's not to say the president's standing is strong right now. It isn't. And the pro-Hamas lobby, with an assist from those just not thinking clearly, is doing its best to exploit his political weakness.

It may be working. TikTok garbage has helped galvanize a vocal and sometimes unhinged hard left that prefers we all just forget about Hamas' invasion on Oct.7 and its slaughter of 1,200 Israelis — the proportional equivalent of about 50,000 Americas — in a matter of hours. Damage has been done to common sense, and Biden's advisers are attuned to it.

An "Abandon Biden" movement initiated by certain Arab Americans has exacerbated fears of losing Michigan's critical electoral votes. Biden's emissaries have fanned out on bended knee to apologize for his support for Israel. Proving that politics can make reprehensible bedfellows, the White House kisses the ring of none other than Rep. Rashida Tlaib, D-Mich., properly censured by her House colleagues for her determined mendacity, who has accused Biden of complicity with "genocide" for supporting Israel's effort to defend its civilians from truly genocidal killers, to wit, Hamas.

Biden's advisers have settled on a strategy of letting it be known once daily that there are "growing divides" with Israel, about which The New York Times duly and enthusiastically reports thrice daily. This is supposed to placate the anti-Israeli left. It may, but signaling a divide bolsters Hamas' resolve, thereby prolonging the war rather than shortening it.

Even Sen. Bernie Sanders, Lord help us, acknowledges that there can't be a ceasefire with Hamas, which seeks Israel's annihilation. What, then, is Israel supposed to do, exactly? Its critics have no answer. One may dislike or even despise Israeli Prime Minister Benjamin Netanyahu and wish him gone for many excellent reasons — but still not scoff when he observes that Hamas must be removed from Gaza if there's ever going to be peace.

He's absolutely right about this. Indeed, every Western leader has publicly stated the same, and most Arab leaders say so privately.

So let us be spared the robotic inanity about a "ceasefire," as though the solution to the horror show caused by Hamas is in Israel's hands, rather than Hamas'. Israel didn't wish for this war. In order for it to end, Hamas has to end it. Or Israel has to end it by ending Hamas.

Qatar Connection: American Universities Have Some Explaining to Do

February 20, 2024

Columbia may be the gem of the ocean, but the Ivy League university in New York that bears its name has become known as American academia's preeminent breeding and stomping ground for antisemites posing as progressives. As a House Committee put it last Monday in a document demand served on Columbia University administrators, "An environment of pervasive antisemitism has been documented at Columbia for more than two decades before the October 7, 2023, terrorist attack" that slaughtered 1,200 Israelis.

Since Oct. 7, Columbia's campus has more nearly resembled 1930's Berlin than an institution of higher learning. Jewish students have been widely victimized by assaults, harassment, intimidation, invective, bullying and ostracism. As the Committee noted, "social media platforms (have been) flooded with antisemitic messages by Columbia students." Columbia Professor Joseph Massad pronounced the decapitation, dismembering, burning alive, blowing to pieces and raping of Israelis "innovative Palestinian resistance," to say nothing of "astonishing," "awesome," "astounding," "incredible" and inspiring "jubilation and awe."

In a recent piece in Tablet Magazine entitled "What Happens When You Teach at Columbia and Reject Hamas," Shai Davidai, a Jewish assistant professor at Columbia Business School, and his wife, both outspoken critics of Benjamin Netanyahu's government, described how they have been subjected to torrential venom since speaking out against the Hamas slaughter. "Every morning, as we sift through the hundreds of hateful emails and online comments that Shai receives each day, we are reminded that life will never be the same again," they write. "From memes of rats with big, curving noses to threats of physical violence, from the publicizing of our personal information to the dissemination of egregious lies about Shai and his parents ... to conspiratorial antisemitic rants, we believe we've seen it all."

"Shai is regularly called a Nazi, a Zionist pig, a genocidal baby murderer, a kike," they write. "Thousands have called for his death."

The U.S. Department of Education has added Columbia to the list of universities it is investigating for potential civil rights violations. Columbia may be in a class by itself in the Vicious Bigotry Department, but it isn't alone. What is happening there is playing out at colleges and universities across America.

Some pronounce themselves aghast at what they regard as the sheer effrontery of Congress for investigating whether or not prominent universities look the other way at rampant abuse and violence in order to placate left wing students and faculty. They shouldn't: American taxpayers pay these institutions tens of billions of dollars a year in subsidies and tax breaks. Congress — which doles out this financial support — is hardly required to stick its head in the sand, or be a potted plant.

Americans aren't the only ones funding these schools. Document Request No. 23 in the House Committee's document demand of Columbia requires evidence of "all donations and funding to Columbia from Qatari sources since January 1, 2021." This is going to engender some queasiness in Doha as well as Morningside Heights. Since Hamas' violent takeover of Gaza in 2007, Qatar has strategically donated almost $6 billion to 61 American schools, including Ivy League ones.

This is not oh-so-generous interest in American education on the part of Qatar, which has all of 313,000 citizens. There may just be a bit of an agenda here, with grateful recipients of Qatari largesse more than happy to be helpful.

After Iran, there is no government on Earth more responsible for Hamas' atrocities than Qatar. Since Hamas overran Gaza in 2007, Qatar has given Hamas some $1.8 billion. It provides safe harbor to Hamas' top leadership, who live in Qatar in luxury while Gazans live in squalor. Its state-owned media mouthpiece, Al Jazeera, glorifies Hamas and amplifies its messages worldwide. On Oct. 7, the very day of Hamas' massacre, Qatar issued a statement holding "Israel alone responsible" for the massacre of Israelis.

Louis Brandeis famously pointed out that "sunlight is the best disinfectant." The House Committee investigation that Columbia and its fellow Ivy League universities face, and fear, seems very likely to shed light on an insidious infection, one that has festered for far too long.

Ostrich Days: Democracy on the Line, Americans Decide Whether to Fight or Fold

February 27, 2024

"Sometimes the more absurd the lie, the more effective it is," observed a former United Nations official in "Kiss the Future," the new documentary produced by Matt Damon and Ben Affleck about the resilience of Sarajevo's residents under fire from Serbian strongman Slobodan Milosevic's killers during the 1990s. The documentary recounts the successful effort of a young and intrepid humanitarian aid worker named Bill Carter to persuade the rock band U2 to shine a spotlight on Milosevic's barbarism, at a time when effective lies, fatigue and apathy combined to keep the world's focus away from Serbian war crimes.

The film ends with images of Vladimir Putin, and not inadvertently. Its release in movie theaters coincides with the marking of two years since Putin invaded Ukraine, an invasion propelled by confidence that the world would dither, look the other way and permit Ukraine to go under. Putin had ample reason to be confident. After all, the world has dithered, looked the other way and permitted wretched regimes to prevail plenty of times before. And he had reasonable basis to believe that the United States would do little more than wag its finger and pronounce itself "deeply concerned" and "greatly troubled" by Russia's invasion.

In the last Democratic administration, for example, President Barack Obama had pooh-poohed the very notion that Russia was a global threat, gone passive when Russia invaded Crimea, first announced that Syria's use of chemical weapons to murder its citizens would cross a "red line" and then mumbled "Never mind" when the red line was crossed, and derided those who warned that funneling tens of billions of dollars to Iran would fund Hamas, Hezbollah and other entities that we have long stipulated are terrorist organizations.

But led by President Joe Biden, an international coalition mobilized to arm Ukraine so that it could defend itself. Ukrainians are in essence fighting not merely to prevent Russia from subjugating them but to prevent Russia from turning its armed forces thereafter on Eastern European nations that it formerly controlled, and which it wishes to control again. Our NATO allies have done what NATO was formed to do. And Biden, with strong bipartisan support from those in Congress not entirely subservient to Donald Trump and Trump's instruction that Putin be coddled, has ensured that Ukraine has had the aid necessary to keep Russia at bay. In the process of inflicting staggering losses in Russia, Ukraine has also sustained staggering losses, and has seen its economy shattered by Russia's onslaught.

But now, on orders from the best friend Vladimir Putin has ever had, a group of MAGA Republicans, perfectly content to see Putin win and Ukraine lose, and perfectly content to see our allies endangered by a bona fide axis of aggressors that includes Russia, Iran and North Korea, is blocking the support Ukraine desperately needs to avoid being plowed under. "It is the tortured people of Ukraine that beg you, but it is also the credibility of your country that is at stake," Poland's Foreign Minister told CNN's Fareed Zakaria on Sunday.

It's not just the far right whose head is deep in the sand, or elsewhere that heads don't belong, when it comes to the real threats posed to democracies by barbaric state and non-state actors. On the far left, the usual feckless wonders see no evil, hear no evil and acknowledge no evil when evil is directly in front of their noses. Self-professed progressives have eviscerated their credibility on human rights by whitewashing Hamas' mass slaughter on Oct.7, a slaughter not merely bestial but patently genocidal. Naturally, they accuse Israel, the victim of the genocidal attack, of genocide, illustrating the point that "sometimes the more absurd the lie, the more effective it is."

America and its democratic allies find themselves at a hinge point. Whether Putin succeeds in overrunning Ukraine, and whether Iran and its proxies succeed in imposing a state of savagery on the Mideast, is up in the air. How it comes out depends on whether we fight for the survival of democracies or simply fold.

College Daze: On Campuses as in Newsrooms, Orthodoxy Rules

March 5, 2024

In a recent piece in The Atlantic, former New York Times staffer Adam Rubenstein went public with his firsthand account of what has become the classic story of the Times' surrender to the orthodoxy of a certain political set. In 2020, after white policemen murdered George Floyd, protests of police brutality, long an under-recognized feature of America's reality, erupted. Most were peaceful. Some were not; in some cities, police stations were torched, police cars firebombed and police officers themselves murdered.

U.S. Sen. Tom Cotton, R-Ark., advocated invoking federal law to quell the violence. His opinion was supported by 53% of Americans at the time, according to a Morning Consult poll. The Times, which had already editorialized in support of Black Lives Matter and had published many columns sharply at variance with Cotton, invited the senator to publish his opinion — on its opinion page.

Hell broke loose in the Times' newsroom at this effrontery. Fifteen-hundred Times employees signed statements furiously demanding retractions, editors' notes and discipline of those "responsible," claiming that the publication of Cotton's opinion placed them "in danger."

Never mind that the Times had had no problem publishing the "opinions" of tyrants like Libya's Moammar Gadhafi, Turkey's Recep Tayyip Erdogan and Russia's Vladimir Putin. No, the publication of a U.S. senator's opinion on stopping urban violence was an impermissible outrage. Times publisher A.G. Sulzberger, seeking to quell a newsroom riot, went into Full Toady mode, stating that the op-ed "did not meet our standards." Opinion editor James Bennet was forced to resign, and other heads rolled as well. Rubenstein, who edited the piece, wrote that even by merely asking questions about the lock-step, left-leaning political orthodoxy reigning at the Times, "I'd revealed that I wasn't on the same team as my colleagues."

The irony couldn't have been thicker. Here was The New York Times, paragon of First Amendment virtue, touting itself as the avatar of free expression, collapsing under incensed criticism from its own journalists for having published a senator's opinion about public policy.

And the message to any Times journalist even contemplating suggesting that the paper publish stories deemed verboten by the prevailing fashion at the paper was clear: if you value your career, keep your mouth shut.

The Times is hardly the only newsroom where orthodoxy reigns and silence is safest. College students writing for their college newspapers would take their social lives into their own hands by proposing articles that run counter to prevailing campus winds.

Consider this.

Qatar, whose emir exercises absolute power over its 315,000 citizens, is massively wealthy thanks to the vast reserves of fossil fuels it possesses. It also possesses a woeful human rights record: serious restrictions of the rights to free expression, peaceful assembly and political activity, flogging and imprisonment for same-sex sexual conduct and adultery, forced labor, and the widespread exploitation and abuse of workers, especially women, for starters.

It is a huge funder of Hamas, which slaughtered some 1,200 Israelis on Oct. 7. It also happens to be a huge funder of some 60 American colleges and universities, and not for no reason. It invests strategically in international relations centers and journalism schools, hoping to advance Qatar's view of the world and to influence American policy for its benefit.

This fairly cries out for college journalists to ask: what are our institutions' ties to Qatar? How much do we receive, with what strings and with what payback? Are we transparent about it, or do we seek to hide it?

At a time when campaigns to divest from Israel are all the rage, would a college journalist have much incentive to risk the wrath of divestment activists by suggesting that questions be asked that would not be popular to ask?

They would not. To ask such questions, as Adam Rubenstein wrote, might suggest that one wasn't on "the right team." In this case, being on the right team would mean advocating for divestment from Israel, rather than from Hamas' staunch ally.

But where question-asking is considered a bad career move, it isn't "just" the truth that suffers. It's all of us.

Hate Rape: The Kids Say It's OK

March 12, 2024

The United Nations has long been so uniformly corrupt on the subject of Israel that anytime it ekes out an acknowledgement of attacks on the Jewish state — however reluctantly, belatedly and perfunctorily it does so — it's a man-bite-dog story. Last week, a U.N. official who had clearly drawn the bureaucratic short straw issued a "report" of sorts, confirming what anyone paying attention already knew: that in the process of slaughtering 1,200 Israelis on Oct. 7, Hamas had also committed mass acts of sadistic, savage sexual violence.

Hamas' barbarism against young Israelis at an all-night dance festival or asleep in their beds had been thoroughly documented for months by the time the poor U.N. functionary was asked by the secretary general to do something that looked as though he were looking into the matter in late January — almost four months after Hamas' slaughter. God-awful evidence, video and audio recordings by Hamas gunmen, firsthand accounts — and confessions — had already been collected and analyzed.

"Everything was an apocalypse of corpses," one survivor has recalled. "Girls without any clothes on. Without tops. Without underwear. People cut in half. Butchered. Some were beheaded. There were girls with a broken pelvis due to repetitive rapes. Their legs were spread wide apart in a split."

One Israeli investigator stated that "our team commander saw several female soldiers who were shot in the crotch, intimate parts, vagina or shot in the breasts. There seemed to be systematic genital mutilation of a group of victims."

The U.N. report did make official what had already been assumed about Hamas' hostages. It found "clear and convincing" evidence that the children and women held by Hamas have been subjected to rape, sexualized torture, and cruel and degrading sexual abuse.

Now, it might be imagined that self-professed progressives on campuses, in social justice organizations and in The New York Times newsroom would find it natural to condemn Hamas, to make sure that the public knew about these outrages, and to demand that Hamas release those it continues to hold captive.

But no.

There are throngs of young feminists who, rightly disgusted by the sheer misogyny on full display in the "Access Hollywood" tape and by Donald Trump's sexual assault on E. Jean Carroll, wouldn't be caught dead breathing a public word about Hamas' rape and torture of Israeli women. We are lucky if young progressives are prepared to acknowledge that it even occurred. As for speaking up about it on campus or in the workplace, forget about it. To say that it isn't fashionable to deplore what Hamas did and pledges to do again doesn't capture it; speaking up about this is considered social suicide.

The current line is that condemning Hamas' rape spree amounts to Zionists "weaponizing" rape — because, you see, it isn't Hamas, which did the raping, which weaponized rape. It's those pointing out what Hamas did. Moreover, condemning Hamas for its bestial violence against women is "playing into an anti-Palestinian narrative." Such is the deeply disturbed state of the left: part Alice-in-Wonderland on steroids, part mind-bending intellectual dishonesty.

Writer Batya Ungar-Sargon, author of "Bad News: How Woke Media Is Undermining Democracy," spoke recently about the video of 25-year-old Noa Argamani dancing at the Nova music festival just before she was executed by Hamas killers, who then carted her body back into Gaza, where a mob cheered. "Can you even imagine a starker contrast between good and evil?" she asked. "Surely, I thought in my naivete, the left would see itself reflected in these music-loving young people. Surely Noa Argamani begging for her life as the butchers made off with her would inspire on the left a sense of identification and a corresponding sense of anger."

"How could it not?" she says she thought. "Friends, it did not."

So many who hold themselves out as progressives remain silent about Hamas. They justify it, contextualize it, even defend it. Historians will look back at them, and pronounce them a disgrace. Justly so.

Blessed Mission: From Soul and Heart They Serve

March 19, 2024

"In order to serve with dignity, you've got to be organized," says Mary Ann Ponti, director of outreach programs and community engagement at St. Anthony's Shrine in downtown Boston. And on a recent morning at the Shrine, dignity and organization are much on display, as several hundred Bostonians line up for food — no questions asked — provided through the Shrine's food pantry. "You have to create a safe environment for people to receive services," says Ponti, whose blend of street smarts and tenderness is the hallmark of programs the Shrine runs to feed the hungry, shelter the homeless and offer women's health services. She is, one of the volunteers staffing the pantry says, "a force of nature."

So is the work of St. Anthony's, which, like Ponti, is a godsend. "In other places it might take a year's worth of meetings to get things done," says Ponti. "Here, somebody calls with a need, we're going to jump all over it. The friars pride themselves on meeting need."

On this morning, after the volunteer team has unloaded a truckload of food from the Greater Boston Food Bank, they start with a prayer ("Lord, it's been a crazy morning") before Ponti calls out, "Let's roll!" A long line of people, most from nearby Chinatown, file in with carts or bags to collect chicken, pork, beans, rice, spinach and blueberries. The volunteers, all regulars, greet them warmly. Three of the Boston Police Department's finest, also regulars, are there, chatting away. One of them is fluent in Chinese; he banters with those on line, and they seem to banter back.

The pantry didn't miss a beat during the pandemic, a testament to the collaboration among the Greater Boston Food Bank, St. Anthony's and the blessed souls who show up to help. "The volunteers definitely serve up love here," Ponti says.

The pantry's monthly food distribution isn't the only St. Anthony's program to combat hunger. Its Homeless to Housing program provides food, household items and toiletries every week to several hundred people transitioning from homelessness to some form of shelter. Ponti has a wide network of caseworkers who contact her to provide help making that transition successful. Pretty much the Mikhail Baryshnikov of need-serving,

Ponti also spends part of each week walking Boston's streets to tend to the homeless, whom she knows by name. She is not entirely tireless ("My fumes are running on fumes," she cracks) but awfully close.

All over Boston the Catholic Church inspires the community to feed the hungry and organizes to do so. Last Saturday, the Mary Ann Brett Food Pantry, affiliated with Saint Teresa of Calcutta Parish in Dorchester, announced it has raised $1 million to supplement the food supplied by the Greater Boston Food Bank every week that helps 550 families. The pantry is named after a much-beloved immigrant who arrived from Ireland as a small girl then washed the floors of downtown office buildings to support her family.

Father Jack Ahern, instrumental in establishing the pantry in honor of Mary Ann Brett's son Jim, says it is aptly named. "Although she was fairly poor herself," says Father Jack, "she and her family made sure there was always room at the table for others." He marvels not only at the pantry's growth but at the volunteers. "They really are a family," he says. "You see people from across the generations serving food."

Jim Brett, longtime CEO of the New England Council, raised the funds from donors large and small, mindful not only of his mother's life but of Matthew 25: "For I was hungry and you gave me something to eat. I was thirsty and you gave me something to drink. I was a stranger and you invited me in."

These are dark, depressing days in plenty of respects. There's no doubt about that. But then there are people like those who make these food pantries and others like them not merely operate but sing. Theirs is a blessed mission, and they put soul and heart on display in impressive, and inspiring, fashion.

The Bibi Bogeyman: Democrats' Feeble Wobble on Hamas Risks Sinking Biden

March 26, 2024

You can blame Israeli Prime Minister Benjamin Netanyahu for plenty of things, and plenty of Israelis do. These include his cynical maneuvering to avoid being held to account on criminal charges, his alliances with nut jobs in his coalition government and the gross negligence that left Israel vulnerable to Hamas' invasion of Israel and its genocidal massacre of Israelis on Oct. 7.

But here's what you can't blame him for: Hamas' invasion itself. Or that Hamas purposefully consigns Palestinians to death by hiding in tunnels underneath their homes, schools and hospitals, making it impossible to stop Hamas without killing innocents. Or that Hamas refuses to release the hostages it holds, or that it has rejected one ceasefire proposal after another. Or that Hamas knows that whatever it does or doesn't do, the world, including many Americans, will blame Israel for the bloodshed that Hamas has caused.

This is patently obvious. But you'd never know it from listening to some Democratic politicians, whose business it is to stick a finger in the air to ascertain which way the hard left's wind is blowing and then to blow in that direction.

The resulting formulaic talking points are increasingly vapid, and utterly predictable. Here goes: "Of course Israel has the right to defend itself. And Hamas can't control Gaza, and they really should release the hostages. But we cannot support Bibi Netanyahu and his extremist right-wing government."

Huh? Let's think: If we stipulate that Hamas invaded Israel, committed a mass slaughter, pledges to keep doing it and is intentionally causing the deaths of Palestinian civilians by making it impossible for Israel to stop Hamas without killing them no matter what steps Israel takes, then what, precisely, is Israel supposed to do to keep Hamas from maintaining control of Gaza and repeating Oct. 7? A rain dance?

The Blame-It-On-Bibi mantra, so feeble, has taken hold among Democrats because it is so convenient. Convenient, yes, but also mindless, for two reasons.

First, all that speeches like that of Sen. Chuck Schumer do is bolster Hamas' strategy of waiting for America to pressure Israel to back down, which would reward Hamas, hand it a victory and enable it to regroup and keep up its slaughter campaign.

Second, it is mindless because Israelis themselves, who dislike Netanyahu, nevertheless agree with Israeli's prosecution of the war, because they believe they have no other choice. And indeed they don't.

Israelis aren't the only ones who see it that way. According to a Pew Research survey released last week, nearly 60% of Americans believe that Israel's reason for fighting Hamas is valid. That's nearly four times the number who disagree. Twenty-six percent of Americans say they're "not sure."

And despite the enviable publicity lavished on American Jews who denounce Israel, a meaningful percentage of whom are asked by The New York Times to publish guest opinion columns, fully 89% of American Jews believe that Israel's fight against Hamas is legitimate — compared with 7% who disagree. Sixty-two percent told Pew they specifically agree with how Israel is conducting the fight.

This is unwelcome news for Jewish Voices for Peace, which wishes to remind us that the fight against Hamas is not in their name, or for commentators like Peter Beinart, whose gig consists of earnestly telling those who ask him to do so that American Jews are abandoning Israel in droves.

The Democrats' wobble on Israel is a nod to the notion that Rep. Rashida Tlaib, D. Mich., has a chokehold on President Joe Biden's reelection prospects. But the data indicates that in their frantic scramble to placate Team Tlaib, Democrats may be dooming the very president they want to see reelected. American Jews, who staunchly support Israel against Hamas, comprise significant voter blocs in states whose electoral votes the president needs — like Pennsylvania, Arizona, Georgia, Nevada and, yes, Michigan.

Blaming Bibi for this conflict is just a thin veil for blaming Israel. It is one part pander, one part blather. Neither is helpful to the president's cause.

Mourning Joe: Losing Lieberman, We Lose a Principled Independent

April 2, 2024

In the summer of 1997, the Republican-controlled Senate Governmental Affairs Committee was investigating whether the Clinton-Gore White House and the Democratic National Committee had engaged in improper, or even illegal, fundraising practices during President Bill Clinton's 1996 reelection campaign. Acrimony was high, and partisan divides were sharp. The storylines were front-page news as the nationally televised hearings began: Had fundraising events at the White House violated the Hatch Act? Had special favors been dispensed to Democratic donors? Had overnights in the Lincoln Bedroom been used to stroke bundlers?

The bottom line was apparent from the outset. Whichever party controls the White House has used comparable money-raising gambits, which only means that there has been enough conduct that is depressing to go around. But there certainly was evidence aplenty that the Clinton campaign had engaged in fundraising that was smarmy, even if the smarm had a long bipartisan heritage.

One could regard the hearings as mere political theater, and it was in the Democrats' interest to look at it just that way — and to urge America to do the same. One Democratic senator on the committee did not. Sen. Joseph Lieberman, D-Conn., was neither a political novice nor a naif, but he took the evidence presented by the Republicans of machinations that ranged between unsavory and shady very seriously. A loyal Democrat who did not place himself on a pedestal, Lieberman nevertheless regarded some of what came before the committee as a moral affront. He declined to whitewash the malodorous facts or to pretend they didn't exist.

One day, the committee's Republican majority subpoenaed a businessman who, ever-so-coincidentally, had received administration approval for a lucrative energy contract contemporaneously with his massive contribution to the Democratic Party. During their questioning, the Democratic senators took turns evading the obvious issue: Everything about the matter screamed three Latin words — quid pro quo.

All except one. When it was his turn to examine the witness, Lieberman walked the unhappy businessman through the timing of

Democratic fundraisers' solicitation of his contribution, the contribution, his company's request for agency approval and the approval. Lieberman, who had once been Connecticut's attorney general, was soft-spoken about it, but unrelenting.

On the dais where the committee sat, just inches from where Lieberman was conducting his cross-examination, a Democratic senator leaned over to the Democrats' Counsel and whispered, with irritation, "What the hell is Joe doing?"

What the hell Joe was doing, of course, was the job of a public-spirited public servant who took his public service seriously. It was what earned him so much respect from Democrats and Republicans alike. Four hours before Lieberman died, a student at a school in Maine asked Republican Sen. Susan Collins, herself the object of plenty of poison arrows from multiple directions, who she enjoyed working with the most during her career. It was Lieberman, she replied.

Lieberman was famously a man of faith, and he bonded quickly with others of faith, whatever that faith happened to be. Terry Segal, a close friend of Lieberman since their days together at Yale University, remembers that Lieberman wouldn't go the Connecticut Democratic Party convention whose nomination for attorney general he was seeking because it fell on Saturday, the Jewish Sabbath. "We said to him 'You could lose!'" Segal recalls. "He said 'Well, so what?'"

The recollections of a good, decent and unpretentious man flooded in after Lieberman's death, and they were of a single piece. "He was always so gracious," said Boston lawyer Keith Carroll, who was among Lieberman's first interns when he was elected to the Senate in 1988. "All of his success never changed who he was."

There were some, to be sure, who despised Lieberman because he rejected their policy prescriptions. "Joe Lieberman never got the war with Iran that he so desperately wanted," posted Matt Duss, Bernie Sanders' former foreign policy adviser, just hours after Lieberman's death. Joe Lieberman would have just shaken his head at the lack of class. A pity that some people couldn't be more like him.

Hot Air Buffoons: Talking Heads Hand Out Hogwash on Gaza

April 9, 2024

MSNBC's talk show "Morning Joe" is catnip for political junkies, especially those who detest Donald Trump. Hundreds of thousands of us, our body clocks by now conditioned to wake in time to grab coffee and hop on the treadmill just before 6 a.m., start each weekday with predictable, comfortable left-of-center patter from the show's regulars.

In fairness to Joe Scarborough, after whom the show is named, the former congressman has consistently condemned Hamas, the genocidal, jihadist organization that launched the Gaza war by invading Israel and massacring every man, woman and child in sight six months ago. He has repeated that Hamas can't be permitted to control Gaza if either Israelis or Palestinians are ever to know peace.

Like an increasing number of people who carefully recite all the right generalities, however, he has descended ever deeper into drivel as the conflict has persisted and as Hamas, holding a winning hand by hiding among civilians and holding hostages in underground dungeons, gloats and rejects Israeli ceasefire proposals.

Scarborough is smart enough not to swallow hooey. But as Hamas eats popcorn watching Democrats mindlessly insist that Israel simply do what Hamas demands and accept whatever it offers, you'd never know it. The civilian suffering that Hamas purposefully triggered in the first place has made it increasingly fashionable in Democratic circles to blame Israel for a war that it did not want, did not cause and does not deserve. But that's MSNBC's market.

Scarborough has joined Democrats whose spines have disintegrated under pressure from the party's left in returning over and again to the fiddlesticks that the Gaza conflict continues because of this Israeli government's refusal to endorse Palestinian statehood.

He knows better.

He knows that Israel — from its very birth — agreed to a two-state solution, and that every time one has been offered in return for peace, Palestinian leaders have blocked it.

He knows that when Hamas sent 3,000 gunmen into Israel to slaughter, mutilate and kidnap innocents, it wasn't in search of a two-state solution. It was to prevent one.

If only the Israelis would agree to a ceasefire, bleat "Morning Joe" hosts and guests alike. Are they not following the repeated rejections by Hamas of proposal after proposal? But when you have a television show, well, you can say these things, and say them bombastically. It may be nonsense, but plenty of people believe it.

Scarborough's responsibilities extend all the way to getting to the set early in the morning. This is no small obligation, but it doesn't necessarily match that of protecting civilians from an attempted annihilation. He has rightly berated the Netanyahu government for its negligence in protecting those civilians, and, going further, demands to know how the Israelis have not already completed an official investigation while simultaneously defending itself on multiple fronts. "Where's the damned investigation?" he sneers.

One of the enviable advantages of having a successful talk show is that no one who wants to return to the set ever calls BS on the host's BS. The 9/11 Commission created by Congress to examine what happened that terrible morning wasn't even created until late 2002, a year after the attack. And the commission did not release its report until July 2004 — three years later.

After the Israel Defense Forces mistakenly fired on a convoy carrying humanitarian aid workers last week, a sputtering Scarborough, knowing that the IDF would not have targeted the convoy knowing it was transporting aid workers, told his viewers that there would not be an investigation until well in the future. The IDF released its report within 72 hours, accepting full responsibility for what it stated was a grave mistake, and detailing how it occurred.

It was left to prominent attorney and anti-Trump advocate George Conway to capture on X, formerly known as Twitter, the inanity that has metastasized. "Still waiting for Hamas's report on what happened on Oct. 7," Conway posted.

Mindless or Spineless: The Unbearable Lightness of Being Elizabeth Warren

April 16, 2024

The 350 missiles fired at Israelis last weekend were fired by Iran, which has consistently pledged to annihilate Israel. This, of course, is a pledge to commit genocide, defined by Oxford Dictionary as "the deliberate killing of a large number of people from a particular nation or ethnic group with the aim of destroying that nation or group." To constitute genocide, the United Nations states, "there must be a proven intent on the part of the perpetrators to physically destroy a national, ethnic, racial or religious group."

Therefore, is Iran pledged to commit genocide? Check.

Since its very founding, Hamas has been doctrinally and operationally devoted to annihilating Israel by murdering Jews. On Oct. 7, when 3,000 Hamas gunmen funded by Iran invaded Israel and slaughtered 1,200 Israelis before being stopped, their mission was to slaughter their way to Tel Aviv, killing as many Jews as possible. Since then, their leaders have vowed to reprise that slaughter over and over until their mission is accomplished.

Attempted genocide? Pledge to achieve genocide? Check. Check.

But when Massachusetts Sen. Elizabeth Warren, running for reelection and eager to placate the untethered wing of her party, stopped at the Islamic Center of Boston last week, she knew just who to charge with genocide.

Here's a hint: It wasn't Iran, and it wasn't Hamas.

Asked about South Africa's charge made in the International Court of Justice that it was actually Israel that, trying to defend itself against a genocidal campaign, was the party guilty of genocide, the oh-so-courageous Warren didn't reply, "Say what?" or, "You've got to be kidding me," or, "That simply isn't a fair charge to make against Israel."

What she said, in order to cave to an audience that demanded that she endorse the charge, was, "If you want to do it as an application of law, I believe that they'll find that it is genocide, and they have ample evidence to do so."

Ample evidence of genocide by Israel? Like what?

Perhaps it was the obvious intent to destroy Palestinians manifested by the young Israelis who were dancing at a festival when they were raped and executed gangland style en masse. Or the plain genocidal intent of the families sleeping in their beds that peaceful Saturday morning who were dismembered, blown to pieces or bound together and burned to death.

Warren occasionally recites the grudging boilerplate that "of course Israel has the right to defend itself." She has "ample evidence" that Hamas deliberately causes the killing of Palestinians that it uses as human shields, and that therefore it isn't possible for Israel to "defend itself" without harming civilians — because that is what Hamas guarantees. First year law students know what "proximate cause" is. A former Harvard Law professor surely does as well.

The charge that Israel seeks to kill civilians is one that is made routinely by Hamas' defenders every time Hamas starts a war, like clockwork. This charge, let alone the risible charge that Israel seeks to destroy Palestinians as a group, has been repeatedly debunked by American military experts, who actually know what they're talking about. Gen. Martin Dempsey, then Chairman of the Joint Chiefs of Staff, rejected the charge shortly after the 2014 war started by Hamas. "I actually do think that Israel went to extraordinary lengths to limit collateral damage and civilian casualties," Dempsey told the Carnegie Council for Ethics in International Affairs.

That was in 2014, back when Hamas was "only" firing thousands of rockets at Israeli civilians, before it violated a ceasefire and actually invaded Israel. Asked just recently by the Senate Armed Services Committee whether Israel was committing genocide in Gaza, Defense Secretary Lloyd Austin, a retired four-star general in the U.S. Army, replied, "We don't have any evidence of genocide being created. We don't have evidence of that."

But Warren, pressured by the far left to recite nonsense, dutifully allowed that there was "ample evidence" that the victim of attempted genocide was actually the perpetrator of one. A cowering pol is what she appears to be. A profile in courage she is not.

Trouble in River City: Elitism and Arrogance Threaten a Backlash Against Democrats

April 23, 2024

"Trouble in River City" goes the famous line in "The Music Man," one of America's best-loved musicals, set in the fictional town of River City, Iowa, meant to represent the country's heartland. It is in America's heartland — not just geographic, but socio-political — that Democrats risk a backlash this November. For it's a heartland that is home to Americans who may be repulsed by Donald Trump for infinite compelling reasons, but whose disgust with the elitism and arrogance of institutions they associate with Democrats may make it impossible for them to vote Democratic.

This past week provided two illustrations of the Democrats' problem.

In an essay published in The Free Press, award-winning National Public Radio editor Uri Berliner detailed the pronounced liberal bias that has turned the once uniformly respected NPR into patently progressive-occupied territory. "People at every level of NPR have comfortably coalesced around the progressive worldview," Berliner wrote. Quite apart from the long list of examples of the political purity test that dictates what stories run and how they are reported, Berliner has the receipts. NPR's editorial staff consists of 87 Democrats and zero Republicans, Berliner wrote in his essay "I've Been at NPR for 25 years; Here's How We Lost America's Trust."

And Berliner is no errant, closeted Foxaphile. He voted against Trump in 2016 and 2020. "I'm Sarah Lawrence-educated, was raised by a lesbian peace activist mother, I drive a Subaru, and Spotify says my listening habits are most similar to people in Berkeley," he wrote.

The financially troubled NPR plays to its customer base, which tunes in because it knows what it wants and it gets it. Once boasting a broad listenership, NPR's reliably liberal take now generates listeners two-thirds of whom identify as either somewhat or very liberal. "There's an unspoken consensus about the stories we should pursue and how they should be framed," Berliner wrote. "It's almost like an assembly line."

Cue the phony-baloney PR hooey from NPR, which deserved every eye-roll it generated. "We believe that inclusion — among our staff, with our sourcing and in our overall coverage — is critical to telling the nuanced stories of this country and our world," was the slick non-sequitur issued by

NPR's leadership, which plainly was unable to deny a single fact presented by Berliner.

Then NPR suspended Berliner without pay for writing his essay. Not exactly a move designed to encourage the honest journalism NPR professes to stand for. Berliner promptly resigned.

Then there was the President of Columbia University, Dr. Nemat Shafik, who finally deigned to appear last Wednesday before the House Committee investigating the virulent antisemitism surging on college campuses. Shafik had cited "scheduling" issues in declining earlier requests that she answer the Committee's questions. Maybe. Or maybe it was because for Jews, Columbia University has come to resemble Nuremberg University circa 1938, minus only the "Sieg Heils." After Hamas' massacre of 1,200 Israelis on Oct. 7 in their attempt to slaughter their way to Tel Aviv, Columbia faculty proclaimed Hamas' gruesome murders of Jews "astonishing," "astounding" and "awesome." Columbia has become a hell for Jewish students, who have been insulted, threatened, bullied, assaulted and forced to run gauntlets of taunting students with masks and kaffiyehs calling for their genocide.

But there Shafik was, assuring congressmen that things at Columbia were copacetic, and that there were no anti-Jewish protests because they were "not labeled" as such. Meanwhile, hundreds of Columbia students thumbed their noses at their own president, making clear that she was dissembling, ramping up the calls for death to Jews to the point that a university rabbi urged Jewish kids to leave Columbia for their own safety.

The NPR debacle and the Columbia riots played out before a heartland already deeply suspicious of the direction the Democratic Party has traveled. And the heartland isn't stupid. It knows that NPR and the Ivy League function as Democratic Party auxiliaries. Many in that heartland fear that the elitism and the arrogance on display last week are indicative of what an America under Democratic governance will look like. Democrats had better hope that it isn't too many.

About Jeff Robbins

Jeff Robbins, a nationally recognized First Amendment lawyer and civil litigator, served as chief counsel for the Democratic senators on the United States Senate Permanent Subcommittee on Investigations, and as deputy chief counsel for the Democratic senators on the United States Senate Governmental Affairs Committee. In 1999 and 2000, he served as a United States delegate to the United Nations Human Rights Commission in Geneva, Switzerland.

Between 1987 and 1990, he was an assistant United States attorney for the District of Massachusetts, where he focused on civil fraud cases and money laundering investigations. There he was tapped to be the district's first chief of the Asset Forfeiture Unit. He was also twice appointed as a special assistant attorney general in Massachusetts, representing the secretary of the commonwealth.

He has written widely on politics, foreign policy and national security matters for the Wall Street Journal, The Boston Globe, the Boston Herald, The Times of Israel and the New York Observer. He is a visiting professor of the practice of political science at Brown University, where he teaches courses on congressional investigations and political journalism. He has received awards for public service from the United States Department of Justice, the Federal Bureau of Investigation, the Drug Enforcement Administration and the General Services Administration. From 2012 to 2014, he was chairman of the Anti-Defamation League's New England board of directors, and from 2001 through 2004, he was president of the World Affairs Council of Boston. He is a frequent contributor to ABC News Live.

He lives in Massachusetts with his wife, Joanne. They have two children, two dogs, one cat and a staggering monthly pet food bill.

Notes From the Brink: A Collection of Columns About Policy at Home and Abroad is also available as an e-book for Kindle, Amazon Fire, iPad, Nook and Android e-readers. Visit creatorspublishing.com to learn more.

CREATORS PUBLISHING

We find compelling storytellers and
help them craft their narrative,
distributing their novels and collections
worldwide.

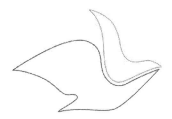

Made in the USA
Monee, IL
22 July 2024

61724131R10275